ORACLE®   *Oracle Press*™

Oracle Wait Interface:
A Practical Guide to Performance Diagnostics & Tuning

Richmond Shee
Kirtikumar Deshpande
K Gopalakrishnan

McGraw-Hill/Osborne

New York   Chicago   San Francisco
Lisbon   London   Madrid   Mexico City   Milan
New Delhi   San Juan   Seoul   Singapore   Sydney   Toronto

The McGraw·Hill Companies

McGraw-Hill/Osborne
2100 Powell Street, 10th Floor
Emeryville, California 94608
U.S.A.

To arrange bulk purchase discounts for sales promotions, premiums, or fund-raisers, please contact
McGraw-Hill/Osborne at the above address. For information on translations or book distributors
outside the U.S.A., please see the International Contact Information page immediately following the
index of this book.

Oracle Wait Interface: A Practical Guide to Performance Diagnostics & Tuning

1234567890 FGR FGR 01987654

ISBN 0-07-222729-X

Publisher
    Brandon A. Nordin

Vice President & Associate Publisher
    Scott Rogers

Editorial Director
    Wendy Rinaldi

Acquisitions Editor
    Lisa McClain

Project Editor
    Jenn Tust

Acquisitions Coordinator
    Athena Honore

Technical Editors
    Scott Gossett, Kyle Hailey, John Kanagaraj,
    Craig Shallahamer, Graham Wood

Copy Editor
    Sally Engelfried

Proofreader
    Marian Selig

Indexer
    Jack Lewis

Composition
    Apollo Publishing Services

Series Design
    Jani Beckwith, Peter F. Hancik

Cover Series Design
    Damore Johann Design, Inc.

This book was composed with Corel VENTURA™ Publisher.

About the Authors

Richmond Shee is a Senior Database Architect for Sprint Corporation (www.sprint.com), a global integrated communications provider serving more than 26 million customers in over 100 countries. Richmond has worked with relational databases since 1984. He mentors DBAs and helps set the direction for implementing Oracle RDBMS technology throughout the company. Richmond leads the tuning efforts on all of Sprint's most critical databases. Among his many accomplishments is pioneering the use of the Oracle Wait Interface at Sprint. He also invented a patent-pending wait-based performance data collector. He is a recognized presenter at the International Oracle Users Group, and he speaks frequently at the Kansas City OUG. He can be reached at richmondshee@yahoo.com.

    Kirtikumar Deshpande (Kirti) has been working in the information technology field for over 24 years, including more than 10 years as an Oracle Database Administrator. He holds Bachelor of Science (Physics) and Bachelor of Engineering (Bio-Medical) degrees. He co-authored an Oracle Press book titled *Oracle Performance Tuning 101*, published in May 2001. He has presented papers in the local Oracle user group meetings and at national and international Oracle user group conferences. He currently works for Verizon Information Services (www.superpages.com) as a Senior Oracle Database Administrator. He can be reached at Kirtikumar_Deshpande@yahoo.com.

    K Gopalakrishnan (Gopal) is a Principal Consultant with Oracle Solution Services (India), specializing exclusively in performance tuning, high availability, and disaster recovery. He is a recognized expert in Oracle RAC and Database Internals and has used his extensive expertise in solving many vexing performance issues all across the world for telecom giants, banks, and universities. He is also a prolific writer and frequently publishes articles in the *Oracle Internals* journal. He has more than eight years of experience backed by a degree in Computer Science and Engineering from the University of Madras, India. He can be reached at kaygopal@yahoo.com.

About the Technical Editors

Scott Gossett is a Technical Manager for Oracle Corporation's Advanced Technology Solutions organization, specializing in performance and high availability. Prior to becoming a technical manager, Scott was a Senior Principal Instructor for Oracle Education for over 12 years, primarily teaching Oracle Internals, performance tuning, RAC, and database administration classes. In addition, Scott Gossett is the architect and one of the primary authors of the Oracle Certified Masters exam.

    Kyle Hailey has worked for Oracle on and off since 1990. He started in Unix support, ported Oracle version 6 onto digital Unix machines, worked in Oracle France on performance and support problems for some of the largest European customers and benchmarks, and worked back in the U.S. in Oracle's kernel development group on performance issues. In between stints at Oracle he worked at a dot-com and at Quest software developing performance monitoring tools. Currently he works in the Enterprise Manager group at Oracle. His personal tuning website, including documentation and tools, can be found at http://oraperf.sourceforge.net.

John Kanagaraj is a Principal Consultant with DBSoft, Inc. He has been working with various flavors of Unix and Oracle since the mid-1980s, mostly as an Oracle DBA and System Administrator in various countries around the world. His specializations are Unix/Oracle performance management, backup and recovery, and system availability. John has been applying the Oracle Wait Interface since version 7 to solve Oracle performance issues with great success. He can be reached via his home page at http://www.geocities.com/john_sharmila.

Craig Shallahamer is a recognized Oracle server authority and "an Oracle performance philosopher who has a special place in the history of Oracle performance management." He is a keynote speaker, teacher, researcher, and publisher who specializes in improving Oracle performance management. He also founded the grid computing company BigBlueRiver. After nine years at Oracle Corporation, Craig started OraPub, Inc., in 1998. OraPub focuses on reactive and proactive Oracle performance management. Craig teaches performance management classes and was the key designer and engineer behind HoriZone, OraPub's web-based capacity planning service.

Graham Wood is an architect in database development at Oracle. Most of his 20 years of Oracle experience have been spent in performance-related areas, including designing and tuning large high-performance systems, benchmarking, and building monitoring tools (such as Statspack). More recently Graham has worked as part of the Oracle 10g Manageability team tasked with simplifying the process of tuning the operation of the database.

Contents at a Glance

Contents

Foreword

wish I had written this book. I don't think I could have done it as well and as thoroughly as K Gopalakrishnan (Gopal), Kirtikumar (Kirti), and Richmond, but I certainly had the opportunity to some years ago. With this book available, and with its contents being so thorough, I don't think there's a need for a second book on the Oracle Wait Interface—ever. At least I won't be writing one, that's for sure.

(If you somehow have managed not to hear about, read about, or work with the Wait Interface, I suggest you start with Chapter 1, which is a good introduction to the topic.)

In the book *Oracle Insights: Tales of The OakTable* (APress, 2004), there are some historic "fun facts" about how the Oracle Wait Interface came out of obscurity and into the mainstream, mainly told by Anjo Kolk, Cary Millsap, and me, so I'm not going to repeat that here.

Instead, I would like to take you on a very personal trip down Memory Lane...

Before I read the now-famous YAPP paper by Shari Yamaguchi and Anjo Kolk, a guy working out of Gold Support in Oracle France, Kyle Hailey, had told me in an intra-Oracle e-mail about the wait stuff and some clever tricks he was using it for, but I didn't really catch the full impact of it. (Kyle, by the way, is one of the technical reviewers of this book and is credited in one of the appendixes with his direct memory access code, and justly so.)

After reading the YAPP paper, which first championed the teaching of this method to the public, I started talking about it to everyone who cared to listen.

Whenever I had questions I would ask Anjo (we both worked at Oracle at that time), and he would usually respond within a few minutes, regardless of the time of day. In fact, I think our first contact happened a few hours after he and his family relocated from Japan to Oracle HQ, and his two sons were still suffering from jet lag.

Soon I was giving small presentations in Denmark. Then bigger presentations in Denmark. In Denmark, people will still refer to it as "Mogens' beloved Wait Interface," as if I had invented it.

Then came the presentations at various user group meetings and conferences. I couldn't talk about much else in that period of my life, and I still find the whole idea and method incredibly compelling.

I had the good fortune of being used by Lex de Haan to present Oracle Technical Seminars in many wonderful countries for a couple of years, and whatever the topic was (7.3 New Features or whatever), I always made sure the audience was also introduced to the YAPP method.

I think I presented technical seminars in close to 30 different countries, and so they heard about this wonder in Argentina, Taiwan, South Africa, Italy, and anywhere in between.

One memorable occasion was presenting at a symposium arranged by Cary Millsap in his then-role as head of Oracle's System Performance Group (SPG) in Las Vegas (in 1998 or 1999, I think). Eighty people attended my presentation (the maximum allowed) and several others wanted in—what a great feeling!

After the presentation, Cary strolled up to me and casually remarked, "I think that was the best presentation I ever saw." Imagine hearing that from one of your absolute heroes. I could have done anything in Las Vegas that night. But I didn't.

Fired up like that, it's hardly surprising that I kept talking about the Oracle Wait Interface whenever I had the chance.

Surprisingly, I was still one of the very few, if not the only one, to talk about the Wait Interface at the IOUG conference in Orlando in 2001. The maximum number of attendees allowed into the room was 400 and still 150 more wanted in.

That presentation went extremely well. Cary Millsap was taking care of my slides, the audience was in a very good mood, and the whole thing rocked. In fact, a nice guy in a wheelchair in the front of the room laughed so hard that at one point his glass of water fell to the floor.

During the same year, Gaja Krishna Vaidyanatha and Kirti wrote a fine performance book, *Oracle Performance Tuning 101* (McGraw-Hill/Osborne, 2001), in which Gaja introduced the unforgettable phrase "Compulsive Tuning Disorder." He should also be credited with spreading the word about the Wait Interface with great enthusiasm.

I didn't participate at the recent IOUG conference in Toronto (2004), but there were a *lot* of presentations about the Wait Interface. The Oracle Wait Interface has truly entered the mainstream of Oracle knowledge, and I must find other things to talk about.

Cary Millsap and Jeff Holt of Hotsos have also written a very fine book, *Optimizing Oracle Performance* (O'Reilly, 2003), on the topic of Oracle performance methodology (including a chapter on queueing theory, which was invented in 1909 by a bored Dane, Agnar Erlang, who worked for the phone monopoly—one day I'll understand it).

So with *Oracle Wait Interface: A Practical Guide to Performance Diagnostics & Tuning* fully (and I mean *fully*!) documenting the Wait Interface, its pitfalls and joys, and many tips and tricks, I think the topic is covered.

This is why I have recently taken up talking to SQL Server audiences about the virtues of a Wait Interface. And you know what? They ask me whether there's a book available on the topic.

The timing of this book is perfect. Any other time would also have been perfect if it wasn't for one important detail: With Oracle Database 10g, Oracle (really Graham Wood, the chief architect of the Manageability area in Oracle Development and another technical reviewer of this book) is finally taking full advantage of the Wait Interface. Oracle is recording the right things, storing them correctly in a repository, and using advisory services and other utilities to use the information to its fullest.

Gopal, Kirti, and Richmond have made sure that their book contains essential details about the usage of the wait information in Oracle Database 10g, while at the same time describing how to use it, what to look out for, and how to understand its output from Oracle 7.0.12 and up to the present. A very impressive piece of work.

The promise of all this is that optimization can be automated, but that's a bit out in the future. Until such time when we can all safely forget about performance problems, this book ought to be the preferred reference on this topic.

If it weren't for the fact that I get a copy for free, I would buy this book.

Denmark, May 2004
Mogens Nørgaard
Technical Director
Miracle A/S

Acknowledgments

ever did I imagine that writing a book could be this involved. It required so much sacrifice, not only on my part, but for everyone who was directly and indirectly involved with it. I am so thankful for my wife, Jody (my crown and joy), for her help and understanding while I spent many nights and weekends clicking away on the keyboard.

I am blessed with excellent co-authors: Kirtikumar Deshpande and K Gopalakrishnan, who readily shared their knowledge and real-life experiences. Their contributions extended the depth and breadth of this book. I am also thankful for the world-class technical editors: Scott Gossett, Graham Wood, Kyle Hailey, John Kanagaraj, and Craig Shallahamer for their invaluable technical contributions and corrections. Scott, I can still vividly remember my first DBA-I class in Chicago. You were an excellent instructor and mentor.

Thanks to my outstanding superiors at Sprint Corporation: Rich Carner and all the managers in Data Management (thank you, John Mueller, for hiring me), David Hanks, David Courtney, and Michael Rapken for their support, encouragement, trust, and management style that fosters innovation. I appreciate the fine DBAs with whom I am privileged to work and share production issues and challenges. Thanks for accepting and using Oracle Wait Interface when I proposed it as a corporate standard.

Finally, thanks to the team at Osborne: Lisa McClain, Athena Honore, Jenn Tust, and Sally Engelfried for their work in preparing and making this book a reality. Although it has been hard work, I have thoroughly enjoyed it and learned much along the way.

—*Richmond Shee*

My sincere thanks go Gaja Krishna Vaidyanatha, my friend and the co-author of *Oracle Performance Tuning 101*. That was the first book that promoted the use of Oracle Wait Interface methodology for Oracle Performance diagnostics. Based on the feedback we received it was apparent that there would be a book on OWI. And here it is. If it wasn't for Gaja I would never have gotten involved with writing books.

As practicing DBAs, Richmond Shee and K Gopalakrishnan have worked extensively with OWI. I am very fortunate to have them as co-authors of this book. They have contributed enormously to this book and I thank them for their invaluable contributions.

Sincere thanks go to our technical editors: Scott Gossett, Kyle Hailey, John Kanagaraj, Craig Shallahamer, and Graham Wood for their help in making sure the technical contents are correct and appropriate.

It was great working with the people at Osborne: Lisa McClain, Athena Honore, Sally Engelfried, and Jenn Tust. Thank you all very much for being so patient with us and for making sure that this project stayed on track and on time.

I would also like to thank my boss Paul Harrill for supporting and encouraging me in this effort. Without his help I am afraid that I would not have found time to work on this book.

I am thankful to everyone who contributed to this book either directly or indirectly. During the past few years I have learned a lot from many people, and my special thanks go to Steve Adams, Wolfgang Breitling, Rachel Carmichael, Dave Ensor, Daniel Fink, Tim Gorman, Anjo Kolk, Jonathan Lewis, Cary Millsap, Mogens Nørgaard, Marlene Theriault, Jared Still, and many members of the *oracle-l* list.

Finally, I must thank my wife, Achala, and our son, Sameer. Both of them have been the true source of support and motivation. I am grateful for their support and understanding when I could not be with them while working on the book.

—*Kirtikumar Deshpande*

It all started during Oracle World 2003. When Kirti asked me whether I would be interested in co-authoring an Oracle Press book on Oracle Wait Interface, it seemed as if some mutual friend had told him of my desire. I immediately agreed but soon realized writing was not so easy after all. Without support from Kirti and Richmond, I doubt that I could have completed the chapters so quickly and so completely. I am grateful to both of them for their invaluable help.

I sincerely thank Steve Adams for getting me interested and rousing my extreme curiosity about Oracle internals, and I thank Vijay Lunawat of Oracle Racpack for directing me in the maze of RAC internals. I wish to express my heartfelt thanks to Vivek Marla, Vice President of Oracle Solution Services, India, for his encouragement and support. I am also grateful to Tarakesh Tummapudi and Muthuvel Arumugam for their valuable guidance. Many thanks to my colleague Jaswinder Singh and my friends at Oracle Support, Sudhi, Vijay, Ram(s), Sunil, and Koushal, for their timely responses to my queries—mostly at odd hours. You guys are simply great!

Needless to say, any technical work needs to be reviewed thoroughly. John Kanagaraj, however, was much more than a reviewer. An Oracle guru himself, he has been an inspiration to me for the past few years. I salute him for his patience and guidance. John kept my sprits up whenever I was running low.

I am truly indebted to the esteemed clients with whom I worked. They not only posed challenges, but also were willing to implement my solutions in their systems. They played a big role in the knowledge acquisition and enhancement that I shared in this book.

Last but not the least, I wish to thank reviewers Scott Gossett, Graham Wood, Kyle Hailey, and Craig Shallahamer, whose great efforts are reflected in the rich content and timely completion of the book. Thanks, too, to Lisa McClain, Jenn Tust, Athena Honore, Sally Engelfried, and the rest of the team from Osborne for their superb work.

—*K Gopalakrishnan*

Introduction

"When the learned discern that the learning, which delights them, also delights the world, they love learning all the more."

—*Kural*: 399 Thiruvalluvar

lobalization of businesses creates new competitive landscapes, and the push to be the first to the market often compromises the conventional and proven application and database development paradigms. To gain a competitive edge, businesses leverage the latest computer hardware and storage technologies to capture and analyze a massive amount of data about their customers and spending patterns. This gives rise to very large databases, complex multitiered applications, and needless to say, performance issues. Database administrators are challenged as never before to troubleshoot and resolve performance issues that are always labeled "database problems."

Prior to Oracle release 7.0.12, Oracle Corporation proposed the ratio-based method as a way to measure database performance. As a result, a model based on various ratios was developed to measure database performance. It was taught and used for a long time, and it is still practiced by some DBAs. However, it proved to be very inadequate in finding even the real bottlenecks in the system, much less finding the solutions. Despite the various ratios, the ratio-based method could not answer the question: what is causing the application to run slowly?

In Oracle release 7.0.12, Oracle Corporation introduced the wait-based method commonly known as the Oracle Wait Interface (OWI) to analyze the performance of the system. For the first time, DBAs could find out how much time processes spent on various resources and what resources were the bottlenecks in the system. The higher the wait time, the slower the process's response time. Now DBAs have a way to relate slow performance to the bottlenecks. The primary bottleneck can easily be identified, whether it is related to the application, database, or network. There is no need for guesswork. However, OWI knowledge was slow in reaching the mass DBA population. In the beginning, knowledge and correct usage of the wait-based performance diagnostics was limited to a handful of people at Oracle Corporation. Very little information was made available to others. Since then, Oracle Corporation has made substantial improvements to OWI, both in terms of the technology and knowledge transfer. It is proving to be an extremely dependable and reliable model for correctly identifying system bottlenecks and finding the corrective solutions. Oracle RDBMS releases 8, 8*i*, 9*i*, and 10*g* have seen considerable improvements in the Oracle kernel to report wait times, and the wait-based model is maturing very rapidly.

During the past 10 years, several authors have written about methods and tools to tune and improve database performance. These range from SQL tuning to database internals. Unfortunately, the Wait Interface model lagged behind. This book is an effort to fill that void.

This book does not teach you how to tune a SQL statement or a PL/SQL program. It does, however, help you identify SQL statements and database structures that may need tuning. This book is for all levels of Oracle DBAs. We are confident that once you have read this book, you will begin using OWI to diagnose your next performance problem. When this happens, the case for writing this book rests.

We would love to hear your success stories and your comments, as well as criticisms and arguments. Learning is a never-ending process. By no means have we attempted to cover all the variables of performance tuning. We believe this is just the beginning. You can contact the authors by e-mail: richmondshee@yahoo.com, Kirtikumar_Deshpande@yahoo.com, and kaygopal@yahoo.com.

How to Use This Book

Very rarely would one read a technical book from cover to cover in one sitting. Technical books are mostly used as references. However, we urge you to read all the chapters and appendixes in this book. You will certainly find something new or different in each chapter, regardless of your level of experience in Oracle Database tuning and performance troubleshooting.

This book has nine chapters and five appendixes as described next.

Chapter 1

Chapter 1 introduces you to the Oracle Wait Interface and lays the foundation for understanding why you should learn and use OWI. It explains why the hit-ratio based methodology does not work when it comes to diagnosing slow application response time.

Chapter 2

Chapter 2 discusses the OWI components in detail. It defines the Oracle wait event, describes the various OWI views and their applications, and explains how to use the extended SQL trace. You will learn where, when, and how to find the wait event information.

Chapter 3

Chapter 3 introduces you to the most commonly seen Oracle wait events. It describes these events in detail and shows what information Oracle provides to analyze these events. In addition, the chapter discusses how you can track CPU usage statistics.

Chapter 4

Chapter 4 explains why it is important to monitor and gather session-level wait event information and discusses the importance of historical performance data. It describes how you can put together a simple data collection tool to capture and store session-level Oracle wait event data.

Chapter 5

Chapter 5 discusses how you can diagnose and solve problems related to the most common I/O related wait events. The events discussed are the *db file sequential read, db file scattered read, direct path read, direct path write, log file parallel write, db file parallel write,* and *control file parallel write.*

Chapter 6

Chapter 6 presents an in-depth discussion of *latch free, enqueue,* and *buffer busy waits* wait events. You will learn just about all there is to learn about these wait events. It discusses the difference between a latch and an enqueue and explains how Oracle serializes access to memory structures. This chapter will teach you how to diagnose and solve problems related to locking and serialization. We believe at the present time there is no other publication with such comprehensive information on these wait events as presented in this chapter.

Chapter 7

Chapter 7 covers common latency-related wait events in detail. You will learn how to diagnose and solve problems related to *log file sync, log buffer space, free buffer waits, write complete waits, log file switch completion,* and *log file switch (checkpoint incomplete)* wait events.

Chapter 8

Chapter 8 explains how buffer cache management works in an Oracle Real Application Clusters environment and discusses the Oracle wait events that are commonly seen in RAC environments. You will learn how to diagnose and solve problems related to global cache wait events.

Chapter 9

Chapter 9 introduces you to the Oracle Database 10*g* new automated features for performance monitoring and diagnostics. It discusses different types of database statistics collected by Oracle Database 10*g*. You will learn how Oracle collects performance statistics data and analyzes it to offer remedial solutions in terms of recommendations and advisories. You will also learn how the Automatic Workload Repository, Active Session History, and Automatic Database Diagnostics and Monitoring work. A series of Oracle Enterprise Manager screen shots will show how easy it is to find the root cause of performance issues.

Appendix A

Appendix A discusses Oracle diagnostic events. These events are different from Oracle wait events. You will learn how and when to use these diagnostic events.

Appendix B

Appendix B lists all the enqueue wait events in Oracle Database 10*g*.

Appendix C

Appendix C introduces you to the utilities and procedures used in producing trace files for various data or memory dumps. Such trace files and dumps are often asked for by Oracle Support to diagnose the root cause of errors, such as ORA-0600 or ORA-7445.

Appendix D

Appendix D describes a method to access Oracle SGA directly through a non-SQL interface, such as a C language program. Such a method is the fastest for sampling performance related information in the SGA without introducing the overhead of parsing, latching, and so forth.

Appendix E

Appendix E lists the reference materials we used for this book.

CHAPTER
1

Introduction to
Oracle Wait Interface

peed is the word that defines the twenty-first century. The previous century's saying, "He who dies with the most toys wins" is now "He who dies with the most high-speed toys wins." We want speed in everything we do, be it in our personal lives or the business we conduct. You name it—fast cars, fast computers, fast lanes, fast Internet connections, fast weight loss, fast cures, fast food, and so on.

Businesses compete with one another to be the first to introduce new products to the marketplace. The speed-to-market demand overrides the conventional process of software engineering that used to include such concepts as application analysis, design, code development, test, and implementation. Nowadays, programmers start coding before the requirements are established. And the requirements keep changing throughout the development lifecycle. Furthermore, the testing phase often is shortened or sacrificed to meet unrealistic production dates. Needless to say, many untested applications interact with production databases for the first time on the release day.

In tandem with today's fast-paced world, database sizes have increased as businesses have found value in keeping historical data longer, sometimes "forever," for various analyses to gain a competitive edge. Databases that do not scale well often result in higher processing time in spite of the availability of better and more reliable hardware.

These issues eventually flow downstream and quite often are relabeled as "database performance" problems. Unfortunately, database administrators (DBAs) have to deal with this on a regular basis and take the blame. Corporate IT organizations expect DBAs to possess the required know-how and be available 24x7 for speedy resolution of all performance problems. Due to this, performance monitoring and optimization functions have gained prominence and consume most of a DBA's time. DBAs need reliable performance monitoring and tuning methods. Oracle fulfilled this requirement by architecting the Oracle Wait Interface (OWI) to help DBAs quickly and effectively diagnose performance problems.

This book is all about the Oracle Wait Interface. It gives DBAs a detailed working knowledge of how to use OWI and a practical approach to performance diagnostics and troubleshooting that is based on real experience with large and complex database installations. DBAs will gain an in-depth knowledge of the OWI methodology and will be able to apply the knowledge to solve performance issues.

In this chapter, we compare the OWI with the ratio-based methodology that is still practiced by many DBAs. We outline the limitations of the ratio-based method and highlight the advantages of OWI, thus establishing it as the methodology of choice. It is our sincere hope that this book will assist DBAs in transitioning to using OWI as the main Oracle performance optimization methodology.

The Old Fashion of Oracle Performance Optimization

Some say you need to know what life was like in the old days before you can really appreciate the life you now have. This is also true in the world of Oracle performance optimization. Early versions of Oracle did not offer a reliable method to identify performance bottlenecks. Performance optimization was a difficult and complicated task. Everyone used cache hit ratios as the yardstick to monitor database performance. To fully appreciate the OWI tuning methodology, you must be aware of the problems and limitations of the hit ratio–based tuning method. For many of us, this is a trip down memory lane, but for those of you who didn't grow up in the ratios-based tuning era, you may embrace this as a piece of your predecessor's history.

Since the beginning of Oracle RDBMS, Oracle DBAs were taught to tune the database and instance by watching a few ratio numbers. The idea was to keep all database elements operating within acceptable ranges or limits. Some of the memorable ratios are the buffer cache hit ratio, library cache hit/miss ratio (Oracle7.0), and latch get/miss ratio. Who can forget these commandments?

- Thou shalt keep thy buffer cache hit ratio in the upper 90 percentile.

- Thy data dictionary misses must be under 10 percent at all times, and thy library cache shall not covet thy data dictionary—it shall have its own ratios.

- Thy SQL area *gethitratio* and *pinhitratio* must also be in the 90 percentile at all times. Furthermore, the ratio of reloads to pins must not be more than 1 percent. If thy ratios are bad, thou shalt increase the shared pool size but thou shalt not steal the memory from the buffer cache. And while you are adding memory to the shared pool, throw some memory at the buffer cache also. It will increase the cache-hit ratio.

- Thy willing-to-wait latch hit ratios shalt be close to 1. If not, thou may increase the SPIN_COUNT but thou must be careful not to kill thy CPUs. And so on.

Lost yet? We are. Life can be much simpler, not to mention better.

Why Are Cache-Hit Ratios Grossly Inefficient?

The hit ratio philosophy is not peculiar to Oracle database administration. It is widely used and ingrained in many aspects of our daily lives. Take your local city water department for example. Their goal is to keep your drinking water quality within the limits that are established by the Environmental Protection Agency. Now, your city may meet or exceed the established limits, but that doesn't mean that everyone is happy. Some people are more vulnerable to substances found in drinking water than the general population. And if you are one of the unfortunate ones, you have to work out your own alternative. Chances are your city is not going to do anything about it if the water quality is already within the acceptable limits.

Like it or not, we gave the same kind of customer service to our database users. If they said their job ran slow, all we did was make sure all the ratios were in line. Among them was the *buffer cache hit* ratio, which was the center of attention. If the ratios were in line, we sent our users away, telling them that they really didn't have a problem. If they continued to complain, we would turn SQL trace on for the job, examine the trace file with *tkprof* (Transient Kernel Profiler), and tune some SQL statements. What else could we do? All the performance tuning books and classes taught us that if the ratios were within their acceptable limits, users should be happy. This kind of service is no different than a doctor who only knows how to treat patients based on their blood pressure numbers. Suppose you slit your wrist, bleed profusely, and squirm in pain. The doctor measures your blood pressure, finds it to be in the acceptable range, and sends you away asking you to come back again when your blood pressure is lower.

If the ratio numbers weren't in line, the common (and perhaps the only) solution was to add more memory. Those of you who have *been there and done that* can certainly remember the painful lesson that a larger buffer cache does not always translate to better performance. Remember when the additional memory was installed and you crossed all your fingers and toes, hoping and praying that performance would get better? Alas, the performance didn't get better, it got worse. Surprised and disbelieving, you were totally lost and didn't know what else to do. You lost your credibility and you were in the hot seat. In the follow-up meeting with your customer, someone suggested, "Why don't we bring in the industry-renowned performance tuning expert?" Of course, your boss was also present in the meeting. You felt so small and wished for a place to hide. The expensive expert came in and performed an analysis of the database while you took a back seat. The expert produced a fancy multi-page, multi-colored report with charts and graphs that dazzled your boss and user and left. Regardless of whether the recommended solution worked or not, your reputation was already damaged. Your tuning methodology let you down and you became a "tuning-phobic."

Ratio numbers were the only form of communication in those days. We had to communicate performance using a few numbers, especially the *buffer cache hit* ratio, and it wasn't easy. We always wondered why we got blank stares and glazes in our users' eyes when we told them that the database cache hit ratio was high and totally ignored their complaint about response time being very slow. Obviously, our language was foreign to them, but we couldn't comprehend why they couldn't comprehend. I mean, how hard could it be? High cache hit ratio is good, and you shouldn't have a problem. Low cache hit ratio is bad, and you should expect problems, right? But ratio numbers don't really make sense to those who want to know why their job ran so slowly. Imagine calling to find out why your pizza delivery is running late and being told the driver's hit-rate ratio is 65 percent. Or suppose your boss asks why you were late to work. You would probably attribute your tardiness to one or more events, such as an accident, treacherous driving conditions, slow traffic, traffic lights, and so on. Chances are you wouldn't explain your tardiness to your boss in some sort of ratio.

The cache-hit ratio method is simply not reliable for performance analysis and tuning, or else Oracle Corporation wouldn't have introduced a new methodology. The doctrine of high cache-hit ratio for good performance is wrong most of the time. In reality, high cache-hit ratio doesn't always mean good performance, and low cache-hit ratio doesn't always mean bad performance. In fact, there were many times when cache-hit ratios hit the floor, yet there was no loss in application performance. Trying to judge performance by a cache-ratio number is like trying to determine the speed of a car by its tachometer reading. You can't tell how fast someone is going at 6000 rpm without the speedometer, can you? The tachometer reading is high, but the car may be in second gear.

The Oracle Database 10*g* Release 1 Performance Tuning Guide states,

> When tuning, it is common to compute a ratio that helps determine whether there is a problem. Such ratios include the buffer cache-hit ratio, the soft-parse ratio, and the latch-hit ratio. These ratios should not be used as 'hard and fast' identifiers of whether there is or is not a performance bottleneck. Rather, they should be used as indicators. In order to identify whether there is a bottleneck, other related evidence should be examined.

The New Fashion of Oracle Performance Optimization

Oracle debuted the Wait Interface in Release 7.0.12 with only 104 wait events. The number of wait events quickly grew to about 140 in Oracle8.0, about 220 in Oracle8*i* Database, about 400 in Oracle9*i* Database, and more than 800 in Oracle Database 10*g* Release 1. (The actual number of wait events depends largely on your RDBMS configuration and the options that are installed.)

For those of you who have never used the OWI, the growth in the number of wait events with each new release should convince you that the OWI is the preferred tuning methodology. Don't forget this is not a cheap proposition for Oracle. OWI instrumentation requires the kernel developers to insert counters or sensors in strategic places within the kernel code to collect statistics whenever a process has to wait for resources. If you are still not convinced, then see if you can find the buffer cache-hit ratio (BCHR) in Oracle Database 10*g* Enterprise Manager Performance screens. It is gone. Oracle has removed it. We'd say that is the nail in the coffin for the cache-hit ratio based tuning method.

So if the OWI is so good, why has the methodology spread so slowly among Oracle DBAs? Why are there so few publications about it? Why doesn't Oracle aggressively promote the OWI? We believe documentation was the main factor that limited the popularity of OWI in the beginning. Initially, there wasn't any documentation, and OWI knowledge was pretty much limited to those in the kernel group at Oracle Corporation. OWI information wasn't made available in the Oracle documentation until version 8.0. Back then, whenever you mentioned OWI, most DBAs said, "What's that?"

However, in the mid-1990s, a group of individuals championed the teaching of OWI to the public with useful white papers, presentations, and training. Anjo Kolk and Shari Yamaguchi wrote the famous YAPP-Method (Yet Another Performance Profiling Method) white paper. Others who have contributed significantly include Juan Loaiza, Mogens Nørgaard, Virag Saksena, Craig Shallahamer, Steve Adams, and Cary Millsap, just to name a few.

The OWI methodology continues to spread and increase in popularity as more DBAs find it to be extremely useful. At the turn of the century, OWI topics popped up all over the place, from local Oracle users groups to the International Oracle Users Group (IOUG), as well as in various magazines and articles. Statspack, introduced with Oracle 8.1.6, proudly displays the Top Wait Events on its summary page. Its documentation and papers published in *Oracle* magazine in November 2000 proposed the wait event-based tuning methodology.

The OWI Philosophy

The OWI is a performance tracking methodology that focuses on process bottlenecks, which are better known as "wait events" and lesser known as symptoms. This includes waits for I/O operations, locks, latches, background processes activities, network latencies, and so on. OWI records and presents all the bottlenecks that a process encounters from start to finish. It keeps track of the number of times and the amount of time a process spent on each bottleneck. Removing or even reducing the impact of major bottlenecks improves performance. For example, if you are to improve your travel time to work, you must first identify the major time-consuming elements on your route such as traffic lights, stop signs, school zones, traffic jams, and so on. Once you are able to remove, bypass, or reduce your major bottlenecks, you will automatically improve your travel time.

In the course of processing, a database process may be actively servicing a request on the CPU, it may be off the CPU waiting for a certain resource to be available or delivered, or it may be waiting for a new instruction on what to do next. Each time a process has to wait for something, Oracle collects statistics about the wait. Wait event statistics are made available in several V$ views, which are discussed in detail in Chapter 2. The wait event information lets you quickly identify the major bottlenecks that plague a process so you can find the appropriate solution to solve the problem. For instance, it doesn't take a rocket scientist to figure out why the following job is running slow if you have these statistics:

```
EVENT                          TIME_WAITED
-----------------------------  -----------
latch free                       1,142,981
db file sequential read            727,075
enqueue                             31,650
db file scattered read               3,712
log file switch completion           2,328
local write wait                       801
direct path write                      138
free buffer waits                       66
control file sequential read            28
direct path read                        21
log file sync                           20
file open                                8
```

It is a no-brainer. The job performed badly because it spent too much time competing for latches.

The ability to quickly identify the major bottlenecks that slow a process down has revolutionized performance tuning and greatly reduced troubleshooting time. Before OWI, troubleshooting was merely following a checklist. That usually involved running a few queries that calculated some ratios and checked for high resource-consuming SQL statements. The problem with checklist tuning was that you almost always found issues with every item on the list. Since the items were not quantified based on time, you simply didn't know which one would yield the best return for your tuning effort. So you usually picked one according to your best judgment, and it was a toss-up. Troubleshooting and problem solving was tedious and time consuming. You spent a lot of time tuning a lot of things in vain. But now, OWI clocks every bottleneck and you easily can sort them to find the significant ones.

Pointing the DBA directly to the major bottlenecks not only saves a lot of troubleshooting time, it also, more importantly, helps the DBA not bark up the wrong tree. If you see that a process spent the majority of its time competing for latches and a minor amount of time waiting for I/Os, should you really spend your time redoing your I/O subsystem? With OWI, you can now focus your effort on the items that yield large performance returns. This translates into lower turnaround time for problem solving, lower operational costs, and better customer service.

The OWI philosophy not only brings with it a new way of monitoring, measuring, and tuning your databases, it also gives you a new way of communicating performance.

Now, you can sit down with your customers and show them the list of bottlenecks or symptoms that their processes encounter, the amount of time wasted, and discuss the plan of action. For example, you can quantify the characteristic of a job, that it spent 60 percent of its time waiting on full table scans (*db file scattered read*) I/Os, 7 percent on index reads (*db file sequential read*), 5 percent on latch free, and so on. You can also show when a problem is not in the database. OWI lets you describe performance in a way that makes sense to everyone. When all the parties see and understand what the main problem is, it helps to bring about a speedy resolution. It also fosters collaboration between the various business entities.

Database Response Time Tuning Model

If you ask your users to describe performance, they will either describe it in terms of response time or throughput. When your users call you about performance problems, it is because they are unhappy with their process's response time or throughput. They don't call you because certain database ratio numbers are bad or some SQL statements are taking a lot of CPU time, having high buffer gets or causing a lot of physical disk reads. Frankly, they don't care.

OWI plays a significant role in determining the database response time. The database response time consists of the "service time" and "wait time" as follows:

$$ResponseTime = ServiceTime + WaitTime$$

The service time is the amount of time a process spends on the CPU. The wait time is the amount of time a process waits for specific resources to be available before continuing with processing. This formula is based on the notion that at any point, a process is either actively servicing a request on the CPU or is off the CPU and in a wait state. You can improve database response time by shortening the service time, the wait time, or both. This is not hard to understand as you also practice this formula in your daily chores. Take your last trip to the grocery store. When you were getting ready to pay, your checkout response time was how long you had to wait in line plus how fast the clerk scanned your items. You normally get bad checkout response time if you shop during peak hours (high wait time), or if you are unlucky enough to get a rookie clerk who needs to look up the code numbers on most of your produce purchases (high service time). So you improve your checkout response time by shopping during off hours (low wait time) and picking an experienced clerk with whom you are familiar (low service time).

However, you should note that a total (or end-user or end-to-end) response time goes beyond the database response time. End-to-end response time includes server latencies such as queue time, context switch, memory management, and so on, as well as network and middle tier latencies, if applicable. But for our purposes, we will look exclusively at the database response time, and we may rewrite the formula in the database terminology as follows:

Response Time = CPU used when call started + Σ TIME_WAITED

At the session level, service time refers to the *CPU used when call started* statistic in the V$SESSTAT view, and wait time is the sum of TIME_WAITED for all foreground-related wait events in the V$SESSION_EVENT view for the particular session. The *CPU used when call started* statistic comprises three categories: CPU used for parsing, CPU used for recursive calls, and CPU used for normal work. The CPU used for parsing is tracked by the statistic *parse time CPU*, while the CPU used for recursive calls is tracked by the statistic *recursive cpu usage*. The CPU used for normal work (CPU_W) can be calculated as follows:

CPU_W = CPU used when call started – parse time CPU – recursive cpu usage

NOTE
There are statistics for CPU used by this session *and* CPU used when call started *in the V$SYSSTAT and V$SESSTAT views. We recommend using the latter because* CPU used by this session *is buggy and the* CPU used when call started *is much more stable. Both statistics show approximately the same value in the absence of the bug, so there is no benefit to using the* CPU used by this session.

NOTE
CPU statistics are only updated at the end of a call, but wait event statistics happen in real time. So a long-running SQL statement will not increment the CPU statistics until it returns from its call. What this means is that the accuracy of the database response-time calculation is highly dependent on when you sample the stats.

The true measure of a session-level database response time should be obtained right before the session disconnects. Obviously, this is quite impossible to do manually. In Chapter 4, we will show you how this can be achieved using the database LOGOFF trigger. For sessions that do not disconnect, it is possible to take snapshots of ongoing session-level database response times using the following query, bearing in mind the nasty trait of CPU time reporting just discussed.

```
select event, time_waited as time_spent
from   v$session_event
where  sid = &sid
and    event not in (
         'Null event',
         'client message',
         'KXFX: Execution Message Dequeue - Slave',
         'PX Deq: Execution Msg',
         'KXFQ: kxfqdeq - normal deqeue',
         'PX Deq: Table Q Normal',
         'Wait for credit - send blocked',
         'PX Deq Credit: send blkd',
         'Wait for credit - need buffer to send',
         'PX Deq Credit: need buffer',
         'Wait for credit - free buffer',
         'PX Deq Credit: free buffer',
         'parallel query dequeue wait',
         'PX Deque wait',
         'Parallel Query Idle Wait - Slaves',
         'PX Idle Wait',
         'slave wait',
         'dispatcher timer',
         'virtual circuit status',
         'pipe get',
         'rdbms ipc message',
         'rdbms ipc reply',
         'pmon timer',
         'smon timer',
         'PL/SQL lock timer',
         'SQL*Net message from client',
         'WMON goes to sleep')
union all
select b.name, a.value
from   v$sesstat a, v$statname b
where  a.statistic# = b.statistic#
and    b.name       = 'CPU used when call started'
and    a.sid        = &sid;
```

NOTE
Oracle Database 10g Release 1 classifies wait events into several classes, one of which is the Idle *class. Rather than listing the unwanted idle events as shown above, you may simply exclude the* Idle *class. Please see Chapter 2 for more information on idle events and wait event classification.*

Following is an example output from the preceding query. If you add up all the numbers in the TIME_SPENT column, you get the process's snapshot response time. In this case, it is 3,199,836 centiseconds or about 8.89 hours.

```
EVENT                         TIME_SPENT
----------------------------- -----------
CPU used when call started     1,358,119
db file sequential read        1,518,787
SQL*Net message from dblink      191,907
db file scattered read            54,949
SQL*Net more data from dblink     44,075
latch free                        12,687
free buffer waits                  9,567
write complete waits               8,970
log file switch completion           553
direct path read                      97
local write wait                      33
log file sync                         32
SQL*Net message to dblink             24
db file parallel read                 14
direct path write                     13
buffer busy waits                      7
file open                              2
```

The Database Response Time tuning model takes performance tuning to new heights by taking you closer to the real end-user performance experience. You should always have response time in mind when you sift through the bottlenecks.

Paradigm Shift

What do you think is the hardest part about eating sushi? Wouldn't you agree that it requires a paradigm shift? You have to get over the raw-fish mentality. If you are stuck thinking of sushi as bait, then you will never be a sushi eater. Likewise, the hardest part of the OWI methodology is not the methodology itself, but the paradigm shift. Once you have developed the mentality to focus on response time, you are home free. Sounds simple, but many DBAs struggle in the transition, mainly due to the mental baggage they carry with them from the old school that mainly relied on ratio-based tuning. (We hasten to clarify that not all of the tuning methods from your old school are useless. Some of the methods, such as capacity utilization and resource consumption are still valid, but those methods must account for response time.)

There are three key behavioral changes that need to happen before you can master the OWI method:

- You must stop measuring performance using non-throughput related ratios, such as the BCHR, sorts-to-disk ratio, and so on.

- You need to start measuring process response time and/or throughput.

- You must look at resource consumption from the response time perspective.

We talked about the first point at length at the beginning of this chapter, so we won't cover that again. Here, we will point out the fallacy of the resource consumption-based tuning and explain why you must evaluate resource consumption with time element.

The old school teaches DBAs to identify and tune SQL statements that consume a lot of CPU, use a lot of buffers, or make a lot of physical I/O calls, because they are a threat to performance and therefore must be eliminated. What is wrong with this concept? It has no regard for bottlenecks and response time. When you judge a SQL statement based on its resource consumption alone, you will not be able to forecast the improvement or the return on your tuning effort because the time element is missing. You can't tell how much faster a process will run after you reduce the level of resource consumption because you don't know what impact the level of consumption has on the process in terms of processing time. You may tune your heart out and still not make a dent in the process response time. With OWI, however, you know what impact each bottleneck has on processing time because every bottleneck is timed. When a bottleneck is removed, the process can potentially run that much faster.

Furthermore, a statement may rank No.1 on CPU used, buffer gets, or I/O calls, but the process that it belongs to may spend the majority of its time on a certain bottleneck that, when removed or reduced, could yield a far greater performance gain than what could be realized by reducing the level of resource consumption. For example, you may reduce your car's gasoline consumption by ensuring that the engine is properly tuned, but that doesn't necessarily guarantee that you will get to your next destination any faster, especially if you are behind a school bus.

You should never base your tuning decisions on quantity; rather, you should focus on response time. In Chapter 2, you will learn to query the V$SYSTEM_EVENT view in the order of TIME_WAITED and not TOTAL_WAITS, because quantity not accompanied by time can be deceiving.

Does this mean that you should ignore high resource-consuming SQL statements all together? No. But you should consider them with response time in mind. Start thinking in terms of response time before you undertake any tuning task. That will help you focus on the "big fish" and prioritize your tuning efforts accordingly. Remember the optimization mantra—response time = service time + wait time—and you won't see much gain if the service time and wait time already are low.

In a Nutshell

Performance optimization, which was once considered an art practiced by a gifted group of highly paid consultants, is now accessible to the common DBA via the Oracle Wait Interface methodology. Using OWI, DBAs can precisely identify the major bottlenecks in the system based on time and resolve performance issues by applying the appropriate solution that reduces or bypasses the bottlenecks. This greatly reduces troubleshooting and problem turnaround time, which translates into better productivity and customer service. The greatest thing about OWI is that it really works consistently and reliably, and you can depend on it!

CHAPTER
2

Oracle Wait Interface Components

racle has always been self-monitoring, but it hasn't always been self-tuning. This means there is a wealth of data in each Oracle instance that can help answer a lot of performance questions. You just need to know where to find the data. There is instance-level and session-level performance data, as well as current and historical activities in various views.

This chapter provides a roadmap into the Oracle Wait Interface. You will be introduced to all the wait event views; their applications, and the extended SQL trace facility (trace event 10046 with appropriate debug level) to capture wait events in a trace file. At the completion of this chapter you will know where, when, and how to find wait event information that will help diagnose performance problems. You will begin your journey by understanding what an Oracle wait event is.

What Is a Wait Event?

An event can be defined as a particular function, or task, that the Oracle kernel performs on behalf of the user session or its own background process. Tasks such as reading and writing data blocks to and from data files, waiting for latch acquisitions before accessing or manipulating data in the memory, interprocess postings and communications, and so on are known as database events, and they have specific names.

But why are these events called *wait events*?

Every session that is connected to an Oracle instance needs resources to perform its tasks. A resource may be a data buffer, a latch, an enqueue (lock), a pin, or a database object. Whenever a session has to wait for something, the wait time is tracked and charged to the event that is associated with that wait. For example, a session that needs an index block that is not in the SGA makes a read call to the operating system and waits for the delivery of the block. The wait time is charged to the *db file sequential read* event. Another session may have completed the last instruction and is now idle, waiting for user input. In this case, the wait time is charged to the *SQL*Net message from client* event. In short, when a session is not using the CPU, it may be waiting for a resource, an action to complete, or simply more work. Hence, events that are associated with all such waits are known as wait events.

NOTE
Oracle wait events are different from Oracle diagnostic events. The diagnostic events are discussed in Appendix A.

OWI Components

Oracle Wait Interface is a collection of a few dynamic performance views and an extended SQL trace file.

Oracle Wait Interface provides statistics for wait events to tell you how many times and how long the session waited for an event to complete. To get the "how long" part, however, you must set the initialization parameter, TIMED_STATISTICS, to TRUE. Old documentation associated high overhead with this parameter and scared a lot of DBAs away. But take comfort: these days, setting this parameter to TRUE does not add any appreciable overhead to the database performance on most platforms because most machines provide hardware support for fast timers. It provides critical and required timing information for all performance improvement efforts.

Since its introduction in Oracle Release 7.0.12, Oracle Wait Interface has had the following four V$ views:

- V$EVENT_NAME

- V$SESSION_WAIT

- V$SESSION_EVENT

- V$SYSTEM_EVENT

In addition to these wait event views, Oracle Database 10*g* Release 1 introduces the following new views to display wait information from several perspectives:

- V$SYSTEM_WAIT_CLASS

- V$SESSION_WAIT_CLASS

- V$SESSION_WAIT_HISTORY

- V$EVENT_HISTOGRAM

- V$ACTIVE_SESSION_HISTORY

However, V$SYSTEM_EVENT, V$SESSION_EVENT, and V$SESSION_WAIT remain the three prominent dynamic performance views that provide wait event statistics and timing information at various levels of granularity. The lowest level of granularity is provided by the V$SESSION_WAIT view. Information from this view is summarized to the V$SESSION_EVENT and then to the V$SYSTEM_EVENT view. You can represent this relationship as follows:

$$V\$SESSION\_WAIT \subset V\$SESSION\_EVENT \subset V\$SYSTEM\_EVENT$$

You may find yourself repeatedly querying these wait event views in short successions when investigating performance bottlenecks. However, there will be times when this is not feasible or practical. In that case, the wait event information can be captured into a trace file using the extended SQL trace facility and analyzed using the *tkprof* (Transient Kernel Profiler) utility.

NOTE
By default, the tkprof *utility in the Oracle9i Database reports summarized wait event information from the extended SQL trace files, including those that are generated from earlier Oracle versions.*

Let's now explore these Oracle Wait Interface components in detail.

V$EVENT_NAME View

Contrary to its naming convention, V$EVENT_NAME is not a dynamic V$ view. The information it provides does not change over time. It is a reference view that contains all the wait events defined for your database instance. The number of wait events varies from version to version and is also dependent on the Oracle options that are installed. Upon its introduction in Oracle Release 7.0.12, there were less than 100 wait events. Oracle Release 7.3.4 contained a little more than 100 wait events. Oracle8i Database had over 200 wait events, while Oracle9i Database has about 400. There are over 800 wait events in Oracle Database 10g Release 1. But don't let these numbers overwhelm you. You need to familiarize yourself with only a handful of common wait events, and they normally cover 80 to 90 percent of your troubleshooting needs. You are not expected to know all of them, but you do need to know where to find them.

V$EVENT_NAME view has the following columns:

Name	Type	Notes
EVENT#	NUMBER	
EVENT_ID	NUMBER	Starting Oracle10g
NAME	VARCHAR2(64)	
PARAMETER1	VARCHAR2(64)	
PARAMETER2	VARCHAR2(64)	
PARAMETER3	VARCHAR2(64)	
WAIT_CLASS_ID	NUMBER	Starting Oracle10g
WAIT_CLASS#	NUMBER	Starting Oracle10g
WAIT_CLASS	VARCHAR2(64)	Starting Oracle10g

How to Use V$EVENT_NAME View

This is where you will discover the number of events that Oracle has defined for your database. If you do not yet know, we suggest you run a quick COUNT (*) against this view.

If you ever forget the exact spelling of an event name, you will find the answer in this view. An event name can change between versions. An example is the null event, which is spelled as "Null event" in versions up to Oracle8*i* Database and spelled as "null event" thereafter.

The column EVENT# is a unique number for the event. This number can change from one Oracle version to another for the same wait event because of the way it is built by the compile time macros in the Oracle code. For better stability, Oracle Database 10*g* Release 1 includes the EVENT_ID column, which contains a hash number that is based on the event name. The hash value will remain the same across versions for as long as the event name does not change. The column NAME contains the wait event name. Each wait event can have up to three attributes that are recorded in the PARAMETER1, PARAMETER2, and PARAMETER3 columns, respectively. These attributes give specific information about the wait event each time it occurs. You can list all the events and their attributes from V$EVENT_NAME view using the following query:

```
select event#, name, parameter1, parameter2, parameter3
from    v$event_name
order by name;
```

The text of PARAMETER1, PARAMETER2, and PARAMETER3 of each event are also displayed in the P1TEXT, P2TEXT, and P3TEXT columns in the V$SESSION_WAIT view whenever a session waits on the event. The actual values for these parameters are shown in P1, P2, and P3 columns of the V$SESSION_WAIT view.

The WAIT_CLASS_ID, WAIT_CLASS#, and WAIT_CLASS columns are added to the V$EVENT_NAME view in Oracle Database 10*g* Release 1 to group wait events by class or category, such as User I/O, Network, Concurrency, etc. The WAIT_CLASS_ID contains the hash value of the wait class name; it will remain the same from version to version as long as the name of the wait class does not change. The column WAIT_CLASS# contains a unique number for the WAIT_CLASS. Just like the EVENT#, it may change from version to version. The column WAIT_CLASS contains the actual name of the wait event class. There are 12 classes of wait events in Oracle Database 10*g* Release 1 as shown next:

```
select wait_class#, wait_class_id, wait_class
from    v$event_name
group by wait_class#, wait_class_id, wait_class;
```

```
WAIT_CLASS# WAIT_CLASS_ID WAIT_CLASS
----------- ------------- ----------------------------------------------
          0    1893977003 Other
          1    4217450380 Application
          2    3290255840 Configuration
          3    4166625743 Administrative
          4    3875070507 Concurrency
          5    3386400367 Commit
          6    2723168908 Idle
          7    2000153315 Network
          8    1740759767 User I/O
          9    4108307767 System I/O
         10    2396326234 Scheduler
         11    3871361733 Cluster
```

Those of you who are not yet using Oracle Database 10g Release 1 don't have to be envious. You can write a simple query using the DECODE function to classify the events in the same manner as Oracle Database 10g Release 1.

V$SYSTEM_EVENT View

The V$SYSTEM_EVENT displays aggregated statistics of all wait events encountered by all Oracle sessions since the instance startup. It keeps track of the total number of waits, total timeouts, and time waited for any wait event ever encountered by any of the sessions.

The V$SYSTEM_EVENT view has the following columns:

```
Name                 Type              Notes
-------------------- ----------------- ----------------
EVENT                VARCHAR2(64)
TOTAL_WAITS          NUMBER
TOTAL_TIMEOUTS       NUMBER
TIME_WAITED          NUMBER
AVERAGE_WAIT         NUMBER
TIME_WAITED_MICRO    NUMBER            Starting Oracle9i
EVENT_ID             NUMBER            Starting Oracle10g
```

The column EVENT contains the name of the wait event, and the column TOTAL_WAITS contains the number of times the sessions waited on this event. If applicable to the event, the TOTAL_TIMEOUTS column records the number of times a session failed to get the requested resource after the initial wait. The column TIME_WAITED reports the total amount of time spent waiting on the event. The column AVERAGE_WAIT gives the average time for each wait and is derived from the TOTAL_WAITS and TIME_WAITED columns.

Before Oracle9i Database, the unit of measure for wait event timing was in centiseconds, that is, 1/100th of a second.

Starting with Oracle9*i* Database, wait time has been tracked in microseconds, that is, 1/1,000,000th of a second, and has been reported in the TIME_WAITED_ MICRO column. The TIME_WAITED and AVERAGE_WAIT columns are derived by dividing TIME_WAITED_MICRO by 10000.

Oracle Database 10*g* Release 1 added a new column, EVENT_ID, which represents a version-independent unique number for the event.

Some wait events have a *wait time* (or timeout time) attribute, which is the maximum slice of time that a session will wait on a particular event before renewing the wait. For example, the wait event *free buffer waits* has 100 centiseconds wait time. This means every session that waits on the *free buffer waits* event will wait for a maximum of 100 centiseconds. If free buffers are not available at the end of this wait time, the wait times out and the session renews its wait for another 100 centiseconds. The TOTAL_TIMEOUTS column keeps track of the number of times the wait was timed out. For some wait events, the wait time increases exponentially in subsequent attempts. Some wait events, particularly those related to I/O operations, do not have a timeout attribute. In this case, a session will wait indefinitely until the resource becomes available.

How to Use V$SYSTEM_EVENT View

The V$SYSTEM_EVENT view is a good place to start if you want to perform a quick health check on the database instance. This quick health check may be helpful when you must diagnose a poorly performing database instance, especially if you are unfamiliar with it and the application. You will quickly discover the top *n* bottlenecks that plague the database instance since startup. However, don't judge performance or make any tuning decisions based on these bottlenecks just yet. The information is cumulative since the instance startup. You must keep the following three things in mind when querying this view:

- The V$SYSTEM_EVENT view provides instance-level wait event statistics. At this level, it does not offer details such as what sessions suffered the major bottlenecks and when they occurred, rendering it unsuitable for root cause analysis. You cannot always associate the worst event reported by this view with a session that is currently running very slowly.

- You should always order the data from this view by the TIME_WAITED column, as shown in the following example. The values in the TOTAL_ WAITS column can easily misguide you. In Chapter 1, we said you should never base your tuning decisions on quantity; rather, you should focus on time. Certain events such as the *latch free* event may show high TOTAL_ WAITS, but each wait is very short and therefore, the TIME_WAITED may be insignificant. Other events, such as *enqueue*, may have low TOTAL_ WAITS, but each wait might be long.

- You need to evaluate the wait time with respect to the instance startup time. Don't be alarmed by high TIME_WAITED values. Chances are, the longer the instance uptime, the more you will see wait events having high TOTAL_ WAITS and TIME_WAITED values.

Prior to Oracle10*g*:

```
set lines 130
set numwidth 18
col event for a30
col total_waits for 999,999,999
col total_timeouts for 999,999,999
col time_waited for 999,999,999,999
col average_wait for 999,999,999,999
select a.*, b.startup_time
from    v$system_event a,
        v$instance b
order by a.time_waited;
```

Starting Oracle10g:

```
set lines 160
set numwidth 18
col class for a15
col event for a30
col total_waits for 999,999,999
col total_timeouts for 999,999,999
col time_waited for 999,999,999,999
col average_wait for 999,999,999,999
select b.class, a.*, c.startup_time
from    v$system_event a,
        v$event_name b,
        v$instance c
where   a.event = b.name
order by b.class, a.time_waited;
```

Pay attention to the AVERAGE_WAIT column of I/O related events (the *User I/O* and *System I/O* classes in Oracle Database 10g Release 1), which are reported in centiseconds. It can shed some light on the speed of your I/O subsystem. More importantly, it represents your average I/O cost.

As shown in the following partial example output from an Oracle8*i* Database instance, on average it costs a session 0.103029259 centiseconds (10ms) for each single block read and 0.061187607 centiseconds (6ms) for each multiblock read. So you may be able to tolerate higher I/O calls if the average costs are low. (There is more discussion on this subject in Chapter 5.)

```
EVENT                      TOTAL_WAITS  TIME_WAITED  AVERAGE_WAIT
-------------------------  -----------  -----------  ------------
db file sequential read       63094601      6500590   .103029259
db file scattered read       103809207      6351837   .061187607
```

NOTE
*Starting from Oracle9i Database, the AVERAGE_
WAIT column always reports integer numbers. This
is because Oracle applies the ROUND function
when dividing the TIME_WAITED by the TOTAL_
WAITS to compute AVERAGE_WAIT.*

The data in the V$SYSTEM_EVENT view persists throughout the life of the instance.
Oracle doesn't store information from this view for historical analysis as it does for
the V$LOG_HISTORY view.

You may want to know what bottlenecks exist between a certain time frame,
which may encompass a load or processing cycle. To get this information, you must
sample this view periodically and compute the differences, commonly known as *delta*.
After reviewing the delta information, you can concentrate on the areas of concern.
You can investigate the wait events that were waited on the most and categorize
them. Are they I/O-based events such as *db file scattered read* and *db file sequential
read*? Or are they memory-based events such as *latch free*? If so, you can zero in on
the system resources that may need augmentation.

The Oracle-supplied Statspack utility simplifies this task. You can take level-0
snapshots over time and produce a Statspack report showing the delta.

If you do not have Statspack installed, you may use the following SQL scripts to
produce similar results. This method was used before Statspack was introduced in
Oracle8i Database. We encourage you to install and use Statspack instead.

```
-- Assumption is that you have TOOLS tablespace in your database.

-- Create Begin and End tables to store V$SYSTEM_EVENT contents for
-- time T1 and T2 to compute delta.
-- =================================
-- You only need to create these tables once.
-- =================================
create table begin_system_event tablespace tools
as
select *
from   v$system_event
where  1=2;

create table end_system_event tablespace tools
as
```

```
select *
from    v$system_event
where   1=2;

-- Take a snapshot of V$SYSTEM_EVENT information at time T1
truncate table begin_system_event;
insert into begin_system_event
 select *
 from    v$system_event;

-- Wait n seconds or n minutes, and then take another snapshot
-- of V$SYSTEM_EVENT at time T2
truncate table end_system_event;
insert into end_system_event
 select *
 from    v$system_event;

-- Report the 'delta' numbers for wait events between times T2 and T1
select t1.event,
       (t2.total_waits - nvl(t1.total_waits,0)) "Delta_Waits",
       (t2.total_timeouts - nvl(t1.total_timeouts,0)) "Delta_Timeouts",
       (t2.time_waited - nvl(t1.time_waited,0)) "Delta_Time_Waited"
from   begin_system_event t1,
       end_system_event t2
where t2.event = t1.event(+)
order by (t2.time_waited - nvl(t1.time_waited,0)) desc;
```

V$SESSION_EVENT View

The V$SESSION_EVENT view contains aggregated wait event statistics by session for all sessions that are currently connected to the instance. This view contains all the columns present in the V$SYSTEM_EVENT view and has the same meaning, but the context is session-level. It keeps track of the total waits, time waited, and maximum wait time of each wait event by session. The SID column identifies individual sessions. The maximum wait time per event per session is tracked in MAX_WAIT column. You can get more information about the session and user by joining V$SESSION_EVENT with V$SESSION using the SID column.

The V$SESSION_EVENT view has the following columns:

Name	Type	Notes
SID	NUMBER	
EVENT	VARCHAR2(64)	
TOTAL_WAITS	NUMBER	
TOTAL_TIMEOUTS	NUMBER	
TIME_WAITED	NUMBER	

```
AVERAGE_WAIT          NUMBER
MAX_WAIT              NUMBER          Starting Oracle8
TIME_WAITED_MICRO     NUMBER          Starting Oracle9i
EVENT_ID             NUMBER          Starting Oracle10g
```

How to Use V$SESSION_EVENT View

The V$SESSION_EVENT view is useful when you know the SID of the session that is currently connected to the instance. Let's say you get a call about a job that is running very slowly. You ask for the USERNAME and find the SID from the V$SESSION view. (Don't ask your user for the SID; you should be thankful if they can give you the USERNAME. Finding the exact SID can still be a challenge if your application connects with a common USERNAME.) You then query the V$SESSION_EVENT view for the particular SID and order the result by the TIME_WAITED column. You can easily pick out the bottlenecks that may be contributing to poor performance.

Finding the major bottlenecks that are slowing a session down is only the first step in OWI performance tuning. The next step is to determine the root cause, which can be rather difficult using data from the V$SESSION_EVENT view for two main reasons:

- The V$SESSION_EVENT view does not keep track of the SQL statements that experience the bottlenecks. Without correlating bottlenecks to the SQL statements, you may not be able to minimize the bottlenecks even if you discover the worst bottleneck for a session. For example, you may discover that the *db file scattered read* wait event is the major performance bottleneck, but without capturing the SQL statement that performs the full table scans, you'll have very little to offer to your unhappy customers.

- It is hard to determine the root cause of a performance problem if you don't have enough information about its symptom. For example, all latch waits are rolled up into the *latch free* wait event, and you cannot tell which one of the several hundred latches the session waited on the most. However, in Oracle Database 10g Release 1 a handful of the latches are broken out into their individual wait events.

Due to the preceding reasons, the V$SESSION_EVENT view is not suitable for root cause analysis, but it is a good place to get an initial idea of the kind of problems you are dealing with when you have the SID of the running session.

Another column that you may find useful is MAX_WAIT, which records the maximum wait time for each event as experienced by each session in centiseconds. For example, you can find out the longest time a session had to wait for a single block read (*db file sequential read*). It is like a high-water mark of the wait time for the wait event. However, there is no timestamp associated with MAX_WAIT, which means you will not know when the MAX_WAIT was reached. However, Oracle has an undocumented procedure, *dbms_system.kcfrms()*, that resets this column to zero. You can then monitor how MAX_WAIT gets populated. Let's say you are about to execute another module or another step within a job, and you want to know the maximum wait time of each wait event encountered during this execution. You can execute the following procedure while connected as sysdba:

```
execute dbms_system.kcfrms;
```

NOTE
This procedure will reset the MAX_WAIT column for all sessions. In addition, it will reset the MAXIORTM and MAXIOWTM columns in the V$FILESTAT view.

If you use earlier releases of Oracle9*i* Database, you should be aware of a bug (#2429929) that causes misalignment of the SID number between the V$SESSION_ EVENT and V$SESSION views. The SID number in the V$SESSION_EVENT view is off by 1, and it does not have statistics for the PMON process, which has the SID value of 1 in the V$SESSION view. The following query helps you get the correct result in versions that are affected by this bug. According to Oracle, this problem is corrected in release 9.2.0.3.

```
break on sid skip 1 dup
col sid        format 999
col event      format a39
col username format a6    trunc
select b.sid,
        decode(b.username,null,
                substr(b.program,18),b.username) username
        a.event,
        a.total_waits,
        a.total_timeouts,
        a.time_waited,
        a.average_wait,
        a.max_wait,
        a.time_waited_micro
from    v$session_event a, v$session b
where   b.sid = a.sid + 1
order by 1, 6;
```

As in all dynamic performance views, the session-level data of each session persists through the life of the session. Oracle does not keep a history for session-level wait event information. However, the V$ACTIVE_SESSION_HISTORY view in Oracle Database10*g* Release 1 keeps about half an hour of session-level wait event history in memory that was sampled every second. We discuss this view in detail in Chapter 9.

V$SESSION_WAIT View

The V$SESSION_WAIT view provides detailed information about the event or resource that each session is waiting for. This view contains only one row of information per session, active or inactive, at any given time. Unlike the other views, this view displays session-level wait information in real time. Because of this, it may very well show different results each time you query the view.

```
Name                    Type              Notes
--------------------    ---------------   ---------------
SID                     NUMBER
SEQ#                    NUMBER
EVENT                   VARCHAR2(64)
P1TEXT                  VARCHAR2(64)
P1                      NUMBER
P1RAW                   RAW(8)
P2TEXT                  VARCHAR2(64)
P2                      NUMBER
P2RAW                   RAW(8)
P3TEXT                  VARCHAR2(64)
P3                      NUMBER
P3RAW                   RAW(8)
WAIT_CLASS_ID           NUMBER            Starting Oracle10g
WAIT_CLASS#             NUMBER            Starting Oracle10g
WAIT_CLASS              VARCHAR2(64)      Starting Oracle10g
WAIT_TIME               NUMBER
SECONDS_IN_WAIT         NUMBER
STATE                   VARCHAR2(19)
```

As you already know, the column SID shows the session identifier, and EVENT contains the name of the event. The columns P1, P2, and P3 contain specific information about the event and identify a specific resource the session is waiting for. The interpretation of these values is event dependent. The columns P1RAW, P2RAW, and P3RAW contain the hexadecimal representation of the values in P1, P2 and P3, respectively. To help you reference what these values pertain to, the columns P1TEXT, P2TEXT, and P3TEXT provide the description for columns P1, P2 and P3, respectively. The column SEQ# is an internal sequence number for the event related to the session. It increments each time the session waits on the event. The WAIT_TIME column records the amount of time the session has waited for. A negative value denotes unknown wait time, a value equal to zero means that the session is still waiting, and a value greater than zero is the actual wait time. The column SECONDS_IN_WAIT shows wait time in seconds while the session is waiting on the event. The STATE column shows the current wait status. The trio of STATE, WAIT_TIME, and SECONDS_IN_WAIT should be evaluated together, and the next section shows you how to do that.

The WAIT_CLASS_ID, WAIT_CLASS#, and WAIT_CLASS columns are introduced in Oracle Database 10g Release 1 to support the wait event classification feature.

NOTE
*In Oracle Database 10g Release 1 the V$SESSION_*
WAIT view is wholly incorporated into the
V$SESSION view so that you can get pertinent
information about the user session without having to
join the two views.

How to Use V$SESSION_WAIT View

A good time to query the V$SESSION_WAIT view is when you get a call about a slow running application and you want to investigate what the application is doing at that particular moment. Due to its real-time nature, you have to query this view repeatedly, most likely in quick successions. You may see different wait events cycle through quickly, which means the application is actively working, or you may see the application continue to wait on the same event, which means it could be idle or actively waiting on a particular resource such as a lock, a latch or, in case of a resumable session (from Oracle9i Database), a disk space–related issue.

NOTE
Resumable sessions will post event statement
suspended, wait error to be cleared when they
encounter disk space problems; they will wait
till the error is cleared or the resumable session
times out.

Obviously, this view is useful only for current waits and does not provide a history of past wait events. However, that is changed in Oracle Database 10g Release 1. See the "V$SESSION_WAIT_HISTORY View" section for more information.

As explained in the previous section, P1, P2, and P3 are attributes that describe the wait event they are associated with. P1RAW, P2RAW, and P3RAW are the hexadecimal equivalents of P1, P2, and P3. You should familiarize yourself with the attributes of common wait events, but in case you forget, you can get their descriptions from the P1TEXT, P2TEXT, and P3TEXT columns. For root-cause analysis, you must translate the attributes into meaningful information. For example, you can obtain the object name that the *db file sequential read* and *db file scattered read* events are referencing by translating their P1 and P2 values. Likewise, you can find out the name of the latch that the session is waiting on by translating the P2 value. No doubt this can be a very tedious task if you try to do it manually. By the time you successfully translate one event, many other events could go by unnoticed. (Chapter 4 discusses wait event monitoring and data collection in great detail.) Oracle Database 10g Release 1 simplifies this task for latch and enqueue wait events. Common latches have their own wait events, for example, *latch: redo copy* and *latch: cache buffers chains.* All enqueues have their own wait events, for example, *enq: TX - row lock contention* and *enq: ST - contention.*

The STATE column has four possible values: WAITED UNKNOWN TIME, WAITED SHORT TIME, WAITING, and WAITED KNOWN TIME, and their meanings are as follows:

- WAITED UNKNOWN TIME simply means that the TIMED_STATISTICS initialization parameter is set to FALSE and Oracle is unable to determine the wait time. In this case, the WAIT_TIME column shows –2.

- WAITED SHORT TIME means the previous wait was less than one centisecond. In this case, the WAIT_TIME column shows –1.

- WAITING means that the session is currently waiting and the WAIT_TIME column shows 0, but you can determine the time spent on this current wait from the SECONDS_IN_WAIT column. (Please note that SECONDS_IN_WAIT is in seconds, but WAIT_TIME is in centiseconds.)

- WAITED KNOWN TIME means Oracle is able to determine the duration of the last wait and the time is posted in the WAIT_TIME column.

When monitoring the V$SESSION_WAIT view, pay particular attention to the events with STATE=WAITING. This indicates the sessions are actively waiting on the event. The SECONDS_IN_WAIT column shows how long the sessions have been waiting. Also, bear in mind that you should not judge performance based on just one wait occasion. If you want to know how much time a session has waited on a particular wait event, you should consult the V$SESSION_EVENT view.

NOTE
A bug (#2803772) in Oracle Release 9.2.0.2 resets the SECONDS_IN_WAIT column to zero each time the SEQ# changes for the event. There is a patch to correct this issue, or you can upgrade your database to Oracle Release 9.2.0.4.

Trace Event 10046—The Extended SQL Trace

As briefly mentioned earlier, there will be times when it is not feasible to monitor wait events interactively by querying the wait event views. Many times the best way to diagnose a performance problem is by recording the wait events in a trace file for further analysis. This is equivalent to setting SQL_TRACE=TRUE for the session. However, the trace event 10046 can provide a lot more information, depending on the trace level, because it is a superset of SQL trace.

Following are the valid trace levels for this event:

- **Level 0**   Tracing is disabled. This is the same as setting SQL_TRACE = FALSE.

- **Level 1**   Standard SQL trace information (SQL_TRACE = TRUE). This is the default level.

- **Level 4**   SQL trace information plus bind variable values.

- **Level 8**   SQL trace information plus wait event information.

- **Level 12**   SQL trace information, wait event information, and bind variable values.

You can use the trace event 10046 to trace user sessions or Oracle background processes. When tracing a user session, the trace file is written to the directory specified by the parameter USER_DUMP_DEST (UDUMP). When tracing background processes, the trace file is written to the directory specified by the parameter BACKGROUND_DUMP_DEST (BDUMP). The size of the trace file depends on four factors: the trace level, the duration of the trace, the session's activity level, and the value of the MAX_DUMP_FILE_SIZE parameter. The higher the trace level, the larger the trace file, as trace event 10046 is very aggressive at higher debug levels, such as 8 and 12. Due to this aggressive nature, the trace event 10046 is nicknamed "SQL trace on steroids."

How to Use Trace Event 10046

There are various ways to enable the trace event 10046 at the instance or session level. You can enable trace event 10046 at instance level by using the EVENT initialization parameter and restarting the instance so the parameter takes effect, but please don't rush and try it out just yet! At this level, Oracle will begin tracing all sessions and can quickly fill up the UDUMP and BDUMP directory. It is not a good idea to set trace event 10046 at an instance level. We discuss this only for academic interest and show the following syntax for completeness, as this is one of the ways to trap wait event information in a trace file:

```
# This enables the trace event 10046 at level 8 for the instance.
# Restart the instance after this change is made to the init.ora file.
EVENT = "10046 trace name context forever, level 8"

# To disable the trace event 10046 at instance level simply delete or
# comment out the EVENT parameter in the init.ora file and restart the
# instance.
## EVENT = "10046 trace name context forever, level 8"
```

The session level is the practical level for enabling the trace event 10046, and the trace level 8 is normally sufficient. You can trace your own or someone else's session. You can enable and disable the trace at any point during the life of the session. Once the trace is disabled, Oracle stops writing to the trace file.

How to Trace Your Own Session

Enabling trace event 10046 for your current session is easy. You can enter the command interactively or embed it in your SQL script or program. Before you enable the trace, it is a good idea to make sure the parameter TIMED_STATISTICS is set to TRUE and that the trace file size governor, the MAX_DUMP_FILE_SIZE parameter, is set sufficiently large. If TIMED_STATISTICS is not set to TRUE, Oracle will not report any timing information. If the MAX_DUMP_FILE_SIZE is not large enough, Oracle will stop writing trace information to the file after it reaches this value. Following example shows the steps to enable trace for your session:

```
alter session set timed_statistics = true;
alter session set max_dump_file_size = unlimited;
-- To enable the trace event 10046 in Oracle 7.3 onwards
alter session set events '10046 trace name context forever, level 8';
-- Run your SQL script or program to trace wait event information
-- To turn off the tracing:
alter session set events '10046 trace name context off';
```

If you have the DBMS_SUPPORT package installed, you can use the following procedure to enable and disable tracing:

```
-- To include Wait Event data with SQL trace (default option)
exec sys.dbms_support.start_trace;
-- To include Bind variable values, Wait Event data with SQL trace
exec sys.dbms_support.start_trace(waits => TRUE, binds=> TRUE)
-- Run your SQL script or program to trace wait event information
-- To turn off the tracing:
exec sys.dbms_support.stop_trace;
```

NOTE
Per MetaLink Note #62294.1, you will need to run dbmssupp.sql to create DBMS_SUPPORT package. The script is located in the rdbms/admin directory under ORACLE_HOME.

How to Trace Someone Else's Session

Tracing someone else's session or program is a bit more of an involved process, and there are several ways to do it.

If you are not sure whether the TIMED_STATISTICS and MAX_DUMP_FILE_SIZE parameters are set appropriately for the session you want to trace, you should get the SID and its serial number (SERIAL#) from the V$SESSION view. You can then make the following procedure calls to set these parameters appropriately before enabling the trace.

```
-- Set TIME_STATISTICS to TRUE for SID 1234, Serial# 56789

exec sys.dbms_system.set_bool_param_in_session( -
    sid => 1234, -
    serial# => 56789, -
    parnam => 'TIMED_STATISTICS', -
    bval => true);
-- Set MAX_DUMP_FILE_SIZE to 2147483647
-- for SID 1234, Serial# 56789
exec sys.dbms_system.set_int_param_in_session( -
    sid => 1234, -
    serial# => 56789, -
    parnam => 'MAX_DUMP_FILE_SIZE', -
    intval => 2147483647);
```

You can use ALTER SYSTEM SET <parameter> command to set these parameters if these procedures are not available in your Oracle version (Oracle Release 8.1.5 and below).

The next step is to enable the trace in the other session and then disable it after you have gathered enough trace information. You can use one of the following ways to do that:

■ Use the DBMS_SUPPORT package procedures:

```
-- Enable 'level 12' trace in session 1234 with serial# 56789
exec dbms_support.start_trace_in_session( -
    sid => 1234, -
    serial# => 56789, -
    waits => true, -
    binds => true);
```

```
-- Let the session execute SQL script or
-- program for some amount of time

-- To turn off the tracing:
exec dbms_support.stop_trace_in_session( -
    sid => 1234, -
    serial# => 56789);
```

■   Use the DBMS_SYSTEM package procedure:

```
-- Enable trace at level 8 for session 1234 with serial# 56789
exec dbms_system.set_ev( 1234, 56789, 10046, 8, '');

-- Let the session execute SQL script or
-- program for some amount of time

-- To turn off the tracing:
exec dbms_system.set_ev( 1234, 56789, 10046, 0, '');
```

NOTE
*Oracle does not officially support the use of DBMS_*
SYSTEM.SET_EV procedure.

■   Use the *oradebug* facility. You need to know the session's OS process ID
    (SPID) or Oracle process ID (PID). You can look them up in the V$PROCESS
    view. Assuming you know the name of the user you want to trace:

```
select s.username,
       p.spid os_process_id,
       p.pid oracle_process_id
from   v$session s, v$process p
where  s.paddr = p.addr
and    s.username = upper('&user_name');
```

Now use SQL*Plus to connect as sysdba and issue following commands:

```
alter system set timed_statistics = true;
oradebug setospid 12345;
-- 12345 is the OS process id for the session
oradebug unlimit;
oradebug event 10046 trace name context forever, level 8;
-- Let the session execute SQL script
-- or program for some amount of time

-- To turn off the tracing:
oradebug event 10046 trace name context off;
```

In Oracle Database 10g Release 1 you can use DBMS_MONITOR package procedures to enable tracing based on the SID, service name, module, or action. The action-based tracing empowers a DBA to trace a specific business function. There is a little catch to this: the procedure requires that the DBA know the module and action names.

■ Use the DBMS_MONITOR package to enable tracing for session 1234 and serial# 56789 as shown below:

```
exec dbms_monitor.session_trace_enable( -
    session_id => 1234, -
    serial_num => 56789, -
    waits => true, -
    binds => true);
-- Let the session execute SQL script or
-- program for some amount of time


-- To turn off the tracing:
exec dbms_monitor.session_trace_disable( -
    session_id => 1234, -
    serial_num => 56789);
```

These procedures look exactly like the ones from DBMS_SUPPORT package. We recommend that you use DBMS_MONITOR package procedures in Oracle Database 10g Release 1.

■ Use the DBMS_MONITOR package for service, module, and action-based tracing:

```
-- Enable Level 12 trace for known Service,
-- Module and Action
exec dbms_monitor.serv_mod_act_trace_enable( -
    service_name => 'APPS1', -
    module_name => 'GLEDGER', -
    action_name => 'DEBIT_ENTRY', -
    waits => true, -
    binds => true, -
    instance_name => null);


-- Let the session execute SQL script or
-- program for some amount of time


-- To turn off the tracing:
exec dbms_monitor.serv_mod_act_trace_disable( -
    service_name => 'APPS1', -
    module_name => 'GLEDGER', -
    action_name => 'DEBIT_ENTRY');
```

NOTE
The module and action name must be set by the
application using either OCI calls or procedures in
the DBMS_APPLICATION_INFO package.

How to Find Your Trace File

When you enable the trace for your session or for someone else's session, the trace
information may get written to a single trace file or multiple trace files. If you do not
use Oracle's multithreaded server (MTS) or shared server setup, only one trace file
will be generated for one SQL*Plus session. In case of MTS or a shared server, the
trace information may be written to multiple trace files.

As mentioned earlier, the trace files for user sessions will be written to the
USER_DUMP_DEST directory, and for background processes they will be written
to the BACKGROUND_DUMP_DEST directory. Trace file names contain the .trc or
.TRC extension on most platforms. The easiest way to find your trace file is to list
the directory contents in the descending order of timestamp as soon as the tracing
is completed. Chances are the newest file is the trace file you are looking for. You
can confirm it by examining the contents of the file.

Finding your trace file is a bit easier with the *oradebug* trace facility because the
SPID number of the dedicated server process is also written to the trace file. In addition,
you can also get the actual trace file name as follows:

```
SQL> oradebug setmypid
Statement processed.
SQL> oradebug event 10046 trace name context forever,level 8
Statement processed.
SQL> oradebug tracefile_name
d:\oracle\admin\or92\udump\or92_ora_171.trc
```

Starting in Oracle Release 8.1.7 you can set TRACEFILE_IDENTIFIER parameter
for your session using ALTER SESSION command, as shown here:

```
alter session set tracefile_identifier = 'MyTrace';
```

The generated trace file will contain "MyTrace" in its name, making it much
easier for you to find the file.

What Does the Trace File Show?

Once you have located your trace file, the next step is to analyze it for wait events
information. The file contains lines starting with WAIT, as shown in the following
output from an Oracle9*i* Database trace file. These lines show the name (nam) of
the event Oracle waited on and the elapsed time (ela) of the wait. Beginning in

Oracle9*i* Database, this time is in microseconds, but prior to Oracle9*i* Database, it is in centiseconds. You will also find the p1, p2, and p3 parameters that are associated with the wait event. This is equivalent to the P1, P2, and P3 of the V$SESSION_WAIT view. Metalink article #39817.1 discusses how to interpret this raw output.

```
PARSE#1:c=710000,e=1061985,p=4,cr=706,cu=0,mis=1,r=0,dep=0,og=4,tim=183749167771
EXEC #1:c=0,e=399,p=0,cr=0,cu=0,mis=0,r=0,dep=0,og=4,tim=183749170861
WAIT #1: nam='SQL*Net message to client' ela= 12 p1=1650815232 p2=1 p3=0
WAIT #1: nam='db file sequential read' ela= 21578 p1=6 p2=130570 p3=1
WAIT #1: nam='db file sequential read' ela= 17009 p1=6 p2=160988 p3=1
. . . . . . .
. . . . . . .
WAIT #1: nam='SQL*Net message from client' ela= 4700 p1=1650815232 p2=1 p3=0
WAIT #1: nam='SQL*Net message to client' ela= 190 p1=1650815232 p2=1 p3=0
FETCH #1:c=0,e=1408,p=0,cr=0,cu=0,mis=0,r=15,dep=0,og=4,tim=183768775984
WAIT #1: nam='SQL*Net message to client' ela= 7 p1=1650815232 p2=1 p3=0
FETCH #1:c=0,e=1221,p=0,cr=0,cu=0,mis=0,r=15,dep=0,og=4,tim=183768909326
. . . . . . .
```

As you can see, it is rather difficult to manually group the events and sum up their wait times to determine the primary bottleneck. As previously mentioned, the Oracle9*i* Database *tkprof* utility summarizes wait event information that is in the trace file. It produces a report, as shown below, making it much easier to focus on the wait events of interest.

```
Elapsed times include waiting on following events:
  Event waited on                     Times    Max. Wait   Total Waited
  ----------------------------        Waited   ----------  ------------
  SQL*Net message to client           1184        0.00          0.00
  db file sequential read             2441        0.08          8.50
  direct path write                     38        0.00          0.00
  direct path write temp                38        0.00          0.00
  direct path read                     143        0.00          0.00
  direct path read temp                143        0.00          0.03
  SQL*Net message from client         1184       23.87        226.31
********************************************************************
```

New OWI Views in Oracle Database 10*g* Release 1

Oracle Database 10*g* Release 1 contains several nice enhancements to the OWI, such as the wait event classification, the wait event history, and wait event metrics. Several new V$ views are also added to OWI, and the V$SESSION view has been enhanced to include wait event information.

V$SESSION_WAIT_HISTORY View

Historical information has been lacking from the Oracle wait events views. Low-level historical data simply doesn't exist, and DBAs have to rely on high-level data from V$SESSION_EVENT, V$SYSTEM_EVENT and the Statspack utility for performance diagnosis. This view retains the 10 most recent wait events for each connected session. This is not a complete history, but it is a step in the right direction.

The V$SESSION_WAIT_HISTORY view contains the following columns:

```
Name                  Type
-------------------   ----------------
SID                   NUMBER
SEQ#                  NUMBER
EVENT#                NUMBER
EVENT                 VARCHAR2(64)
P1TEXT                VARCHAR2(64)
P1                    NUMBER
P2TEXT                VARCHAR2(64)
P2                    NUMBER
P3TEXT                VARCHAR2(64)
P3                    NUMBER
WAIT_TIME             NUMBER
WAIT_COUNT            NUMBER
```

How to Use V$SESSION_WAIT_HISTORY View

As you noticed, most of the columns in this view are identical to the ones in V$SESSION_WAIT except for the SEQ#, EVENT#, and WAIT_COUNT columns.

The value in column SEQ# indicates the order in which the session encountered the wait events. The most recent event will have a value of 1, while the oldest event will have a value of 10. The column EVENT# identifies the event in the instance. Please note that in Oracle Database 10g Release 1 there is no EVENT_ID in this view. The WAIT_TIME column shows the session wait time for the event. A value of zero means the session was waiting for the event to complete when this information was captured. A value greater than zero denotes the session's last wait time.

The WAIT_COUNT column shows the number of times the session waited for this event. However, we failed to notice any value other than 1 in this column in Oracle Database 10g Release 1.

This view comes in handy when you don't want to keep querying V$SESSION_ WAIT view in quick successions to see what events get posted by the session but would like to quickly get a peek at what events the session has posted recently. The view refreshes the information when the session posts the next event. The oldest event is removed, and the newest one is displayed with a SEQ# of 1.

You can view the history of wait events for a particular session using the following query:

```
select sid, seq#, event, p1, p2, p3, wait_time
from   v$session_wait_history
where  sid = <sid>;
```

Following is a sample output from the above query for SID 20:

```
SID SEQ# EVENT                           P1        P2     P3  WAIT_TIME
--- ---- ------------------------------- ---------- ------- ----- ----------
 20    1 db file scattered read                  6 192033     8          1
 20    2 db file scattered read                  6 192025     8          0
 20    3 db file scattered read                  6 192017     8          0
 20    4 db file scattered read                  6 192009     8          0
 20    5 db file scattered read                  6 192001     8          0
 20    6 SQL*Net message to client       1650815232      1     0          0
 20    7 SQL*Net message from client     1650815232      1     0          0
 20    8 db file scattered read                  6 192057     8          0
 20    9 db file scattered read                  6 192049     8          0
 20   10 db file scattered read                  6 192041     8          0
10 rows selected.
```

This information is good, but 10 slots are too few for an active session because events roll off too quickly. We hope Oracle will provide more slots in future releases. However, as we said earlier, this is the first step in the right direction in providing online historical data for performance diagnosis.

The V$ACTIVE_SESSION_HISTORY view in Oracle Database 10*g* Release 1 also offers historical performance data, which we will discuss in Chapter 9. The information is based on 1-second sampling intervals versus the most recent 10 waits, as in the V$SESSION_WAIT_HISTORY view. We prefer the V$ACTIVE_SESSION_HISTORY because it gives more historical data.

V$SYSTEM_WAIT_CLASS View

This V$SYSTEM_WAIT_CLASS shows the instance-level total waits and time waited by wait class since instance startup.

The view V$SYSTEM_WAIT_CLASS has the following columns:

```
Name                  Type
--------------------- ----------------
WAIT_CLASS_ID         NUMBER
WAIT_CLASS#           NUMBER
WAIT_CLASS            VARCHAR2(64)
TOTAL_WAITS           NUMBER
TIME_WAITED           NUMBER
```

How to Use V$SYSTEM_WAIT_CLASS View

As with the V$SYSTEM_EVENT view, the information displayed by V$SYSTEM_WAIT_CLASS view can be used to quickly check the health of the database instance. Instead of focusing on individual events, you are focusing on the class level.

You can find out what wait classes posted the most wait times since the instance startup. The view will have at most 12 rows, so a simple SELECT * order by TIME_WAITED against this view will reveal the class that has the most waits since instance startup. However, sampling the information between two points of time will show you which wait classes are contributing to the wait times for that period.

You can use a similar method to the one discussed in the "V$SYSTEM_EVENT View" section for computing the delta. Following is a sample output from one of our tests. Ignoring the *Idle* wait class for the time being, you can see that the *System I/O* wait class has the most time. You can now focus only on those wait events that are classified as *System I/O*. You can use this information to track down the sessions that may be contributing wait times to this wait class.

```
WAIT_CLASS# WAIT_CLASS      Delta_Waits Delta_Time_Waited
----------- --------------- ----------- -----------------
          6 Idle                  15107           4210778
          9 System I/O             5116              1926
          8 User I/O              3456              1480
          0 Other                   83               344
          7 Network               2038                 2
          4 Concurrency              3                 1
          5 Commit                   7                 1
          1 Application              7                 0
          2 Configuration            0                 0
```

Interestingly enough, *User I/O* is not far behind *System I/O*. If I/O related wait classes consistently show high wait times, this may indicate an under performing I/O subsystem or I/O bound application code. As it turned out, the server we were using for our tests had only two internal disk drives, and the I/O subsystem was heavily loaded. It was not surprising to us to see this delta information correctly identifying I/O related classes as the potential hot spots.

V$SESSION_WAIT_CLASS View

The view V$SESSION_WAIT_CLASS is similar to the V$SYSTEM_WAIT_CLASS view, but it gives session-level information for all sessions that are currently connected to the instance.

The view V$SESSION_WAIT_CLASS has the following columns:

```
Name                 Type
-------------------- ----------------
SID                  NUMBER
```

```
SERIAL#              NUMBER
WAIT_CLASS_ID        NUMBER
WAIT_CLASS#          NUMBER
WAIT_CLASS           VARCHAR2(64)
TOTAL_WAITS          NUMBER
TIME_WAITED          NUMBER
```

How to Use V$SESSION_WAIT_CLASS View

The V$SESSION_WAIT_CLASS view is useful when you know the SID (and maybe the SERIAL#) of the session that is connected to the instance. You can simply query this view for the SID to quickly find out what wait class has the most waits. Further drilling down using V$SESSION_EVENT view allows you to identify the wait events that may need further investigation.

If you identified a particular wait class as a potential problem by sampling the V$SYSTEM_WAIT_CLASS view as just shown, you can find out all the current sessions contributing to this wait class by querying V$SESSION_WAIT_CLASS view using the WAIT_CLASS#. Once the SID is known, you can find out the user and the SQL that is causing the waits.

V$EVENT_HISTOGRAM View

This is a very interesting and informational view in Oracle Database 10*g* Release 1 when it comes to analyzing wait time per wait event over the life of the instance. It shows a histogram of the number of waits, the total wait time, and the maximum wait for each event. The bucket sizes, or the time intervals in this case, for the histograms are predefined. They cannot be changed. The bucket time intervals are from < 1 ms, < 2 ms, < 4 ms, < 8 ms, < 16 ms, and so on, increasing with the power of 2 up to >= 2^{22} ms. The buckets will be populated accordingly and only when TIMED_STATISTICS is set to TRUE.

The view V$EVENT_HISTOGRAM has the following columns:

```
Name                  Type
--------------------  ---------------
EVENT#                NUMBER
EVENT                 VARCHAR2(64)
WAIT_TIME_MILLI       NUMBER
WAIT_COUNT            NUMBER
```

How to Use V$EVENT_HISTOGRAM View

The event number is shown in the EVENT# column, while the event name is shown in the EVENT column. The column WAIT_TIME_MILLI defines the amount of the time the histogram bucket represents. As the name suggests, the time is in milliseconds. This is similar to how you define the range partitions with a partition key. Still confused?

We'll illustrate this with an example. Once you understand how to read this information, we are confident that you will like this view a lot.

The following simple query selects only two common wait events from this view. Event number 290 and 291 correspond to the *db file sequential read* and *db file scattered read* in our database instance. They may be different in your database instance; check V$EVENT_NAME for the correct numbers in your Oracle version.

```
select *
from   v$event_histogram
where  event# in (290,291);

    EVENT# EVENT                     WAIT_TIME_MILLI WAIT_COUNT
---------- ------------------------- --------------- ----------
       290 db file sequential read                 1       5928
       290 db file sequential read                 2       6099
       290 db file sequential read                 4        509
       290 db file sequential read                 8        640
       290 db file sequential read                16       1653
       290 db file sequential read                32       2327
       290 db file sequential read                64        506
       290 db file sequential read               128         67
       290 db file sequential read               256         20
       290 db file sequential read               512         13
       290 db file sequential read              1024          2

    EVENT# EVENT                     WAIT_TIME_MILLI WAIT_COUNT
---------- ------------------------- --------------- ----------
       291 db file scattered read                  1       4228
       291 db file scattered read                  2       2230
       291 db file scattered read                  4       1002
       291 db file scattered read                  8       2875
       291 db file scattered read                 16        616
       291 db file scattered read                 32       1040
       291 db file scattered read                 64        655
       291 db file scattered read                128        144
```

Let us review the preceding output for event #290, the *db file sequential read*. The values in column WAIT_TIME_MILLI vary from 1 to 1024, comprising 11 histogram buckets. The values in column WAIT_COUNT vary from 5928 to 2. From the first bucket, you see that there were 5928 waits of duration less than 1ms each; from the second bucket, you see that there were 6099 waits of duration more than 1ms but less than 2ms; and so on. In the last bucket, you see that there were 2 waits of duration greater than 512ms but less than 1024ms.

For event #291, there are only 8 histogram buckets because the longest wait time never exceeded 128ms.

What can you learn from this?

You can tell if there are smaller numbers of long waits or a large number of shorter waits.

For any event, the fewer buckets the better because the wait time they represent is shorter. The bucket boundaries are preset, and you cannot change their values. Also, high WAIT_COUNT numbers should be in the buckets with lower WAIT_TIME_MILLI values. If you have it the other way around, then that's the event you need to investigate further! Got it?

Another good application of this view is to monitor the *SQL*Net message from client* event. If the WAIT_COUNT is high for the low-end buckets, it could mean that the application is communicating a lot with the client. This may cause excessive network traffic, which could be reduced with higher ARRAYSIZE or server-side processing. On the other hand, if the WAIT_COUNT is high for the high-end buckets, it is more likely due to user lag time, for example, user think time, coffee time, and so on.

Types of Wait Events

Long before Oracle Database 10g, DBAs have been classifying wait events into four main categories: Foreground, Background, Idle, and Non-Idle events. Foreground events are posted by sessions that have V$SESSION.TYPE ='USER', otherwise referred to as foreground processes. Background events are posted by sessions t hat have V$SESSION.TYPE='BACKGROUND', otherwise known as background processes. Both the foreground and background event categories can have the same wait events. For example, you will find the *latch free, direct path read, direct path write, db file sequential read, db file scattered read* events, among others, posted by both foreground and background processes. Moreover, foreground and background events can further be classified into subcategories, such as I/O, latency, locks, and so on.

Idle events are normally ignored. There is not an industry standard list of common and idle wait events. Oracle Database 10g Release 1 has 58 events listed in wait class #6, the Idle Wait Class.

Table 2-1 shows an example of some of the non-idle wait events that can be posted by foreground (F) and background (B) processes.

Table 2-2 shows some of the idle wait events defined in Oracle Database 10g Release 1.

NOTE
It is important to note that "idle" does not mean that the wait can be ignored—it just means that the user session is not doing work in the database instance.

db file sequential read (F, B)	db file scattered read (F, B)
direct path read (F, B)	direct path write (F, B)
db file parallel write (B)	log file parallel write (B)
control file parallel write (B)	write complete waits (F, B)
free buffer waits (F)	log buffer space (F)
latch free (F, B)	log file sync (F)
enqueue (F, B)	buffer busy waits (F, B)
SQL*Net more data to client (F)	SQL*Net message to client (F)
SQL*Net more data from client (F)	

TABLE 2-1.   *Non-Idle Wait Events (Not a Complete List)*

Whether or not the event *SQL*Net message from client* (and *SQL*Net message from dblink*) should be ignored depends on how the application works. Foreground processes post this event when they wait for instructions from client processes. In other words, the foreground processes are sitting idle waiting for more work to do. For example, a user may run a short query and spend time looking at the result or go out to lunch without logging off. All the while, the foreground process faithfully

PL/SQL lock timer	all events beginning with PX Deq
PX idle wait	SQL*Net message from client
SQL*Net message from dblink	dispatcher timer
jobq slave wait	pipe get
pmon timer	queue messages
rdbms ipc message	single-task message
smon timer	virtual circuit status
wait for activate message	wait for transaction
wakeup event for builder	wakeup event for preparer
wakeup event for reader	wakeup time manager
Null event	

TABLE 2-2.   *Idle Wait Events (Not a Complete List)*

waits for the user to return, posting the *SQL*Net message from client* event and increasing the value in the TIME_WAITED column. Therefore, the *SQL*Net message from client* is the most prevalent event in OLTP systems, and this is why many DBAs choose to ignore this event.

However, this event may provide proof that the bottlenecks are on the client side. Let's say a job ran for a total of 100 seconds, but every 2 seconds it waited on the *SQL*Net message from client* event for another 8 seconds. This shows that whenever a command hit the database, it finished in 2 seconds and the client process took 8 seconds to deal with the result before sending another command to the database. In this case, it is clear that the bulk of the processing time belongs to the client. You can show this timing information to your customers and politely state that the performance of the database instance is not a problem but that the client process needs to be reviewed. In a client/server environment, one should not ignore the SQL*Net, Net8, or Oracle Net–related wait events.

You can safely ignore the *Null* event but you may not want to ignore the *null* event. No, this is not a typo. Pay attention to the case. The *Null* event becomes *null* event starting in Oracle9*i* Database, and it is a major nuisance. It not so much because the case is changed; it's mainly because a bug #2843192 causes many events to be inaccurately reported as the *null* event in the V$SESSION_WAIT view. This is an important view for root cause analysis. You can quickly find out if this bug affects your version of Oracle. Query the V$SESSION_WAIT view in a few quick successions during active processing. If you see the *null* event reported in the output, you should obtain and apply the appropriate patch for the bug, or upgrade to Oracle Release 9.2.0.4. Some patch numbers are listed in Table 2-3, but you should always consult Oracle Support for the right patch, or patchset, for your platform.

Platform	Patch Number
IBM AIX (64-bit) 5L	3073015
IBM RS/6000 AIX 64-bit	3064001
HP Tru64 UNIX	3073015
HP 9000 Series HP-UX 64bit	3055343
Sun Solaris OS (SPARC) 64-bit Sun Solaris OS (SPARC)	3095277

TABLE 2-3. *Patch Numbers for Oracle9i Database for Bug #2843192.*

OWI Limitations

As good as the OWI is, it has a few issues and limitations. We would do you a disservice if we left them out of our discussion because being aware of them will help you better understand how OWI works and how to use it. In the next few sections are some of the issues and limitations of OWI not discussed elsewhere.

No CPU Statistics

We introduced response time tuning methodology in Chapter 1, which takes into account the service time. Service time is the CPU time, but OWI does not offer the CPU time information. However, this information can be obtained from the V$SESSTAT view.

No End-to-End Visibility

One thing you may hear a lot from software vendors that sell proprietary performance monitoring tools is that OWI is limited to the database and has no end-to-end visibility. They emphasize the importance of end-to-end monitoring in today's complex N-tier application architectures, many involving middle-tier connection pooling, XA, Tuxedo, and so on. This is a valid concern. Performance-impacting bottlenecks exist in many areas outside the database instance. As we mentioned in Chapter 1, the end-user response time goes beyond the database response time. If you are to put yourself in the end-users' shoes, you need to experience performance as they experience it—the end-user response time. To calculate the end-user response time, you need to be able to access and account for the latencies in every layer of the application architecture, and this is not possible with OWI. This is where some of the third-party vendors find their niche.

A good end-to-end performance-monitoring tool is indeed appealing, but don't expect your management to rush into buying it—for two main reasons. One, the vendor normally wants an arm and a leg for this kind of tool, and two, the jurisdiction issue. In most companies, the database department is responsible only for the database and not the hardware, network, middle tier products, application codes, and so on. So why should the database department spend the money from its budget to buy an end-to-end monitoring tool? Unless you have a corporate-level "Uncle Sam" department, you are not likely to have such a tool. Even if you do have such a tool and are able to find problems in other areas, you are still limited to your jurisdiction and may find it difficult to bring about changes to correct the problems.

OWI is useful and powerful within the database, and seasoned DBAs practicing OWI will tell you that it is easy to deal with database-related performance problems. The challenge is when the performance problem is outside the database. However, OWI is still useful as a tool to conclusively prove whether the problem is within the database or not: if the problem is not within the database, it has to be somewhere else.

No Historical Data

A big missing piece from OWI is the historical data feature. When a performance issue is raised, DBAs have no way to find out what happened to the session or the database. Unfortunately, this happens far too often and DBAs are always in the dark. The only advice they can give to their unhappy customers is to rerun the job and offer to baby-sit it. Many DBAs resort to developing homegrown monitoring programs or using a high overhead utility, such as the extended SQL trace, to obtain historical data. (Chapter 4 discusses historical data collection in detail.)

This deficiency also opens a wide door of opportunity for third-party vendors, and needless to say, they cash in on it. The performance-monitoring tools market is a fierce battleground, with each vendor offering its bells and whistles. Oracle Corporation noticed this deficiency and is offering many good self-managing features in Oracle Database 10*g* Release 1 that shake the battleground and cause many third-party vendors to tremble. Oracle has always been self-monitoring, it just hasn't always been self-tuning—but that is changing in Oracle Database 10*g* Release 1. The Active Session History (ASH) component collects OWI data every second. The Automatic Workload Repository (AWR) and Automatic Database Diagnostic Monitor (ADDM) provide history and advisories. You can read more about these features in Chapter 9.

Inaccuracies

One of the main complaints among the Wait Interface believers is that OWI statistics are not 100 percent accurate. This is true. Some of the inaccuracies are bug-related, and some are architecture-related. We won't discuss the bug-related inaccuracies here because Oracle will correct them sooner or later, but the architecture-related inaccuracies that are commonly sighted by OWI DBAs are listed here:

- **Inaccurate timing**   The centisecond unit of measurement used in versions prior to Oracle9*i* Database is too coarse for today's fast computers. Many activities are completed in less than one centisecond, and those times are reported as zero. In this case, Oracle misses the time. Whenever an activity begins and ends across a centisecond tick mark but the elapsed time for the activity is less than one centisecond, Oracle counts the time as a full centisecond. In this case, Oracle overcharges the time. You should not be concerned with such under- and overcharging because in the big picture, over time, they do average out. However, Oracle resolved this problem with the microsecond timing, which was first introduced in Oracle9*i* Database, to report timing more accurately. Unfortunately, the microsecond timing is not used across the board. Wait event timeouts and CPU timings in the V$SYSSTAT and V$SESSTAT views are still reported in centiseconds; you must remember to convert the CPU time into microseconds when calculating response time in Oracle version 9*i* and 10*g* if you are using the TIME_WAITED_MICRO for your wait time. However, you need not do so if you take your wait time from the TIME_WAITED column because it is already in the centisecond unit. The CPU_TIME in the V$SQL and V$SQLAREA views is reported in microsecond, but it is "fake" in the sense that it is derived from centisecond. You will always see four significant zeros (1 centisecond * 10,000 = 1 microsecond). In other words, you will never see any row returning from the following query:

```
select  cpu_time
from    v$sqlarea
where   cpu_time between 1 and 999;
```

■ **Incomplete total wait time**   This comes from the fact that not all waits are accounted for. OWI reports waits that are architected in the Oracle kernel, so, obviously, the waits that are not architected are missed. This problem is more significant in earlier versions such as Oracle7 and Oracle8.0, but not as much in Oracle9*i* Database and Oracle Database 10*g*. In Oracle Database 10*g*, Oracle keeps track of over 800 different wait events compared to only 104 in release 7.0.12.

■ **Accounting discrepancies**   No, we are not talking about Enron or WorldCom! What we are talking about is that you may see different results from different views that are reporting on the same thing. For example, there are four views in Oracle9*i* Database that show the magnitude of the *buffer busy waits* contention in the database instance. If you looked at the output from these views, as shown next, you will see how the results vary. Such discrepancies occur mainly because Oracle does not maintain read consistency for V$ views and not all X$ structures are protected by latches. Therefore, in a high concurrency environment, you are bound to see this kind of accounting discrepancy. You should note that this is not an OWI methodology problem, rather it is an Oracle architectural problem that affects V$ views and X$ structures.

```
select  a.value A, b.value B, c.value C, d.value D
from    (select sum(bbwait) AS value
          from   x$kcbwds) a,
        (select total_waits AS value
          from   v$system_event
          where  event = 'buffer busy waits') b,
        (select sum(count) AS value
          from   v$waitstat) c,
        (select sum(value) AS value
          from   v$segment_statistics
          where  statistic_name = 'buffer busy waits') d;

         A           B           C           D
---------- ---------- ---------- ----------
  48216984    48221287    48155238    40947971
```

There you have it. Once you begin working with OWI, you may run into the preceding issues or limitations. If you have been working with OWI for some time, you can probably list a few more. However, Oracle Database 10*g* Release 1 does a better a job of keeping such discrepancies to a minimum.

Even with these limitations and issues, the V$ wait event views and the OWI methodology is the only way to quickly identify performance bottlenecks. In the grand scheme of things, if you have a batch job that runs for hours or days, a few seconds or even a few minutes of discrepancy is not going to misguide you down the wrong path when diagnosing performance problems. Using OWI, you will still be able to find the major bottlenecks that plague the session. Database administration and performance troubleshooting do not require rocket science precision.

In a Nutshell

All Oracle sessions will encounter waits for required resources. You cannot eliminate such waits entirely. OWI enables measurement of all such waits and provides a mechanism to report them. This information is critical to troubleshooting the root cause of such waits and to minimizing them. The less time a session spends waiting for a resource, the faster it may run, improving the response time to the end users, and that is the goal you are after.

The wait event views V$SYSTEM_EVENT, V$SESSION_EVENT, and V$SESSION_WAIT provide various levels of information that you can use to quickly identify sessions contributing to the wait times. The extended SQL trace (trace event 10046) facility nicely supplements these views to report all wait event–related information in a trace file. The wait event information in this trace file can be summarized using the Oracle9*i* Database *tkprof* utility.

Oracle Database 10*g* Release 1 enhances OWI by classifying wait events into categories, such as I/O, Network, Application, Configuration, Idle, and so on. These classifications are useful for focusing your troubleshooting efforts on the affected areas. The new views V$SYSTEM_WAIT_CLASS, and V$SESSION_WAIT_CLASS provide wait time information by wait classes. The view V$SESSION_WAIT_HISTORY displays the 10 latest wait events encountered by each session, and the view V$EVENT_HISTOGRAM provides a nice analysis of the wait times for an event by showing how many times the event waited for a particular time interval. A quick glance at this information will tell you which events might be the possible hot spots.

As the number of wait events tracked in the Oracle kernel keeps increasing with each release, OWI will become increasingly more important. Wait event information is now part of V$SESSION view in Oracle Database 10*g* Release 1. There is no doubt in our minds that OWI is here to stay, and it is the only way to quickly identify performance bottlenecks.

CHAPTER
3

Common Wait Events

ou learned about the components of the OWI. Now, you are ready to explore some of the common Oracle wait events. Of the numerous wait events, only a few common wait events are of importance to the DBA. The wait events in your database will depend on how the application works in your database environment. You should familiarize yourself with the wait events you see in your environment. Many environments will have a handful of the wait events described in the following sections.

The section titled "Common Wait Events in Oracle Real Application Clusters Environment" discusses the wait events seen in the RAC environment.

Introduction to Common Wait Events

We will describe what the event means, what information Oracle provides you in the additional wait parameters, P1, P2 and P3 in the V$SESSION_WAIT view, the extended SQL trace file and the V$SESSION view in Oracle Database 10*g* Release 1. We will also discuss the wait time, or the timeout value for these wait events. Subsequent chapters will discuss in detail the common causes of these events and actions to take to minimize them.

We will also discuss the importance of tracking CPU usage statistics in conjunction with the wait event information.

buffer busy waits

The *buffer busy waits* event occurs when a session wants to access a data block in the buffer cache that is currently in use by some other session. The other session is either reading the same data block into the buffer cache from the datafile, or it is modifying the one in the buffer cache.

In order to guarantee that the reader session has a coherent image of the block with either all of the changes or none of the changes, the session modifying the block marks the block header with a flag letting other sessions know that a change is taking place and to wait until the complete change is applied.

Prior to Oracle Database 10*g* Release 1, *buffer busy waits* event was posted by the session when it had to wait for the other session to read the same data block into the buffer cache. However, starting with Oracle Database 10*g* Release 1, such waits are now posted as *read by other session* event. The *buffer busy waits* event denotes the waits by a session for data block change completion by some other session.

Oracle Database 10*g* Release 1 has another event titled *buffer busy*. Do not confuse this event with *buffer busy waits*. The *buffer busy* event is posted by sessions accessing cached metadata in a database using Automatic Storage Management (ASM).

Although the view V$WAITSTAT is not a component of Oracle Wait Interface, it provides valuable wait statistics for each class of buffer. The most common buffer classes that encounter *buffer busy waits* are data blocks, segment header, undo blocks, and undo header.

The following example shows a sample output from querying V$WAITSTAT view:

```
select *
from   v$waitstat
where  count > 0;

CLASS                  COUNT       TIME
------------------ ---------- ----------
data block            4170082    1668098
segment header            116         98
undo header               916       1134
undo block               2087       1681
```

Wait Parameters

Wait parameters for *buffer busy waits* are described here:

- **P1** From Oracle8 Database onwards, P1 shows the absolute file number where the data block in question resides.

- **P2** The actual block number the processes need to access.

- **P3** Prior to Oracle Database 10*g* Release 1, this is a number indicating the reason for the wait. Oracle posts this event from multiple places in the kernel code with different reason code. The value of this reason code depends on the Oracle release—that is, the reason code changed from pre-Oracle8 Database to Oracle9*i* Database. Oracle Database 10*g* Release 1 does not use reason code anymore, and P3 refers to the *class* in the V$WAITCLASS view in Oracle Database 10*g*. Chapter 6 has more details about how to interpret this information.

For Oracle releases prior to Oracle Database 10*g* Release 1, Table 3-1 lists the reason codes and their descriptions. The reason code in parentheses applies to Oracle releases 8.1.5 and below.

Wait Time

100cs or 1 second

control file parallel write

The *control file parallel write* event occurs when the session waits for the completion of the write requests to all of the control files. The server process issues these write requests in parallel. Starting with Oracle 8.0.5, the CKPT process writes the checkpoint

Reason Code	Description
100 (1003)	The blocking session is reading the block into cache, most likely the undo block for rollback; the waiting session wants exclusive access to create a new block for this information.
110 (1014)	The blocked or waiting session wants to access the current image of the block in either shared (to read) or exclusive (to write) mode, but the blocking session is reading the block into cache.
120 (1014)	The blocked session wants to access the block in current mode; the blocking session is reading the block in the cache. This happens during buffer lookups.
130 (1013)	One or more sessions want to access the same block, but it is not in the buffer. One session will perform the I/O operation and post either a *db file sequential read* or a *db file scattered read* event, while the waiting sessions will post *buffer busy waits* with this reason code.
200 (1007)	The blocking session is modifying the block in the cache; the waiting session wants exclusive access to create a new block.
210 (1016)	The blocking session is modifying the block, while the blocked session wants the current version of the block in exclusive mode. This happens when two processes want to update the same block.
220 (1016)	The blocking session is modifying the block, while the blocked session wants to access the block in current mode during buffer lookup.
230 (1010)	The blocking session is modifying the block, while the blocked session wants shared access of a coherent version of the block.
231 (1012)	The blocking session is modifying the block, while the blocked session is the reading current version of the block when shared access of a coherent version of the block was wanted.

TABLE 3-1. *buffer busy waits Reason Codes*

position in the online redo logs to the control files every three seconds. Oracle uses this information during database recovery operation. Also, when you perform DML operations using either the NOLOGGING or UNRECOVERABLE option, Oracle records the unrecoverable SCN in the control files. The Recovery Manager (RMAN) records backup and recovery information in control files.

There is no blocking session for *control file parallel write*. The session is blocked waiting on the OS and its I/O subsystem to complete the write to all control files. The session performing the write to the control files will be holding the CF enqueue so other sessions may be waiting on this enqueue. If systemwide waits for this wait event are significant, this indicates either numerous writes to the control file, or slow performance of writes to the control files.

Wait Parameters
Wait parameters for *control file parallel write* are described here:

- **P1**   Number of control files the server process is writing to
- **P2**   Total number of blocks to write to the control files
- **P3**   Number of I/O requests

Wait Time
The actual elapsed time to complete all I/O requests.

db file parallel read
Contrary to what the name suggests, the *db file parallel read* event is not related to any parallel operation—neither parallel DML nor parallel query. This event occurs during the database recovery operation when database blocks that need changes as a part of recovery are read in parallel from the datafiles. This event also occurs when a process reads multiple noncontiguous single blocks from one or more datafiles.

Wait Parameters
Wait parameters for *db file parallel read* are described here:

- **P1**   Number of files to read from
- **P2**   Total number of blocks to read
- **P3**   Total number of I/O requests (the same as P2 since multiblock read is not used)

Wait Time
No timeouts. The session waits until all of the I/Os are completed.

db file parallel write
Contrary to what the name suggests, the *db file parallel write* event is not related to any parallel DML operation. This event belongs to the DBWR process, as it is the

only process that writes the dirty blocks to the datafiles. The blocker is the operating system I/O subsystem. This can also have an impact on the I/O subsystem in that the writes may impact read times of sessions reading from the same disks.

DBWR compiles a set of dirty blocks into a "write batch". It issues multiple I/O requests to write the write batch to the datafiles and waits on this event until the I/O requests are completed. However, when using asynchronous I/O, DBWR does not wait for the whole batch write to complete, it waits only for a percentage of the batch to complete before pushing the free buffers back onto the LRU chain so that they can be used. It may also issue more write requests.

Wait Parameters

Wait parameters for *db file parallel write* are described here:

- **P1** Number of files to write to
- **P2** Total number of blocks to write
- **P3** From Oracle9*i* Release 9.2 onward, P3 shows the timeout value in centiseconds to wait for the I/O completion; prior to this release, P3 indicates the total number of I/O requests, which is the same as P2 (blocks).

Wait Time

No timeouts. The session waits until all the I/Os are completed.

db file scattered read

The *db file scattered read* event is posted by the session when it issues an I/O request to read multiple data blocks. The blocks read from the datafiles are scattered into the buffer cache. These blocks need not remain contiguous in the buffer cache. The event typically occurs during full table scans or index fast full scans. The initialization parameter, DB_FILE_MULTIBLOCK_READ_COUNT determines the maximum number of data blocks to read.

Waiting on datafile I/O completion is normal in any Oracle database. The presence of this wait event does not necessarily indicate a performance problem. However, if the time spent waiting for multiblock reads is significant compared to other waits, you must investigate the reason for it.

Wait Parameters

Wait parameters for *db file scattered read* are described here:

- **P1** File number to read the blocks from
- **P2** Starting block number to begin reading
- **P3** Number of blocks to read

Wait Time

No timeouts. The session waits until all of the I/Os are completed to read specified number of blocks.

db file sequential read

The *db file sequential read* wait event occurs when the process waits for an I/O completion for a sequential read. The name is a bit misleading, suggesting a multiblock operation, but this is a single block read operation. The event gets posted when reading from an index, rollback or undo segments, table access by rowid, rebuilding control files, dumping datafile headers, or the datafile headers.

Waiting on datafile I/O completion is normal in any Oracle Database. The presence of this wait event does not necessarily indicate a performance problem. However, if the time spent waiting for single block reads is significant compared to other waits, you must investigate the reason for it.

Wait Parameters

No timeouts. Wait parameters for *db file sequential read* are described here:

- **P1** File number to read the data block from
- **P2** Starting block number to read
- **P3** 1 in most cases, but for temporary segments can be more than 1

Wait Time

No timeouts. The session waits until the I/O is completed to read the block.

NOTE
In a paper titled "Why are Oracle's Read Events 'Named Backwards'?" Jeff Holt explains how the events db file sequential read *and* db file scattered read *got their names. Basically, the* db file sequential read *happens when the buffer cache memory locations that receive data from disk are contiguous. In the case of* db file scattered read *those are not guaranteed to be contiguous. The paper is available at www.hotsos.com.*

db file single write

The *db file single write* event is posted by DBWR. It occurs when Oracle is updating datafile headers, typically during a checkpoint. You may notice this event when your database has an inordinate number of database files.

Wait Parameters

Wait parameters for *db file single write* are described here:

- **P1** File number to write to

- **P2** Starting block number to write to

- **P3** The number of blocks to write, typically 1

Wait Time

No timeouts. Actual time it takes to complete the I/O operation.

direct path read

The *direct path read* event occurs when Oracle is reading data blocks directly into the session's PGA instead of the buffer cache in the SGA. Direct reads may be performed in synchronous I/O or asynchronous I/O mode, depending on the hardware platform and the value of the initialization parameter, DISK_ASYNCH_IO. Direct read I/O is normally used while accessing the temporary segments that reside on the disks. These operations include sorts, parallel queries, and hash joins.

The number of waits and time waited for this event are somewhat misleading. If the asynchronous I/O is not available, the session waits till the I/O completes. But these are not counted as waits at the time the I/O request is issued. The session posts a *direct path read* wait event when accessing the data after the completion of the I/O request. In this case, the wait time will be negligibly small.

If the asynchronous I/O is available and in use, then the session may issue multiple direct path read requests and continue to process the blocks that are already cached in the PGA. The session will register *direct path read* wait event only when it cannot continue processing because the required block has not been read into the buffer. Therefore, the number of read requests may not be the same as the number of waits. Due to these anomalies, it is unlikely that you will see this wait event reported in V$SYSTEM_EVENT and V$SESSION_EVENT views.

Starting from Oracle Release 8.1.7 there is a separate *direct path read (lob)* event for reading LOB segments.

Wait Parameters

Wait parameters for *direct path read* are described here:

- **P1** Absolute file number to read from

- **P2** Starting block number to read from

- **P3** Number of blocks to read

Wait Time
No timeouts. Actual time until the outstanding I/O request completes.

direct path write

The *direct path write* wait event is just an opposite operation to that of *direct path read.* Oracle writes buffers from the session's PGA to the datafiles. A session can issue multiple write requests and continue processing. The OS handles the I/O operation. If the session needs to know if the I/O operation was completed, it will wait on *direct path write* event.

The direct path write operation is normally used when writing to temporary segments, in direct data loads (inserts with APPEND hint, or CTAS), or in parallel DML operations.

As with the *direct path write* event, the number of waits and time waited for this event can be misleading when asynchronous I/O is in use.

Starting from Oracle 8.1.7 there is a separate *direct path write (lob)* event for writing to uncached LOB segments.

Wait Parameters
Wait parameters for *direct path write* are described here:

- **P1** Absolute file number to write to
- **P2** Starting block number to write from
- **P3** Number of blocks to write

Wait Time
No timeouts. Actual time until the outstanding I/O request completes.

enqueue

An enqueue is a shared memory structure used by Oracle to serialize access to the database resources. The process must acquire the enqueue lock on the resource to access it. The process will wait on this event if the request to acquire the enqueue is not successful because some other session is holding a lock on the resource in an incompatible mode. The processes wait in queue for their turn to acquire the requested enqueue. A simple example of such an enqueue wait is a session waiting to update a row when some other session has updated the row and not yet committed (or rolled back) its transaction and has a lock on it in an exclusive mode.

There are various types of enqueue to serialize access to various resources, uniquely identified by a two-character enqueue name. For example:

- **ST** Enqueue for Space Management Transaction

■ **SQ** Enqueue for Sequence Numbers

■ **TX** Enqueue for a Transaction

NOTE
In Oracle Database 10g Release 1, each enqueue type is represented by its own wait event, which makes it much easier to understand exactly what type of enqueue the session is waiting for. Please refer to Appendix B for a complete list of these enqueue waits.

Wait Parameters

Wait parameters for *enqueue* are described here:

■ **P1** Enqueue name and mode requested by the waiting process.
This information is encoded in ASCII format. The following SQL statement shows how you can find out the enqueue name and mode requested by the waiting process:

```
col Name format a4
select sid,
        chr(bitand(p1, -16777216)/16777215) ||
        chr(bitand(p1,16711680)/65535) "Name",
        (bitand(p1, 65535)) "Mode"
from    v$session_wait
where   event = 'enqueue';

        SID Name         Mode
---------- ---- ----------
        64 TX              6
```

■ **P2** Resource identifier ID1 for the requested lock, same as V$LOCK.ID1

■ **P3** Resource identifier ID2 for the requested lock, same as V$LOCK.ID2

The values for resource identifiers ID1 and ID2 are dependent on the enqueue name.

Wait Time

The wait time is dependent on enqueue name, but in most cases Oracle waits for up to three seconds or until the enqueue resource becomes available, whichever occurs first. When the wait event times out, Oracle will check that the session holding the lock is still alive and, if so, wait again.

free buffer waits

The *free buffer waits* event occurs when the session cannot find free buffers in the database buffer cache to read in data blocks or to build a consistent read (CR) image of a data block. This could mean either the database buffer cache is too small, or the dirty blocks in the buffer cache are not getting written to the disk fast enough. The process will signal DBWR to free up dirty buffers but will wait on this event.

Wait Parameters

Wait parameters for *free buffer waits* are described here:

■ **P1** File number from which Oracle is reading the block

■ **P2** Block number from the file that Oracle wants to read into a buffer

■ **P3** Not used prior to Oracle Database 10*g* Release 1; in this release it shows the SET_ID# for the LRU and LRUW lists in the buffer cache

Wait Time

Oracle will wait up to one second for free buffers to become available and then try to find a free buffer again.

latch free

The *latch free* wait occurs when the process waits to acquire a latch that is currently held by other process. Like enqueue, Oracle uses latches to protect data structures. One process at a time can either modify or inspect the data structure after acquiring the latch. Other processes needing access to the data structure must wait till they acquire the latch. Unlike enqueue, processes requesting latch do not have to wait in a queue. If the request to acquire a latch fails, the process simply waits for a short time and requests the latch again. The short wait time is called "spin". If the latch is not acquired after one or more spin iterations, the process sleeps for a short time and tries to acquire the latch again, sleeping for successively longer periods until the latch is obtained.

The most common latches you need to know are *cache buffer chains, library cache,* and *shared pool.* These and other latches are discussed in detail in Chapter 6.

Wait Parameters

Wait parameters for *latch free* are described here:

■ **P1** Address of the latch for which the process is waiting

- **P2** Number of the latch, same as V$LATCHNAME.LATCH#.
  To find out the latch name waited on, you can use the following SQL statement:

```
select *
from   v$latchname
where  latch# = &p2_value;
```

- **P3** Number of tries; a counter showing the number of attempts the process made to acquire the latch

Wait Time

The wait time for this event increases exponentially. It does not include the time the process spent spinning on the latch.

In Oracle Database 10*g* Release 1, most latches have their own wait events. Table 3-2 lists the wait events associated with latches.

library cache pin

The *library cache pin* wait event is associated with library cache concurrency. It occurs when the session tries to pin an object in the library cache to modify or

latch: In memory undo latch	latch: messages
latch: KCL gc element parent latch	latch: object queue header heap
latch: cache buffer handles	latch: object queue header operation
latch: cache buffers chains	latch: parallel query alloc buffer
latch: cache buffers lru chain	latch: redo allocation
latch: checkpoint queue latch	latch: redo copy
latch: enqueue hash chains	latch: redo writing
latch: gcs resource hash	latch: row cache objects
latch: ges resource hash list	latch: session allocation
latch: library cache	latch: shared pool
latch: library cache lock	latch: undo global data
latch: library cache pin	latch: virtual circuit queues

TABLE 3-2. *Latch Events in Oracle Database 10*g

examine it. The session must acquire a pin to make sure that the object is not updated by other sessions at the same time. Oracle posts this event when sessions are compiling or parsing PL/SQL procedures and views.

What actions to take to reduce these waits depend heavily on what blocking scenario is occurring. A common problem scenario is the use of DYNAMIC SQL from within a PL/SQL procedure where the PL/SQL code is recompiled and the DYNAMIC SQL calls something that depends on the calling procedure. If there is general widespread waiting, the shared pool may need tuning. If there is a blocking scenario, the following SQL can be used to show the sessions that are holding and/ or requesting pins on the object that are given in P1 in the wait:

```
select s.sid, kglpnmod "Mode", kglpnreq "Req"
from   x$kglpn p, v$session s
where  p.kglpnuse=s.saddr
and    kglpnhdl='&P1RAW' ;
```

Wait Parameters
Wait parameters for *library cache pin* are described here:

- **P1** Address of the object being examined or loaded

- **P2** Address of the load lock

- **P3** Contains the mode plus the namespace (mode indicates which data pieces of the object are to be loaded; namespace is the object namespace as displayed in V$DB_OBJECT_CACHE view)

Wait Time
For the PMON process it is one second; for all others it is three seconds.

library cache lock
The *library cache lock* event is also associated with library cache concurrency. A session must acquire a library cache lock on an object handle to prevent other sessions from accessing it at the same time, or to maintain a dependency for a long time, or to locate an object in the library cache.

Wait Parameters
Wait parameters for *library cache lock* are described here:

- **P1** Address of the object being examined or loaded

- **P2** Address of the load lock

- **P3** Contains the mode plus the namespace (mode indicates which data pieces of the object are to be loaded; namespace is the object namespace as displayed in V$DB_OBJECT_CACHE view)

Wait Time
For the PMON process it is one second; for all others it is three seconds.

log buffer space

The *log buffer space* wait occurs when the session has to wait for space to become available in the log buffer to write new information. The LGWR process periodically writes to redo log files from the log buffer and makes those log buffers available for reuse. This wait indicates that the application is generating redo information faster than LGWR process can write it to the redo files. Either the log buffer is too small, or redo log files are on disks with I/O contention.

Wait Parameters
Wait parameters are not used for *log buffer space*.

Wait Time
Normally one second, but five seconds if the session has to wait for a log file switch to complete.

log file parallel write

The *log file parallel write* wait occurs when the session waits for LGWR process to write redo from log buffer to all the log members of the redo log group. This event is typically posted by LGWR process. The LGWR process writes to the active log file members in parallel only if the asynchronous I/O is in use. Otherwise, it writes to each active log file member sequentially.

   The waits on this event usually indicate slow disk devices or contention where the redo logs are located.

Wait Parameters
Wait parameters for *log parallel write* are described here:

- **P1** Number of log files to write to

- **P2** Number of OS blocks to write to

- **P3** Number of I/O requests

Wait Time

Actual elapsed time it takes to complete all I/Os. Although the log files are written to in parallel, the write is not complete till the last I/O operation is complete.

log file sequential read

The *log file sequential read* wait occurs when the process waits for blocks to be read from the online redo logs files. The ARCH process encounters this wait while reading from the redo log files.

Wait Parameters

Wait parameters for *log file sequential read* are described here:

- **P1**   Relative sequence number of the redo log file within the redo log group
- **P2**   Block number to start reading from
- **P3**   Number of OS blocks to read starting from P2 value

Wait Time

Actual elapsed time it takes to complete the I/O request to read.

log file switch (archiving needed)

The *log file switch* wait indicates that the ARCH process is not keeping up with LGWR process writing to redo log files. When operating the database in archive log mode, the LGWR process cannot overwrite or switch to the redo log file until the ARCH process has archived it by copying it to the archived log file destination. A failed write to the archive log file destination may stop the archiving process. Such an error will be reported in the alert log file.

Wait Parameters

Wait parameters are not used for *log file switch (archiving needed)*.

Wait Time

One second

log file switch (checkpoint incomplete)

The *log file switch* wait indicates that the process is waiting for the log file switch to complete, but the log file switch is not possible because the checkpoint process for that log file has not completed. You may see this event when the redo log files are sized too small.

Wait Parameters
Wait parameters are not used for *log file switch (checkpoint incomplete)*.

Wait Time
One second

log file switch completion
This wait event occurs when the process is waiting for log file switch to complete.

Wait Parameters
Wait parameters are not used for *log file switch completion*.

Wait Time
One second

log file sync
When a user session completes a transaction, either by a commit or a rollback, the session's redo information must be written to the redo logs by LGWR process before the session can continue processing. The process waits on this event while LGWR process completes the I/O to the redo log file.

If a session continues to wait on the same buffer#, the SEQ# column of V$SESSION_WAIT view should increment every second. If not, then the local session has a problem with wait event timeouts. If the SEQ# column is incrementing, the blocking process is the LGWR process. Check to see what LGWR process is waiting on because it may be stuck.

Tune LGWR process to get good throughput to disk; for example, do not put redo logs on RAID-5 disk arrays. If there are lots of short-duration transactions see if it is possible to BATCH transactions together so there are fewer distinct COMMIT operations. Each COMMIT has to have it confirmed that the relevant REDO is written to disk. Although commits can be *piggybacked* by Oracle, reducing the overall number of commits by batching transactions can have a very beneficial effect.

Wait Parameters
Wait parameters for *log file sync* are described here:

- ■ **P1** The number of the buffer in the log buffer that needs to be synchronized

- ■ **P2** Not used

- ■ **P3** Not used

Wait Time
One second

SQL*Net message from client

This wait event is posted by the session when it is waiting for a message from the client to arrive. Generally, this means that the session is sitting idle. Excessive wait time on this event in batch programs that do not interact with an end user at a keyboard may indicate some inefficiency in the application code or in the network layer. However, the database performance is not degraded by high wait times for this wait event, because this event clearly indicates that the perceived database performance problem is actually not a database problem.

Wait Parameters
Wait parameters for *SQL*Net message from client* are described here:

■ **P1**   Prior to Oracle8*i* release, the value in this parameter was not of much use. Since Oracle8*i*, the P1RAW column contains an ASCII value to show what type of network driver is in use by the client connections; for example, bequeath, and TCP.

■ **P2**   The number of bytes received by the session from the client—generally one, even though the received packet will contain more than 1 byte.

■ **P3**   Not used.

Wait Time
The actual time it takes for the client message to arrive since the last message the session sent to the client.

SQL*Net message to client

This wait event is posted by the session when it is sending a message to the client. The client process may be too busy to accept the delivery of the message, causing the server session to wait, or the network latency delays may be causing the message delivery to take longer.

Wait Parameters
Wait parameters for *SQL*Net message to client* are described here:

■ **P1**   Prior to Oracle8*i* Database, the value in this parameter was not of much use. Since Oracle8*i*, the P1RAW column contains an ASCII value to show what type of network driver is in use by the client connections, for example, bequeath and TCP.

- ■ **P2** Number of bytes sent to client. This is generally one even though the sent packet will contain more than 1 byte.

- ■ **P3** Not used.

Wait Time
Actual elapsed time it takes to complete the message delivery to the client.

Common Wait Events in Oracle Real Application Clusters Environment

In this section we will discuss some of the common wait events that you will see in Oracle Real Application Clusters (RAC) environment.

global cache cr request

When a session is looking for a consistent read (CR) copy of the buffer cached by the remote instance, it waits on the *global cache cr request* event till the buffer is available in the local instance. Normally the holder constructs the CR version of the buffer and ships it to the requesting instance through the high speed interconnect. The wait ends when the CR buffer arrives at the local buffer cache.

From Oracle Database 10*g* Release 1, *global cache cr request* waits are known as *gc cr request waits*.

Depending on the mode of the buffer held in the remote instance and the number of times the remote instance ships the CR copy to the local instance, one of the following will happen:

1. The CR copy of the buffer is sent to the requesting instance and the "fairness counter" is incremented for that buffer. Subsequently the *global cache cr blocks received* statistic is incremented.

2. If the buffer is not cached by the remote instance (but mastered by the remote instance), it grants it to the requesting instance. The session can read the block from the disk and the *global cache gets* statistic is incremented.

3. If the number of CR copies for that particular buffer reaches the *_fairness_ threshold* limit, the remote instance downgrades the lock to null mode and flushes the redo to the disk. The session can do the disk I/O to get the block from the disk.

In cases 2 and 3, the *global cache cr requests* waits are typically followed by the *db file sequential reads* and/or *db file scattered read* waits.

Wait Parameters
Wait parameters for *global cache cr request* are described here:

- **P1**   File number from which Oracle is reading the block
- **P2**   Block number from the file that Oracle wants to read into a buffer
- **P3**   The lock element number or class of the buffer

Table 3-3 lists the most commonly seen block classes.

Wait Time
The wait is up to one second between timeouts. The actual wait time will be until the buffer is cached at the requesting instance in required compatible mode.

Block Class	Description
0	System rollback segment
1	Data blocks
2	Sort blocks
3	Deferred rollback segment blocks (save undo)
4	Segment header blocks
5	Deferred rollback segment header blocks
6	Freelist blocks
7	Extent map blocks
8	Bitmapped space management blocks
9	Space management index blocks
10	Unused

TABLE 3-3.   *Common Block Classes*

buffer busy global cache

When a session wants to modify a buffer that is cached in the remote instances, it waits on the *buffer busy global cache* event. This is similar to *buffer busy wait* in single instance architecture. This wait happens at cache layer. In other words, the session is waiting for a buffer in local cache, which is busy because it is waiting for a global cache request to complete. The wait at the RAC layer is accounted in the *global cache busy* wait event.

From Oracle Database10g Release 1, *buffer busy global cache* waits are known as *gc buffer busy* waits.

Wait Parameters

Wait parameters for *buffer busy global cache* are described here:

- **P1** File number from which Oracle is reading the block
- **P2** Block number from the file that Oracle wants to read into a buffer
- **P3** The numeric code indicating the reason

Wait Time

The wait time is one second between timeouts.

buffer busy global cr

When more than one session is queued for a CR copy of the buffer in a same instance, and the CR copy is expected from the remote instance, the session waits on the *buffer busy global cr* wait event. Once the CR copy from the remote instance arrives at the local cache, the block SCN is compared with the snapshot SCN before the buffer can be used.

From Oracle Database 10g Release 1, this wait event is known as *gc cr block busy* waits.

Wait Parameters

Wait parameters for *buffer busy global cr* are described here:

- **P1** File number from which Oracle is reading the block
- **P2** Block number from the file that Oracle wants to read into a buffer
- **P3** The numeric code indicating the reason

Wait Time

The wait time is one second between timeouts.

global cache busy

When a session wants to modify a buffer that is held in a shared mode, it waits on the *global cache busy* wait event till it gets the buffer in current mode. This normally happens when an instance wants to acquire a buffer from a remote instance and the lock convert or acquisition process is in progress. Normally, the segment header blocks, index branch blocks, and bitmap segment blocks are held in the shared mode. During addition of new blocks to the segment, the buffer is transformed from shared current mode to exclusive current mode.

Waits for *global cache busy* are usually followed by the *global cache s to x* waits. Excessive waits for these waits could be an indicator of slow interconnect or a delay in flushing the redo for that particular block on the remote instance.

Wait Parameters

Wait parameters for *global cache busy* are described here:

■ **P1** File number from which Oracle is reading the block

■ **P2** Block number from the file that Oracle wants to read into a buffer

■ **P3** The lock element number or class of the buffer

Wait Time

The wait time is one second between timeouts.

global cache null to x

When a session wants to modify a block, it must hold that block in exclusive mode in its local cache. The session will wait for *global cache null to x* wait when the buffer is not in its local cache in any other mode. If the buffer is in the global cache at the remote instance, the buffer is shipped to the local cache and the exclusive lock for that buffer is granted. The statistics *global cache current blocks served* is incremented after the transfer.

If it is not held in any other mode in remote cache, the lock is granted for that buffer from the Global Cache Service (GCS) at the appropriate mode. Once the lock is granted for the buffer, disk I/O is done to read the buffer from the disk.

Wait Parameters

Wait parameters for *global cache null to x* are described here:

■ **P1** File number from which Oracle is reading the block

■ **P2** Block number from the file that Oracle wants to read into a buffer

■ **P3** The lock element number or class of the buffer

Wait Time
One second

global cache null to s

When a session wants to read a buffer, it has to convert from NULL mode to SHARED mode. The buffer can be read from the disk if it is not cached globally or can be obtained from the other instance's cache through the interconnect.

Wait Parameters

Wait parameters for *global cache null to s* are described here:

- **P1**   File number from which Oracle is reading the block

- **P2**   Block number from the file that Oracle wants to read into a buffer

- **P3**   The lock element number or class of the buffer

Wait Time
One second

global cache s to x

The session waits for *global cache s to x* when it holds the buffer in SHARED mode and wants to convert it to EXCLUSIVE (X) mode. If no other instances are holding that buffer in SHARED or EXCLUSIVE mode, the lock is immediately upgraded to X mode after incrementing the *global cache converts* counter. If any other instance is holding the buffer in SHARED mode, the lock mode is downgraded to *null* mode.

Typically, index updates will result in *global cache s to x* waits as you lock the buffer for SHARED mode while traversing in the index tree. It will update the leaf block address in the branch block after holding the buffer in EXCLUSIVE mode.

Wait Parameters

Wait parameters for *global cache s to x* are described here:

- **P1**   File number from which Oracle is reading the block

- **P2**   Block number from the file that Oracle wants to read into a buffer

- **P3**   The lock element number or class of the buffer

Wait Time
One second

global cache open x

A session waits for the *global cache open x* wait when it wants to modify the current block (usually for inserts and bulk loads), which is not cached in the local instance in any mode. The current block has to come from the remote instance or from the disk. If the block is not cached in any of the caches and if that is a new block to the global cache, there is no lock conversion involved. The process is called block "newing," and it happens during the new blocks allocated to the freelist chain or bitmap segments.

Wait Parameters

Wait parameters for *global cache open x* are described here:

- **P1**   File number from which Oracle is reading the block
- **P2**   Block number from the file that Oracle wants to read into a buffer
- **P3**   The lock element number or class of the buffer

Wait Time

One second

global cache open s

A session waits for the *global cache open s* when it reads the block in the buffer cache for the first time. This can happen during the startup or while reading a block that is the first-time read into the local buffer cache. The block can either be read from the disk or shipped from the other instance cache.

Wait Parameters

Wait parameters for *global cache open s* are described here:

- **P1**   File number from which Oracle is reading the block
- **P2**   Block number from the file that Oracle wants to read into a buffer
- **P3**   The lock element number or class of the buffer

Wait Time

One second

row cache lock

The dictionary cache is known as row cache because it keeps the information at row level, as opposed to the buffer cache, which keeps the information at block level. The locks, which protect the definition of the data dictionary objects, are called *row cache locks*. Normally, DDL statements require *row cache lock*, and the session will wait for the *row cache lock* to lock the data dictionary information.

This wait is not a RAC-specific wait. It is applicable in single instance also but has a bigger impact in the RAC environment because the library cache and row cache are globally coordinated.

Wait Parameters

Wait parameters for *row cache lock* are described here:

- **P1**   Cache ID of the row cache lock the session is waiting for; can be obtained from V$ROWCACHE

- **P2**   The mode in which the lock is held

- **P3**   The mode in which the lock is requested

The following SQL can be used to find cache number from the V$ROWCACHE:

```
select cache#, type, parameter
from   v$rowcache
where  cache# = &P1;
```

Wait Time

Three seconds between timeouts. After 100 timeouts, the process is rolled back and the session writes: WAITED TOO LONG FOR A ROW CACHE ENQUEUE LOCK in the alert.log, and the process is aborted.

Tracking CPU and Other Statistics

We briefly mentioned in Chapter 2 that OWI does not capture any CPU statistics. Fortunately, this, along with myriad other statistics is exposed via the V$SYSSTAT view at the system level and the V$SESSTAT view at the session level. The V$STATNAME view provides a list of statistics that can be used to resolve the statistic name for V$SESSTAT. In short, V$SYSSTAT shows cumulative instance-wide statistics since the instance started, while V$SESSTAT shows cumulative session-wide statistics since the session started. The number and names of these statistics vary from version to version, just as with the wait events. However, the structure and meaning has mostly remained the same through the versions.

The meaning is usually the same whether you are looking at V$SESSTAT for the session-level statistics or whether you are looking at V$SYSSTAT for the system-level statistics. While there are a large number of statistics, we will look into only those

CPU used by this session	Amount of CPU time (in tens of milliseconds) used by a session from the time a user call starts until it ends. If a user call completes within 10 milliseconds, the start and end user-call time are the same for purposes of this statistic, and 0 milliseconds are added.
CPU used when call started	The CPU time used when the call is started. See also *CPU used by this session*, above.
recursive cpu usage	Total CPU time used by nonuser calls (recursive calls). Subtract this value from *CPU used by this session* to determine how much CPU time was used by the user calls.
parse time cpu	Total CPU time used for parsing (hard and soft) in tens of milliseconds.
parse time elapsed	Total elapsed time for parsing, in tens of milliseconds. Subtract *parse time cpu* from this statistic to determine the total waiting time for parse resources.
session logical reads	The sum of *db block gets* plus *consistent gets*. Simply put, *db block gets* is the number of requests for an "unchanged" lock and *consistent gets* is the number of requests for a block that was "changed" and then reconstructed.

TABLE 3-4.   *CPU Usage*

that pertain either directly or indirectly to CPU usage and I/O requests. Tables 3-4 and 3-5 list these, with explanations from the *Oracle Reference Guide* along with our notes.

physical reads	Total number of data blocks read from disk. This number equals the value of *physical reads direct* plus all reads into buffer cache, where *physical reads direct* are reads that bypassed the buffer cache.
physical writes	Total number of data blocks written to disk. This number equals the value of *physical writes direct* plus all writes from buffer cache, where *physical writes direct* are writes that were written directly to disk.

TABLE 3-5.   *Physical I/O Requests*

The name *CPU used by this session* is probably incorrect when applied to systemwide statistics from V$SYSSTAT. However, the meaning is the same—that is, it is the systemwide CPU usage at that point of time. You will also observe that while the values of *CPU used when call started* and *CPU used by this session* will be more or less the same for a particular session in V$SESSTAT, they may differ slightly when looking at V$SYSSTAT, especially on a database that is prone to long running queries. This is because *CPU used when call started* in V$SYSSTAT is a snapshot of CPU time used before the currently executing calls *started*, while *CPU used by this session* records the incremental CPU time of sessions that have already completed.

The CPU usage of a session is mainly accounted under two areas:

■ **Access to blocks in the buffer cache**   Requires a complex set of operations including determining the location, computing the address, holding a latch to get to the block, and requesting a physical I/O if the block is not present in the buffer cache. This is termed a logical I/O (LIO) and consumes significant amount of CPU. The *session logical reads* is thus a very valid statistic that keeps track of this.

■ **Parsing the query**   Requires another complex set of operations including checking the syntax and semantics of the query, allocating and loading Data Dictionary and Library cache entries, and so on, which again needs significant latching.

All these actions, of course, precipitate wait time for events to occur, which OWI exposes so well.

The *physical reads* and *physical writes* are a measure of physical I/O requested by the session in the case of V$SESSTAT or summed across the database in V$SYSSTAT. Note that this may not directly equate to the actual I/O operations performed, as the OS buffer cache, the volume manager cache and even the disk storage array cache may have satisfied these I/O requests.

To some extent, the value of these statistics as an aid to tuning is in their absolute numbers. However, they fully serve the purpose when you look at the *delta* values between specific times to fully understand what happened in-between the start and end of those times. This way, they complement the information obtained by using OWI and provide some crosschecking that can be performed.

In a Nutshell

We discussed some wait events that are commonly seen in many databases, including the Real Application Clusters environment.

The wait parameters P1, P2, and P3 in the V$SESSION_WAIT view, or the V$SESSION view in Oracle Database 10*g* Release 1, provide more information to find the cause of the wait event. For some events, the columns P1RAW, P2RAW, and P3RAW of these views contain the needed information. The wait time, or timeout value, varies for various wait events. The event waits until the required action is completed or the required resource becomes available. The views V$SYSSTAT and V$SESSTAT are not part of the OWI. However, those provide vital information about CPU usage and other statistics.

CHAPTER
4

OWI Monitoring and Collection Methods

rescribing the right solution for performance problems the first time is the ultimate goal of every tuning practitioner. This may be relatively easy if the problem is a current one, but it could be daunting if the performance problem happened in the past, and you are called upon to determine the root cause and provide a solution to prevent it from happening again. This task can be unbearable when pressure is added because the severity and visibility levels of the performance problem are high and the whole organization is watching and expecting only positive results, especially if your boss is breathing down your neck.

Performance diagnosis is a major part of tuning, and a good collection of historical performance data improves root cause analysis and identification. History is relevant and important because most performance tuning exercises are reactive in nature. Without a history of every foreground process that connects to the database, you are limited to the current status of processes and their activities and a few views that provide high-level performance statistics, which may not necessarily reveal or represent the true problem. Often jobs must be re-executed to reproduce the symptoms, assuming they are reproducible and you know when they are going to resurface. Performing tuning exercises without the guidance of symptoms is like shooting in the dark and is dangerous because such exercises are likely to lead you down the wrong path and cause unnecessary reworks. Obviously, such attempts are also costly to the business as they increase the problem turnaround time. Also, while you are looking for the root cause of the performance problem, blame usually is placed on the database, and no DBA likes to hear that.

This chapter deals with the importance of session-level wait event monitoring and historical data collection for root cause analysis. It shows you how to put together a data collector that complements trace event 10046 using Oracle-supplied resources in a relatively short time. We hope you will use and benefit from these resources and that you will always be ready to give an answer to anyone who inquires about database performance.

Why Is Historical Performance Data Important?

A DBA is in his cube waiting for an export job to finish when the developer calls. The developer claims he ran a job around midnight the night before that took two hours when it should have run in about 20 minutes. He wants the DBA to explain why the job ran for so long. When the DBA asks him if he had made any code changes, he quickly says, "No". However, the DBA is almost certain that he is hiding codes capable of mass destruction. So, the DBA says he doesn't know the cause of the performance problem and offers to monitor the job if the developer will run it again. Having worked with the developer for a long time, the DBA knows what he is thinking: "First, ask the DBA what's wrong with the database. If the DBA can't provide an immediate answer, blame the database, otherwise, find others to blame."

A question from a customer such as, "Why did the job run so slowly?" is not only a loaded question, it has to be the most challenging question a DBA can face. This kind of question catches many DBAs helpless like a deer in the headlights; not because they can't tune, but they have no historical data to show what went on in the database.

Corporate IT organizations seem to think that DBAs are omniscient creatures and don't need sleep. They expect speedy answers from their DBAs when they inquire about database performance no matter what time of day or day of the year it is. That's why you carry a pager, right? (Sometimes two or even three pagers!) However, without reliable historical performance data, you simply cannot tell them why a job ran slowly. If you fail to provide an answer, the performance problem usually is labeled as a database problem. You are guilty until you prove yourself innocent. The burden of proof always falls on the DBA.

Are you tired of being blamed for problems unrelated to the database? Ask yourself what percentage of the performance calls you receive are truly database problems. Why is it that the database is such a magnet for blame? Perhaps being downstream may have something to do with it—or could it be that you simply have no way to find out what happened, making you an easy target for abuse? The truth is that nowadays application codes are moved into production systems with very little review and testing, and when there is a performance issue, the common question is what's wrong with the database. You can defend yourself only when you are armed with session-level historical performance data. For this, you need a data collector that collects session-level performance data continuously.

Fast and Accurate Root Cause Analysis

Now that you understand the importance of historical performance data, the next step is to establish the characteristics of the data collector suitable for ongoing data collection as well as the kind of information you need to effectively perform root cause analyses of performance problems. You need to be able to look back in time to discover what each foreground process did in the database. The facts should either lead you to the problem in the database or help you prove that the problem is external. If the facts reveal that the problem is outside the database, you can use these facts to encourage the other teams to review their processes and systems and prevent finger pointing at the database. The following is our recommended list of data collector characteristics:

- **Wait-based methodology**   Root cause analyses rely heavily on session-level wait events data. Therefore, the data collector of choice must subscribe to the Oracle Wait Interface.

■ **Session-level granularity** Performance root cause analyses also require raw (low-level) session-level data. Summarized session-level data has some value, but instance-level granularity is too coarse and is not suitable for this purpose.

■ **Always-on and low overhead** Because no one knows when a performance problem will occur, the data collector must be running at all times (meaning continuous collection or sampling). The collector must also be able to simultaneously monitor all foreground database connections. Therefore, low processing overhead is extremely important.

■ **Historical repositories** Repositories are important because they allow you to look back in time to discover what went on in the database, just like surveillance tapes that investigators rely on to solve a crime or mystery. You should have a separate repository for sessions or connections, wait events, and SQL statements. There is more discussion on repositories in the "Sampling for Performance Using PL/SQL Procedure" section.

Why Trace Event 10046 Is Not a Suitable Data Collector

Trace event 10046, not to be confused with wait events, is the best utility to trace processes, bar none. The trace file contains information on SQL statements, parses and executions, bind variables, and wait events. You can trace foreground and background processes with it. It is perfect for ad hoc tracing when you need runtime information at the lowest granular level and you have established the tracing timeframe. We showed you how to use this trace facility in Chapter 2.

However, the 10046 trace facility does not meet the always-on and low overhead requirement established in the previous section. There are two main reasons why you cannot use this trace facility as a continuous performance data collector:

■ *It generates too much data.* The fine-grain data that it offers is synonymous with high volume, especially at levels 8 and 12. The amount of trace data generated at these levels can quickly consume all the space in your UDUMP/BDUMP directory. For this reason, trace event 10046 is seldom enabled at the instance level. If it is, it is only for a brief moment, usually at the request and guidance of Oracle Support. Forget about enabling this for all processes on a 24x7 basis. It is not even practical to trace one long-running session from start to finish. You have to be very selective about when to start and stop tracing, which means you need to have a rough idea of when the problem will arise.

■ *It is expensive.* The comprehensiveness of this trace facility is synonymous with overhead. The overhead will further degrade the performance of an already slow-running process.

Besides these reasons, there are other reasons the trace event 10046 is unsuitable for the task, including the following:

■ Despite the vast amount of data generated at levels 8 and 12, it is still not enough. You will only find raw event data in the trace file. You may see something like "*WAIT #12: nam='db file scattered read' ela= 0 p1=106 p2= 60227 p3=8*". Obviously, it is not user-friendly and there is no value-added interpretation. You have to manually translate P1 and P2 to discover the object name, which is a laborious task, especially when many objects are present. Furthermore, translations performed after the fact can be erroneous if the object is dropped and/or the same space is occupied by another object. There is also no cross-referencing in the trace file. For example, when there is an *enqueue* wait, the trace file records the P1, P2, and P3 values for the *enqueue* event, but there is no data about the blocking session or the SQL statement that the blocker executes. In this case, you only get half of the story.

■ Depending on the Oracle version, the trace files may be bug prone and are not always reliable. Consider the following snippet of an event 10046 trace file that belongs to the DBWR process in Oracle Release 9.2.0.1.0. Notice the negative P1 values. (This bug is fixed in 9.2.0.4.)

```
WAIT #0: nam='db file parallel write' ela= 1166386 p1=143 p2=1 p3=2147483647
WAIT #0: nam='db file parallel write' ela= 2 p1=-144 p2=1 p3=0
WAIT #0: nam='db file parallel write' ela= 3947659 p1=204 p2=1 p3=2147483647
WAIT #0: nam='db file parallel write' ela= 3 p1=-205 p2=1 p3=0
WAIT #0: nam='db file parallel write' ela= 1793305 p1=204 p2=1 p3=2147483647
WAIT #0: nam='db file parallel write' ela= 2 p1=-205 p2=1 p3=0
```

■ Perhaps the biggest drawback with the trace event 10046 facility is that it is impractical as an ongoing data collector, though it is technically possible.

Why Statspack Is Not a Suitable Data Collector

Oracle Corporation introduced Statspack in Oracle 8.1.6 as a tool to collect and store performance data. Statspack provides instance-level diagnostic data, which is too coarse for root cause analysis. Although it is possible to take session-level snapshots with Statspack, it is not designed for tracking every database connection. Therefore, we do not consider Statspack a suitable data collector. To find out more about why Statspack is not suitable for collecting session-level performance data, refer to the "10046 Alternatives" white paper at www.ioug.org.

Database Logoff Trigger as a Data Collector

Prior to Oracle8i Database, database triggers could only be created on tables and views and fired on DML events. In Oracle8i Database, Oracle extended its database trigger capability so that database triggers can be defined at the database or schema level and can fire on certain database and DDL events. The database events include STARTUP, SHUTDOWN, SERVERERROR, LOGON, and LOGOFF. The DDL events include CREATE, DROP, and ALTER.

The database trigger of interest here is the BEFORE LOGOFF trigger. It can be used to collect summarized session-level wait event data and CPU statistics from the V$SESSION_EVENT and V$SESSTAT views when sessions log off. Among the benefits, you can see all the events that belong to every foreground process that was connected to the database. You can easily discover the worst bottleneck within each session and give an answer to the person who asks why the process ran so slowly. This is a good application for the database logoff trigger, especially if you manage many databases and are only interested in summarized session-level performance data. You may not know what caused the performance problem, but at least you'll be able to tell what the major symptoms were.

The database logoff trigger as a performance data collector is attractive because it fulfills one of the critical requirements previously established: it's always on and has a low overhead. This method allows for instance-wide monitoring. You don't need to be selective as to which session to monitor or baby-sit any of them into the wee hours of the morning. The database logoff trigger will automatically fire and collect data when sessions log off, relieving you from time-consuming monitoring. However, bear in mind that the logoff trigger will not fire if the session is killed. This includes sessions that are killed by the operating system, ALTER SYSTEM KILL SESSION and SHUTDOWN IMMEDIATE/ABORT commands, as well as sessions that are sniped for exceeding resource limits and then removed by PMON. The initialization parameter _SYSTEM_TRIG_ENABLED will also prevent the logoff trigger from firing if it's set to FALSE.

Another nice thing about the database logoff trigger is that there is no overhead until a session logs off because that is the only time the trigger goes to work. Of course, the overhead depends mainly on what you put inside the trigger body. Sessions that are logging off will experience a slight delay because they must wait for the inserts into the repository tables to complete. If you have a busy system, you should expect many concurrent logoffs. This means expect many concurrent inserts into the repository tables. Therefore, you should build the repository tables with multiple INITRANS, FREELIST, and FREELIST GROUPS. By default, INITRANS is set to 2 in Oracle9i Database even though the DBA_TABLES view shows only one entry. You do not need to set FREELIST and FREELIST GROUPS if the tablespace is created with the Automatic Segment Space Management (ASSM) option. ASSM was introduced in Oracle9i Database.

```
-- This script creates a database logoff trigger for the purpose of
-- collecting historical performance data during logoffs.
-- It is applicable to Oracle8i Database and above.
-- You must be connected as "/ as sysdba" to create this trigger.

create or replace trigger sys.logoff_trig
before logoff on database
declare
  logoff_sid    pls_integer;
  logoff_time   date          := sysdate;
begin
  select sid
  into   logoff_sid
  from   v$mystat
  where  rownum < 2;

  insert into system.session_event_history
         (sid, serial#, username, osuser, paddr, process,
          logon_time, type, event, total_waits, total_timeouts,
          time_waited, average_wait, max_wait, logoff_timestamp)
  select a.sid, b.serial#, b.username, b.osuser, b.paddr, b.process,
         b.logon_time, b.type, a.event, a.total_waits, a.total_timeouts,
         a.time_waited, a.average_wait, a.max_wait, logoff_time
  from   v$session_event a, v$session b
  where  a.sid      = b.sid
  and    b.username = login_user
  and    b.sid      = logoff_sid;
-- If you are on earlier releases of Oracle9i Database, you should check to
-- see if your database is affected by bug #2429929, which causes
-- misalignment of SID numbers between the V$SESSION_EVENT and V$SESSION
-- views. The SID number in the V$SESSION_EVENT view is off by 1.
-- If your database is affected, please replace the above
-- "where a.sid = b.sid" with "where b.sid = a.sid + 1".

  insert into system.sesstat_history
         (username, osuser, sid, serial#, paddr, process, logon_time,
          statistic#, name, value, logoff_timestamp)
  select c.username, c.osuser, a.sid, c.serial#, c.paddr, c.process,
         c.logon_time, a.statistic#, b.name, a.value, logoff_time
  from   v$sesstat a, v$statname b, v$session c
  where  a.statistic# = b.statistic#
  and    a.sid        = c.sid
  and    b.name       in ('CPU used when call started',
                          'CPU used by this session',
                          'recursive cpu usage',
                          'parse time cpu')
  and    c.sid        = logoff_sid
  and    c.username   = login_user;
end;
/
```

In order for the preceding script to work, you must precreate two repository tables that are owned by the SYSTEM user. If you choose another user, you must modify the code appropriately. The first table, SESSION_EVENT_HISTORY, stores all the wait events, while the second table, SESSTAT_HISTORY stores the CPU statistics of sessions that are logging off. Again, you may choose another name for the tables and modify the code appropriately. Following are the DDLs to create the repository tables:

```
create table system.session_event_history
tablespace <name>
storage (freelist groups <value>)
initrans <value>
as
select b.sid,
       b.serial#,
       b.username,
       b.osuser,
       b.paddr,
       b.process,
       b.logon_time,
       b.type,
       a.event,
       a.total_waits,
       a.total_timeouts,
       a.time_waited,
       a.average_wait,
       a.max_wait,
       sysdate as logoff_timestamp
from   v$session_event a, v$session b
where  1 = 2;

create table system.sesstat_history
tablespace <name>
storage (freelist groups <value>)
initrans <value>
as
select c.username,
       c.osuser,
       a.sid,
       c.serial#,
       c.paddr,
       c.process,
       c.logon_time,
       a.statistic#,
       b.name,
       a.value,
       sysdate as logoff_timestamp
from   v$sesstat a, v$statname b, v$session c
where  1 = 2;
```

Before we discuss more aspects of the database logoff trigger, this is a good place to show you a real-life example of how this trigger can be used. Following are the runtime statistics of a conventional SQL*Loader load job that were collected using the database logoff trigger method:

```
EVENT                                   TIME_WAITED
-------------------------------------- -----------
log file sync                               101,232
log file switch completion                   21,865
log file switch (checkpoint incomplete)      15,630
SQL*Net message from client                  13,019
SQL*Net more data from client                 1,021
db file sequential read                          68
SQL*Net message to client                        39
CPU used when call started                   20,481
```

Clearly, the main bottlenecks were related to commit (*log file sync*) and log switch (*log file switch completion*). The fix was simple and mundane, but the fun part was dealing with a fierce DBA wannabe application developer who came from the bigger-is-better school. This person wasn't satisfied with the load performance and continually pressured a junior DBA to increase the buffer cache size. Ultimately, the SGA was at 3GB, up from about 256MB originally, and there was no performance improvement. In frustration, this person escalated the issue to the director level and demanded the system administrator to install more memory in the server. A senior DBA assigned to resolve the issue created the database logoff trigger. Using the wait event data collected by the trigger, the senior DBA discovered that the redo log size was only 4MB, and redo logs were switching at the rate of 7 or 8 times per minute. Further investigation also revealed that the SQL*Loader *bindsize* was only 64K. After resizing the SGA back down to 256MB, replacing the redo logs with larger ones, and increasing the SQL*Loader *bindsize* to 3MB, the load elapsed time went from 33 minutes to under 4 minutes.

How about that for a few lines of code? You may enhance this application with a data purge routine for the repository tables, and the right partitioning scheme allows you to quickly purge old data. (The Oracle partitioning option is available since Oracle8.0 and it is a separately licensed product.)

On the other hand, we want you to be aware that you may not always be able to nail down the root cause of a performance problem using this method because the data is summarized at the session-level. For example, if the *latch free* event shows up to be the primary bottleneck, the summarized data will not reveal which latch was contended for, when it happened, the number of tries, and the session that held the latch. Or if the *db file scattered read* is the primary bottleneck, you will not be able to pinpoint the SQL statement and the object that participated in the full table scans.

Now, some of you may have storage concerns. The logoff trigger disk space requirement depends on the session logoff rate and the amount of history you plan

Database Logoff Trigger	Trace Event 10046
Fire once for the lifetime of a session	Continuous tracing
Summarized performance data	Fine-grain performance data
Low overhead	High overhead
Low storage requirement	High storage requirement
Instance-wide monitoring capability	Commonly enabled at session level
Limited root cause analysis capability	Best for root cause analysis

TABLE 4-1. *Differences Between Database Logoff Trigger and Trace Event 10046*

to keep. A seven-day history should be sufficient because if there is a performance problem you should hear about it within a day. The logoff rate depends on the behavior of the application. Some applications spawn multiple sessions aggressively connecting and disconnecting from the database. If you have scheduled background jobs, don't forget to account for the logoff rate of SNP processes. The logoff trigger fires each time an SNP background process completes its scheduled job and goes back to sleep. You may start with a 512MB tablespace and monitor the space usage.

Lastly, we give you yet another application for the database logoff trigger. It is perfect for benchmarking when you are only interested in the end result. For example, say you want to see what kind of impact the Oracle9*i* FAST_START_MTTR_TARGET feature has on a process by comparing the summarized session-level wait events of the same process with and without the feature.

In many ways, the database logoff trigger is the opposite of the trace event 10046. Table 4-1 gives a quick comparison. If everything that has been said about the database logoff trigger sounds really good to you but your database version is prior to Oracle8*i* Database, then you are unfortunate. As mentioned earlier, Oracle introduced the database logoff trigger in version 8*i*.

Sampling for Performance Data Using PL/SQL Procedure

The database logoff trigger method for collecting historical performance data comes close to meeting all the requirements for root cause analysis established previously, except it lacks fine-grain data and a SQL statement repository. It looks like you need something between the trace event 10046 and the database logoff trigger. We can live with near fine-grain data, but we must absolutely have low overhead ongoing monitoring capability as well as wait event and SQL statement repositories. To achieve this, sampling may be the best approach. If you can sample every foreground process that connects to the instance at regular intervals and write the data to repository tables, you will have a history of what each process does in the database from about the time it starts to the time it completes. This ability is critical; otherwise you have no history and remain in the dark. The goal is to collect just enough information for root cause analysis.

Some of you may have heard that the Oracle Database 10*g* Active Session History (ASH) feature also samples for performance data. That is correct, and we are glad that Oracle is on the same page as we are. The sampling methodology that we are about to share with you is proven and is implemented in many of our databases since Oracle 7.3.4. The DBAs of those databases are less dependent on the trace event 10046 because the data collected through sampling is sufficient for them to perform root cause analyses. This sampling methodology does not replace the event 10046 trace facility; rather, it complements it. Those of you who are not using Oracle Database 10*g* can certainly benefit from this method.

We will now show you how to develop this performance data collector in PL/SQL. We will guide you step by step, and provide examples. For the purpose of our discussion, we will refer to this data collector as DC. Following are four areas you must consider when developing DC:

- Data source

- Sampling frequency

- Repositories

- Events to monitor

Data Source

The best data source for this task is the V$SESSION_WAIT view. This view shows the resources or events for which active sessions are currently waiting. The quality of data that it offers is fine grain, which is most suitable for root cause analysis.

```
Name                     Type              Notes
-------------------      ---------------   ---------------
    SID                  NUMBER
    SEQ#                 NUMBER
    EVENT                VARCHAR2(64)
    P1TEXT               VARCHAR2(64)
    P1                   NUMBER
    P1RAW                RAW(8)
    P2TEXT               VARCHAR2(64)
    P2                   NUMBER
```

```
P2RAW               RAW(8)
P3TEXT              VARCHAR2(64)
P3                  NUMBER
P3RAW               RAW(8)
WAIT_CLASS_ID       NUMBER          In Oracle Database 10g
WAIT_CLASS#         NUMBER          In Oracle Database 10g
WAIT_CLASS          VARCHAR2(64)    In Oracle Database 10g
WAIT_TIME           NUMBER
SECONDS_IN_WAIT     NUMBER
STATE               VARCHAR2(19)
```

Sampling Frequency

The frequency of sampling affects the quantity of the historical data and determines the type of scheduler. You must choose a sampling frequency that is appropriate for your environment. A batch process can tolerate lower frequency sampling, while an OLTP process needs higher frequency sampling. Lower sampling frequencies yield lesser data volume while higher frequencies yield higher data volume.

If you chose a sampling frequency that is less than a minute, you would probably use a simple Unix shell script that wakes up at the preset intervals to execute the DC procedure to collect performance data. But if you chose a low sampling frequency such as the one-minute intervals, then you could also use the Unix *cron* or an Oracle SNP process to kick off the DC procedure. One bad thing about the Oracle SNP process, however, is that it is not reliable. It is notorious for sleeping on the job, causing loss of valuable data.

DBAs have the tendency to choose high-frequency sampling, and some may be shocked by the one-minute intervals. Again, don't forget that the goal is to collect just enough information for root cause analysis and not run into a space problem as you would with the trace event 10046. In batch environments where jobs usually run for over half an hour, it is sufficient to take a snapshot of the V$SESSION_WAIT view at the top of every minute. This provides a minute-by-minute picture or history of what happened to every process in the database. If you supplement this sampling with the database logoff trigger discussed earlier, you will get both the summarized wait events and the detailed minute-by-minute events of all sessions, and you should be able to perform root cause analysis. If your users are unhappy with the performance of a short running job (say, less than 15 minutes), you can still use the trace event 10046 to trace the session.

Before we get into the crux of what to monitor, we want to show you two examples to give you an idea of how this sampling method can help you identify the root causes of performance problems.

In the following real-life example, user ULN8688 wanted to know why his job was taking an unusually long time to complete. He assured the DBA that he didn't make any code changes. He said the same code had been running for over a year and suddenly it was very slow. The on-call DBA pulled out the minute-by-minute history for that job as shown below and discovered that it was performing full table scans on the ADJUSTMENTS table. The DBA also discovered that all indexes were invalid. It turned out that another DBA had reorganized the table the night before with the ALTER TABLE MOVE command and had not rebuilt the indexes.

```
              SmplTme
Usernam SID DD/HHMI  EVENT                OBJECT_NAME          HASH_VALUE
------- --- -------  -------------------  -------------------  ----------
ULN8688   9 31/0808  db file scattered    ADJUSTMENTS           159831610
ULN8688   9 31/0809  db file scattered    ADJUSTMENTS           159831610
ULN8688   9 31/0810  db file scattered    ADJUSTMENTS           159831610
ULN8688   9 31/0811  db file scattered    ADJUSTMENTS           159831610
ULN8688   9 31/0812  db file scattered    ADJUSTMENTS           159831610
ULN8688   9 31/0813  db file scattered    ADJUSTMENTS           159831610
ULN8688   9 31/0814  db file scattered    ADJUSTMENTS           159831610
ULN8688   9 31/0815  db file scattered    ADJUSTMENTS           159831610
ULN8688   9 31/0816  db file scattered    ADJUSTMENTS           159831610
ULN8688   9 31/0817  db file scattered    ADJUSTMENTS           159831610
ULN8688   9 31/0818  db file scattered    ADJUSTMENTS           159831610
ULN8688   9 31/0819  db file scattered    ADJUSTMENTS           159831610
ULN8688   9 31/0820  db file scattered    ADJUSTMENTS           159831610
ULN8688   9 31/0821  db file scattered    ADJUSTMENTS           159831610
ULN8688   9 31/0822  db file scattered    ADJUSTMENTS           159831610
ULN8688   9 31/0823  db file scattered    ADJUSTMENTS           159831610
. . .
```

Following is another real-life example of a minute-by-minute history of a process that belonged to the GATEWAY user. The process began execution shortly before 1:59 A.M. The first event captured was the *latch free* event. A quick glance over the report showed the *latch free* was the primary wait event in terms of the number of occurrences. By the way, this event also ranked the highest in terms of time waited according to the summarized wait event data collected by the database logoff trigger.

```
              SmplTme
Usernam SID DD/HHMI EVENT                 OBJECT_NAME          HASH_VALUE
------- --- ------- -------------------   -------------------  ----------
GATEWAY  13 04/0159 latch free            cache buffers chain   249098659
GATEWAY  13 04/0200 latch free            cache buffers chain   249098659
GATEWAY  13 04/0201 db file sequential    PRODUCT_MASTER       4120235380
GATEWAY  13 04/0202 SQL*Net more data                          249098659
GATEWAY  13 04/0203 latch free            cache buffers chain   249098659
GATEWAY  13 04/0204 SQL*Net more data                          249098659
GATEWAY  13 04/0205 latch free            cache buffers chain  4120235380
GATEWAY  13 04/0206 latch free            cache buffers chain   249098659
GATEWAY  13 04/0207 db file sequential    ORDERDATA_IX04        249098659
GATEWAY  13 04/0208 db file sequential    ORDERDATA_IX04        249098659
GATEWAY  13 04/0209 latch free            cache buffers chain  4120235380
GATEWAY  13 04/0210 latch free            cache buffers chain   249098659
GATEWAY  13 04/0211 latch free            cache buffers chain   249098659
GATEWAY  13 04/0212 db file sequential    PRODUCT_MASTER_IX02   249098659
```

```
GATEWAY  13 04/0213  enqueue               TX4                  249098659
GATEWAY  13 04/0214  latch free            cache buffers chain  4120235380
GATEWAY  13 04/0215  db file sequential    ORDERDATA_IX04        249098659
GATEWAY  13 04/0216  enqueue               TX4                  249098659
GATEWAY  13 04/0217  latch free            cache buffers chain  249098659
GATEWAY  13 04/0218  db file sequential    ORDERDATA_IX04        249098659
GATEWAY  13 04/0219  latch free            cache buffers chain  249098659
GATEWAY  13 04/0220  latch free            cache buffers chain  249098659
GATEWAY  13 04/0221  db file sequential    RMORDDTL_01           249098659
. . .
```

Also notice that the *latch free* waits were competitions for the *cache buffers chains* child latches. This was discovered by translating the P2 parameter value in the V$SESSION_WAIT view. We will show you how to do the translation in the "Events to Monitor" section. Based on the latch addresses (P1 parameter) that were collected, we also learned that the contentions were focused on one particular child *cache buffers chains* latch. (The latch address is not shown in the preceding example due to space constraints.) The information was important because it helped the DBA better understand and deal with the problem by informing that the sessions were competing for one or more blocks that were hashed to the same latch.

Another critical piece of data was the SQL hash value. The SQL statement with hash value 249098659 was a query, and it was associated with most of the *latch free* wait events and a few *db file sequential read* events on the ORDERDATA_IX04 object, which was an index. The DBA realized that it normally takes at least two active processes to create a *latch free* contention, so the DBA queried the repository tables to see if there were concurrent processes that executed the same hash value. The DBA found 14 concurrent processes and all of them executed the same SQL hash value. Bingo! That was a classic case of an application spawning multiple concurrent sessions to execute the same code.

Many application designers and developers fail to understand that only one process can acquire an Oracle latch at any one time and when a process holds a latch, it prevents all other processes from accessing any data blocks that are hashed to the same latch. In their logic, if a single-threaded process completes a task in an hour, then the same task can be completed in six minutes by ten parallel processes. This logic is too simplistic and does not always work when latches are involved.

Repositories

Repository tables are the core components of this sampling methodology. They allow you to look back in time to discover what transpired in the database. The DC data collector populates these tables at predetermined intervals. The following repositories are recommended. You may normalize or denormalize them as you see fit.

■ **Wait events repository** Keeps track of the wait events that appear in the V$SESSION_WAIT view as encountered by each session chronologically.

Therefore, the wait event repository table will have the same attributes as the V$SESSION_WAIT view. Additionally, it should include attributes that define:

■ The sampling date and time.

■ The hash value of the SQL statement that is associated with the wait event.

■ The key that identifies the session (not just the SIDs because they are recycled when sessions log off and are not always associated with the same database users). The key that uniquely identifies a session comprises of SID, SERIAL#, and LOGON_TIME and can be extended to include USERNAME, OSUSER, PADDR (process address), and PROCESS.

■ The database object name that belongs to the wait event. This may be the table name, table partition name, index name, or index partition name for events such as *db file scattered read*, *db file sequential read*, *buffer busy waits*, and *free buffer waits*; or the latch name for the *latch free* wait event; or the enqueue name for the *enqueue* wait event; or the SQL text, procedure name, function name, or package name for events such as *library cache pin*, *library cache lock*, and *library cache load lock*; or the file name for events such as *direct path read* and *direct path write*; and so on. The reason this is so important is that it enhances the readability and user-friendliness of the history. Otherwise, the history will show only P1, P2, and P3 values much like the event 10046 trace files, and you will waste a lot of precious troubleshooting time in translating those values, assuming the objects still exist in the database. You can see what we mean by this in the OBJECT_NAME column of the two minute-by-minute examples we discussed earlier.

■ The primary key of the wait event repository table.

■ **SQL statement repository**   Wait events by themselves are of little value. You must evaluate wait events with the SQL statement that generates them. This means each time you capture a wait event, you must also capture the SQL statement that is associated with (or causing) the wait event. Remember, the wait event wouldn't have occurred without the SQL statement. Together, they can help define the context and get you closer to the real problem. For example, a process waits on the *buffer busy waits* wait event for a data block that belongs to the EMP table, according to the P1 and P2 parameter values. Let's say the P3 parameter value is 220, which means multiple sessions are competing to perform DML operations within the same block. Now, that can be an insert, update, or delete statement. You can't be certain unless you have the SQL statement that is associated with that *buffer busy waits* wait event. Another important reason for capturing SQL statements is so that you can take them back to the application team and the developers can correctly identify the modules. The SQL statement repository should have the same attribute as the V$SQLTEXT view. In addition, for each SQL statement, the repository should include statistics such as the DISK_READS and BUFFER_GETS from the V$SQLAREA view, and the application module name from the V$SESSION view. Of course, don't forget the primary key for the repository itself.

Using the information from the wait event and SQL statement repositories, you can investigate what users were doing in the database and the kind of bottlenecks they encountered. The bottlenecks can lead you to the root cause of the performance problem.

Events to Monitor

Lastly, you must decide what wait events you want to monitor. Don't be too aggressive in the beginning. Start with a few common wait events to get a feel for the historical data and then gradually add new wait events to the list. Fortunately, there are only a handful of common wait events, and they are sufficient for most diagnostics. There are also idle events that you may ignore; we discussed this in Chapter 2. You can begin by making your own list of events that you want to monitor, or simply use the following list:

- db file sequential read
- db file scattered read
- latch free
- direct path read
- direct path write
- enqueue
- library cache pin
- buffer busy waits
- free buffer waits

Once you have decided on the list, it is time to start coding! Once you have created your own tool, you can take it with you anywhere you go, and you don't have to rely on expensive monitoring tools. Begin by setting up a PL/SQL cursor that camps at the V$SESSION_WAIT view to collect and translate the relevant wait events. You may join the V$SESSION_WAIT view to the V$SESSION view to get the user's information. An example of the cursor follows:

```
-- Remark: This is an incomplete procedure.
create or replace procedure DC
as
   cursor current_event is
   select a.sid,          a.seq#,           a.event,      a.p1text,
          a.p1,           a.p1raw,          a.p2text,     a.p2,
          a.p2raw,        a.p3text,         a.p3,         a.p3raw,
          a.wait_time,    a.seconds_in_wait, a.state,     b.serial#,
          b.username,     b.osuser,         b.paddr,      b.logon_time,
          b.process,      b.sql_hash_value, b.saddr,      b.module,
          b.row_wait_obj#, b.row_wait_file#, b.row_wait_block#,
          b.row_wait_row#
   from   v$session_wait a, v$session b
   where  a.sid       = b.sid
   and    b.username is not null
   and    b.type      <> 'BACKGROUND'
   and    a.event in (
          'db file sequential read',
          'db file scattered read',
          'latch free',
          'direct path read',
          'direct path write',
          'enqueue',
          'library cache pin',
          'library cache load lock',
          'buffer busy waits',
          'free buffer waits');
. . .
```

Using the SQL hash value from the CURRENT_EVENT cursor, you can capture the SQL text from the V$SQLTEXT view as shown next and store it in the appropriate history table. If you are also interested in the SQL statistics, you can get the information from the V$SQLAREA using the same SQL hash value from the cursor.

```
-- To extract the SQL text for a given hash value.
select hash_value, address, piece, sql_text
from   v$sqltext
where  hash_value = <cursor hash value>
order by piece;
```

For each wait event supplied by the CURRENT_EVENT cursor, the DC procedure should translate the event parameters into meaningful names. For example, in case of *db file scattered read* wait event, the DC procedure should translate the P1 and P2 parameters into the object name and partition name if applicable and store the information in the history table. This value-added feature not only improves the readability of the history but, more importantly, it also allows you to focus on troubleshooting. Following is a list of common events and examples of the kind of information that the DC procedure should translate and store in the repository tables.

db file sequential read and db file scattered read
The *db file sequential read* and *db file scattered read* are I/O related wait events.

1. Determine the object name and partition name (if applicable) using the P1 and P2 values supplied by the CURRENT_EVENT cursor:

```
select  segment_name, partition_name
from    dba_extents
where   <cursor P2> between block_id and (block_id + blocks - 1)
and     file_id = <cursor P1>;
```

Querying the DBA_EXTENTS view in this manner can be slow, especially when many sessions are waiting on *db file sequential read* and *db file scattered read* events. This is because DBA_EXTENTS is a complex view that is comprised of many views and base tables. The performance gets worse when the number of extents in the database is high. The following are two alternatives that improve performance.

■ Precreate a working table (regular heap or global temporary table) with the same structure as the DBA_EXTENTS view. Then take a snapshot of the DBA_EXTENTS view once at the beginning of each sampling interval (or once a day depending on the number of extents and their volatility) and insert the data into the working table. In this case, the preceding query can be rewritten to go against the working table instead of the DBA_EXTENTS view.

■ Obtain the object number (OBJ) from the X$BH view using the P1 and P2 from the CURRENT_EVENT cursor. With the object number, you can resolve the object name (NAME) and subobject name (SUBNAME) by querying the DBA_OBJECTS view. An example of the query follows. The caveat to this method is that you must wait for the block to be read into the SGA; otherwise, the X$BH view has no information on the block that is referenced by the P1 and P2. Also, you may not be quick enough to catch the blocks that are being read in by a full table scan operation. This is because full table scans against NOCACHE objects do not flood the buffer cache. A small number of blocks are quickly reused. By the time you get the P1 and P2 values from the V$SESSION_WAIT view, the block in X$BH could have been reused by another block from subsequent reads.

```
select  distinct a.object_name, a.subobject_name
from    dba_objects a, sys.x$bh b
where   (a.object_id = b.obj or a.data_object_id = b.obj)
  and     b.file#  = <cursor P1>
and     b.dbablk = <cursor P2>;
```

2. Obtain the SQL statement that is associated with the *db file sequential read* or *db file scattered read* event using the hash value supplied by the CURRENT_EVENT cursor:

```
select hash_value, address, piece, sql_text
from   v$sqltext
where  hash_value = <cursor hash value>
order by piece;
```

latch free
The *latch free* wait event is related to concurrency and serialization.

1. Get the name of the latch that is being competed for using the P2 value supplied by the CURRENT_EVENT cursor:

```
select name
from   v$latchname
where  latch# = <cursor P2>;
```

2. Obtain the SQL statement that is associated with the *latch free* event using the hash value supplied by the CURRENT_EVENT cursor:

```
select hash_value, address, piece, sql_text
from   v$sqltext
where  hash_value = <cursor hash value>
order by piece;
```

direct path read
The *direct path read* wait event is related to direct read operations that read data into the session's PGA.

1. Find out the name of the object the session is reading from using the P1 and P2 values supplied the CURRENT_EVENT cursor:

```
select segment_name, partition_name
from   dba_extents
where  <cursor P2> between block_id and (block_id + blocks - 1)
and    file_id    = <cursor P1>;
```

2. You can get a rough idea of what the session is doing from the type of database file from which it reads. If the file is a TEMPFILE, then you know the session is reading temporary segments that it previously created through *direct path write* operations. However, if it is a data file, it is probably the parallel query slave at work. The following query

determines the database file name using the P1 value supplied by the CURRENT_EVENT cursor:

```
select name
from   v$datafile
where  file# = <cursor P1>
union all
select a.name
from   v$tempfile a, v$parameter b
where  b.name = 'db_files'
and    a.file# + b.value = <cursor P1>;
```

3. If the session is reading from the temporary tablespace, find out what type of segment it is as this can also give you an idea of what the session is doing. For example, if the segment is SORT, then you know the sort batch is larger than your SORT_AREA_SIZE (or work area size), and you may have a SQL statement that employs one or more aggregate functions or the merge-join operation. If the segment is HASH, then you know your HASH_AREA_SIZE is too small for the SQL statement that employs the hash-join operation. However, this doesn't mean you simply increase the sort and hash memory. You should first optimize the SQL statements. The following query reveals the type of segment that the session is reading using the SADDR (session address) and SERIAL# supplied by the CURRENT_EVENT cursor:

```
select distinct decode(ktssosegt, 1,'SORT', 2,'HASH', 3,'DATA',
4,'INDEX', 5,'LOB_DATA', 6,'LOB_INDEX', 'UNDEFINED')
from   sys.x$ktsso
where  inst_id = userenv('instance')
and    ktssoses = <cursor session address>
and    ktssosno = <cursor serial#>;
```

4. Obtain the SQL statement that is associated with the *direct path read* event using the hash value supplied by the CURRENT_EVENT cursor:

```
select hash_value, address, piece, sql_text
from   v$sqltext
where  hash_value = <cursor hash value>
order by piece;
```

direct path write
The *direct path write* wait event is related to direct write operations.

1. Ascertain the name of the object the session is writing to using the P1 and P2 values supplied by the CURRENT_EVENT cursor:

```
select segment_name, partition_name
from   dba_extents
```

```
where   <cursor P2> between block_id and (block_id + blocks - 1)
and     file_id     = <cursor P1>;
```

2. You can get a rough idea of what the session is doing from the type of
   database file it writes to. If the file is a TEMPFILE, then you know the SQL
   statement that the session is executing is creating temporary segments. But
   if it is a data file, then the session is performing a direct path load operation.
   The following query determines the database file name using the P1 value
   supplied by the CURRENT_EVENT cursor:

```
select  name
from    v$datafile
where   file# = <cursor P1>
union all
select  a.name
from    v$tempfile a, v$parameter b
where   b.name = 'db_files'
and     a.file# + b.value = <cursor P1>;
```

3. If the session is writing to the temporary tablespace, find out what type of
   segment it is. If the segment is SORT, then you know the sort batch is larger
   than the SORT_AREA_SIZE (or work area size) in memory and sort runs are
   being written to the temporary tablespace. You may have a SQL statement
   that employs one or more aggregate functions or the merge-join operation.
   If the segment is HASH, then you know the HASH_AREA_SIZE is too small
   for the SQL statement that performs the hash-join operation. It is also possible
   for a SQL statement to create both SORT and HASH segments in the temporary
   tablespace. This is common when the execution plan contains both the hash
   and merge join, or a hash join with an aggregate function. The following query
   reveals the type of segment that the session is writing to using the SADDR
   (session address) and SERIAL# supplied by the CURRENT_EVENT cursor:

```
select distinct decode(ktssosegt, 1,'SORT', 2,'HASH', 3,'DATA',
4,'INDEX', 5,'LOB_DATA', 6,'LOB_INDEX', 'UNDEFINED')
from    sys.x$ktsso
where   inst_id  = userenv('instance')
and     ktssoses = <cursor session address>
and     ktssosno = <cursor serial#>;
```

4. Obtain the SQL statement that is associated with the *direct path write* event
   using the hash value supplied by the CURRENT_EVENT cursor:

```
select hash_value, address, piece, sql_text
from    v$sqltext
where   hash_value = <cursor hash value>
order by piece;
```

enqueue
The *enqueue* wait event is related to transaction locking.

1. Discover the requested lock type and mode by deciphering the P1 value supplied by the CURRENT_EVENT cursor.

```
select  chr(bitand(<cursor P1>,-16777216)/16777215) ||
        chr(bitand(<cursor P1>,16711680)/65535) lock_type,
        mod(<cursor P1>,16) lock_mode
from    dual;
```

2. Determine the name of the object the enqueue is for using the ROW_WAIT_OBJ# supplied by the CURRENT_EVENT cursor:

```
select  object_name, subobject_name
from    dba_objects
where   object_id = <cursor row_wait_obj#>;
```

3. Identify the blocking session and the information about the lock that is being held, such as the lock type and lock mode and time held using the P2 and P3 values supplied by the CURRENT_EVENT cursor:

```
select  a.sid,   a.serial#,   a.username,   a.paddr,   a.logon_time,
        a.sql_hash_value,   b.type,        b.lmode,   b.ctime
from    v$session a, v$lock b
where   a.sid   = b.sid
and     b.id1   = <cursor P2>
and     b.id2   = <cursor P3>
and     b.block = 1;
```

4. Obtain the SQL statement that is associated with the *enqueue* event using the hash value supplied by the CURRENT_EVENT cursor:

```
select  hash_value, address, piece, sql_text
from    v$sqltext
where   hash_value = <cursor hash value>
order by piece;
```

buffer busy waits
The *buffer busy waits* event is related to read/read, read/write, and write/write contention.

1. Establish the name of the object that the buffer lock contention is for using the P1 and P2 values supplied by the CURRENT_EVENT cursor:

```
select  segment_name, partition_name
from    dba_extents
where   <cursor P2> between block_id and (block_id + blocks - 1)
and     file_id   = <cursor P1>;
```

2. Find out the type of block using the P1 and P2 values provided by the CURRENT_EVENT cursor. The contention may be for a segment header block, freelist group block, or data block. In Oracle Database 10g, this information is provided by the P3 parameter. See the "*buffer busy waits*" section in Chapter 6 for more details.

```
select segment_type || ' header block'
from    dba_segments
where   header_file  = <cursor P1>
and     header_block = <cursor P2>
union all
select segment_type || ' freelist group block'
from    dba_segments
where   header_file    = <cursor P1>
and     <cursor P2> between header_block + 1 and
                              (header_block + freelist_groups)
and     freelist_groups > 1
union all
select segment_type || ' data block'
from    dba_extents
where   <cursor P2> between block_id and (block_id + blocks - 1)
and     file_id    = <cursor P1>
and     not exists (select 1
                    from    dba_segments
                    where   header_file  = <cursor P1>
                    and     header_block = <cursor P2>);
```

3. Obtain the SQL statement that is associated with the *buffer busy waits* event using the hash value supplied by the CURRENT_EVENT cursor:

```
select hash_value, address, piece, sql_text
from   v$sqltext
where  hash_value = <cursor hash value>
order by piece;
```

free buffer waits

The *free buffer waits* is latency related wait event. Obtain the SQL statement that is associated with the *free buffer waits* event using the hash value supplied by the CURRENT_EVENT cursor:

```
select hash_value, address, piece, sql_text
from   v$sqltext
where  hash_value = <cursor hash value>
order by piece;
```

che pin

cache pin wait event is related to contention for library cache objects.

1. Look up the name of the object that the pin is for using the P1RAW value supplied by the CURRENT_EVENT cursor:

```
select kglnaobj
from    x$kglob
where   inst_id  = userenv('instance')
and     kglhdadr = <cursor P1RAW>;
```

2. Find out who is blocking, the statement that is executing, and the mode in which the object is being held using the P1RAW value supplied by the CURRENT_EVENT cursor:

```
select a.sid,  a.serial#,  a.username,  a.paddr,  a.logon_time,
       a.sql_hash_value,   b.kglpnmod
from    v$session a, sys.x$kglpn b
where   a.saddr     = b.kglpnuse
and     b.inst_id   = userenv('instance')
and     b.kglpnreq  = 0
and     b.kglpnmod not in (0,1)
and     b.kglpnhdl  = <cursor P1RAW>;
```

3. Obtain the SQL statement that is associated with the *library cache pin* event using the hash value supplied by the CURRENT_EVENT cursor:

```
select hash_value, address, piece, sql_text
from    v$sqltext
where   hash_value = <cursor hash value>
order by piece;
```

Pros and Cons

This sampling method is truly a great complement to the event 10046 trace facility. It lets you monitor all foreground connections to the database 24x7 and gives you a snapshot-by-snapshot history of the bottlenecks that each session encountered. When your user inquires why a particular job ran like molasses, you can look into the history to discover the bottlenecks and determine the root cause. The history also enables you to proactively monitor production critical processes and inform your users when you see anomalies. For instance, you may notice a session clocked a lot of time on a particular SQL hash value and the main event was the *db file scattered read*, so you fetch the SQL text from the history table and tune it. Then you call and offer the user a more efficient SQL statement. What an exceptional level of service! You will have also turned the tide. Instead of the user calling you and blaming the database, you will be calling the user to complain about their SQL code! Needless to say, soon you will be a respected (and perhaps feared) DBA.

Another nice feature is that you can determine the elapsed time of every session from the history by a simple calculation. Let's say you use the one-minute sampling interval. You can compute the session's elapsed time by comparing the first and the last historical record of the session. In this case, the margin of error is at most two minutes. The elapsed time can be used to validate users' claims and keep them honest. Many times, when asked how long their job ran, they will give you a highly inflated number.

The disk space requirement depends on the number of connections that are active, their processing time, the number of events you are monitoring, and the amount of history you plan on keeping. If you ignore idle events and limit your history to seven days, this method normally takes less than half a gigabyte of disk space as experienced in our installation sites.

This sampling method requires you to possess a basic working PL/SQL knowledge. This is a mini-development project, and it involves some amount of coding. The overhead introduced by this method strictly depends on the quality of your PL/SQL code. If quality is not an issue, this method has far less overhead than the trace event 10046. You should also implement maintenance and purge routines for the history tables. Consider using partitioning to help maintenance.

Sampling for Performance Data with SQL-less SGA Access

The critics of the SQL or PL/SQL sampling method contend that the sampling interval is too coarse and that there is a low limit on the number of times a program can sample data through views every second. There is a way to sample Oracle performance data at a high frequency without using SQL in Unix-like systems. This method is known as SGA Direct Access. It uses an external program, typically written in the C language, to obtain Oracle data by reading the SGA shared memory segment directly. This method is a little more complex than the rest of the monitoring methods, but it has advantages over them. Because this is an uncommon method, we provide the details in Appendix D.

In a Nutshell

A database performance problem may easily be diagnosed if the DBA knows what each session is doing or has done in the database. In practice, however, a DBA normally administers many databases, and it is impossible to baby-sit each one. Therefore, a question such as, "Why did the job run so slowly?" is challenging to even the most competent DBA. The Oracle Wait Interface is great at finding the root causes of performance problems, provided the DBA is aware of the bottlenecks. Tuning exercises without the guidance of bottlenecks (or symptoms) is almost always unprofitable and a waste of time.

This chapter offers a couple of methods for capturing performance data—that is, using the database logoff trigger and PL/SQL procedure. In addition, it is also possible to sample performance data by accessing the SGA directly with an external program. These methods are a good complement to the event 10046 trace facility. The historical data allows the DBA to perform root cause analyses of performance problems.

The ability to monitor all active processes on a 24x7 basis is good. Having repositories to help answer why a particular job ran slowly is great. But having the evidence to prove that the performance problem is not in the database and that you are innocent is PRICELESS! The historical data gives DBAs the evidence they need to confirm or refute the common accusation from developers and business users: "It is a database problem."

CHAPTER
5

Interpreting Common I/O Related Wait Events

/O operations are an essential part of processing and often represent a major portion of processing time. This is because I/Os are complicated operations involving many layers and components of a computer system, including software components such as Oracle, the disk volume manager, the server operating system, and the disk operating system, as well as hardware components such as buffers, I/O cards, cables, networks, routers, switches, storage controllers, and physical disks. Every component has its own attributes. There are many places that a mismatch or misconfiguration can easily degrade the I/O throughput and application performance.

There are also two basic types of I/O operations: synchronous and asynchronous, which differ in performance. Although hardware engineers have been working for the past decade or so to beef up I/O throughput with various offerings, I/O operations remain the slowest activity in a computer system.

Everyone that touches the computer system needs to be conscientious of the high cost of I/Os. Applications and databases must be designed with efficient data access in mind. Unfortunately, this concept exists mostly in schools and textbooks and seldom in the real business world. Not that there is anything wrong with the concept, but in practice, data access design is often pushed to the back seat because of the unrealistic application delivery dates that are derived from pressure to be the first to the market. As a result, the quality of code suffers and DBAs find numerous SQL statements with poor access paths and joins in the production databases.

This chapter equips you to diagnose and solve problems related to seven common I/O related wait events: *db file sequential read, db file scattered read, direct path read, direct path write, log file parallel write, db file parallel write,* and *controlfile parallel write.* You can find their descriptions in Chapter 3.

db file sequential read

The *db file sequential read* wait event has three parameters: file#, first block#, and block count. In Oracle Database 10*g*, this wait event falls under the User I/O wait class. Keep the following key thoughts in mind when dealing with the *db file sequential read* wait event.

- The Oracle process wants a block that is currently not in the SGA, and it is waiting for the database block to be read into the SGA from disk.

- The two important numbers to look for are the TIME_WAITED and AVERAGE_WAIT by individual sessions.

- Significant *db file sequential read* wait time is most likely an application issue.

Common Causes, Diagnosis, and Actions

The *db file sequential read* wait event is initiated by SQL statements (both user and recursive) that perform single-block read operations against indexes, rollback (or undo) segments, and tables (when accessed via rowid), control files and data file headers. This wait event normally appears as one of the top five wait events, according to systemwide waits.

Physical I/O requests for these objects are perfectly normal, so the presence of the *db file sequential read* waits in the database does not necessarily mean that there is something wrong with the database or the application. It may not even be a bad thing if a session spends a lot of time on this event. In contrast, it is definitely bad if a session spends a lot of time on events like *enqueue* or *latch free*. This is where this single-block read subject becomes complicated. At what point does the *db file sequential read* event become an issue? How do you define excessive? Where do you draw the line? These are tough questions, and there is no industry standard guideline. You should establish a guideline for your environment. For example, you may consider it excessive when the *db file sequential read* wait represents a large portion of a process response time. Another way is to simply adopt the nonscientific hillbilly approach—that is, wait till the users start screaming.

You can easily discover which session has high TIME_WAITED on the *db file sequential read* wait event from the V$SESSION_EVENT view. The TIME_WAITED must be evaluated with the LOGON_TIME and compared with other nonidle events that belong to the session for a more accurate analysis. Sessions that have logged on for some time (days or weeks) may accumulate a good amount of time on the *db file sequential read* event. In this case, a high TIME_WAITED may not be an issue. Also, when the TIME_WAITED is put in perspective with other nonidle events, it prevents you from being blindsided. You may find another wait event which is of a greater significance. Based on the following example, SID# 192 deserves your attention and should be investigated:

```
select a.sid,
       a.event,
       a.time_waited,
       a.time_waited / c.sum_time_waited * 100 pct_wait_time,
       round((sysdate - b.logon_time) * 24) hours_connected
from   v$session_event a, v$session b,
       (select sid, sum(time_waited) sum_time_waited
        from   v$session_event
        where  event not in (
                   'Null event',
                   'client message',
                   'KXFX: Execution Message Dequeue - Slave',
                   'PX Deq: Execution Msg',
                   'KXFQ: kxfqdeq - normal deqeue',
```

```
                      'PX Deq: Table Q Normal',
                      'Wait for credit - send blocked',
                      'PX Deq Credit: send blkd',
                      'Wait for credit - need buffer to send',
                      'PX Deq Credit: need buffer',
                      'Wait for credit - free buffer',
                      'PX Deq Credit: free buffer',
                      'parallel query dequeue wait',
                      'PX Deque wait',
                      'Parallel Query Idle Wait - Slaves',
                      'PX Idle Wait',
                      'slave wait',
                      'dispatcher timer',
                      'virtual circuit status',
                      'pipe get',
                      'rdbms ipc message',
                      'rdbms ipc reply',
                      'pmon timer',
                      'smon timer',
                      'PL/SQL lock timer',
                      'SQL*Net message from client',
                      'WMON goes to sleep')
           having sum(time_waited) > 0 group by sid) c
where    a.sid        = b.sid
and      a.sid        = c.sid
and      a.time_waited > 0
and      a.event      = 'db file sequential read'
order by hours_connected desc, pct_wait_time;

 SID EVENT                    TIME_WAITED PCT_WAIT_TIME HOURS_CONNECTED
---- ---------------------- ----------- ------------- ----------------
 186 db file sequential read       64446    77.0267848              105
 284 db file sequential read     1458405    90.992838               105
 194 db file sequential read     1458708    91.0204316              105
 322 db file sequential read     1462557    91.1577045              105
 139 db file sequential read      211325    52.6281055               11
 256 db file sequential read      247236    58.0469755               11
 192 db file sequential read      243113    88.0193625                2
```

There are two things you can do to minimize the *db file sequential read* waits:

■ Optimize the SQL statement that initiated most of the waits by reducing the number of physical and logical reads.

■ Reduce the average wait time.

Unless you trace a session with the event 10046 or have a continuously running wait event data collector as discussed in Chapter 4, it is difficult to determine the SQL statement that is responsible for the cumulated wait time. Take the preceding

SID #192 again, for example. The 243113 centiseconds wait time may be caused by one long-running or many fast SQL statements. The latter case may not be an issue. Furthermore, the SQL statement that is currently running may or may not be the one that is responsible for the waits. This is why interactive diagnosis without historical data is often unproductive. You can query the V$SQL view for statements with high average DISK_READS, but then how can you tell they belong to the session? Due to these limitations, you may have to identify and trace the session the next time around to nail down the offending SQL statement. Once you have found it, the optimization goal is to reduce the amount of physical and logical reads.

NOTE
In addition to the DISK_READS column, the V$SQL and V$SQLAREA views in Oracle Database 10g have exciting new columns: USER_IO_WAIT_TIME, DIRECT_WRITES, APPLICATION_WAIT_TIME, CONCURRENCY_WAIT_TIME, CLUSTER_WAIT_TIME, PLSQL_EXEC_TIME, and JAVA_EXEC_TIME. You can discover the SQL statement with the highest cumulative or average USER_IO_WAIT_TIME.

Another thing you can do to minimize the impact of the *db file sequential read* event is reduce the AVERAGE_WAIT time. This is the average time a session has to wait for a single block fetch from disk; the information is available in the V$SESSION_EVENT view. In newer storage subsystems, an average single-block read shouldn't take more than 10ms (milliseconds) or 1cs (centisecond). You should expect an average wait time of 4 to 8ms (0.4 to 0.8cs) with SAN (storage area network) due to large caches. The higher the average wait time, the costlier it is to perform a single-block read, and the overall process response time will suffer. On the other hand, a lower average wait time is more forgiving and has a lesser impact on the response times of processes that perform a lot of single-block reads. (We are not encouraging you to improve the average wait time to avoid SQL optimization. If the application has SQL statements that perform excessive amounts of single-block reads, they must first be inspected and optimized.) The *db file sequential read* "System-Level Diagnosis" section has some ideas on how to improve the AVERAGE_WAIT time.

As you monitor a session and come across the *db file sequential read* event, you should translate its P1 and P2 parameters into the object that they represent. You will find that the object is normally an index or a table. The DBA_EXTENTS view is commonly used for object name resolution. However, as mentioned in Chapter 4, the DBA_EXTENTS is a complex view and is not query-friendly in regards to performance. Object name resolution is much faster using the X$BH and DBA_OBJECTS views. The caveat is that you must wait for the block to be read into the buffer cache; otherwise the X$BH view has no information on the buffer that is referenced by the P1 and P2 parameters. Also, the DBA_OBJECTS view does not contain rollback or undo segment objects that the P1 and P2 parameters may be referencing.

```
select  b.sid,
        nvl(substr(a.object_name,1,30),
                   'P1='||b.p1||' P2='||b.p2||' P3='||b.p3) object_name,
        a.subobject_name,
        a.object_type
from    dba_objects a, v$session_wait b, x$bh c
where   c.obj = a.object_id(+)
and     b.p1 = c.file#(+)
and     b.p2 = c.dbablk(+)
and     b.event = 'db file sequential read'
union
select  b.sid,
        nvl(substr(a.object_name,1,30),
                   'P1='||b.p1||' P2='||b.p2||' P3='||b.p3) object_name,
        a.subobject_name,
        a.object_type
from    dba_objects a, v$session_wait b, x$bh c
where   c.obj = a.data_object_id(+)
and     b.p1 = c.file#(+)
and     b.p2 = c.dbablk(+)
and     b.event = 'db file sequential read'
order   by 1;

  SID OBJECT_NAME              SUBOBJECT_NAME           OBJECT_TYPE
----- ----------------------- ------------------------ ----------------
   12 DVC_TRX_REPOS           DVC_TRX_REPOS_PR64       TABLE PARTITION
  128 DVC_TRX_REPOS           DVC_TRX_REPOS_PR61       TABLE PARTITION
  154 ERROR_QUEUE             ERROR_QUEUE_PR1          TABLE PARTITION
  192 DVC_TRX_REPOS_1IX       DVC_TRX_REPOS_20040416   INDEX PARTITION
  194 P1=22 P2=30801 P3=1
  322 P1=274 P2=142805 P3=1
  336 HOLD_Q1_LIST_PK                                  INDEX
```

Sequential Reads Against Indexes

The main issue is not index access; it is waits that are caused by excessive and unwarranted index reads. If the *db file sequential read* event represents a significant portion of a session's response time, all that tells you is that the application is doing a lot of index reads. This is an application issue. Inspect the execution plans of the SQL statements that access data through indexes. Is it appropriate for the SQL statements to access data through index lookups? Is the application an online transaction processing (OLTP) or decision support system (DSS)? Would full table scans be more efficient? Do the statements use the right driving table? And so on. The optimization goal is to minimize both the number of logical and physical I/Os.

If you have access to the application code, you should examine the application logic. Look at the overall logic and understand what it is trying to do. You may be able to recommend a better approach.

Index reads performance can be affected by slow I/O subsystem and/or poor database files layout, which result in a higher average wait time. However, I/O tuning should not be prioritized over the application and SQL tuning, which many DBAs often do. I/O tuning does not solve the problem if SQL statements are not optimized and the demand for physical I/Os remains high. You should also push back when the application team tries to circumvent code changes by asking for more powerful hardware. Getting the application team to change the code can be like pulling teeth. If the application is a rigid third-party solution, you may explore the stored outline feature, introduce new indexes, or modify the current key compositions whenever appropriate.

In addition to SQL tuning, it may also be worthwhile to check the index's clustering factor if the execution plan calls for *table access by index rowid*. The clustering factor of an index defines how ordered the rows are in the table. It affects the number of I/Os required for the whole operation. If the DBA_INDEXES.CLUSTERING_FACTOR of the index approaches the number of blocks in the table, then most of the rows in the table are ordered. This is desirable. However, if the clustering factor approaches the number of rows in the table, it means the rows in the table are randomly ordered. In this case, it is unlikely for the index entries in the same leaf block to point to rows in the same data block, and thus it requires more I/Os to complete the operation. You can improve the index's clustering factor by rebuilding the table so that rows are ordered according to the index key and rebuilding the index thereafter. What happens if the table has more than one index? Well, that is the downside. You can only cater to the most used index.

Also check to see if the application has recently introduced a new index using the following query. The introduction of a new index in the database may cause the optimizer to choose a different execution plan for SQL statements that access the table. The new plan may yield a better, neutral, or worse performance than the old one.

```
select owner,
       substr(object_name,1,30) object_name,
       object_type,
       created
from   dba_objects
where  object_type in ('INDEX','INDEX PARTITION')
order by created;
```

The OPTIMIZER_INDEX_COST_ADJ and OPTIMIZER_INDEX_CACHING initialization parameters can influence the optimizer to favor the nested loops operation and choose an index access path over a full table scan. The default value for the OPTIMIZER_INDEX_COST_ADJ parameter is 100. A lower value tricks the optimizer into thinking that index access paths are cheaper. The default value for the OPTIMIZER_INDEX_CACHING parameter is 0. A higher value informs the optimizer that a higher percentage of index blocks is already in the buffer cache and that nested loops operations are cheaper. Some third-party applications use this method to promote index usage. Inappropriate use of these parameters can cause significant I/O wait time. Find out what values the sessions are running with. Up to Oracle9*i* Database, this information could only be obtained by tracing the sessions with the trace event 10053 at level 1 and examining the trace files. In Oracle Database 10*g*, this is as simple as querying the V$SES_OPTIMIZER_ENV view.

Make sure all object statistics are representative of the current data, as inaccurate statistics can certainly cause the optimizer to generate poor execution plans that call for index reads when they shouldn't. Remember, statistics need to be representative and not necessarily up-to-date, and execution plan may change each time statistics are gathered.

NOTE
When analyzing tables or indexes with a low ESTIMATE value, Oracle normally uses single block reads, and this will add to the db file sequential read *statistics for the session (V$SESSION_EVENT) and instance (V$SYSTEM_EVENT).*

Sequential Reads Against Tables

You may see *db file sequential read* wait events in which the P1 and P2 parameters resolve to a table instead of an index. This is normal for SQL statements that access tables by rowids obtained from the indexes, as shown in the following explain plan. Oracle uses single-block I/O when reading a table by rowids.

```
LVL OPERATION                            OBJECT
--- ----------------------------------   ----------------------
  1 SELECT STATEMENT
  2   TABLE ACCESS BY INDEX ROWID        RESOURCE_ASGN_SNP
  3     INDEX RANGE SCAN                 RESOURCE_ASGN_SNP_4IX
```

System-Level Diagnosis

The V$SYSTEM_EVENT view provides the data for system-level diagnosis. For I/O related events, the two columns of interest are the AVERAGE_WAIT and TIME_WAITED.

Remember to evaluate the TIME_WAITED with the instance startup in mind. It is normal for an older instance to show a higher *db file sequential read* wait time. Also, always query the V$SYSTEM_EVENT view in the order of TIME_WAITED such as in the following example. This allows you to compare the *db file sequential read* waits with other significant events in the system. If the *db file sequential read* wait time is not in the top five category, don't worry about it because you have bigger fish to fry. Even if the *db file sequential read* wait time *is* in the top five category, all it tells you is that the database has seen a lot of single-block I/O calls. The high wait time may be comprised of waits from many short-running OLTP sessions or a few long-running batch processes, or both. At the system level, there is no information as to who made the I/O calls, when the calls were made, what objects were accessed, and the SQL statements that initiated the calls. In other words, system-level statistics offer very limited diagnosis capability.

```
select a.event,
       a.total_waits,
       a.time_waited,
       a.time_waited/a.total_waits average_wait,
       sysdate - b.startup_time days_old
from   v$system_event a, v$instance b
order by a.time_waited;
```

The AVERAGE_WAIT column is more useful. We showed what you should consider as normal in the preceding paragraphs. If your average single-block read wait time exceeds this allowance, you may have a problem in the I/O subsystem or hot spots on disk. If your database is built on file systems, make sure the database mount points contain only Oracle files. Do not share your database mount points with the application or another database. Also, if possible, avoid sharing I/O devices. Several mount points can be mapped to the same I/O device. According to the following Veritas *vxprint* output, mount points u02, u03, u04, and u05 are all mapped to device c2t2d0. You should find out how your database files are mapped to I/O controllers and I/O devices or physical disks. For databases on the Veritas file system, the *vxprint –ht* command shows the mount point mappings.

```
v  oracle_u02    -               ENABLED  ACTIVE   20480000 fsgen   -           SELECT
pl oracle_u02-01 oracle_u02  ENABLED  ACTIVE   20482560 CONCAT  -           RW
sd oracle01-01   oracle_u02-01 oracle01 0       20482560 0        c2t2d0 ENA

v  oracle_u03    -               ENABLED  ACTIVE   20480000 fsgen   -           SELECT
pl oracle_u03-01 oracle_u03  ENABLED  ACTIVE   20482560 CONCAT  -           RW
sd oracle01-02   oracle_u03-01 oracle01 20482560 20482560 0        c2t2d0 ENA

v  oracle_u04    -               ENABLED  ACTIVE   20480000 fsgen   -           SELECT
pl oracle_u04-01 oracle_u04  ENABLED  ACTIVE   20482560 CONCAT  -           RW
sd oracle01-03   oracle_u04-01 oracle01 40965120 20482560 0        c2t2d0 ENA

v  oracle_u05    -               ENABLED  ACTIVE   30720000 fsgen   -           SELECT
pl oracle_u05-01 oracle_u05  ENABLED  ACTIVE   30723840 CONCAT  -           RW
sd oracle01-04   oracle_u05-01 oracle01 266273280 30723840 0       c2t2d0 ENA
```

Make sure the database files are properly laid out to avoid hot spots. Monitor I/O activities using operating system commands such as *iostat* and *sar*. Pay attention to disk queue length, disk service time, and I/O throughput. If a device is particularly busy, then consider relocating some of the data files that are on the device. On the Solaris operating system, you can get I/O statistics on controllers and devices with the *iostat –dxnC* command. However, hot spots tuning is easier said than done. You need to know how the application uses I/O. Furthermore, if the application is immature and new functionalities are constantly being added, the hot spots may be moving targets. DBAs are normally not apprised of new developments and often have to discover them reactively. This is why I/O balancing can be a never ending task. If you can upgrade to Oracle Database 10*g*, ASM (Automatic Storage Management) can help with I/O balancing.

By the way, in addition to the systemwide *db file sequential read* average wait time from the V$SYSTEM_EVENT view, Oracle also provides single-block read statistics for every database file in the V$FILESTAT view. The file-level single-block average wait time can be calculated by dividing the SINGLEBLKRDTIM with the SINGLEBLKRDS, as shown next. (The SINGLEBLKRDTIM is in centiseconds.) You can quickly discover which files have unacceptable average wait times and begin to investigate the mount points or devices and ensure that they are exclusive to the database.

```
select a.file#,
       b.file_name,
       a.singleblkrds,
       a.singleblkrdtim,
       a.singleblkrdtim/a.singleblkrds average_wait
from   v$filestat a, dba_data_files b
where  a.file# = b.file_id
and    a.singleblkrds > 0
order by average_wait;

FILE# FILE_NAME                      SINGLEBLKRDS SINGLEBLKRDTIM AVERAGE_WAIT
----- ------------------------------ ------------ -------------- ------------
  367 /dev/vgEMCp113/rPOM1P_4G_039           5578            427  .076550735
  368 /dev/vgEMCp113/rPOM1P_4G_040           5025            416   .08278607
  369 /dev/vgEMCp113/rPOM1P_4G_041          13793           1313  .095193214
  370 /dev/vgEMCp113/rPOM1P_4G_042           6232            625  .100288832
  371 /dev/vgEMCp113/rPOM1P_4G_043           4663            482  .103366931
  372 /dev/vgEMCp108/rPOM1P_8G_011         164828         102798  .623668309
  373 /dev/vgEMCp108/rPOM1P_8G_012         193071         125573   .65039804
  374 /dev/vgEMCp108/rPOM1P_8G_013         184799         126720  .685717996
  375 /dev/vgEMCp108/rPOM1P_8G_014         175565         125969  .717506337
```

db file scattered read

The *db file scattered read* wait event has three parameters: file#, first block#, and block count. In Oracle Database 10*g*, this wait event falls under the User I/O wait class. Keep the following key thoughts in mind when dealing with the *db file scattered read* wait event.

■ The Oracle session has requested and is waiting for multiple contiguous database blocks (up to DB_FILE_MULTIBLOCK_READ_COUNT) to be read into the SGA from disk.

- Multiblock I/O requests are associated with full table scans and index fast full scans (FFS) operations.

- The two important numbers to look for are the TIME_WAITED and AVERAGE_ WAIT by individual sessions.

- Significant *db file scattered read* wait time is most likely an application issue.

Common Causes, Diagnosis, and Actions

The *db file scattered read* wait event is much like the *db file sequential read* event. Instead of single-block read, this is multiblock read. The *db file scattered read* wait event is initiated by SQL statements (both user and recursive) that perform full scans operations against tables and indexes. Contrary to some teaching, full scans are not always bad; they are good when the SQL statement needs most of the rows in the object. Full scans on tables and indexes are normal and are not the main issue. You want to avoid having full scans on objects when SQL predicates can be better served by single-block reads. Following are some helpful tips for diagnosing and correcting *db file scattered read* waits.

Session-Level Diagnosis

When do multiblock reads become an issue? As with the *db file sequential read* event, you must also establish a guideline for your environment. The amount of time a process spends on the *db file scattered read* event is always a good indicator, bearing in mind the LOGON_TIME and the significance of the wait time in relation to other nonidle events. A high wait time is normally caused by inefficient SQL statements and therefore is most likely an application issue.

In addition to the V$SESSION_EVENT view, the V$SESSTAT view also has full table scans statistics of current sessions. However the time element is missing, so the V$SESSION_EVENT view is better. Following is an example query:

```
select a.sid, b.name, a.value
from   v$sesstat a, v$statname b
where  a.statistic# = b.statistic#
and    a.value      <> 0
and    b.name = 'table scan blocks gotten'
order by 3,1;

SID NAME                                VALUE
---- -------------------------- ----------
111 table scan blocks gotten          59,535
  8 table scan blocks gotten         567,454
164 table scan blocks gotten       5,978,579
158 table scan blocks gotten      14,798,247
```

You can minimize the *db file scattered read* waits the same way you do *db file sequential read* waits:

- Optimize the SQL statement that initiated most of the waits. The goal is to minimize the number of physical and logical reads.

- Reduce the average wait time.

As we discussed in the *db file sequential read* section, you must first find the SQL statement that is responsible for most of the waits, and this is challenging if you do not have a wait event data collector that monitors processes from start to finish. (The Active Session History [ASH] in Oracle Database 10*g* automatically collects SQL execution information, and you can easily identify the offending SQL statement using the Enterprise Manager.) Once the SQL statement is identified, examine its execution plan. Should the statement access the data by a full table scan or index FFS? Would an index range or unique scan be more efficient? Does the query use the right driving table? Are the SQL predicates appropriate for hash or merge join? If full scans are appropriate, can parallel query improve the response time? The objective is to reduce the demands for both the logical and physical I/Os, and this is best achieved through SQL and application tuning.

Prior to Oracle9*i* Database, generating accurate explain plans for SQL statements could be a painstaking task, especially if your schema was not privileged to the objects accessed by the SQL statements. This task is now a breeze, however, beginning in Oracle9*i* Database with the V$SQL_PLAN view. The following query extracts the execution plans of SQL statements that are currently performing full scans:

```
set linesize 132
break on hash_value skip 1 dup
col child_number format 9999     heading 'CHILD'
col operation      format a55
col cost           format 99999
col kbytes         format 999999
col object         format a25
select hash_value,
       child_number,
       lpad(' ',2*depth)||operation||' '||options||decode(id, 0,
substr(optimizer,1,6)||' Cost='||to_char(cost)) operation,
       object_name object,
       cost,
       cardinality,
       round(bytes / 1024) kbytes
from   v$sql_plan
where  hash_value in (select  a.sql_hash_value
                      from    v$session a, v$session_wait b
```

```
                      where    a.sid   = b.sid
                      and      b.event = 'db file scattered read')
order by hash_value, child_number, id;

-- Not all the columns are shown due to space constraints.
HASH_VALUE CHILD OPERATION                                 OBJECT
---------- ----- ----------------------------------- ----------------
 138447424     0 DELETE STATEMENT CHOOSE Cost=5
 138447424     0  DELETE
 138447424     0   INDEX FAST FULL SCAN                HOLD_Q1_LIST_PK

4246069598     0 SELECT STATEMENT CHOOSE Cost=4075
4246069598     0  NESTED LOOPS ANTI
4246069598     0   MERGE JOIN ANTI
4246069598     0    SORT JOIN
4246069598     0     PARTITION RANGE ALL
4246069598     0      TABLE ACCESS FULL                 SRV_TRX_REPOS
4246069598     0     SORT UNIQUE
4246069598     0      PARTITION RANGE ALL
4246069598     0       INDEX FAST FULL SCAN             Q3_PK
4246069598     0    PARTITION RANGE ALL
4246069598     0     INDEX FAST FULL SCAN               ERROR_QUEUE_PK
```

If an application that has been running fine for a while suddenly clocks a lot of time on the *db file scattered read* event and there hasn't been a code change, you might want to check to see if one or more indexes has been dropped or become unusable. To determine which indexes have been dropped, you can compare the development, test, and production databases. Also, check when the LAST_DDL_TIME of the table was in the DBA_OBJECTS view. When an index is created or dropped, Oracle stamps the date and time in the LAST_DDL_TIME column. The ALTER TABLE MOVE command marks all indexes associated with the table as unusable. Certain partitioning operations can also cause indexes to be marked unusable. This includes adding a new partition or coalescing partitions in a hash-partitioned table; dropping a partition from a partitioned table or global partitioned index; modifying partition attributes; and merging, moving, splitting, or truncating table partitions. A direct load operation that fails also leaves indexes in an unusable state. This can easily be fixed by rebuilding the indexes.

There are initialization parameters that, when increased in value, can skew the optimizer toward full scans: DB_FILE_MULTIBLOCK_READ_COUNT (MBRC), HASH_AREA_SIZE, and OPTIMIZER_INDEX_COST_ADJ. Find out the values the sessions are running with and make appropriate adjustments to the parameters so they do not adversely affect application runtimes.

Yet another factor that can adversely affect the quality of execution plans and cause excessive I/Os is having inaccurate statistics. When the optimizer sees a table with statistics that say it has only a few rows, it will choose the full table scan access path. If the table has millions of rows in reality, the SQL statement is in for a rude awakening at execution time, especially if the table is an inner table of a nested loops join. Make sure all statistics are representative of the actual data. Check the LAST_ ANALYZED date. If you suspect the statistics are stale, you can count the current number of rows in the table and compare it with the NUM_ROWS value. Alternatively, you can let Oracle decide if statistics need to be refreshed by executing the DBMS_ STATS.GATHER_TABLE_STATS with the GATHER STALE option, but only if table monitoring is enabled for the table. Oracle considers the statistics stale when 10 percent of the rows are changed. Table monitoring is enabled by default in Oracle Database 10*g*.

NOTE
When analyzing tables or indexes with the COMPUTE option, Oracle normally performs full table scans. This will add to the db file scattered read *statistics for the session (V$SESSION_EVENT) and instance (V$SYSTEM_EVENT).*

System-Level Diagnosis
Query the V$SYSTEM_EVENT view in the order of TIME_WAITED and find the *db file scattered read* wait event. The columns of interest are the AVERAGE_WAIT and TIME_WAITED. Handling the *db file scattered read* waits on systemlevel is similar to handling the *db file sequential read* waits on system level, so you should refer to the "System-Level Diagnosis" section of the *db file sequential read* wait event.

Why Does *db file sequential read event* Show Up in a Full Table Scan Operation
If you trace or monitor a full table scan operation closely, you may find *db file sequential read* events sandwiched between *db file scattered read* events. This may or may not be a problem depending on the circumstance of the single-block read. Following are the four primary reasons why you see *db file sequential read* events in a full scan operation.

- **Extent boundary**   When the last set of blocks in an extent is only 1 block, Oracle fetches that block with a single-block read call. This is normally not a problem unless your extent size is too small. Following is an event 10046 trace file that shows *db file sequential read* events embedded in a full table scan operation. The table block size is 8K, the MBRC is 8 blocks, and the extent size is 72K (9 blocks). A full table scan against the table will result in many *db file sequential read* events if the table is large. If this is the case, the full table scan operation will complete faster if the table is rebuilt with a larger extent size.

```
WAIT #1: nam='db file scattered read' ela= 470 p1=7 p2=18 p3=8
WAIT #1: nam='db file sequential read' ela= 79 p1=7 p2=26 p3=1
WAIT #1: nam='db file scattered read' ela= 459 p1=7 p2=27 p3=8
WAIT #1: nam='db file sequential read' ela= 82 p1=7 p2=35 p3=1
WAIT #1: nam='db file scattered read' ela= 466 p1=7 p2=36 p3=8
WAIT #1: nam='db file sequential read' ela= 79 p1=7 p2=44 p3=1
WAIT #1: nam='db file scattered read' ela= 460 p1=7 p2=45 p3=8
WAIT #1: nam='db file sequential read' ela= 60 p1=7 p2=53 p3=1
WAIT #1: nam='db file scattered read' ela= 779 p1=7 p2=54 p3=8
WAIT #1: nam='db file sequential read' ela= 78 p1=7 p2=62 p3=1
. . .
```

- **Cached blocks** See explanation in the "Why Does a Full Scan Operation Request Fewer Blocks than the MBRC" section. This is not a problem.

- **Chained or migrated rows** It is a problem if you see many *db file sequential read* waits against a table when the execution plan of the SQL statement calls for a full table scan. This indicates the table has many chained or migrated rows. Oracle goes after each chained or migrated row with the single-block I/O call. Check the table's CHAIN_CNT in the DBA_TABLES view. Of course, the CHAIN_CNT is as of the LAST_ANALYZED date. Migrated rows can be corrected by reorganizing the table (export and import, or ALTER TABLE MOVE).

- **Index entry creation** It is not a problem if you see many *db file sequential read* waits against an index when the execution plan of the SQL statement calls for a full table scan. In the following example, TABLE_A has an index and the *db file sequential read* waits were the result of reading index blocks into the SGA to be filled with data from TABLE_B. Notice the magnitude of the *db file sequential read* waits versus the *db file scattered read* in the statistics. This means you cannot always assume which bottlenecks you will see from looking at an execution plan. Most DBAs would expect to see a lot of *db file scattered read* events. Another point worth noting is that the *db file sequential read* wait event does apply to insert statements. The common misconception is that it only applies to update and delete statements.

```
-- SQL statement
insert into table_A
select * from table_B;

-- Explain plan
LVL OPERATION              OBJECT
--- -------------------- --------------------
  1  INSERT STATEMENT
  2    TABLE ACCESS FULL   TABLE_B
```

```
-- Wait event statistics
SID EVENT                               TIME_WAITED
--- ------------------------------- -----------
  7 SQL*Net message from client               5
  7 latch free                               11
  7 log file switch completion              155
  7 log buffer space                        205
  7 log file sync                           467
  7 db file scattered read                1,701
  7 db file sequential read             185,682
```

Why Does a Full Scan Operation Request Fewer Blocks than the MBRC?

If you monitor a full table scan operation closely by repeatedly querying the V$SESSION_WAIT view in quick successions or by tracing the session with trace event 10046, you may see some *db file scattered read* events that request fewer blocks than the MBRC. This irregularity is due to any of the following reasons:

■ The last set of blocks in an extent is less than the MBRC. If the MBRC is set to 8 and every extent has 10 blocks, Oracle will issue two multiblock read calls for each extent—one read call for 8 blocks and the other read call for 2 blocks—because the MBRC factor cannot span across extents.

■ One or more blocks in the multiblock read set is already in the buffer cache, so Oracle breaks the fetch into two or more reads, which may be comprised of a single or multiblock I/Os. For example, if the MBRC is 8 and blocks 3 and 7 are in the cache, Oracle will issue three read calls—the first for blocks 1 and 2, the second for blocks 4 through 6, and the third for block 8. Since the third fetch is for a single database block, the wait event is *db file sequential read*. However, for the first two read calls, the wait event is *db file scattered read* because the number of blocks is greater than 1. Therefore, cached blocks can cause full table scans operations to perform more reads than required.

Setting the DB_FILE_ MULTIBLOCK_ READ_ COUNT (MBRC)

As mentioned, a higher MBRC number can influence the optimizer to lean toward full scans. The right number for the database depends on the application (DSS or OLTP). Batch processes can benefit from a higher MBRC as it allows full scan operations to complete faster. If the database serves both batch and OLTP processes, you must find a balance. The default value of 8 is rather conservative.

If full scans are the best way to go, you want SQL statements to scan the objects with the maximum value supported by your system. Why waste time with a smaller value? You should find out what the maximum value is and dynamically apply this value to processes that perform large full scans.

There is a limit on MBRCs. It depends on several factors, including *sstiomax*, DB_BLOCK_SIZE, and DB_BLOCK_BUFFERS. The *sstiomax* is an Oracle internal limit, which limits the amount of data that can be transferred in a single I/O of a read or write operation. The value is internally set in the Oracle code and varies with the Oracle version. The limit is 128K in earlier versions of Oracle and 1MB beginning in version 8. The product of DB_BLOCK_SIZE and MBRC cannot exceed the port-specific definition for *sstiomax*. MBRC must also be smaller than DB_BLOCK_BUFFERS / 4. Furthermore, MBRC is subject to hardware limits such as the Solaris *maxphys* and file system *maxcontig* values. Does this sound like too much to you? It is! The good news is there is a shortcut to finding the limit for your platform. You can set the MBRC to a ridiculously high number for your session, as shown next, and let Oracle figure out what the system can handle. You then simply run a query that scans a table and monitor the progress from another session by querying the V$SESSION_WAIT view in quick successions. The maximum P3 value of the *db file scattered read* events that belong to the first session is the MBRC limit for your platform. Alternatively, you can monitor the full table scans with trace event 10046. This maximum value is not meant to be set at the database level; rather, it may be applied at the session level to speed up full scans when that is the best way to go.

```
alter session set db_file_multiblock_read_count = 1000;
select /*+ full(a) */ count(*) from big_table a;

-- This following is an excerpt from the 10046 trace file.
-- It shows that the largest MBRC the system can bear is 128 blocks.
WAIT #1: nam='db file scattered read' ela= 17946 p1=6 p2=56617 p3=128
WAIT #1: nam='db file scattered read' ela= 21055 p1=6 p2=56745 p3=128
WAIT #1: nam='db file scattered read' ela= 17628 p1=6 p2=56873 p3=128
WAIT #1: nam='db file scattered read' ela= 29881 p1=6 p2=57001 p3=128
WAIT #1: nam='db file scattered read' ela= 33220 p1=6 p2=57129 p3=128
WAIT #1: nam='db file scattered read' ela= 33986 p1=6 p2=57257 p3=96
WAIT #1: nam='db file scattered read' ela= 46372 p1=6 p2=65577 p3=128
WAIT #1: nam='db file scattered read' ela= 33770 p1=6 p2=65705 p3=128
WAIT #1: nam='db file scattered read' ela= 41750 p1=6 p2=65833 p3=128
WAIT #1: nam='db file scattered read' ela= 34914 p1=6 p2=65961 p3=128
WAIT #1: nam='db file scattered read' ela= 33326 p1=6 p2=66089 p3=128
```

Why Physical I/Os Are Expensive

Whenever most DBAs hear that physical I/Os are costly, they immediately train their thoughts toward the physical disks and I/O subsystem. Yes, the storage layer is the slowest component, but that is only half of the story. The other half is about the stuff that goes on inside Oracle when blocks are being read into the SGA.

There are numerous operations that have to take place. For brevity's sake, among them, the foreground process must first scan the free buffer list. If a free buffer is not found when the maximum scan limit is reached, the foreground process posts the DBWR process to make free buffers. Then the foreground process has to retry for the free buffer. Once it finds a free buffer, it unlinks it from the free lists chain and relinks the buffer in at the top of the LRU (Least Recently Used) or the midpoint insertion of the LRU (depending on the version). Then the pointers for the buffer header must be adjusted accordingly. There are at least two sets of pointers, and each change requires a latch get. The header structure of the block must also be initialized and updated. The bits in the block header must also be set and changed during the allocation of the buffer, the read of the block into the buffer, and the completion of a read in order to prevent other processes from using the block while it is influx.

Therefore the best way to combat the *db file sequential read* and *db file scattered read* waits is to reduce the demand for both the logical and physical I/Os. This can be best achieved through application and SQL tuning. Now that you have been informed how expensive physical I/Os are, you should also know that logical I/Os are not that cheap either. We will discuss this in Chapter 6.

direct path read

The *direct path read* wait event has three parameters: file#, first block#, and block count. In Oracle Database 10*g*, this wait event falls under the User I/O wait class. Keep the following key thoughts in mind when dealing with the *direct path read* wait event.

- These are waits that are associated with direct read operations. An Oracle direct read operation reads data directly into the session's PGA (Program Global Area), bypassing the SGA. The data in the PGA is not shared with other sessions.

- Direct reads may be performed in synchronous or asynchronous mode, depending on the platform and the value of the DISK_ASYNC_IO parameter. The systemwide *direct path read* wait event statistics can be very misleading when asynchronous I/O is used.

- A significant number of *direct path read* waits is most likely an application issue.

Common Causes, Diagnosis, and Actions

The *direct path read* waits are driven by SQL statements that perform direct read operations from the temporary or regular tablespaces.

SQL statements with functions that require sorts, such as ORDER BY, GROUP BY, UNION, DISTINCT, and ROLLUP, write sort runs to the temporary tablespace when the input size is larger than the work area in the PGA. The sort runs in the temporary tablespace are subsequently read and merged to provide the final result. An Oracle session waits on the *direct path read* wait event while the sort runs are being read. SQL statements that employ the merge join, either through a hint or as decided by the optimizer, also require sort.

SQL statements that employ the hash join, either as directed by a hint or the optimizer, flush the hash partitions that don't fit in memory to the temporary tablespace. The hash partitions in the temporary tablespace are read back into the memory to be probed for rows that match the SQL predicates. An Oracle session waits on the *direct path read* wait event while the hash partitions are being read.

SQL statements that employ parallel scans also contribute to the systemwide *direct path read* waits. In a parallel execution, the *direct path read* waits are associated with the query slaves and not the parent query. The session that runs the parent query waits mostly on the *PX Deq: Execute Reply* wait event (in Oracle8*i* Database and above).

NOTE
As of Oracle 8.1.7, there is a separate direct read wait event for LOB segments: direct path read (lob). *This wait event applies to LOBs that are stored as NOCACHE. When LOBs are stored as CACHE, reads and writes go through the buffer cache and waits show up as* db file sequential read.

Session-Level Diagnosis

It is highly unlikely that the *direct path read* wait event will show up as the leading bottleneck within a session even though it may actually be it. The reasons are as follows:

- The way Oracle accounts for the waits, as discussed in Chapter 3.

- Sessions that perform parallel processing using parallel query do not wait on the *direct path read* wait event, which normally represents the bulk of the time. The *direct path read* waits are associated with the query slaves' sessions that scan the tables. The only time the *direct path read* wait event shows up within a parent session is when the parent session itself has read activities against the temporary tablespace. This is driven by SQL functions, such as ORDER BY, GROUP BY, and DISTINCT, or hash partitions that spill to disk but not parallel scans.

Therefore you shouldn't evaluate *direct path read* waits based on the TOTAL_WAITS or TIME_WAITED in the V$SESSION_EVENT view. Instead, you can find current sessions that perform a lot of direct read operations from the V$SESSTAT view using the following query. The *physical reads direct* is comprised of the direct reads that are originated by the parent session itself as well as the sum of all direct reads that are originated by the query slaves that the parent session employs. The direct reads that are initiated by query slaves are only reflected in the parent session when the slaves complete their jobs. The downside to this approach is that there is no time element.

```
select a.name, b.sid, b.value,
       round((sysdate - c.logon_time) * 24) hours_connected
from   v$statname a, v$sesstat b, v$session c
where  b.sid       = c.sid
and    a.statistic# = b.statistic#
and    b.value     > 0
and    a.name      = 'physical reads direct'
order by b.value;

NAME                          SID     VALUE HOURS_CONNECTED
------------------------- ---- ---------- ---------------
physical reads direct           2        41             980
physical reads direct           4        41             980
physical reads direct           5    445186             980
```

Apart from finding the sessions that perform a lot of direct reads, you must also find out where the sessions are reading from (temporary tablespace or data files), the SQL statements that initiate the waits, and the type of segments being read. The following query gives you the answers. Sessions that read from the temporary tablespace may be reading sort or hash segments. Sessions that read from data files normally belong to parallel query slaves.

```
select a.event,
       a.sid,
       c.sql_hash_value hash_value,
       decode(d.ktssosegt,
              1,'SORT', 2,'HASH',    3,'DATA',
              4,'INDEX',5,'LOB_DATA',6,'LOB_INDEX',
              null) as segment_type,
       b.tablespace_name,
       b.file_name
```

```
from     v$session_wait a, dba_data_files b, v$session c, x$ktsso d
where    c.saddr       = d.ktssoses(+)
and      c.serial#     = d.ktssosno(+)
and      d.inst_id(+) = userenv('instance')
and      a.sid         = c.sid
and      a.p1          = b.file_id
and      a.event       = 'direct path read'
union all
select a.event,
       a.sid,
       d.sql_hash_value hash_value,
       decode(e.ktssosegt,
              1,'SORT', 2,'HASH',    3,'DATA',
              4,'INDEX',5,'LOB_DATA',6,'LOB_INDEX',
              null) as segment_type,
       b.tablespace_name,
       b.file_name
from     v$session_wait a, dba_temp_files b, v$parameter c,
         v$session d, x$ktsso e
where    d.saddr       = e.ktssoses(+)
and      d.serial#     = e.ktssosno(+)
and      e.inst_id(+) = userenv('instance')
and      a.sid         = d.sid
and      b.file_id     = a.p1 - c.value
and      c.name        = 'db_files'
and      a.event       = 'direct path read'
order by 1,2;

-- File name output is edited to fit page.
EVENT                    SID HASH_VALUE SEGMENT TABLESPACE_N FILE_NAME
------------------------ --- ---------- ------- ------------ ----------------
direct path read           8  511952958 SORT    TEMP_BATCH   temp_batch_01.dbf
direct path read           9 3138787393         ORDERS       orders_01.dbf
direct path read          11 3138787393         ORDERS       orders_01.dbf
direct path read          12 3138787393         ORDERS       orders_01.dbf
direct path read          14 3138787393         ORDERS       orders_01.dbf
```

If you catch a session reading sort segments from the temporary tablespace, this indicates the SORT_AREA_SIZE (or work area size if you use the PGA_AGGREGATE_ TARGET in Oracle9*i* Database) is not large enough to accommodate a cache sort (or in memory sort). This is fine. It is unrealistic to expect all SQL statements to perform cache sorts. However, you should avoid multipass sorts because they create a lot of I/Os to the temporary tablespace and are very slow. How can you tell if a SQL statement is doing a multipass sort? Well, it is not that easy in versions prior to Oracle9*i* Database. You have to trace the session with the event 10032 and examine the trace file. However, beginning in Oracle9*i* Database, you can simply query the V$SQL_WORKAREA or V$SQL_WORKAREA_ACTIVE views with the SQL hash value that performs the sort. For a more in-depth discussion on sort, please review the "If Your Memory Serves You Right" white paper from the International Oracle Users Group (IOUG) 2004 conference proceedings at www.ioug.org.

The goal of tuning in this case is to minimize the number of sorts as a whole and, more specifically, disk sorts. Increasing the SORT_AREA_SIZE (or PGA_AGGREGATE_TARGET) may help reduce the number of disk sorts, but that's usually the workaround rather than the cure, unless your SORT_AREA_SIZE is unreasonably small to begin with. You should examine the application and the SQL statements to see if sorts are really necessary. Applications have the tendency to abuse the DISTINCT and UNION functions. Whenever possible use UNION ALL instead of UNION, and where applicable use HASH JOIN instead of SORT MERGE and NESTED LOOPS instead of HASH JOIN. Make sure the optimizer selects the right driving table. Check to see if the composite index's columns can be rearranged to match the ORDER BY clause to avoid sort entirely. Also, consider automating the SQL work areas using PGA_AGGREGATE_TARGET in Oracle9*i* Database. Statistically, the automatic memory management delivers a higher percentage of cache sorts.

NOTE
Be careful when switching from UNION to UNION ALL as this can produce different results depending on the data. The UNION operator returns only distinct rows that appear in either result, while the UNION ALL operator returns all rows.

NOTE
By default, the HASH_AREA_SIZE is twice the SORT_AREA_SIZE. A larger HASH_AREA_SIZE will influence the optimizer toward the hash joins (full table scan) rather than nested loops operation.

Similarly, if you catch a session reading hash segments from the temporary tablespace, all that tells you is that the HASH_AREA_SIZE (or work area size in case of the PGA_AGGREGATE_TARGET in Oracle9*i* Database) is not big enough to accommodate the hash table in memory. The solution is similar to the one just mentioned: cure it from the application and SQL tuning before adjusting the HASH_AREA_SIZE (or PGA_AGGREGATE_TARGET). Unless, of course, your HASH_AREA_SIZE is too small to begin with.

If you discover that the direct reads belong to parallel query slaves, you should verify if parallel scans are appropriate for the parent SQL statement and that the degree of parallelism is right. Make sure the query slaves do not saturate your CPUs or disks. Identifying the parent SQL statement can be a bit tricky because the hash value of the parent statement is not the same as the hash value of child statements that the query slaves execute. It was even trickier before the V$PX_SESSION view was introduced in Oracle 8.1.5. Following are two examples, one for versions prior to 8.1.5 and the other for version 8.1.5 and greater, that can help you identify the parent SQL statements when parallel queries are involved:

```
-- For versions prior to 8.1.5.
-- Note: This query is not able to differentiate parallel query statements
--       that are executed by multiple SYS users as they all share a common
--       AUDSID.
select decode(ownerid,2147483644,'PARENT','CHILD') stmt_level,
       audsid,
       sid,
       serial#,
       username,
       osuser,
       process,
       sql_hash_value hash_value,
       sql_address
from   v$session
where  type <> 'BACKGROUND'
and    audsid in (select audsid
                  from   v$session
                  group by audsid
                  having count(*) > 1)
order by audsid, stmt_level desc, sid, username, osuser;
```

```
STMT_L   AUDSID   SID SERIAL# USERNAME OSUSER  PROCESS HASH_VALUE SQL_ADDR
------   -------- ---- ------- -------- ------- ------- ---------- --------
PARENT   3086501   20     779 INTREPID cdh8455 16537   3663187692 A0938E54
CHILD    3086501   12     841 INTREPID cdh8455 16544    817802256 A092E1CC
CHILD    3086501   14    2241 INTREPID cdh8455 16546    817802256 A092E1CC
CHILD    3086501   17    3617 INTREPID cdh8455 16540    817802256 A092E1CC
CHILD    3086501   21     370 INTREPID cdh8455 16542    817802256 A092E1CC
```

The following query applies to version 8.1.5 and higher.

```
select decode(a.qcserial#, null, 'PARENT', 'CHILD') stmt_level,
       a.sid,
       a.serial#,
       b.username,
       b.osuser,
       b.sql_hash_value,
       b.sql_address,
       a.degree,
       a.req_degree
from   v$px_session a, v$session b
where  a.sid = b.sid
order by a.qcsid, stmt_level desc;
```

```
STMT_L  SID  SERIAL#  USERNAME  OSUSER   HASH_VALUE   SQL_ADDR  DEG  REQ_DEG
------  ---  -------  --------  -------  ----------   --------  ---  -------
PARENT   20      779  INTREPID  cdh8455  3663187692   A0938E54
CHILD    17     3617  INTREPID  cdh8455   817802256   A092E1CC    4        4
CHILD    21      370  INTREPID  cdh8455   817802256   A092E1CC    4        4
CHILD    12      841  INTREPID  cdh8455   817802256   A092E1CC    4        4
CHILD    14     2241  INTREPID  cdh8455   817802256   A092E1CC    4        4
```

Initialization Parameters of Interest

The DB_FILE_DIRECT_IO_COUNT initialization parameter can impact the *direct path read* performance. It sets the maximum I/O buffer size for direct reads and writes operations. Up to Oracle8*i* Database, the default value on most platforms is 64 blocks. So if the DB_BLOCK_SIZE is 8K, the maximum I/O buffer size for direct reads and writes operations is 512K. This number is further subject to hardware limits.

The DB_FILE_DIRECT_IO_COUNT parameter is hidden in Oracle9*i* Database, and the value is expressed in bytes instead of blocks. The default value in Oracle9*i* Database is 1MB. The actual direct I/O size depends on your hardware configuration and limits.

You can discover the actual direct read I/O size in three ways:

■ Trace the Oracle session that performs direct reads operations using the trace event 10046 at level 8. The P3 parameter indicates the number of blocks read. Based on the following example, the *direct path read* I/O size is 64K since the block size is 8K. Alternatively, you can query the V$SESSION_ WAIT view for the P3 value of the *direct path read* event.

```
WAIT #1: nam='direct path read' ela= 4 p1=4 p2=86919 p3=8
WAIT #1: nam='direct path read' ela= 5 p1=4 p2=86927 p3=8
WAIT #1: nam='direct path read' ela= 10 p1=4 p2=86935 p3=8
WAIT #1: nam='direct path read' ela= 39 p1=4 p2=86943 p3=8
WAIT #1: nam='direct path read' ela= 5 p1=4 p2=86951 p3=8
WAIT #1: nam='direct path read' ela= 38 p1=4 p2=86959 p3=8
. . .
```

■ Trace the Unix session that performs direct reads or writes operations using the operating system trace facility such as *truss, tusc, trace,* or *strace.* The snippet of the *truss* report from an Oracle9*i* Database reveals the direct I/O size is 65536 bytes or 64K:

```
9218/6:        kaio(AIONOTIFY, -14712832)              = 0
9218/1:        kaio(AIOWAIT, 0xFFBECE98)               = 1
9218/1:        lwp_cond_signal(0xFEB7BFA0)             = 0
9218/3:        pread64(256, "0602\0\001\0 ~13C19AEE }".., 65536, 0x0FC26000) = 65536
9218/1:        lwp_cond_signal(0xFEB69FA0)             = 0
9218/4:        pread64(256, "0602\0\001\0 ~1BC19AEFE7".., 65536, 0x0FC36000) = 65536
. . .
```

■ Enable the debug information for the session that performs direct I/O operations using the trace event 10357 at level 1. Example: *alter session set events '10357 trace name context forever, level 1'*. The snippet of the trace file is provided here:

```
Unix process pid: 4375, image: oracle@kccdeds73 (P000)
*** SESSION ID:(9.18) 2004-02-08 21:47:01.908
DBA Range Initialized: length is 1570, start dba is 0100602b
kcblin: lbs=fc86c1cc  flag=8 slot_cnt=32 slot_size=65536 state obj=24321224
kcblin: state objects are: Call=243a2210,Current Call=243a2210, Session=24321224
kdContigDbaDrCbk:starting from tsn 5
kdContigDbaDrCbk:starting from rdba 0100602b
kdContigDbaDrCbk:returning 1570 blocks
kcblrs:issuing read on slot : 0
kcbldio:lbs=fc86c1cc slt=fc86408c typ=0 async=1 afn=4 blk=602b cnt=8 buf=fc87fe00
kcblrs:issuing read on slot : 1
kcbldio:lbs=fc86c1cc slt=fc864210 typ=0 async=1 afn=4 blk=6033 cnt=8 buf=fc89fe00
kcblcio: lbs=fc86c1cc slt=fc86408c type=0 afn=4 blk=602b cnt=8 buf=fc87fe00
. . .
```

In the preceding example, the trace file belongs to query slave #0 (P000). There are 32 I/O slots available for the direct read operation (slot_cnt=32). A slot is a unit of I/O, and each slot is 65536 bytes (slot_size=65536). Asynchronous I/O is enabled during the read operation (async=1). The query slave reads data file #4 (afn=4). The number of blocks read is 8 (cnt=8). Since the block size is 8K, this translates to 65536 bytes.

In this case, the direct I/O slot size prevents the process from achieving the full 1MB, which is the default limit of the _DB_FILE_DIRECT_IO_COUNT parameter. The slot size can be modified by event 10351. The number of slots can be modified by event 10353.

CAUTION
The preceding information gives you a sense of the direct I/O throughput in your system. Don't simply change the default slot size or the number of direct I/O slots. You need to know your hardware limits before doing so. Besides, you should focus on optimizing the application and SQL statements first.

Lastly, in Oracle8*i* Database, direct reads can also be enabled for serial scans with the _SERIAL_DIRECT_READ initialization parameter. Earlier releases may do the same by setting event 10355. Doing so will cause data from full scans to be read into the session's PGA and not shared with other sessions. This can sharply increase memory usage.

direct path write

The *direct path write* wait event has three parameters: file#, first block#, and block count. In Oracle Database 10*g*, this wait event falls under the User I/O wait class. Keep the following key thoughts in mind when dealing with the *direct path write* wait event.

- These are waits that are associated with direct write operations that write data from users' PGAs to data files or temporary tablespaces. Oracle direct I/O is not the same as Unix operating system's direct I/O. Oracle direct I/O bypasses the SGA, while the Unix operating system direct I/O bypasses the file system cache.

- Direct writes may be performed in synchronous or asynchronous mode, depending on the platform and the value of the DISK_ASYNC_IO parameter. The systemwide *direct path write* wait event statistics can be very misleading when asynchronous I/O is used.

- A significant number of *direct path write* waits is most likely an application issue.

Common Causes, Diagnosis, and Actions

The *direct path write* waits are driven by SQL statements that perform direct write operations in the temporary or regular tablespaces. This includes SQL statements that create temporary segments such as SORT, HASH, INDEX, DATA, LOB_DATA, and LOB_INDEX in the temporary tablespace, and statements that perform direct load operations such as CTAS (create table as select), INSERT /*+ APPEND */... SELECT, and SQL loader running in direct load mode. Oracle sessions wait on the *direct path write* event to confirm that the operating system has completed all outstanding I/Os, or they wait for I/O slots to become available so that more writes can be issued.

 NOTE
As of Oracle 8.1.7, there is a separate direct write wait event for LOB segments—direct path write (lob). This wait event applies to LOBs that are stored as NOCACHE.

Session-Level Diagnosis

Like the *direct path read* wait event, the *direct path write* wait event is also unlikely to show up as the leading bottleneck within a session due to the way the waits are accounted for, especially when asynchronous I/O is used. This means you shouldn't rely on the V$SESSION_EVENT view for diagnostic data. Instead, you can find current sessions that perform a lot of direct write operations from the V$SESSTAT view using the following query. The downside to this approach is that there is no time element.

```
select a.name, b.sid, b.value,
       round((sysdate - c.logon_time) * 24) hours_connected
from   v$statname a, v$sesstat b, v$session c
where  b.sid        = c.sid
and    a.statistic# = b.statistic#
and    b.value      > 0
and    a.name       = 'physical writes direct'
order by b.value;

NAME                         SID      VALUE HOURS_CONNECTED
------------------------- ---- ---------- ---------------
physical writes direct       4         39             980
physical writes direct       5     445480             980
```

The next step is to discover if the direct writes are going to the temporary tablespace or data files. You can do this by monitoring the P1 values of the *direct path write* events. If they mostly go to the temporary tablespace, you have to find out what kind of temporary segments are being created and the SQL statements that initiate them. The solution is the same as with the *direct path read*: cure it from the application before you decide to increase the SORT_AREA_SIZE, HASH_AREA_SIZE, or PGA_AGGREGATE_TARGET parameters. Tune the application and SQL statements to reduce the number of sort runs or hash partitions. Remember, when you reduce direct writes, you will also reduce the number of direct reads. This is because the temporary segments that are created must be read back.

If the direct writes are mostly going to data files, then one or more SQL statements are performing direct load operations. In this case, you may monitor the I/O operations from the operating system using *sar –d* or *iostat –dxnC*. Make sure the disk service time is acceptable and there is no hot spot.

You can discover the direct write I/O size from the P3 parameter of the *direct path write* event. You can do this by querying the V$SESSION_WAIT view or by tracing the Oracle session that performs direct writes with the trace event 10046 at level 8. Alternatively, you can get the same answer by tracing the Unix session that performs direct writes with *truss, tusc, trace,* or *strace* by enabling the debug information for the session that performs direct writes with the trace event 10357 at level 1. Following is a snippet of the event 10046 and 10357 trace file that belongs to a session that performs direct writes. The wait event trace data and the direct write debug information are mixed because both traces are enabled at the same time. From it, you learn that there are two I/O slots available (slot_cnt=2), and an I/O slot size is 8K (slot_size=8192), which limits the write to one Oracle block (also indicated by cnt=1 and p3=1). The direct writes are going to file #51 as indicated by P1=51 and AFN=33HEX.

```
kcblin: lbs=fc855d08  flag=10 slot_cnt=2 slot_size=8192 state obj=243a1f54
kcblin: state objects are: Call=243a1f54,Current Call=243a1f54, Session=243208b4
```

```
kcbldio:lbs=fc855d08 slt=fc8858bc typ=1 async=1 afn=33 blk=f409 cnt=1 buf=fc8f2a00
kcbldio:lbs=fc855d08 slt=fc885a40 typ=1 async=1 afn=33 blk=f40a cnt=1 buf=fc90da00
kcblcio: lbs=fc855d08 slt=fc8858bc type=1 afn=33 blk=f409 cnt=1 buf=fc8f2a00
kcblcio: lbs=fc855d08 slt=fc8858bc type=1 afn=33 blk=f409 cnt=1 buf=fc8f2a00
WAIT #1: nam='direct path write' ela= 9702 p1=51 p2=62473 p3=1
kcbldio:lbs=fc855d08 slt=fc8858bc typ=1 async=1 afn=33 blk=f40b cnt=1 buf=fc8f2a00
kcblcio: lbs=fc855d08 slt=fc885a40 type=1 afn=33 blk=f40a cnt=1 buf=fc90da00
kcblcio: lbs=fc855d08 slt=fc885a40 type=1 afn=33 blk=f40a cnt=1 buf=fc90da00
WAIT #1: nam='direct path write' ela= 5577 p1=51 p2=62474 p3=1
```

db file parallel write

In Oracle8*i* Database, the *db file parallel write* wait event parameters according to the V$EVENT_NAME view are files, blocks, and requests. Starting in Oracle9*i* Database, the parameters are requests, interrupt, and timeout. However, according to event 10046 trace, the first parameter has always been the block count or the DBWR write batch size. In Oracle Database 10*g*, this wait event falls under the System I/O wait class. Keep the following key thoughts in mind when dealing with the *db file parallel write* wait event.

- The *db file parallel write* event belongs only to the DBWR process.

- A slow DBWR can impact foreground processes.

- Significant *db file parallel write* wait time is most likely an I/O issue.

Common Causes, Diagnosis, and Actions

The DBWR process performs all database writes that go through the SGA. When it is time to write, the DBWR process compiles a set of dirty blocks and issues system write calls to the operating system. The DBWR process looks for blocks to write at various times, including once every three seconds, when posted by a foreground process to make clean buffers, at checkpoints, when the _DB_LARGE_DIRTY_QUEUE, _DB_BLOCK_ MAX_DIRTY_TARGET, and FAST_START_MTTR_TARGET thresholds are met, etc.

Although user sessions never experience the *db file parallel write* wait event, this doesn't mean they will not be impacted by it. A slow DBWR process can cause foreground sessions to wait on the *write complete waits* or *free buffer waits* events. DBWR write performance can be impacted by, among other things, the type of I/O operation (synchronous or asynchronous), storage device (raw partition or cooked file system), database layout, and I/O subsystem configuration. The key database statistics to look at are the systemwide TIME_WAITED and AVERAGE_WAIT of the *db file parallel write, free buffer waits,* and *write complete waits* wait events as they are interrelated.

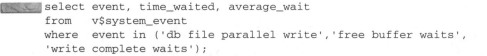

```
select event, time_waited, average_wait
from   v$system_event
where  event in ('db file parallel write','free buffer waits',
'write complete waits');
```

```
EVENT                    TIME_WAITED AVERAGE_WAIT
------------------------ ----------- ------------
free buffer waits             145448   69.8597502
write complete waits          107606   101.228598
db file parallel write       4046782   13.2329511
```

NOTE
Don't be surprised if the db file parallel write *event is
absent in your instance. Most likely this is because the
DISK_ASYNCH_IO is FALSE. This scenario is normally
seen in the HPUX and AIX platforms. Oracle does not
consider this to be a bug. However, in the absence of*
db file parallel write *event, Oracle also could not show
where the DBWR process is charging its wait time to
when waiting for writes to complete. Just because the*
db file parallel write *event is missing, doesn't mean the
DBWR process has no waits.*

If the *db file parallel write* average wait time is greater than 10 centiseconds (or
100ms), this normally indicates slow I/O throughput. You can improve the average
wait time in a number of ways. The main one is to use the right kind of I/O operation.
If your data files are on raw devices and your platform supports asynchronous I/O,
you should use asynchronous writes. But if your database is on file systems, you
should use synchronous writes and direct I/O (this is the operating system direct I/O).
There is more discussion on asynchronous and direct I/O later in this section. Besides
making sure you are using the right kind of I/O operation, check your database
layout and monitor I/O throughput from the operating system using commands such
as *sar −d* or *iostat −dxnC*. Make sure there is no hot spot.

When the *db file parallel write* average wait time is high and the system is busy,
user sessions may begin to wait on the *free buffer waits* event. This is because the
DBWR process can't catch up with the demand for free buffers. If the TIME_WAITED
of the *free buffer waits* event is high, you should address the DBWR I/O throughput
issue before increasing the number of buffers in the cache. Chapter 7 has more details
on the *free buffer waits* event.

Another repercussion of high *db file parallel write* average wait time is high
TIME_WAITED on the *write complete waits* wait event. Foreground processes are
not allowed to modify the blocks that are in transit to disk. In other words, the blocks
that are in the DBWR write batch. They must wait for the blocks to be written and
for the DBWR process to clear the bit in the buffer header. The foreground sessions
wait on the *write complete waits* wait event. So the appearance of the *write complete
waits* event is a sure sign of a slow DBWR process. You fix this latency by improving
the DBWR I/O throughput.

NOTE
Beginning in Oracle8i Database, a new cloning algorithm clones the current buffers that are in the DBWR write batch. The newly cloned buffers can be modified while the originals become consistent read (CR) buffers and are written to disk. This reduces the write complete waits *latency.*

```
select *
from    v$sysstat
where   name in ('write clones created in foreground',
                 'write clones created in background');

STATISTIC# NAME                                  CLASS   VALUE
---------- ----------------------------------- ----- -------
        82 write clones created in foreground      8  241941
        83 write clones created in background      8    5417
```

NOTE
A larger DBWR write batch can also increase the foreground waits on the write complete waits *event. This is because the DBWR process will need more time to write a larger batch of blocks, and when this is coupled with poor I/O performance, the result is a high* write complete waits. *Prior to Oracle8i Database, DBAs tweaked the DB_BLOCK_WRITE_BATCH parameter, which sets the DBWR write batch size. The value can also be seen in the X$KVII view. It is listed as* DB writer IO clump. *Oracle drastically improved the checkpointing architecture in Oracle8i Database, and DBAs shouldn't have to mess with the DBWR write batch anymore. Beginning in Oracle8i Database, the write batch size is controlled by the _DB_WRITER_CHUNK_WRITES parameter, and the maximum number of outstanding DBWR I/Os is controlled by the _DB_WRITER_MAX_WRITES parameter. The DBWR write batch size is also revealed by the P1 parameter of the* db file parallel write *event.*

```
-- Prior to Oracle8i Database
select * from x$kvii where kviitag = 'kcbswc';
ADDR       INDX  INST_ID  KVIIVAL KVIITAG   KVIIDSC
--------  ------- -------- -------- ---------- ------------------------
00E33628        6        1     4096 kcbswc     DB writer IO clump
```

```
-- Beginning in Oracle8i Database
select * from x$kvii where kviitag in ('kcbswc','kcbscw');
ADDR       INDX  INST_ID  KVIIVAL  KVIITAG   KVIIDSC
--------  ------  -------- -------- ---------- ----------------------------
01556808     4       1      4096   kcbswc    DBWR max outstanding writes
01556818     6       1       204   kcbscw    DBWR write chunk
```

Some initialization parameters can increase DBWR checkpoint activities. While a more active DBWR process is beneficial for reducing the number of *free buffer waits* events, it will not improve the *db file parallel write* average wait time if the I/O throughput remains slow. It may not even reduce the *write complete waits* latency. You still need to improve the DBWR average write time. Check the settings of LOG_CHECKPOINT_TIMEOUT, LOG_CHECKPOINT_INTERVAL, FAST_START_IO_TARGET, _DB_BLOCK_MAX_DIRTY_TARGET, and FAST_START_MTTR_TARGET parameters. Starting in Oracle9i Database, you can see if the target recovery time is causing excessive DBWR checkpoint activity (CKPT_BLOCK_WRITES) by querying the V$INSTANCE_RECOVERY view.

So, how can you improve DBWR average write time?

The quick answer is to turn on asynchronous writes if the hardware supports it; if it doesn't, use synchronous writes and multiple database writer processes. Unfortunately, enabling asynchronous I/O is not as simple as setting the DISK_ASYNCH_IO parameter to TRUE. This means nothing if the operating system does not support asynchronous I/O. The HP-UX operating system supports asynchronous I/O on raw devices only. The Solaris operating system supports asynchronous I/O on both raw devices and file systems. However, on raw devices, it uses the kernel asynchronous I/O (KAIO) system call, but on file systems, it spawns several light-weight processes (LWP) that make synchronous I/O calls (read(), write(), pwrite(), pread(), pwrite64(), pread64()) to simulate asynchronous I/O. The AIX operating system also supports asynchronous I/O on both raw devices and file systems. On raw devices, asynchronous I/O is handled by the kernel (also known as the *fastpath AIO*), but on file systems, it is handled by AIO servers through *kprocs* kernel processes. It is beyond the scope of this book to cover what is and is not supported and how to implement asynchronous I/O, as there are many peculiarities. You can get the details from your system administrator, the system engineer of the hardware vendor, or Oracle Support.

It is important to point out that asynchronous I/O is not always faster and better. Asynchronous I/O operations are unstable on some platforms. Synchronous I/O is more reliable. If you see high TIME_WAITED on the *async disk IO* wait event in the V$SYSTEM_EVENT view or many AIOWAIT in a *truss* output, it is a good sign that asynchronous I/O is not working well for you. The *async disk IO* wait event is instrumented in Oracle9i Database. If your entire database is on file systems, you may get better DBWR I/O performance in synchronous mode. The following shows the *db file parallel write* AVERAGE_WAIT time with and without asynchronous I/O.

```
-- database on file systems, disk_asynch_io = true
EVENT                          AVERAGE_WAIT
------------------------------ ------------
db file parallel write            12.8993168

-- the same database on file systems, disk_asynch_io = false,
-- db_writer_processes = 4
EVENT                          AVERAGE_WAIT
------------------------------ ------------
db file parallel write           .000908619
```

Following are our recommendations if your database is on file systems. Before you shut down the database to make the changes, make sure you take a snapshot of the V$SYSTEM_EVENT as a baseline.

- Set DISK_ASYNCH_IO parameter to FALSE.

- If the operating system supports direct I/O to file systems, set the FILESYSTEMIO_OPTIONS parameter to DIRECTIO, otherwise set it to NONE. This parameter is exposed in Oracle9*i* Database but hidden in Oracle8*i* Database.

- For *vxfs* (Veritas file system), ask your system administrator to mount the file system with the MINCACHE=DIRECT option. For *ufs* (Unix file system), mount the file system with the FORCEDIRECTIO option. Check with your system administrator for the specific direct I/O mount option for your file system.

- Spawn multiple DBWR processes with the DB_WRITER_PROCESSES parameter.

NOTE
If your redo logs are on raw devices but the datafiles are on file systems, you can set the FILESYSTEMIO_ OPTIONS to DIRECTIO and DISK_ASYNCH_IO to TRUE. With this, you can get kernel asynchronous I/O to the raw devices and direct I/O to the file systems.

log file parallel write

The *log file parallel write* wait event has three parameters: files, blocks, and requests. In Oracle Database 10g, this wait event falls under the System I/O wait class. Keep the following key thoughts in mind when dealing with the *log file parallel write* wait event.

- The *log file parallel write* event belongs only to the LGWR process.

- A slow LGWR can impact foreground processes commit time.

- Significant *log file parallel write* wait time is most likely an I/O issue.

Common Causes, Diagnosis, and Actions

As the *db file parallel write* wait event belongs only to the DBWR process, the *log file parallel write* wait event belongs only to the LGWR process. When it is time to write, the LGWR process writes the redo buffer to the online redo logs by issuing a series of system write calls to the operating system. The LGWR process waits for the writes to complete on the *log file parallel write* event. The LGWR process looks for redo blocks to write once every three seconds, at commit, at rollback, when the _LOG_IO_SIZE threshold is met, when there is 1MB worth of redo entries in the log buffer, and when posted by the DBWR process.

Although user sessions never experience the *log file parallel write* wait event, they can be impacted by a slow LGWR process. A slow LGWR process can magnify the *log file sync* waits, which user sessions wait on during commits or rollbacks. User sessions will not get the commit or rollback complete acknowledgement until the LGWR has completed the writes. Chapter 7 has more details on the *log file sync* wait event.

The key database statistics to look at are the systemwide TIME_WAITED and AVERAGE_WAIT of the *log file parallel write* and *log file sync* wait events because they are interrelated:

```
select event, time_waited, average_wait
from    v$system_event
where   event in ('log file parallel write','log file sync');

EVENT                    TIME_WAITED AVERAGE_WAIT
------------------------ ----------- ------------
log file parallel write     11315158    .508570816
log file sync                7518513    .497255756
```

If the *log file parallel write* average wait time is greater than 10ms (or 1cs), this normally indicates slow I/O throughput. The cure is the same as for the *db file parallel write* waits. Enable asynchronous writes if your redo logs are on raw devices and the operating system supports asynchronous I/O. For redo logs on file systems, use synchronous direct writes. Unfortunately, you cannot spawn more than one LGWR process. In this case, it is critical that nothing else is sharing the mount point of the redo log files. Make sure the controller that services the mount point is not overloaded. Moving the redo logs to higher speed disks will also help. We strongly suggest that you avoid putting redo logs on RAID5 disks, but we also understand that many times you don't have a choice or a say in it. You can vent your frustration at www.baarf.com.

Besides improving the I/O throughput, you can also work on lowering the amount of redo entries. This will provide some relief, but not the cure. Whenever possible, use the NOLOGGING option. Indexes should be created or rebuilt with the NOLOGGING option. CTAS operations should also use this option.

NOTE
The NOLOGGING option doesn't apply to normal DML operations such as inserts, updates, and deletes. Objects created with the NOLOGGING option are unrecoverable unless a backup is taken prior to the corruption. If you have to take an additional backup, then the I/Os that you save by not logging will be spent on backup. Database in FORCE LOGGING mode will log all changes (except for changes in temporary tablespaces), regardless of the tablespace and object settings.

A lower commit frequency at the expense of higher rollback segment usage can also provide some relief. A high commit frequency causes the LGWR process to be overactive and when coupled with slow I/O throughput will only magnify the *log file parallel write* waits. The application may be processing a large set of data in a loop and committing each change, which causes the log buffer to be flushed too frequently. In this case, modify the application to commit at a lower frequency. There could also be many short sessions that log in to the database, perform a quick DML operation, and log out. In this case, the application design may need to be reviewed. You can find out who is committing frequently with the following query:

```
select sid, value
from    v$sesstat
where   statistic# = (select statistic#
                      from    v$statname
                      where   name = 'user commits')
order by value;
```

```
-- Another evidence of excessive commits is high redo wastage.
select b.name, a.value, round(sysdate - c.startup_time) days_old
from    v$sysstat a, v$statname b, v$instance c
where   a.statistic# = b.statistic#
and     b.name       in ('redo wastage','redo size');

NAME                    VALUE         DAYS_OLD
--------------- --------------- ---------------
redo size          249289419360          5
redo wastage         2332945528          5
```

Check the job scheduler to see if hot backups run during peak hours. They can create large amounts of redo entries, which in turn increases the *log file parallel write* waits. Hot backups should run during off-peak hours, and tablespaces should be taken out of hot backup mode as soon as possible.

Lastly, be careful not to jam the LGWR with too many redo entries at one time. This can happen with large log buffer because the one-third threshold is also larger and holds more redo entries. When the one-third threshold is met, the LGWR process performs a background write if it is not already active. And the amount of redo entries may be too much for the LGWR to handle at one time, causing extended *log file parallel write* waits. So the idea is to stream the LGWR writes. This can be done by lowering the one-third threshold, which is controlled by the initialization parameter _LOG_IO_SIZE. By default the _LOG_IO_SIZE is one-third of the LOG_BUFFER or 1MB, whichever is less, expressed in log blocks. Query the X$KCCLE.LEBSZ for the log block size. Typically, it is 512 bytes. For example, if the LOG_BUFFER is 2,097,152 bytes (2MB), and the log block size is 512 bytes, then the default value for _LOG_IO_SIZE is 1,365 used log blocks. At this size, the LGWR process becomes lazy and normally writes only on transaction terminations (sync writes) or when it wakes up from its three-second timeouts. You should set the _LOG_IO_SIZE at the equivalent of 64K. That way, you can still have a larger log buffer to accommodate the spikes for buffer space after checkpoints, but the writes will start when there is 64K worth of redo entries in the buffer, assuming there is no user commit or rollback, and the LGWR sleep hasn't timed out during that time.

NOTE
This method is not without overhead. The LGWR write operation requires the redo copy and redo writing latches. So a more active LGWR process will increase the load on these latches. Do not reduce the _LOG_IO_SIZE if these latches currently have high SLEEPS. However, if the condition allows you to change the _LOG_IO_SIZE, you must monitor its impact over time by querying the V$LATCH view. Make sure you obtain a baseline before implementing the change.

You can use the following query to find the average number of redo log blocks per write and the average LGWR I/O size in bytes:

```
select  round((a.value / b.value) + 0.5,0) as avg_redo_blks_per_write,
        round((a.value / b.value) + 0.5,0) * c.lebsz as avg_io_size
from    v$sysstat a, v$sysstat b, x$kccle c
where   c.lenum = 1
and     a.name  = 'redo blocks written'
and     b.name  = 'redo writes';

AVG_REDO_BLKS_PER_WRITE AVG_IO_SIZE
----------------------- -----------
                      8        8192
```

control file parallel write

The *control file parallel write* wait event has three parameters: files, blocks, and requests. In Oracle Database 10*g*, this wait event falls under the System I/O wait class. Keep the following key thought in mind when dealing with the *control file parallel write* wait event.

■ The *control file parallel write* waits usually are symptomatic of high log switches.

Common Causes, Diagnosis, and Actions

A session with the *control file parallel write* wait event indicates that it has performed control file transactions. Operations such as log switching and adding or removing data files require the control file to be updated. Control file writes are also performed for some LOB operations.

Both the foreground and background processes can write to the control file. Every three seconds the CKPT background process updates the control files with the checkpoint position that is in the online redo logs. In normal circumstances, the CKPT process should have the highest time waited on the *control file parallel write* event. The ARCH background process updates the control file with information related to archive logs, and the LGWR background process updates the control file each time a log switch occurs. The following query reveals the sessions that performed control file transactions:

```
select /*+ ordered */
       a.sid,
       decode(a.type, 'BACKGROUND', 'BACKGROUND-' ||
substr(a.program,instr(a.program,'(',1,1)), 'FOREGROUND') type,
       b.time_waited,
```

```
         round(b.time_waited/b.total_waits,4) average_wait,
         round((sysdate - a.logon_time)*24) hours_connected
from     v$session_event b, v$session a
where    a.sid   = b.sid
and      b.event = 'control file parallel write'
order by type, time_waited;

SID TYPE                    TIME_WAITED AVERAGE_WAIT HOURS_CONNECTED
--- -------------------     ----------- ------------ ---------------
 10 BACKGROUND-(ARC0)               525        .3431             117
 11 BACKGROUND-(ARC1)               519        .3390             117
  7 BACKGROUND-(CKPT)             64147        .3431             117
  6 BACKGROUND-(LGWR)              1832        .3011             117
517 FOREGROUND                        2        .5120               1
```

If the LGWR process shows a high TIME_WAITED on this event, it means there are too many log switches, and you should check the redo log size by querying the V$LOG view. The logs may be too small for the amount of transactions that come in to the database. Check how often the logs are switching with the following query:

```
select thread#,
       to_char(first_time,'DD-MON-YYYY') creation_date,
       to_char(first_time,'HH24:MI')        time,
       sequence#,
       first_change# lowest_SCN_in_log,
       next_change#  highest_SCN_in_log,
       recid         controlfile_record_id,
       stamp         controlfile_record_stamp
from   v$log_history
order by first_time;
```

If a foreground process shows a high TIME_WAITED on the *control file parallel write* event, check to see if the application is making changes to NOLOGGING LOBs. When a data file is changed by a NOLOGGING operation, its unrecoverable SCN that is in the control file must be updated for RMAN purpose. If the time waited is high, you may consider turning off updates to the control file with event 10359. The following excerpt is from the $ORACLE_HOME/rdbms/mesg/*oraus.msg*:

```
10359, 00000, "turn off updates to control file for direct writes"
// *Cause:
// *Action:  Control files won't get updated for direct writes for LOBs
//           when NOCACHE NOLOGGING is set. The only bad impact that it
//           can have is that if you are using the recovery manager,
//           it may affect a warning that says that the user should
//           back everything up. Now the recovery manager won't know
//           to tell you that the files that were updated with
//           unrecoverable events should be backed up.
```

In a Nutshell

I/O operations are a necessity of every process that reads from or writes to the database. Database reads and writes are simple on the surface, but the path between the database and the physical disks can be a convoluted mess of software and hardware from various manufacturers, each with its own limitations. With all the handshakes that have to take place, it is a miracle that you get your data accurately! Although a DBA is not required to know the hardware layer intimately, a good knowledge of the system will definitely help you better manage the database and enrich your database administration experience.

In this chapter, we covered seven common I/O related wait events: *db file sequential read, db file scattered read, direct path read, direct path write, log file parallel write, db file parallel write,* and *controlfile parallel write.* The first four events are normally indicative of problems within the application. As such, the cure should come from the application and not the database.

The type of I/O operation (synchronous or asynchronous) makes a difference in I/O performance. Asynchronous I/O is not always faster and it may not be supported on your platform. You must choose the I/O operation that is right for your platform.

CHAPTER
6

Interpreting Locks-Related Wait Events

oncurrent database access in its simplest form can be defined as multiple sessions simultaneously reading from or writing to the database. The Oracle SGA architecture can be a lot simpler if concurrent access is the only goal of the RDBMS. However, there is another goal that supersedes concurrency in terms of importance and significance: data integrity.

The integrity of any data structure in the SGA cannot be guaranteed if multiple processes are allowed to modify the same data structure at the same time. Oracle ensures data integrity by serializing access to SGA data structures and database objects with latches and locks. In the DBMS concept, this is the "I" of the ACID properties (Atomicity, Consistency, Isolation, and Durability). Isolation is the safeguard that prevents conflicts between concurrent transactions. So, what happens to concurrency? In this case, concurrency must be sacrificed for the sake of integrity.

Unfortunately, most developers who attempt to improve application performance by increasing the level of concurrency are not aware of the serialization factors. This misunderstanding usually results in poorer application performance because more processes must compete for serialized resources such as latches and contented resources such as locks. The symptoms are usually *latch free*, *buffer busy waits*, and *enqueue* waits. This chapter tells you how to diagnose and solve problems related to locking and serialization.

Latch Free

The *latch free* wait event has three parameters: latch address, latch number, and the number of tries. In Oracle Database 10*g*, depending on the latch wait event, it can fall under the Concurrency, Configuration, or Other wait class. Keep the following key thoughts in mind when dealing with the *latch free* wait event.

- Latches apply only to memory structures in the SGA. They do not apply to database objects. An Oracle SGA has many latches, and they exist to protect various memory structures from potential corruption by concurrent access.

- The Oracle session is waiting to acquire a specific latch. The appropriate action to take depends on the type of latch the process competes for.

- Up to Oracle9*i* Database, the *latch free* wait event represents all latch waits, but starting in Oracle Database 10*g*, common latches are broken out and have independent wait events.

What Is a Latch?

A latch is a form of lock. You should be very familiar with its concept and usage because you use it in your daily routines and conversations, whether you realize it or not. Each time you lock a door, you essentially apply a latch. Each time you get into your vehicle and buckle up, you latch yourself in.

In Oracle RDBMS, latches are simple locking devices. They are nothing more than memory elements that typically consist of three parts: PID (process ID), memory address, and length. They enforce exclusive access to shared data structures in the SGA and thereby protect the integrity of the memory structures against corruption. Access to data structures in the SGA must be serialized to prevent corruption that can result from multiple sessions modifying the same structure at the same time. The integrity of data structures must also be preserved while they are being inspected.

Differences between a Latch and a Lock

Latches are different from locks (enqueues) in several ways, although both are locking mechanisms. Table 6-1 compares latches and locks.

	Latches	**Locks**
Purpose	Serve a single purpose: to provide exclusive access to memory structures. (Starting in Oracle9i Database, the *cache buffers chains* latches are shareable for read-only.)	Serve two purposes: to allow multiple processes to share the same resource when the lock modes are compatible and to enforce exclusive access to the resource when the lock modes are incompatible.
Jurisdiction	Apply only to data structures in the SGA. Protect memory objects, which are temporary. Control access to a memory structure for a single operation. Not transactional.	Protect database objects such as tables, data blocks, and state objects. Application driven and control access to data or metadata in the database. Transactional.
Acquisition	Can be requested in two modes: willing-to-wait or no-wait.	Can be requested in six different modes: null, row share, row exclusive, share, share row exclusive, or exclusive.

TABLE 6-1. *Latches vs. Locks*

	Latches	**Locks**
Scope	Information is kept in the memory and is only visible to the local instance—latches operate at instance level.	Information is kept in the database and is visible to all instances accessing the database—locks operate at database-level.
Complexity	Implemented using simple instructions, typically, test-and-set, compare-and-swap, or simple CPU instructions. Implementation is port specific because the CPU instructions are machine dependent. Lightweight.	Implemented using a series of instructions with context switches. Heavyweight.
Duration	Held briefly (in microseconds).	Normally held for an extended period of time (transactional duration).
Queue	When a process goes to sleep after failing to acquire a latch, its request is not queued and serviced in order (with a few exceptions—for example, the *latch wait list* latch has a queue). Latches are fair game and up for grabs.	When a process fails to get a lock, its request is queued and serviced in order, unless the NOWAIT option is specified.
Deadlock	Latches are implemented in such a way that they are not subject to deadlocks.	Locks support queuing and are subject to deadlocks. A trace file is generated each time a deadlock occurs.

TABLE 6-1. *Latches vs. Locks* (continued)

Latch Family

There are three types of latches: parent, child, and solitary latches. The parent and solitary latches are fixed in the Oracle kernel code. Child latches are created at instance startup. The V$LATCH_PARENT and V$LATCH_CHILDREN views contain the statistics for parent and child latches, respectively. The V$LATCH view contains the statistics for solitary latches as well as the aggregated statistics of the parent latches and their children.

Latch Acquisition

A process may request a latch in the willing-to-wait or no-wait (immediate) mode. The no-wait mode is used on only a handful of latches. Latches that are acquired in the no-wait mode have statistics in the IMMEDIATE_GETS and IMMEDIATE_MISSES columns. These columns are part of the latch family of views: V$LATCH, V$LATCH_PARENT, and V$LATCH_CHILDREN. Generally, a no-wait mode is first used on latches with multiple children such as the *redo copy* latches. If a process fails to get one of the child latches in the first attempt, it will ask for the next, also with the no-wait mode. The willing-to-wait mode is used only on the last latch when all no-wait requests against other child latches have failed.

Latches that are acquired in the willing-to-wait mode have statistics in the GETS and MISSES columns. The GETS of a particular latch are incremented each time a process requests the latch in the willing-to-wait mode.

If the latch is available on the first request, the process acquires it. Before modifying the protected data structure, the process writes the recovery information in the latch recovery area so that PMON knows what to clean up if the process dies while holding the latch.

If the latch is not available, the process spins on the CPU for a short while and retries for the latch. This spin and retry activity can be repeated up to _SPIN_COUNT times, which normally defaults to 2000. Briefly, if the latch is obtained in one of the retries, the process increments the SPIN_GETS and MISSES statistics by 1; otherwise, the process posts the *latch free* wait event in the V$SESSION_WAIT view, yields the CPU, and goes to sleep. At the end of the sleep cycle, the process wakes up and retries the latch again for up to another _SPIN_COUNT times. This spin, retry, sleep, and wake up gyration must be performed until the latch is eventually acquired. The SLEEPS statistics (SLEEPS and SLEEP1 through SLEEPS3 only—SLEEP4 through SLEEP11 are never updated) are updated only when the latch GET succeeds, not on each attempt.

The only way out of the latch GET routine is to get the latch. So, what happens if the process holding the latch is dead? When a process fails to get a latch after a few tries, it will post the PMON process to check up on the latch holder. If the latch holder is dead, PMON will cleanup and release the latch.

Every latch is associated with a level number ranging from 0 to 13 (depending on the version). The levels for solitary and parent latches are fixed in the Oracle kernel code. Child latches are created at instance startup and inherit the level number from their parent. The levels are used to prevent latch deadlocks. The following two rules govern how latches may be acquired so that deadlocks will be prevented:

- When a process requests a latch in the no-wait mode, any level is allowed provided one pair of the latches shares the same level.

- When a process requests a latch in the willing-to-wait mode, its level must be higher than the levels of all the latches currently held.

Short- and Long-Wait Latches

Most latches are short-wait latches, therefore, processes shouldn't have to wait very long to acquire them. For these latches, Oracle processes go to sleep using the exponential backoff sleep algorithm, which means every other sleep time is doubled (1, 1, 2, 2, 4, 4, 8, 8, 16, 16, 32, 32, 64, 64 centiseconds, and so on). The maximum exponential sleep time is internally set by the _MAX_EXPONENTIAL_SLEEP parameter, which usually defaults to 2 seconds but will be reduced to _MAX_SLEEP_HOLDING_LATCH, which defaults to 4 centiseconds if the sleeping process has one or more latches in possession. A process that owns a latch cannot be allowed to sleep for too long or it will increase the chances of other processes missing on their latch requests.

Some latches are long-wait latches. This means they are generally held longer, and Oracle processes that sleep on these latches depend on another process to wake them up. This is known as *latch wait posting,* and this behavior is controlled by the _LATCH_WAIT_POSTING parameter. There should be only two long-wait latches in Oracle8*i* Database, as shown in the following listing (there are more in Oracle9*i* Database and Oracle Database 10*g*). The _LATCH_WAIT_POSTING parameter is obsolete in Oracle9*i* Database. Latches that use latch wait posting have statistics in the WAITERS_WOKEN column.

```
select name, immediate_gets, immediate_misses,
       gets, misses, sleeps, waiters_woken
from   v$latch
where waiters_woken > 0;
```

NAME	IMMEDIATE GETS	IMMEDIATE MISSES	GETS	MISSES	SLEEPS	WAITERS WOKEN
shared pool	0	0	18464156	3124	1032	485
library cache	85508	124	1564400540	4334362	1516400	690419

Latch Classification

Starting in Oracle9*i* Database Release 2, latches can be assigned to classes, and each class can have a different _SPIN_COUNT value. In earlier releases, whenever the _SPIN_COUNT value is changed to benefit one latch, it applies to all latches. This can increase the overall CPU utilization quite a bit, but the new latch classes feature solves this problem. Let's say the *cache buffers chains* latches have high SLEEPS numbers and CPU resources are not an issue. You can assign the *cache buffers chains* latches to a class with a higher _SPIN_COUNT value. A larger _SPIN_COUNT value reduces the number of MISSES and SLEEPS at the expense of CPU time. The X$KSLLCLASS (kernel service lock latches class) view contains the class metadata (or attributes) for all eight classes. The latch class is represented by the INDX column in the following listing:

```
select indx, spin, yield, waittime
from   x$ksllclass;

      INDX        SPIN       YIELD   WAITTIME
---------- ---------- ---------- ----------
         0       20000           0          1
         1       20000           0          1
         2       20000           0          1
         3       20000           0          1
         4       20000           0          1
         5       20000           0          1
         6       20000           0          1
         7       20000           0          1

8 rows selected.
```

Each row in the X$KSLLCLASS view corresponds to a _LATCH_CLASS_*n* initialization parameter, which allows you to change the _SPIN_COUNT, YIELD and WAITTIME values. For example, latch class 0 corresponds to _LATCH_CLASS_0, latch class 1 corresponds to _LATCH_CLASS_1, and so on up to _LATCH_CLASS_7. Let's say you decide to increase the _SPIN_COUNT of the *cache buffers chains* latches to 10,000. To do so, you need to know the latch number and make the following two entries in the INIT.ORA file:

```
select latch#, name
from   v$latchname
where name = 'cache buffers chains';

    LATCH# NAME
---------- ------------------------------
        97 cache buffers chains

# Make these two entries in the INIT.ORA file and bounce the instance.
# This modifies the spin count attribute of class 1 to 10000.
_latch_class_1 = "10000"
# This assigns latch# 97 to class 1.
_latch_classes = "97:1"

select indx, spin, yield, waittime
from   x$ksllclass;

      INDX        SPIN       YIELD   WAITTIME
---------- ---------- ---------- ----------
         0       20000           0          1
         1       10000           0          1
         2       20000           0          1
         3       20000           0          1
```

```
       4        20000           0          1
       5        20000           0          1
       6        20000           0          1
       7        20000           0          1
8 rows selected.

select a.kslldnam, b.kslltnum, b.class_ksllt
from   x$kslld a, x$ksllt b
where  a.kslldadr = b.addr
and    b.class_ksllt > 0;


KSLLDNAM                         KSLLTNUM CLASS_KSLLT
------------------------         --------- -----------
process allocation                      3           2
cache buffers chains                   97           1
```

NOTE
*Do not increase the _SPIN_COUNT value if the
server does not have spare CPU resources. New and
faster CPUs should be able to bear a higher _SPIN_
COUNT value. The default value of 2000 was
established a long time ago when CPU speeds were
much slower.*

What Does the Latch Free Wait Event Tell You?

When you see a *latch free* wait event in the V$SESSION_WAIT view, it means the process failed to obtain the latch in the willing-to-wait mode after spinning _SPIN_COUNT times and went to sleep. When processes compete heavily for latches, they will also consume more CPU resources because of spinning. The result is a higher response time. Remember the response time formula from Chapter 1? In this case, the high CPU utilization is a secondary symptom. This false CPU utilization level can falsely impress your capacity planner that the server needs faster or more CPUs.

The TOTAL_WAITS statistic of the *latch free* wait event in the V$SYSTEM_EVENT view tracks the number of times processes fail to get a latch in the willing-to-wait mode. The SLEEPS statistic of a particular latch in the V$LATCH view tracks the number of times processes sleep on that latch. Because a process has nothing else to do but sleep when it fails to get the latch after spinning for _SPIN_COUNT times, the TOTAL_WAITS should equal the sum of SLEEPS as shown in the following code. However, there are times where TOTAL_WAITS is greater than the sum of SLEEPS. This is because SLEEPS statistics are only updated when the latch GET operation succeeds, and not on each attempt.

```
select a.total_waits, b.sum_of_sleeps
from  (select total_waits from v$system_event where event = 'latch free') a,
      (select sum(sleeps) sum_of_sleeps from v$latch) b;

TOTAL_WAITS SUM_OF_SLEEPS
----------- -------------
  414031680      414031680
```

Because *latch free* waits are typically quite short, it is possible to see a large number of waits (TOTAL_WAITS) that only account for a small amount of time. You should only be concerned when the TIME_WAITED is significant.

of V$ system-event

Latch Miss Locations

The V$LATCH_MISSES view keeps information on the locations within the Oracle kernel code where latch misses occur. This information is helpful to Oracle Support in diagnosing obscure latch wait cases. You can see the location information with the following query. Steve Adams has an excellent article on this subject at http:// www.ixora.com.au/newsletter/2001_02.htm.

```
select location,
       parent_name,
       wtr_slp_count,
       sleep_count,
       longhold_count
from   v$latch_misses
where  sleep_count > 0
order by wtr_slp_count, location;
```

LOCATION	PARENT_NAME	WTR_SLP_COUNT	SLEEP_COUNT	LONGHOLD COUNT
. . .				
kglupc: child	library cache	7879693	11869691	0
kghupr1	shared pool	8062331	5493370	0
kcbrls: kslbegin	cache buffers chains	9776543	14043355	0
kqrpfl: not dirty	row cache objects	15606317	14999100	0
kqrpre: find obj	row cache objects	20359370	20969580	0
kglhdgn: child:	library cache	23782557	9952093	0
kcbgtcr: fast path	cache buffers chains	26729974	23166337	0
kglpnc: child	library cache	27385354	7707204	0

Latches in Oracle Database 10*g* Release 1

Prior to Oracle Database 10*g*, all latch waits show up as the *latch free* wait event. You can determine the name of the latch that a process contended for by querying the V$LATCH view using the P2 parameter value of the *latch free* event from the V$SESSION_WAIT view or the event 10046 trace file. The P2 parameter contains the specific latch number. In Oracle Database 10*g*, common latches are broken out and have independent wait event names and statistics. Following is a listing from Oracle Database 10*g* Release 1.

```
select name
from    v$event_name
where   name like 'latch%'
order by 1;

NAME
----------------------------------------------------------------
latch activity
latch free
latch: In memory undo latch
latch: KCL gc element parent latch
latch: MQL Tracking Latch
latch: cache buffer handles
latch: cache buffers chains
latch: cache buffers lru chain
latch: checkpoint queue latch
latch: enqueue hash chains
latch: gcs resource hash
latch: ges resource hash list
latch: latch wait list
latch: library cache
latch: library cache lock
latch: library cache pin
latch: messages
latch: object queue header heap
latch: object queue header operation
latch: parallel query alloc buffer
latch: redo allocation
latch: redo copy
latch: redo writing
latch: row cache objects
latch: session allocation
latch: shared pool
latch: undo global data
latch: virtual circuit queues
28 rows selected.
```

Common Causes, Diagnosis, and Actions

A latch contention indicates that a latch is held by another process for too long. When coupled with high demands, the contention is magnified to noticeable performance degradation. Latch contentions are common in high concurrency environments. You shouldn't plan on eliminating *latch free* waits from your database; that is unreasonable. The *latch free* wait event will always show up in the V$SYSTEM_EVENT view; the question is *where* in relation to other wait events in terms of TIME_WAITED. You should be concerned only when the TIME_WAITED is high, bearing in mind the instance startup time. If the systemwide time waited for latches is high, you can discover the hot latches that the processes competed for from the number of SLEEPS in the V$LATCH view with the following code:

```
select name, gets, misses, immediate_gets, immediate_misses, sleeps
from   v$latch
order by sleeps;
```

NAME	GETS	MISSES	IMMEDIATE GETS	IMMEDIATE MISSES	SLEEPS
enqueue hash chains	42770950	4279	0	0	1964
shared pool	9106650	5400	0	0	2632
row cache objects	69059887	27938	409	0	7517
enqueues	80443314	330167	0	0	13761
library cache	69447172	103349	465827	190	44328
cache buffers chains	1691040252	1166249	61532689	5909	127478

. . .

Due to the variety of latches, the common causes and appropriate action to take depends on the type of latch that is being competed for. A detailed discussion on all the latches would take more space than we have available. We picked the five most common latches: *shared pool, library cache, cache buffers chains, cache buffers lru chain,* and *row cache objects,* and we'll show you how to diagnose and fix problems related to them.

Shared Pool and Library Cache Latches

The Oracle shared pool consists of many structures. The prominent ones are the dictionary cache, SQL area, and library cache. You can see other structures by querying the V$SGASTAT view. The *shared pool* latch protects the shared pool structures, and it is taken when allocating and freeing memory heaps. For example, it is taken when allocating space for new SQL statements (hard parsing), PL/SQL procedures, functions, packages, and triggers as well as when it is aging or freeing chunks of space to make room for new objects.

Prior to Oracle9*i* Database, the shared pool memory structures were protected by a solitary shared pool latch. Beginning with Oracle9*i* Database, up to seven child *shared pool* latches can be used to protect the shared pool structures. This is possible because Oracle9*i* Database can break the shared pool into multiple subpools if the server has at least four CPUs and the SHARED_POOL_SIZE is greater than 250MB. The number of subpools can be manually adjusted by the _KGHDSIDX_COUNT initialization parameter, which also supplies the appropriate number of child *shared pool* latches. If you manually increase the number of subpools, you should also increase the SHARED_POOL_SIZE because each subpool has its own structure, LRU list, and *shared pool* latch. Otherwise, the instance may not start due to the error *ORA-04031: unable to allocate 32 bytes of shared memory ("shared pool","unknown object","sga heap(5,0)","fixed allocation callback")*.

The following statistics are from an Oracle9*i* Database running on a 16-CPU server and using 256MB of SHARED_POOL_SIZE. The shared pool is broken into two subpools as shown by the _KGHDSIDX_COUNT parameter. There are two LRU lists as shown by the X$KGHLU (*kernel generic heap lru*) view, and two of the seven child latches are used as shown by the V$LATCH_CHILDREN view.

```
select  a.ksppinm, b.ksppstvl
from    x$ksppi a, x$ksppsv b
where   a.indx = b.indx
and     a.ksppinm = '_kghdsidx_count';

KSPPINM            KSPPSTVL
------------------ ----------
_kghdsidx_count    2

select addr, kghluidx, kghlufsh, kghluops, kghlurcr, kghlutrn, kghlumxa
from    x$kghlu;

ADDR              KGHLUIDX  KGHLUFSH   KGHLUOPS  KGHLURCR KGHLUTRN  KGHLUMXA
----------------- --------  ---------- ---------- -------- -------- ----------
80000001001581B8        2  41588416   496096025    14820    17463 2147483647
8000000100157E18        1  46837096  3690967191    11661    19930 2147483647

select addr, name, gets, misses, waiters_woken
from    v$latch_children
where name = 'shared pool';

ADDR              NAME               GETS      MISSES WAITERS_WOKEN
----------------- ------------ ----------- ---------- -------------
C00000004C5B06B0  shared pool            0          0             0
C00000004C5B0590  shared pool            0          0             0
C00000004C5B0470  shared pool            0          0             0
C00000004C5B0350  shared pool            0          0             0
C00000004C5B0230  shared pool            0          0             0
C00000004C5B0110  shared pool   1385021389   90748637      12734879
C00000004C5AFFF0  shared pool   2138031345  413319249      44738488
```

The library cache structures are the home for cursors, SQL statements, execution plans, and parsed trees among other things. The structures are protected by the *library cache* latch. Oracle processes acquire the *library cache* latch when modifying, inspecting, pinning, locking, loading, or executing objects in the library cache structures. The number of child *library cache* latches that exist in an instance can be discovered by querying the V$LATCH_CHILDREN view as shown next. The number is usually the smallest prime number that is greater than the CPU_COUNT. This number can be modified by the _KGL_LATCH_COUNT parameter. Starting in

Oracle9*i* Database, the V$SQLAREA has a CHILD_LATCH column, which allows you to see how cursors are distributed across the *library cache* latches.

```
select count(*)
from   v$latch_children
where  name = 'library cache';
```

Contention for Shared Pool and Library Cache Latches—Parsing

Contentions for the *shared pool* and *library cache* latches are mainly due to intense hard parsing. A hard parse applies to new cursors and cursors that are aged out and must be re-executed. Excessive hard parsing is common among applications that primarily use SQL statements with literal values. A hard parse is a very expensive operation, and a child *library cache* latch must be held for the duration of the parse.

- Discover the magnitude of hard parsing in your database using the following query. The number of soft parses can be determined by subtracting the hard parse from the total parse.

```
select a.*, sysdate-b.startup_time days_old
from   v$sysstat a, v$instance b
where  a.name like 'parse%';
```

STATISTIC#	NAME	CLASS	VALUE	DAYS_OLD
230	parse time cpu	64	33371587	4.6433912
231	parse time elapsed	64	63185919	4.6433912
232	parse count (total)	64	2137380227	4.6433912
233	parse count (hard)	64	27006791	4.6433912
234	parse count (failures)	64	58945	4.6433912

NOTE
A parse failure is related to the "ORA-00942: table or view does not exist" error or out of shared memory.

- Discover the current sessions that perform a lot of hard parses:

```
select a.sid, c.username, b.name, a.value,
       round((sysdate - c.logon_time)*24) hours_connected
from   v$sesstat a, v$statname b, v$session c
where  c.sid       = a.sid
and    a.statistic# = b.statistic#
and    a.value     > 0
and    b.name      = 'parse count (hard)'
order by a.value;
```

```
SID USERNAME    NAME                         VALUE HOURS_CONNECTED
---- ---------- ------------------- ---------- ----------------
 510 SYS        parse count (hard)          12               4
 413 PMAPPC     parse count (hard)         317              51
  37 PMHCMC     parse count (hard)       27680             111
 257 PMAPPC     parse count (hard)       64652              13
 432 PMAPPC     parse count (hard)      105505              13
```

The V$SESS_TIME_MODEL view in Oracle Database 10*g* shows where the hard parses are coming from by providing the elapsed time statistics on hard and failed parses. Following is a sample from the V$SESS_TIME_MODEL view for a particular session:

```
select *
from   v$sess_time_model
where  sid = (select max(sid) from v$mystat);

SID     STAT_ID STAT_NAME                                             VALUE
---- ---------- -------------------------------------------------- ----------
 148 3649082374 DB time                                            11141191
 148 2748282437 DB CPU                                              9530592
 148 4157170894 background elapsed time                                   0
 148 2451517896 background cpu time                                       0
 148 4127043053 sequence load elapsed time                               0
 148 1431595225 parse time elapsed                                  3868898
 148  372226525 hard parse elapsed time                            3484672
 148 2821698184 sql execute elapsed time                           9455020
 148 1990024365 connection management call elapsed time                6726
 148 1824284809 failed parse elapsed time                                0
 148 4125607023 failed parse (out of shared memory) elapsed time          0
 148 3138706091 hard parse (sharing criteria) elapsed time            11552
 148  268357648 hard parse (bind mismatch) elapsed time               4440
 148 2643905994 PL/SQL execution elapsed time                         70350
 148  290749718 inbound PL/SQL rpc elapsed time                           0
 148 1311180441 PL/SQL compilation elapsed time                      268477
 148  751169994 Java execution elapsed time                               0
```

The hard parse statistics in the preceding output can be grouped as such:

1. parse time elapsed
   2. hard parse elapsed time
      3. hard parse (sharing criteria) elapsed time
         4. hard parse (bind mismatch) elapsed time
2. failed parse elapsed time
   3. failed parse (out of shared memory) elapsed time

■ Identify literal SQL statements that are good candidates for bind variables. The following query searches the V$SQLAREA view for statements that are identical in the first 40 characters and lists them when four or more instances of the statements exist. The logic assumes the first 40 characters of most of your application's literal statements are the same. Obviously, longer strings (for example, *substr(sql_text,1,100)*) and higher occurrences (for example, *count(*) > 50*) will yield a shorter report. Once you have identified the literal statements, you can advise the application developers on which statements to convert to use bind variables.

```
select hash_value, substr(sql_text,1,80)
from   v$sqlarea
where  substr(sql_text,1,40) in (select substr(sql_text,1,40)
                                 from   v$sqlarea
                                 having count(*) > 4
                                 group by substr(sql_text,1,40))
order by sql_text;


HASH_VALUE SUBSTR(SQL_TEXT,1,80)
---------- --------------------------------------------------------------------
2915282817 SELECT revenue.customer_id, revenue.orig_sys, revenue.service_typ
2923401936 SELECT revenue.customer_id, revenue.orig_sys, revenue.service_typ
 303952184 SELECT revenue.customer_id, revenue.orig_sys, revenue.service_typ
 416786153 SELECT revenue.customer_id, revenue.orig_sys, revenue.service_typ
2112631233 SELECT revenue.customer_id, revenue.orig_sys, revenue.service_typ
3373328808 select region_id from person_to_chair where chair_id = 988947
 407884945 select region_id from person_to_chair where chair_id = 990165
3022536167 select region_id from person_to_chair where chair_id = 990166
3204873278 select region_id from person_to_chair where chair_id = 990167
 643778054 select region_id from person_to_chair where chair_id = 990168
2601269433 select region_id from person_to_chair where chair_id = 990169
3453662597 select region_id from person_to_chair where chair_id = 991393
3621328440 update plan_storage set last_month_plan_id = 780093, pay_code
2852661466 update plan_storage set last_month_plan_id = 780093, pay_code
 380292598 update plan_storage set last_month_plan_id = 780093, pay_code
2202959352 update plan_storage set last_month_plan_id = 780093, pay_code
  . . .
```

In Oracle9*i* Database, you can query the V$SQL view for SQL statements that share the same execution plan, as the statements may be identical except for the literal values. They are the candidates for bind variables.

```
select plan_hash_value, hash_value
from   v$sql
order by 1,2;
```

You should see significant reduction in the contention for the *shared pool* and *library cache* latches when you convert literal SQL statements to use bind variables. The conversion is best done in the application. The workaround is to set the initialization parameter CURSOR_SHARING to FORCE. This allows statements that differ in literal values but are otherwise identical to share a cursor and therefore reduce latch contention, memory usage, and hard parse.

CAUTION
The CURSOR_SHARING feature has bugs in the earlier releases of Oracle8i Database. It is not recommended in environments with materialized views because it may cause prolonged library cache pin waits. Also, setting the CURSOR_SHARING to FORCE may cause the optimizer to generate unexpected execution plans because the optimizer does not know the values of the bind variables. This may positively or negatively impact the database performance. Starting in Oracle9i Database, the optimizer will peek at the bind variable values in the session's PGA before producing an execution plan. This behavior is controlled by the parameter _OPTIM_PEEK_USER_ BINDS. However, this applies to statements that require hard parsing only, which means the execution plan is based on the first value that is bound to the variable.

Whenever a SQL statement arrives, Oracle checks to see if the statement is already in the library cache. If it is, the statement can be executed with little overhead; this process is known as a soft parse. While hard parses are bad, soft parses are not good either. The *library cache* latch is acquired during a soft parse operation. Oracle still has to check the syntax and semantics of the statement, unless the statement is cached in the session's cursor cache. You can reduce the *library cache* latch hold time by properly setting the SESSION_CACHED_CURSORS parameter. (See Oracle Metalink notes #30804.1 and #62143.1 for more information.) However, the best approach is to reduce the number of soft parses, which can only be done through the application. The idea is to parse once, execute many instead of parse once, execute once. You can find the offending statements by querying the V$SQLAREA view for statements with high numbers of PARSE_CALLS.

Contention for Shared Pool Latch—Oversized Shared Pool
Thanks to the new multiple subpools architecture, large shared pools are not as bad starting in Oracle9i Database. However, if your database is not yet on Oracle9i Database, an oversized shared pool can increase the contention for the *shared pool* latch. This is because free memory in the shared pool is categorized and maintained on a number of buckets or free lists according to the chunk size. Larger *shared pools* tend to have long free lists and processes that need to allocate space in them must spend extra time scanning the long free lists while holding the *shared pool* latch. In a high concurrency environment, this can result in serious *shared pool* latch contention (high SLEEPS and MISSES), especially if the application uses primarily literal SQL. If this is the case, there is no need for a large shared pool. Why keep unshared statements in the shared pool?

The *alter session set events 'immediate trace name heapdump level 2'* command lets you see the shared pool free lists. The command generates a trace file in the UDUMP directory. Search the trace file for the word "Bucket" and you will see the free memory chunks that are associated with each bucket. Alternatively, you can use the following script to help generate a query to list the shared pool free memory chunks. Once the query is generated, it is reusable in the database that generates the trace file. Do not use it in another database of a different version because this can produce wrong results. Also, this query will not run in Oracle Database 10*g* Release 1 because it limits the number of arguments in a case expression to 128. (See Oracle Metalink note #131557.1 and bug #3503496.) You may work around this limitation by rewriting the query using the DECODE and SIGN functions.

```
SQL> oradebug setmypid
Statement processed.
SQL> oradebug dump heapdump 2
Statement processed.
SQL> oradebug tracefile_name
/u01/admin/webmon/udump/orcl_ora_17550.trc
SQL> exit

$ grep Bucket /u01/admin/webmon/udump/orcl_ora_17550.trc > tmp.lst
$ sed 's/size=/ksmchsiz>=/' tmp.lst > tmp2.lst
$ sed 's/ Bucket //' tmp2.lst | sort -nr > tmp.lst

# Create a shell script based on the following and run it to generate
# the reusable query for the database.
echo 'select ksmchidx, (case'
cat tmp.lst | while read LINE
do
  echo $LINE | awk '{print "when " $2 " then " $1}'
done
echo 'end) bucket#,'
echo '        count(*) free_chunks,'
echo '        sum(ksmchsiz) free_space,'
echo '        trunc(avg(ksmchsiz)) avg_chunk_size'
echo 'from    x$ksmsp'
echo "where  ksmchcls = 'free'"
echo 'group by ksmchidx, (case';
cat tmp.lst | while read LINE
do
  echo $LINE | awk '{print "when " $2 " then " $1'}
done
echo 'end);'
```

If you discover the database has long shared pool free lists and the application uses literal SQL, then you should consider reducing the SHARED_POOL_SIZE. This will reduce the contention for the shared pool latch. Be careful not to make the shared pool too small, as this can cause the application to fail on the ORA-04031 error. You should also pin reusable objects in the shared pool using the DBMS_SHARED_POOL.KEEP procedure. The V$DB_OBJECT_CACHE view has information on kept objects.

Contention for Library Cache Latches—Statements with High Version Counts

Oracle uses multiple child cursors to distinguish SQL statements that are identical in their characters but cannot be shared because they refer to different underlying objects. For example, if there are three CUSTOMER tables in the database and each table is owned by a different schema, the SELECT * FROM CUSTOMER issued by each owner will have the same hash value but different child numbers. When a hash value of a statement being parsed matches the hash value of a statement with a high number of children or version count, Oracle has to compare the statement with all the existing versions. The library cache latch must be held for the duration of the inspection, and this may cause other processes to miss on their library cache latch requests. You can minimize this problem by having unique object names in the database. The following query lists all SQL statements in the V$SQLAREA with version counts greater than 20:

```
select version_count, sql_text
from   v$sqlarea
where  version_count > 20
order by version_count, hash_value;
```

NOTE
High version counts may also be caused by a bug related to the SQL execution progression monitoring feature in Oracle8i Database. (See Oracle Metalink note #62143.1) The bug prevents SQL statements from being shared. This feature can be turned off by setting the _SQLEXEC_PROGRESSION_COST parameter to 0, which in turn suppresses all data in the V$SESSION_LONGOPS view.

Oracle provides the V$SQL_SHARED_CURSOR view to explain why a particular child cursor is not shared with existing child cursors. Each column in the view identifies a specific reason why the cursor cannot be shared.

```
-- The columns in uppercase are relevant to Oracle9i Database.
-- Oracle Database 10g Release 1 has eight additional columns and it
```

```
-- also contains the child cursor address and number.
select a.*, b.hash_value, b.sql_text
from   v$sql_shared_cursor a, v$sqltext b, x$kglcursor c
where  a.unbound_cursor          || a.sql_type_mismatch       ||
       a.optimizer_mismatch      || a.outline_mismatch        ||
       a.stats_row_mismatch      || a.literal_mismatch        ||
       a.sec_depth_mismatch      || a.explain_plan_cursor      ||
       a.buffered_dml_mismatch   || a.pdml_env_mismatch        ||
       a.inst_drtld_mismatch     || a.slave_qc_mismatch        ||
       a.typecheck_mismatch      || a.auth_check_mismatch      ||
       a.bind_mismatch           || a.describe_mismatch        ||
       a.language_mismatch       || a.translation_mismatch     ||
       a.row_level_sec_mismatch  || a.insuff_privs             ||
       a.insuff_privs_rem        || a.remote_trans_mismatch    ||
       a.LOGMINER_SESSION_MISMATCH || a.INCOMP_LTRL_MISMATCH    ||
       a.OVERLAP_TIME_MISMATCH     || a.sql_redirect_mismatch   ||
       a.mv_query_gen_mismatch     || a.USER_BIND_PEEK_MISMATCH ||
       a.TYPCHK_DEP_MISMATCH       || a.NO_TRIGGER_MISMATCH     ||
       a.FLASHBACK_CURSOR <> 'NNNNNNNNNNNNNNNNNNNNNNNNNNNNNNN'
and    a.address = c.kglhdadr
and    b.hash_value = c.kglnahsh
order by b.hash_value, b.piece;
```

Cache Buffers Chains Latches

When data blocks are read into the SGA, their buffer headers are placed on linked lists (hash chains) that hang off hash buckets. This memory structure is protected by a number of child *cache buffers chains* latches (also known as hash latches or CBC latches). Figure 6-1 illustrates the relationships between hash latches, hash buckets, buffer headers, and hash chains.

A process that wants to add, remove, search, inspect, read, or modify a block on a hash chain must first acquire the *cache buffers chains* latch that protects the buffers on the chain. This guarantees exclusive access and prevents other processes from reading or changing the same chain from beneath. Concurrency is hereby sacrificed for the sake of integrity.

NOTE
Starting in Oracle9i Database, the cache buffers chains *latches can be shared for read-only. This reduces some contention, but will by no means eliminate the contention all together. We have many Oracle9i production databases that are plagued by the* cache buffers chains *latch contention.*

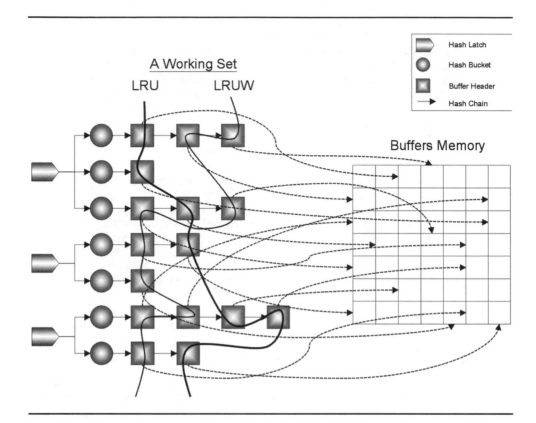

FIGURE 6-1. *A depiction of the buffer cache in Oracle8i Database and above*

The hash bucket for a particular block header is determined based on the modulus of the Data Block Address (DBA) and the value of the _DB_BLOCK_HASH_BUCKETS parameter. For example, hash bucket = MOD(DBA, _DB_BLOCK_HASH_BUCKETS). The contents of the buffer header are exposed through the V$BH and X$BH views. You can dump the buffer headers using the following command:

```
alter system set events 'immediate trace name buffers level 1';
```

Up to Oracle8.0, there is one *cache buffers chains* latch (hash latch) per hash bucket, and each hash bucket has one chain. In other words, the relationship between hash latches, hash buckets, and hash chains is 1:1:1. The default number of hash buckets is DB_BLOCK_BUFFERS / 4, rounded up to the next prime number. This value can be adjusted by the _DB_BLOCK_HASH_BUCKETS parameter. For example, if the DB_BLOCK_BUFFERS is 50000, this means the instance has 12501 hash latches, 12501 hash buckets, and 12501 hash chains.

Up to Oracle8.0: Hash latch ← (1:1) → hash bucket ← (1:1) → hash chain

Starting in Oracle8i Database: Hash latch ← (1:m) → hash bucket ← (1:1) → hash chain

Starting in Oracle8*i* Database, Oracle changed the nexus between hash latches and hash buckets to 1:m, but kept the nexus between hash buckets and hash chains unchanged at 1:1. Multiple hash chains could now be protected by a single hash latch. In doing this, Oracle drastically reduced the default number of hash latches. The default number of hash latches depends on the value of the DB_BLOCK_BUFFERS parameter. Usually, the number is 1024 when the buffer cache size is less than 1GB. The number of hash latches can be adjusted by the _DB_BLOCKS_HASH_LATCHES parameter. You can quickly discover the number of hash latches in the instance in one of the following ways:

```
select  count(distinct(hladdr))
from    x$bh;

COUNT(DISTINCT(HLADDR))
-----------------------
                   1024

select  count(*)
from    v$latch_children
where   name = 'cache buffers chains';

  COUNT(*)
----------
      1024
```

The default number of hash buckets is 2 * DB_BLOCK_BUFFERS, and the value is adjustable by the _DB_BLOCK_HASH_BUCKETS parameter. So, if the DB_BLOCK_BUFFERS is 50000, this means the instance has 100000 hash buckets and 100000 hash chains but only 1024 hash latches (assuming the block size is 8K). As you can see, there is a drastic change in the number of hash buckets and hash latches from Oracle8.0 to Oracle8*i* Database. Many DBAs think this new architecture seems backward and that it will increase *latch free* contention because there are far fewer latches. However, Oracle was hoping that by increasing the number of hash chains by a factor of 8, each chain would be shorter and compensate for a lower number of latches. Don't bet on this; you will still see *cache buffers chains* latch contentions.

Oracle Database 10*g* uses a different algorithm to determine the default number of hash buckets. Initially, it seems to be 1/4 of the DB_CACHE_SIZE, but further tests reveal that a hash bucket value remains constant over multiple DB_CACHE_SIZEs. For example, there are 65536 hash buckets when the DB_CACHE_SIZE is between 132MB and 260MB. This new algorithm also does not use prime numbers. Table 6-2 shows the default number of hash buckets in Oracle8*i* Database through Oracle Database 10*g* in various buffer cache sizes. In all cases, the DB_BLOCK_SIZE is 8K.

Oracle Database 10*g* on the Solaris Operating System

db_cache_size	32M	64M	128M	256M	512M	1024M	2048M
_ksmg_granule_size	4M	4M	4M	4M	4M	16M	16M
_db_block_buffers	3976	7952	15904	31808	63616	127232	254464
_db_block_hash_buckets	8192	16384	32768	65536	131072	262144	524288
_db_block_hash_latches	1024	1024	1024	1024	1024	1024	2048

Oracle9*i* Database on the Solaris Operating System

db_cache_size	32M	64M	128M	256M	512M	1024M	2048M
_ksmg_granule_size	4M	4M	16M	16M	16M	16M	16M
_db_block_buffers	4000	8000	16016	32032	64064	128128	256256
_db_block_hash_buckets	8009	16001	32051	64067	128147	256279	512521
_db_block_hash_latches	1024	1024	1024	1024	1024	1024	2048

Oracle8*i* Database on the Solaris Operating System

db_block_buffers	4000	8000	16016	32032	64064	128128	192192
_db_block_hash_buckets	8000	16000	32032	64064	128128	256256	384384
_db_block_hash_latches	1024	1024	1024	1024	1024	1024	2048

TABLE 6-2. *Default Number of Hash Buckets in Select Oracle Databases*

Contention for Cache Buffers Chains Latches— Inefficient SQL Statements

Inefficient SQL statements are the main cause of *cache buffers chains* latch contentions. When mixed with high concurrency, the time spent on *latch free* waits can be rather significant. This is a familiar scene in environments where the application opens multiple concurrent sessions that execute the same inefficient SQL statements that go after the same data set.

You will do well if you keep these three things in mind:

- Every logical read requires a latch get operation and a CPU.

- The only way to get out of the latch get routine is to get the latch.

- Only one process can own a *cache buffers chains* latch at any one time, and the latch covers many data blocks, some of which may be needed by another process. (Again, as mentioned in a previous note, Oracle9*i* Database allows the *cache buffers chains* latches to be shared for read-only.)

Naturally, fewer logical reads means fewer latch get operations, and thus reduces latch competition, which translates to better performance. Therefore, you must identify the SQL statements that contend for the *cache buffers chains* latches and tune them to reduce the number of logical reads. SQL statements with high BUFFER_GETS (logical reads) per EXECUTIONS are the main culprits.

NOTE
Many DBAs make a grave mistake by simply increasing the number of cache buffers chains *latches with the _DB_BLOCKS_HASH_LATCHES parameter without first optimizing the SQL statements. While additional latches may provide some relief, these DBAs treat the symptom without fixing the problem.*

NOTE
We experienced a lot of cache buffers chains *latch contentions after upgrading a database from Oracle8.1.7.4 to Oracle9.2.0.5 on the Sun Solaris platform. The new optimizer was generating and using poor execution plans for the application. Several hidden optimizer-related parameters that are by default disabled in Oracle8i Database are enabled Oracle9i Database. The problem was fixed by unsetting some of the parameters. If you are having the same problem, the best way is to handle it through Oracle Support.*

Contention for Cache Buffers Chains Latches—Hot Blocks

Hot blocks are another common cause of *cache buffers chains* latch contention. This happens when multiple sessions repeatedly access one or more blocks that are protected by the same child *cache buffers chains* latch. This is mostly an application issue. In most cases, increasing the number of *cache buffers chains* latches will do little to improve performance. This is because blocks are hashed to hash buckets and chains based on the block address and the number of hash buckets, and not the number of *cache buffers chains* latches. If the block address and the number of hash buckets remain the same, chances are those few hot blocks will still be covered by one *cache buffers chains* latch, unless the number of latches is drastically increased.

When sessions compete for the *cache buffers chains* latches, the best way to find out if you have a hot blocks situation is to examine the P1RAW parameter value of the *latch free* wait event. (Remember, in Oracle Database 10*g* this event is *latch: cache buffers chains*.) The P1RAW parameter contains the latch address. If the sessions are waiting on the same latch address, you have hot blocks. Based on the following example, there are hot blocks on chains covered by the 00000400837D7800 and 00000400837DE400 latches:

```
select sid, p1raw, p2, p3, seconds_in_wait, wait_time, state
from    v$session_wait
where   event = 'latch free'
order by p2, p1raw;

SID P1RAW                P2  P3 SECONDS_IN_WAIT  WAIT_TIME STATE
---- ---------------- --- --- ---------------- ---------- ----------------
  38 00000400837D7800  98   1                1          2 WAITED KNOWN TIME
  42 00000400837D7800  98   1                1          2 WAITED KNOWN TIME
  44 00000400837D7800  98   3                1          4 WAITED KNOWN TIME
  58 00000400837D7800  98   2                1         10 WAITED KNOWN TIME
  85 00000400837D7800  98   3                1         12 WAITED KNOWN TIME
 214 00000400837D7800  98   1                1          2 WAITED KNOWN TIME
 186 00000400837D7800  98   3                1         14 WAITED KNOWN TIME
 149 00000400837D7800  98   2                1          3 WAITED KNOWN TIME
 132 00000400837D7800  98   2                1          2 WAITED KNOWN TIME
 101 00000400837D7800  98   3                1          4 WAITED KNOWN TIME
 222 00000400837D7800  98   3                1         12 WAITED KNOWN TIME
 229 00000400837D7800  98   3                1          4 WAITED KNOWN TIME
 230 00000400837D7800  98   3                1         11 WAITED KNOWN TIME
 232 00000400837D7800  98   1                1         20 WAITED KNOWN TIME
 257 00000400837D7800  98   3                1         16 WAITED KNOWN TIME
 263 00000400837D7800  98   3                1          5 WAITED KNOWN TIME
 117 00000400837D7800  98   4                1          4 WAITED KNOWN TIME
 102 00000400837D7800  98   3                1         12 WAITED KNOWN TIME
  47 00000400837D7800  98   3                1         11 WAITED KNOWN TIME
  49 00000400837D7800  98   1                1          2 WAITED KNOWN TIME

  99 00000400837D9300  98   1                1         32 WAITED KNOWN TIME

  51 00000400837DD200  98   1                1          1 WAITED KNOWN TIME

  43 00000400837DE400  98   1                1          2 WAITED KNOWN TIME
 130 00000400837DE400  98   1                1         10 WAITED KNOWN TIME
  89 00000400837DE400  98   1                1          2 WAITED KNOWN TIME
  62 00000400837DE400  98   0                1         -1 WAITED KNOWN TIME
 150 00000400837DE400  98   1                1          9 WAITED KNOWN TIME
 195 00000400837DE400  98   1                1          3 WAITED KNOWN TIME
  67 00000400837DE400  98   1                1          2 WAITED KNOWN TIME
```

The next step is to see what blocks are covered by the latch. You should also capture the SQL statements that participate in the competition. This is because a *cache buffers chains* latch covers many blocks, and you can identify the hot blocks by the tables that are used in the SQL statements. In Oracle8*i* Database and above, you can identify the hot blocks based on their TCH (touch count) values using the following query. Generally, hot blocks have higher touch count values. However, bear in mind that the touch count is reset to 0 when a block is moved from the cold to the hot end of the LRU list. Depending on the timing of your query, a block with a 0 touch count value is not necessarily cold.

```
-- Using the P1RAW from the above example (00000400837D7800).
select a.hladdr, a.file#, a.dbablk, a.tch, a.obj, b.object_name
from   x$bh a, dba_objects b
where  (a.obj = b.object_id  or  a.obj = b.data_object_id)
and    a.hladdr = '00000400837D7800'
union
select hladdr, file#, dbablk, tch, obj, null
from   x$bh
where  obj in (select obj from x$bh where hladdr = '00000400837D7800'
               minus
               select object_id from dba_objects
               minus
               select data_object_id from dba_objects)
and    hladdr = '00000400837D7800'
order by 4;
```

```
HLADDR            FILE#  DBABLK  TCH          OBJ  OBJECT_NAME
---------------- ----- ------- ---- ----------- --------------------
00000400837D7800    16  105132    0        19139  ROUTE_HISTORY
00000400837D7800    16  106156    0        19163  TELCO_ORDERS
00000400837D7800    26   98877    0        23346  T1
00000400837D7800    16   61100    0        19163  TELCO_ORDERS
00000400837D7800    16   26284    0        19059  FP_EQ_TASKS
00000400837D7800     7  144470    0        18892  REPORT_PROCESS_QUEUE
00000400837D7800     8  145781    0        18854  PA_EQUIPMENT_UNION
00000400837D7800   249  244085    0   4294967295
00000400837D7800     7   31823    1        18719  CANDIDATE_EVENTS
00000400837D7800    13  100154    1        19251  EVENT
00000400837D7800     7   25679    1        18730  CANDIDATE_ZONING
00000400837D7800     7    8271    1        18719  CANDIDATE_EVENTS
00000400837D7800     7   32847    2        18719  CANDIDATE_EVENTS
00000400837D7800     8   49518    2        18719  CANDIDATE_EVENTS
00000400837D7800     7   85071    2        18719  CANDIDATE_EVENTS
00000400837D7800   275   76948    2   4294967295
00000400837D7800     7   41039    3        18719  CANDIDATE_EVENTS
00000400837D7800     7   37967    4        18719  CANDIDATE_EVENTS
00000400837D7800     8   67950    4        18719  CANDIDATE_EVENTS
00000400837D7800     7   33871    7        18719  CANDIDATE_EVENTS
00000400837D7800     7   59471    7        18719  CANDIDATE_EVENTS
00000400837D7800     8    8558   24        18719  CANDIDATE_EVENTS
```

As previously mentioned, hot blocks are an application issue. Find out why the application has to repeatedly access the same block (or blocks) and check if there is a better alternative.

As for the workaround, the idea is to spread the hot blocks across multiple *cache buffers chains* latches. This can be done by relocating some of the rows in the hot blocks. The new blocks have different block addresses and, with any luck, they are hashed to buckets that are not covered by the same *cache buffers chains* latch. You can spread the blocks in a number of ways, including:

■ Deleting and reinserting some of the rows by ROWID.

■ Exporting the table, increasing the PCTFREE significantly, and importing the data. This minimizes the number of rows per block, spreading them over many blocks. Of course, this is at the expense of storage and full table scans operations will be slower.

■ Minimizing the number of records per block in the table. This involves dumping a few data blocks to get an idea of the current number of rows per block. Refer to the "Data Block Dump" section in Appendix C for the syntax. The "nrow" in the trace file shows the number of rows per block. Export and truncate the table. Manually insert the number of rows that you determined is appropriate and then issue the ALTER TABLE *table_name* MINIMIZE RECORDS_PER_BLOCK command. Truncate the table and import the data.

■ For indexes, you can rebuild them with higher PCTFREE values, bearing in mind that this may increase the height of the index.

■ Consider reducing the block size. Starting in Oracle9*i* Database, Oracle supports multiple block sizes. If the current block size is 16K, you may move the table or recreate the index in a tablespace with an 8K block size. This too will negatively impact full table scans operations. Also, various block sizes increase management complexity.

For other workarounds, if the database is on Oracle9*i* Database Release 2 or higher, you may consider increasing the _SPIN_COUNT value as discussed earlier. As a last resort, you may increase the number of hash buckets through the _DB_ BLOCK_HASH_BUCKETS parameter. This practice is rarely necessary starting in Oracle8*i* Database. If you do this, make sure you provide a prime number—if you don't, Oracle will round it up to the next highest prime number

Contention for Cache Buffers Chains Latches—Long Hash Chains

Multiple data blocks can be hashed to the same hash bucket, and they are linked together with pointers on the hash chain that belong to the hash bucket. The number of blocks on a hash chain can run into hundreds for large databases. A process has to sequentially scan the hash chain for the required block while holding the *cache buffers chains* latch. We call this "chasing the chain." The latch must be held longer when scanning a long chain and may cause another process to miss on its *cache buffers chains* latch request.

Up to Oracle8.0, it is easy to determine the length of a particular hash chain because the relationships between hash latches, hash buckets, and hash chains are 1:1:1, and the length of a hash chain is equal to the number of blocks protected by its latch. The following query reports the number of blocks per hash chain. Chains with 10 or more blocks are considered long.

```
select hladdr, count(*)
from    x$bh
group by hladdr
order by 2;
```

Oracle8*i* Database changed the nexus between hash latches and hash buckets to 1: m. This means you can no longer determine the length of a particular hash chain. Rather, you can only determine the number of blocks covered by a particular hash latch, and a hash latch covers multiple hash chains. The preceding query will now report the number of blocks on each hash latch. Before you can determine if a hash latch is overloaded, the ratio between hash latches and hash buckets must first be determined. According to the following example, each hash latch protects 125 hash chains. If you allow up to 10 blocks per hash chain, you should only be concerned when you see values close to or more than 1250 from the preceding query. The hash chain length can be reduced by increasing the number of hash buckets through the _DB_BLOCK_HASH_BUCKETS parameter. You will find that this is rarely necessary in the newer releases of Oracle.

```
_DB_BLOCK_HASH_BUCKETS = 128021
_DB_BLOCK_HASH_LATCHES = 1024
Ratio = 128021 / 1024 = 125
```

Cache Buffers Lru Chain Latches

In addition to the hash chains, buffer headers are also linked to other lists such as the LRU, LRUW, and CKPT-Q. The LRU and LRUW lists are nothing new—they are the two original lists in the buffer cache. The LRU list contains buffers in various states, while the LRUW list contains only dirty buffers. The LRU and LRUW lists are mutually exclusive, and they are called a working set. Each working set is protected by a *cache buffers lru chain* latch. In other words, the number of working sets in the buffer cache is determined by the number of *cache buffers lru chain* latches. You can see the working sets by querying the X$KCBWDS (kernel cache buffer working sets descriptors) view as follows. Notice the child latch ADDR is the SET_LATCH address.

LRU + LRUW = A Working Set

```
select set_id, set_latch
from   x$kcbwds
order by set_id;

    SET_ID SET_LATC
---------- --------
         1 247E299C
         2 247E2E68
         3 247E3334
         4 247E3800
         5 247E3CCC
         6 247E4198
         7 247E4664
         8 247E4B30


select addr
from   v$latch_children
where name = 'cache buffers lru chain'
order by addr;

ADDR
--------
247E299C
247E2E68
247E3334
247E3800
247E3CCC
247E4198
247E4664
247E4B30
```

Typically, foreground processes access the LRU lists when looking for free buffers. The DBWR background process accesses the LRU lists to move cleaned buffers from the LRUW and move the dirty ones to the LRUW list. All processes must acquire the *cache buffers lru chain* latch before performing any kind of operation on a working set.

Buffers in the DB_2K_CACHE_SIZE, DB_4K_CACHE_SIZE, DB_8K_CACHE_SIZE, DB_16K_CACHE_SIZE, DB_32K_CACHE_SIZE, DB_CACHE_SIZE, DB_KEEP_CACHE_SIZE, and DB_RECYCLE_CACHE_SIZE pools are divided among the *cache buffers lru chain* latches. You should have at least one *cache buffers lru chain* latch per buffer pool or DBWR process, whichever is higher; otherwise, the working set can be too long. In Oracle9*i* Database and Oracle Database 10*g*, the default number of *cache buffers lru chain* latches is 4 times the CPU_COUNT, unless the DB_WRITER_PROCESSES is greater than 4, in which case the default is the product of DB_WRITER_PROCESSES and CPU_COUNT. The number of *cache buffers lru chain* latches can be adjusted upward by the _DB_BLOCK_LRU_LATCHES parameter in CPU_COUNT increments.

Competition for the *cache buffers lru chain* latch is symptomatic of intense buffer cache activity caused by inefficient SQL statements. Statements that repeatedly scan large unselective indexes or perform full table scans are the prime culprits. Capture the active SQL statement that is associated with the *latch free* wait event of the *cache buffers lru chain* latch. (Oracle Database 10*g* has a separate wait event for this latch called *latch: cache buffers lru chain*.) Tune the statement to reduce the number of logical and physical reads.

Row Cache Objects Latches

The *row cache objects* latch protects the Oracle data dictionary (or row cache because information is stored as rows instead of blocks). Processes must obtain this latch when loading, referencing, or freeing entries in the dictionary. This latch is a solitary latch up to Oracle8*i* Database. With the new multiple subpools architecture in Oracle9*i* Database, multiple copies of child *row cache objects* latches exist. Oracle Database 10*g* has a separate wait event for this latch known as *latch: row cache objects*.

Starting in Oracle7.0, the data dictionary became part of the shared pool; before that every dictionary object had a separate DC_* initialization parameter. The change in Oracle 7.0 means the data dictionary can no longer be tuned directly; it can only be tuned indirectly through the SHARED_POOL_SIZE parameter. The V$ROWCACHE has statistics for every data dictionary object. You can discover the hottest object using the following query:

```
select cache#, type, parameter, gets, getmisses, modifications mod
from    v$rowcache
where   gets > 0
order by gets;
```

CACHE#	TYPE	PARAMETER	GETS	GETMISSES	MOD
7	SUBORDINATE	dc_user_grants	1615488	75	0
2	PARENT	dc_sequences	2119254	189754	100
15	PARENT	dc_database_links	2268663	2	0
10	PARENT	dc_usernames	7702353	46	0
8	PARENT	dc_objects	11280602	12719	400
7	PARENT	dc_users	81128420	78	0
16	PARENT	dc_histogram_defs	182648396	51537	0
11	PARENT	dc_object_ids	250841842	3939	75

Row cache tuning is very limited. The best solution is to reduce dictionary access based on the output from the V$ROWCACHE. For example, if sequences are the problem, consider caching the sequences. Views that contain multiple table joins and view-on-views will increase this latch contention. The common workaround is simply to increase the SHARED_POOL_SIZE.

Enqueue

Until Oracle9*i* Database, the *enqueue* wait event parameters are name and mode, ID1, and ID2. In Oracle Database 10*g*, the first parameter remains the same, but the second and third parameters provide specific information about the enqueue they represent. Depending on the *enqueue* wait event, it can fall under the Administrative, Application, Configuration, Concurrency, or Other wait class. Keep the following key thoughts in mind when dealing with the *enqueue* wait event.

■ Enqueues are locks that apply to database objects.

■ Enqueues are transactional, initiated by the application.

■ The Oracle session is waiting to acquire a specific enqueue. The enqueue name and mode is recorded in the P1 parameter. The appropriate action to take depends on the type of enqueue being competed for.

■ Up to Oracle9*i* Database, the *enqueue* wait event represents all *enqueue* waits; starting in Oracle Database 10*g*, all enqueues are broken out and have independent wait events.

What Is an Enqueue?

What an enqueue is depends on the context in which it is used. When used as a verb, it refers to the act of placing a lock request in a queue. When used as a noun, it refers to a specific lock, such as the TX enqueue.

Enqueues are sophisticated locking mechanisms for managing access to shared resources such as schema objects, background jobs, and redo threads. Oracle uses enqueues for two purposes. First, they prevent multiple concurrent sessions from sharing the same resource when their lock modes are incompatible. Second, they allow sessions to share the same resource when their lock modes are compatible. When a session requests a lock on the whole or part of an object, and if the requested lock mode is incompatible with the mode held by another session, the requesting session puts its lock request in a queue (hence enqueue) and waits to be served in order. This event is known as an *enqueue* wait. *Enqueue* waits are waits for a variety of local locks, except for buffer locks (discussed in the "Buffer Busy Waits" section), library cache locks, row cache locks, and PCM (Parallel Cache Management) locks.

What Is an Enqueue Resource?

An *enqueue resource* is a database resource that is affected by an enqueue lock. Oracle manages the enqueue resources using an internal array structure that can be seen through the X$KSQRS (kernel service enqueue resource) or V$RESOURCE view as follows:

```
select * from v$resource;

ADDR                TY        ID1        ID2
----------------    --  ----------  ----------
C000000047BE4D40    TX     4980825      115058
C00000003FEB4A58    TM        6112           0
C00000004262E758    WL           1       25603
C00000004AD99538    TX      327726      202076
C00000004A5C6CE8    TM        5507           0
C00000003FB7C4F8    TX     5898241       23053
C00000004BB3A968    DX          28           0
. . .
```

According to the preceding output, the enqueue resource structure consists of a lock type and two numeric identifiers. The lock type is represented by a two-character code such as TX, TM, TS, MR, RT, etc. The two numeric identifiers ID1 and ID2 have different meanings depending on the lock type. Table 6-3 gives a few examples. Prior to Oracle Database 10g, the meaning of ID1 and ID2 for each lock type was not readily available to the general public. Because all enqueues have independent wait events in Oracle Database 10g, you can easily find out what ID1 and ID2 means from the PARAMETER2 and PARAMETER3 parameters of the particular *enqueue* wait event in the V$EVENT_NAME view.

The maximum number of enqueue resources that can be concurrently locked by the lock manager is controlled by the ENQUEUE_RESOURCES parameter. The default value is normally sufficient, but you may need to increase it if the application uses parallel DML operations. Parallel DML operations use more locks than serial DML operations. Processes that fail to obtain an enqueue resource will get the *ORA-00052: "maximum number of enqueue resources exceeded"* error. The V$RESOURCE_LIMIT view provides important utilization statistics, such as current utilization and how far the high watermark (MAX_UTILIZATION) is from the limit (LIMIT_VALUE). Up to Oracle8i Database, the ENQUEUE_RESOURCES parameter also sets the size of the X$KSQRS array. But starting in Oracle9i Database, Oracle seems to use a different algorithm for establishing the X$KSQRS array size.

```
select *
from    v$resource_limit
where   resource_name in ('enqueue_resources','enqueue_locks',
'dml_locks','processes','sessions');

RESOURCE_NAME      CURRENT_UTILIZATION MAX_UTILIZATION INITIAL_AL LIMIT_VALU
-----------------  ------------------- --------------- ---------- ----------
processes                          438             643       2000       2000
sessions                           443             664       2205       2205
enqueue_locks                      402             465      27101      27101
enqueue_resources                  449             584        800  UNLIMITED
dml_locks                           68             778        600  UNLIMITED
```

Lock type	TX
ID1	ID1 indicates the rollback segment and the slot number. On 32-bit machines, you must convert ID1 into hexadecimal and left pad with zeros up to 8 characters. The high order 2 bytes give the rollback segment number, and the low order 2 bytes give the rollback slot number. The values can be seen in the XIDUSN and XIDSLOT columns of the V$TRANSACTION view.
ID2	Rollback segment wrap or sequence number. This value can be seen in the XIDSQN column of V$TRANSACTION view.
Lock type	**TM**
ID1	ID1 indicates the object ID of the table, which can be found in DBA_OBJECTS.OBJECT_ID.
ID2	Always 0.
Lock type	**TS**
ID1	This is the tablespace number, which can be found in the TS$.TS#.
ID2	This is the relative Database Block Address (DBA).
Lock type	**JQ**
ID1	Always 0.
ID2	ID2 indicates the job number.
Lock type	**MR**
ID1	Data file ID. Oracle takes up to one MR enqueue per data file (including temp files).
ID2	Always 0.
Lock type	**RT**
ID1	Redo thread number.
ID2	Always 0.

TABLE 6-3. *ID1 and ID2 Meanings Depending on the Lock Type*

What Is an Enqueue Lock?

An enqueue lock is the lock itself. Oracle uses a separate array than the enqueue resources array to manage the enqueue locks. This structure can be seen through the X$KSQEQ (kernel service enqueue object) view or the V$ENQUEUE_LOCK view as follows. The size of this structure is influenced by the _ENQUEUE_LOCKS parameter. You can check how close the maximum utilization is to the limit value from the V$RESOURCE_LIMIT view as shown in the preceding code.

```
select *
from   x$ksqeq
where  bitand(kssobflg,1)!=0
and    (ksqlkmod!=0 or ksqlkreq!=0);

-- or simply query from V$ENQUEUE_LOCK
select * from v$enqueue_lock;
```

ADDR	KADDR	SID	TY	ID1	ID2	LMODE	REQUEST	CTIME	BLOCK
243F8368	243F8378	2	MR	51	0	4	0	349520	0
243F831C	243F832C	2	MR	6	0	4	0	349520	0
243F82D0	243F82E0	2	MR	5	0	4	0	349520	0
243F8284	243F8294	2	MR	4	0	4	0	349520	0
243F8238	243F8248	2	MR	3	0	4	0	349520	0
243F81EC	243F81FC	2	MR	2	0	4	0	349520	0
243F81A0	243F81B0	2	MR	1	0	4	0	349520	0
243F80BC	243F80CC	3	RT	1	0	6	0	349521	0
243F7F8C	243F7F9C	4	XR	4	0	1	0	349524	0
243F8108	243F8118	5	TS	2	1	3	0	349519	0
243F7FD8	243F7FE8	9	TX	393241	875	0	6	2651	0

The enqueue lock structure contains information such as the session ID (SID), lock type, database resource (identified by ID1 and ID2), lock mode, request mode, current mode time (CTIME), and blocking flag. This structure is used for managing and servicing lock requests in the order of request, not lock mode. This means if one of the waiters needs a particular lock and the mode is compatible with the current mode, but the waiter is behind another waiter whose lock mode is incompatible with the current mode, the waiter's request cannot be served.

Don't be surprised if you don't see the normal transaction (TX) and DML (TM) locks in V$ENQUEUE_LOCKS. They are not in the X$KSQEQ structure, unless there is an *enqueue* wait for them. Oracle uses different structures to manage the TX and TM enqueues: the X$KTCXB (kernel transaction control transaction object—the base view for V$TRANSACTION_ENQUEUE) and X$KTADM (kernel transaction access definition dml lock). You can find the entries using the following queries. The structures are sized by the TRANSACTIONS and DML_LOCKS parameters. The V$LOCK is the best view because it shows all the locks.

```
select *
from   x$ktcxb
```

```
where   KTCXBLKP in (select kaddr from v$lock where type = 'TX');

select  *
from    x$ktadm
where   KSQLKADR in (select kaddr from v$lock where type = 'TM');
```

Enqueue Architecture

Internally, the *enqueue architecture* is very similar to the cache buffers architecture. The main components are enqueue hash chains latches, enqueue hash table, enqueue hash chains, and enqueue resources. The relationship between the enqueue hash chains latches, enqueue hash table, and enqueue hash chains is as follows:

enqueue hash chains latch ← (1:m) → hash bucket ← (1:1) → enqueue hash chain

Child enqueue hash chains latches protect the enqueue hash table and hash chains. By default, the number of child enqueue hash chains latches is equal to the CPU_COUNT. This number can be adjusted by the initialization parameter _ENQUEUE_HASH_CHAIN_LATCHES.

Enqueue resources are hashed to the enqueue hash table based on the resource type and identifiers and are placed on the appropriate enqueue hash chains. The default length of the enqueue hash table is derived from the SESSIONS parameter and can be adjusted by the _ENQUEUE_HASH parameter. If you ever need to increase the ENQUEUE_RESOURCES parameter significantly from its default value, you might want to keep an eye on the sleep rate of the enqueue hash chains latches. This is because the enqueue hash table length will remain the same because it is derived from SESSIONS, not from ENQUEUE_RESOURCES. The combination of a high demand for enqueue resources and a small enqueue hash table will result in a higher hash collision rate and potentially lengthy hash chains. This problem manifests itself as latch contentions for the enqueue hash chains latches. In this case, you need to increase the _ENQUEUE_HASH.

*enqueue hash table length = ((SESSIONS – 10) * 2) + 55*

To learn more about the enqueue hash table, the resources and queues, you can dump the enqueue structure to a trace file with the following command:

```
alter session set events 'immediate trace name enqueues level 3';
```

Decoding Enqueue Type and Mode

Oracle encodes the enqueue type and mode in the P1 column of the *enqueue* wait event. When deciphered, you will get a two-character enqueue (lock) type and a numeric mode number. The enqueue type can be deciphered by the following query:

```
select sid, event, p1, p1raw,
     chr(bitand(P1,-16777216)/16777215)||chr(bitand(P1,16711680)/65535) type,
       mod(P1, 16) "MODE"
from   v$session_wait
where  event = 'enqueue';

 SID EVENT                P1 P1RAW               TY      MODE
 ---- --------------- ---------- ---------------- --   ----------
 405 enqueue         1213661190 0000000048570006 HW          6
 132 enqueue         1397817350 0000000053510006 SQ          6
  43 enqueue         1413677062 0000000054430006 TC          6
  44 enqueue         1415053316 0000000054580004 TX          4
  40 enqueue         1415053318 0000000054580006 TX          6
. . .
```

Alternatively, the enqueue type can also be discovered from the P1RAW column of the *enqueue* wait event. The values from the above example are from a 64-bit Oracle Database. You can ignore the leading zeros and focus on the last 4 bytes (that is, the last eight numbers). The high order 2 bytes give the enqueue type. Using 54580006 as an example, the 2 high order bytes are 0x5458Hex. Now, 54Hex is decimal 84 and 58Hex is decimal 88, so the enqueue type can be discovered as follows: (Appendix B has a complete list of enqueue types.)

```
select chr(84) || chr(88) from dual;
CH
--
TX
```

Decoding enqueue type is a no-brainer in Oracle Database 10*g* because the enqueue type is part of the *enqueue* wait event name itself, since all enqueues are broken out. The following are a few examples:

```
enq: ST - contention
enq: TX - allocate ITL entry
enq: TX - contention
enq: TX - index contention
enq: TX - row lock contention
```

Processes request enqueue locks in one of these six modes: Null (N), Row Share (RS), Row Exclusive (RX), Share (S), Share Row Exclusive (SRX), or Exclusive (X). These modes are represented by a single numeric digit from 0 to 6, as shown in Table 6-4. The lock mode is encoded in the low order 2 bytes of P1RAW, and it is easily spotted. Using the same 54580006 as an example, the 2 low order bytes are 0006Hex, so the lock mode is 6 (exclusive). Alternatively, the lock mode can be deciphered from the P1 column using *mod(P1, 16)* or *to_char(bitand(P1, 65535)*.

Mode	Description
0	None
1	Null (N)
2	Row-Share (RS), also known as Subshare lock (SS)
3	Row-Exclusive (RX), also known as Subexclusive lock (SX)
4	Share (S)
5	Share Row Exclusive (SRX), also known as Share-Subexclusive lock (SSX)
6	Exclusive (X)

TABLE 6-4. *Lock Modes and Descriptions*

Oracle uses the lock mode to determine if a resource can be shared by multiple concurrent processes. Table 6-5 is the compatibility chart.

Statement	Mode	N	RS	RX	S	SRX	X
SELECT	N	Yes	Yes	Yes	Yes	Yes	Yes
SELECT ... FOR UPDATE	RS	Yes	Yes*	Yes*	Yes*	Yes*	No
lock table in row share mode	RS	Yes	Yes	Yes	Yes	Yes	No
INSERT	RX	Yes	Yes	Yes	No	No	No
UPDATE	RX	Yes	Yes*	Yes*	No	No	No
DELETE	RX	Yes	Yes*	Yes*	No	No	No
lock table in row exclusive mode	RX	Yes	Yes	Yes	No	No	No
lock table in share mode	S	Yes	Yes	No	Yes	No	No
lock table in share row exclusive mode	SRX	Yes	Yes	No	No	No	No
lock table in exclusive mode	X	Yes	No	No	No	No	No

*Yes means sharing is possible if no conflicting row lock is held by another session.

TABLE 6-5. *Lock Mode Compatibility Chart*

Common Causes, Diagnosis, and Actions

Due to the variety of enqueue types, an *enqueue* wait event can occur for many different reasons. The common causes and the appropriate action to take depend on the enqueue type and mode that the sessions are competing for. For each type of enqueue, Oracle keeps an instance-level statistics on the number of requests and waits in the X$KSQST structure. Oracle9*i* Database exposes this structure through the V$ENQUEUE_STAT view. A new column is also added to the X$KSQST structure to keep the cumulative wait time as shown next.

```
-- Oracle9i Database and above
select *
from    v$enqueue_stat
where   cum_wait_time > 0
order by inst_id, cum_wait_time;

    INST_ID EQ TOTAL_REQ# TOTAL_WAIT#   SUCC_REQ# FAILED_REQ# CUM_WAIT_TIME
---------- -- ---------- ----------- ---------- ----------- -------------
          1 SQ      66551         437       66551           0           498
          1 CU      64353         133       64353           0          1616
          1 HW     453067       18683      453067           0         11811
          1 CF     119748          76      119605         143         37842
          1 TX   22687836        9480    22687758          71        672435
          1 TC       3620         724        3620           0        679237
          1 TM   89822967          91    89817200           5       4056333


-- Oracle 7.1.6 to 8.1.7
select inst_id,
       ksqsttyp "Lock",
       ksqstget "Gets",
       ksqstwat "Waits"
from    x$ksqst
where   ksqstwat > 0
order by inst_id, ksqstwat;
```

You should realize how interactive users experience *enqueue* waits. They receive no messages and their sessions freeze up. That is what they will tell you when they call. Don't expect them to tell you that they are waiting on enqueues. You should be thankful they are not that sophisticated.

A detailed discussion on all the enqueues is impractical. However, the most common *enqueue* waits are discussed next.

Wait for TX Enqueue in Mode 6

A wait for the TX enqueue in mode 6 (P1= 1415053318, P1RAW= 54580006) is the most common *enqueue* wait. (In Oracle Database 10*g*, the wait event name is *enq: TX—row lock contention*.) This indicates contention for row-level lock. This wait occurs when a transaction tries to update or delete rows that are currently locked by another transaction. This usually is an application issue. The waiting session will wait until the blocking session commits or rolls back its transaction. There is no other way to release the lock. (Killing the blocking session will cause its transaction to be rolled back.)

The following listing shows an example of TX *enqueue* wait in mode 6 as seen in the V$LOCK view:

```
ADDR      KADDR     SID TY    ID1     ID2 LMODE REQUEST CTIME BLOCK
-------- -------- --- -- ------ ------ ----- ------- ----- -----
A3950688 A395069C  10 TM 188154      0     3       0     3     0
A304E2A0 A304E2B0  10 TX  65585 147836     0       6     3     0
01AD23D4 01AD24A4  20 TX  65585 147836     6       0    10     1
A3950A28 A3950A3C  20 TM 188154      0     3       0    10     0
```

Whenever you see an *enqueue* wait event for the TX enqueue, the first step is to find out who the blocker is and if there are multiple waiters for the same resource by using the following query. If the blocking session is an ad-hoc process, then the user may be taking a break. In this case, ask the user to commit or roll back the transaction. If the blocking session is a batch or OLTP application process, then check to see if the session is still "alive." It may be a live Oracle session, but its parent process may be dead or hung. In this case, chances are you will have to kill the session to release the locks. Be sure to confirm with the application before killing a production process.

```
select /*+ ordered */
        a.sid         blocker_sid,
        a.username    blocker_username,
        a.serial#,
        a.logon_time,
        b.type,
        b.lmode       mode_held,
        b.ctime       time_held,
        c.sid         waiter_sid,
        c.request     request_mode,
        c.ctime       time_waited
from    v$lock b, v$enqueue_lock c, v$session a
where   a.sid     = b.sid
and     b.id1     = c.id1(+)
and     b.id2     = c.id2(+)
and     c.type(+) = 'TX'
and     b.type    = 'TX'
and     b.block   = 1
order by time_held, time_waited;
```

You can discover the resource that is being competed for. The resource ID is available in the V$LOCK.ID1 column of the DML lock (TM) for that transaction. It is also available in the V$SESSION.ROW_WAIT_OBJ# of the waiting session. The following query retrieves the resource of the TX *enqueue* wait:

```
select  c.sid waiter_sid, a.object_name, a.object_type
from    dba_objects a, v$session b, v$session_wait c
where   (a.object_id = b.row_wait_obj# or
         a.data_object_id = b.row_wait_obj#)
and     b.sid       = c.sid
and     chr(bitand(c.P1,-16777216)/16777215) ||
        chr(bitand(c.P1,16711680)/65535) = 'TX'
and     c.event     = 'enqueue';
```

Don't forget to extract the SQL statement that is executed by the waiting session as well as the SQL statement that is executed by the blocking session. These statements will give you an idea of what the waiting session is trying to do and what the blocking session is doing. They are also important points of reference for the application developers so that they can quickly locate the modules. (By the way, the SQL statement that is currently being executed by the blocking session is not necessarily the statement that holds the lock. The statement that holds the lock might have been run a long time ago.)

Wait for TX Enqueue in Mode 4—ITL Shortage

A wait for the TX enqueue in mode 4 is normally due to one of the following reasons:

- ITL (interested transaction list) shortage
- Unique key enforcement
- Bitmap index entry

Here, we will talk about the ITL, which is a transaction slot in a data block. The initial number of ITL slots is defined by the INITRANS clause and is limited by the MAXTRANS clause. By default, a table has 1 ITL and an index has 2 ITLs. Each ITL takes up 24 bytes and contains the transaction ID in the format of USN.SLOT#.WRAP#. Every DML transaction needs to acquire its own ITL space within a block before data can be manipulated. Contention for ITL occurs when all the available ITLs within a block are currently in use and there is not enough space in the PCTFREE area for Oracle to dynamically allocate a new ITL slot. In this case, the session will wait until one of the transactions is committed or rolled back, and it will reuse that ITL slot. ITL is like a building parking space. Everyone who drives to the building needs a parking space. If the parking lot is full, you have to circle the lot until someone leaves the building.

NOTE
Starting in Oracle9i Database, each data block has a minimum of two ITL slots by default. Even if you specify one, you still get two. The DBA_TABLES view will show just one, but the block dump will show two.

The following listing shows an example of the TX *enqueue* wait in mode 4 that is caused by ITL shortage, as seen in the V$LOCK view.

```
ADDR      KADDR     SID TY    ID1    ID2 LMODE REQUEST CTIME BLOCK
--------  --------  --- --  ------  ----- ----- ------- ----- -----
8A2B6400  8A2B6414    8 TM    3172      0     3       0   248     0
89EF3A0C  89EF3A1C    8 TX  131147     13     0       4   248     0
01A4177C  01A41848    9 TX  131147     13     6       0   376     1
8A2B6388  8A2B639C    9 TM    3172      0     3       0   376     0
```

Because a TX *enqueue* wait in mode 4 is not always caused by ITL shortage, your first step should be to validate this premise. (You do not have to do this exercise in Oracle Database 10*g* because the enqueue name is *enq: TX—allocate ITL entry*, and you know it right off the bat.) The V$SESSION row of the waiting session contains the information about the object of the enqueue. The columns in particular are ROW_WAIT_FILE# and ROW_WAIT_BLOCK#. Using these values, you can dump the block and see the number of active ITLs ("--U-") in the block and decide if ITL is the problem. If it is, the fix is to recreate the object with a higher INITRANS value. (Recreating the object with a higher PCTFREE value will also help because Oracle can dynamically allocate new ITL slots in the area.)

```
alter system dump datafile <file#> block <block#>;
```

```
-- The ITL portion of a block dump
 Itl        Xid                       Uba     Flag  Lck      Scn/Fsc
0x01 0x000a.051.0001fcf2 0x07ca2145.4e11.18 --U-    0  scn 0x070e.03df2f08
0x02 0x0005.049.00022d46 0x090618b7.5967.1c C---    0  scn 0x070e.03df2f6a
0x03 0x0012.008.0001244b 0x0580a510.26ac.0c --U-    0  scn 0x070e.03df2f7b
0x04 0x0014.00d.00012593 0x090d4f93.28d3.1e C---    0  scn 0x070e.03e08919
 . . .
```

Starting in Oracle9*i* Database, Oracle keeps track of the number of ITL waits by object and publishes the information in the V$SEGMENT_STATISTICS view. Execute the following query to see the magnitude of ITL waits in your database:

```
select owner,
       object_name,
       subobject_name,
       object_type,
       tablespace_name,
```

```
        value,
        statistic_name
from    v$segment_statistics
where   statistic_name = 'ITL waits'
and     value > 0
order by value;
```

Wait for TX Enqueue in Mode 4—Unique Key Enforcement

Unique or primary key enforcement is yet another reason you might see contention for the TX enqueue in mode 4. (In Oracle Database 10*g*, the wait event name is *enq: TX—row lock contention*.) This only occurs when multiple concurrent sessions insert the same key value into a table that has one or more unique key constraints. The first session to insert the value succeeds, but the rest freeze and wait until the first session commits or rolls back to see if "*ORA-00001 unique constraint (%s.%s) violated*" should be raised.

The following listing shows an example of a TX *enqueue* wait in mode 4 as seen in the V$LOCK view that is due to unique key enforcement. What is the difference between this listing and the one caused by ITL shortage? Notice that the waiter (SID=8) has two TX entries in the V$LOCK view. This doesn't mean that it owns two transactions. In fact, the V$TRANSACTION view shows only two transactions—one for SID 8 and another for SID 9. This shows SID 8 is waiting for the TX lock held by SID 9, and it wants a share lock (mode 4) on the object. SID 8 also holds a TX lock for its own transaction. Another thing you should be aware of is the object ID that is recorded in ID1 of the DML transaction (TM) is always the table ID, not the index ID, although a unique key is enforced through an index.

ADDR	KADDR	SID	TY	ID1	ID2	LMODE	REQUEST	CTIME	BLOCK
01AF6120	01AF61EC	8	TX	131099	14	6	0	4051	0
8A2B6388	8A2B639C	8	TM	3176	0	3	0	4051	0
89EF37CC	89EF37DC	8	TX	131094	14	0	4	4051	0
01AF6120	01AF61EC	9	TX	131094	14	6	0	4461	1
8A2B6400	8A2B6414	9	TM	3176	0	3	0	4461	0

Your action items are the same as before—find out who is blocking, the name of the resource being competed for, and the SQL statements executed by the waiting and the blocking session. This is an application issue, and the fix must come from the application.

Wait for TX Enqueue in Mode 4—Bitmap Index Entry

A wait for the TX enqueue in mode 4 can also occur when multiple sessions try to update or delete different rows that are covered by the same bitmap entry. Of course, this does not apply if the application does not use bitmap indexes.

Unlike the B-tree index entry, which contains a single ROWID, a bitmap entry can potentially cover a range of ROWIDs. So when a bitmap index entry is locked, all the ROWIDs that are covered by the entry are also locked.

The following listing shows an example of a TX *enqueue* wait in mode 4 as seen in the V$LOCK view due to bitmap entry. What is the difference between this listing and the preceding one in the unique key enforcement? Can you tell if you are dealing with a bitmap index entry or unique key enforcement issue by looking at the V$LOCK view output? No, you can't. The object ID in the TM lock doesn't help either, as it is the object ID of the table and not the index. That is why it is very important for you to capture the SQL statement of the waiting and blocking sessions. If the waiting session is attempting an insert, you are dealing with a unique key enforcement issue. If the waiting session is attempting an update or delete, most likely you are dealing with a bitmap entry issue.

ADDR	KADDR	SID	TY	ID1	ID2	LMODE	REQUEST	CTIME	BLOCK
01A52DB4	01A52E80	7	TX	131120	14	6	0	31	1
8A2B6310	8A2B6324	7	TM	3181	0	3	0	31	0
01A52DB4	01A52E80	9	TX	131107	14	6	0	9	0
8A2B6388	8A2B639C	9	TM	3181	0	3	0	9	0
89EF3A4C	89EF3A5C	9	TX	131120	14	0	4	9	0

In order to resolve the contention, you have to hunt down the offending user. However, the offending user is not always the user who holds the lock. That user was there first, for crying out loud. If the user has a legitimate reason to hold the lock, the waiters should back out of their transactions.

Wait for ST Enqueue

There is only one ST lock per database. Database actions that modify the UET$ (used extent) and FET$ (free extent) tables require the ST lock, which includes actions such as drop, truncate, and coalesce. Contention for the ST lock indicates there are multiple sessions actively performing dynamic disk space allocation or deallocation in dictionary managed tablespaces. Temporary tablespaces that are not created with the TEMPORARY clause and dictionary managed tablespaces that undergo high extent allocation or deallocation are the principal reasons for ST lock contention. Following are some of the things you can do to minimize ST lock contention in your database. The first two items are critical, and you should implement them in your database. They will significantly reduce the ST lock contentions.

■ Use locally managed tablespaces. In Oracle9*i* Database Release 2, all tablespaces including SYSTEM can be locally managed. There is no reason not to use locally managed tablespaces. (If the SYSTEM tablespace is locally managed, you cannot have any dictionary managed tablespaces that are read/write.)

- Recreate all temporary tablespaces using the CREATE TEMPORARY TABLESPACE TEMPFILE... command.

- For dictionary managed tablespaces, increase the next extent sizes of segments that experienced high dynamic allocations. Also, preallocate extents for the segments that are frequently extended.

Wait for TM Enqueue in Mode 3

Unindexed foreign key columns are the primary cause of TM lock contention in mode 3. However, this only applies to databases prior to Oracle9*i* Database. Depending on the operation, when foreign key columns are not indexed, Oracle either takes up a DML share lock (S – mode 4) or share row exclusive lock (SRX – mode 5) on the child table whenever the parent key or row is modified. (The share row exclusive lock is taken on the child table when the parent row is deleted and the foreign key constraint is created with the ON DELETE CASCADE option. Without this option, Oracle takes the share lock.) The share lock or share row exclusive lock on the child table prohibits other processes from getting a row exclusive lock (RX—mode 3) on the table. The waiting session will wait until the blocking session commits or rolls back its transaction.

Here is a philosophical question for you: Are you going to start building new indexes for all the foreign key columns in your databases? DBAs are divided on this. Our take is that you should hold your horses and don't get carried away building new indexes just yet. If you do, you will introduce many new indexes to the database, some that are unnecessary. For example, you don't need to create new indexes on foreign key columns when the parent tables they reference are static. You only need to create indexes on foreign key columns of the child table that is being identified by the *enqueue* wait event. The object ID for the child table is recorded in the P2 column, which corresponds to the ID1 column of the V$LOCK view. Query the DBA_OBJECTS view using the object ID and you will see the name of the child table. Yes, you will be operating in reactive mode, but it beats creating unnecessary indexes in the database, which not only wastes storage and increases maintenance, but may open up another can of worms for SQL tuning.

Following is an Oracle8*i* Database V$LOCK view output of a TM *enqueue* wait in mode 3 that is caused by an unindexed foreign key column. Notice the blocking session holds two TM locks: one for the parent table (ID1=3185) and the other for the child table (ID=3187). The share row exclusive lock (mode 5) on the child table prevents the row exclusive lock (mode 3) request from the waiting session (SID=9).

ADDR	KADDR	SID	TY	ID1	ID2	LMODE	REQUEST	CTIME	BLOCK
01A52DB4	01A52E80	7	TX	131155	14	6	0	603	0
8A2B6388	8A2B639C	7	TM	3187	0	5	0	603	1
8A2B6310	8A2B6324	7	TM	3185	0	3	0	603	0
8A2B6400	8A2B6414	9	TM	3187	0	0	3	758	0

The same steps that are used to produce the preceding TM enqueue contention are repeated in an Oracle9*i* Database; following is the output. In this case, the ID of the child table is 128955 and the ID of the parent table is 128953. Notice that there is no blocking lock. Unindexed foreign keys are no longer an issue starting in Oracle9*i* Database.

KADDR	SID	TY	ID1	ID2	LMODE	REQUEST	CTIME	BLOCK
C00000003B1F7230	295	TM	128953	0	2	0	21	0
C00000003B1F73B0	295	TM	128955	0	3	0	21	0
C000000036F5F2F0	295	TX	4391002	145885	6	0	21	0
C00000003B1F6CF0	465	TM	128953	0	3	0	27	0
C00000003B29B118	465	TX	1310720	143517	6	0	27	0
C00000003B1F6DB0	465	TM	128955	0	3	0	27	0

Finally, TM enqueue contention in mode 3 can also occur when a table is explicitly locked in the share mode or higher and there are concurrent DML activities against the table. This is common with applications that use old third-party vendor codes. You can query the V$SQLAREA view for the LOCK TABLE statement. Following is an example of what this contention will look like in the V$LOCK view:

KADDR	SID	TY	ID1	ID2	LMODE	REQUEST	CTIME	BLOCK
C00000003B1F6B70	295	TM	128956	0	0	3	12	0
C00000003B1F75F0	465	TM	128956	0	4	0	18	1

Buffer Busy Waits

Until Oracle9*i* Database, the *buffer busy waits* event parameters are file#, block#, and ID (reason code). In Oracle Database 10*g* Release 1, the first two parameters remain the same, but the third parameter gives the block class#. This wait event falls under the Concurrency wait class. Keep the following key thoughts in mind when dealing with the *buffer busy waits* event.

- The Oracle session is waiting to pin a buffer. A buffer must be pinned before it can be read or modified. Only one process can pin a buffer at any one time.

- *buffer busy waits* indicate read/read, read/write, or write/write contention.

- The appropriate action to take depends on the reason encoded in the P3 parameter.

A session that reads or modifies a buffer in the SGA must first acquire the cache buffers chains latch and traverse the buffer chain until it finds the necessary buffer header. Then it must acquire a buffer lock or a pin on the buffer header in shared or exclusive mode, depending on the operation it intends to perform. Once the buffer header is pinned, the session releases the cache buffers chains latch and performs the intended operation on the buffer itself. If a pin cannot be obtained, the session waits on the *buffer busy waits* wait event. This wait event does not apply to read or write operations that are performed in sessions' private PGAs.

Common Causes, Diagnosis, and Actions

The following four pieces of information are essential for diagnosing the *buffer busy waits* problem when it is the leading bottleneck that slows a process down.

- The primary reason code that represents why a process fails to get a buffer pin.

- The class of block that the *buffer busy waits* wait event is for.

- The SQL statement that is associated with the *buffer busy waits* event.

- The segment that the buffer belongs to.

Of the four, the first two are the most important as they reveal the reason a process fails to get a buffer pin and what class of block it is. Your corrective action depends on what they are, not on the number of *buffer busy waits* that a segment has encountered as tracked by the V$SEGMENT_STATISTICS in the Oracle9*i* Database. Shortly, we will show you how to correct the *buffer busy waits* problem, but first let us talk about the reason code.

A session may fail to get a pin on a buffer header for various reasons. The reasons are represented by a set of codes. Up to Oracle9*i* Database, a process that waits on the *buffer busy waits* event publishes the reason code in the P3 parameter of the wait event. Oracle uses a four-digit code in versions up to Oracle 8.0.6 and a three-digit code starting in Oracle 8.1.6. The Oracle Metalink note #34405.1 provides a table of reference. The codes are also listed in Chapter 3. Although there are at least 10 different reasons why a *buffer busy waits* wait event can occur, codes 130 and 220 (equivalent to codes 1013 and 1016 in Oracle8.0) are most common. Basically, a code number that is less than 200 means the wait is I/O related.

Reason code 130 means there are multiple sessions concurrently requesting the same data block that is not already in the buffer cache and has to be read from disk. This is typical in applications that spawn multiple concurrent threads or sessions, and each one executes the same query that goes after the same data set. In this case, you can check the sessions' logon time in the V$SESSION view, and chances are you will find them only a few seconds apart. When multiple sessions request the same data block that is not in the buffer cache, Oracle is smart enough to prevent every session from making the same operating system I/O call. Otherwise, this can severely increase the number of system I/Os. Instead, Oracle allows only one of the sessions to perform the actual I/O, while others wait for the block to be brought into the buffer cache. The other sessions wait for the block on the *buffer busy waits* event and the session that performs the I/O waits on the *db file sequential read* (or the *db file scattered read*) wait event. You will notice that the *buffer busy waits* and the *db file sequential read* events share the same P1 (file#) and P2 (block#) values.

Reason code 220 indicates there are multiple sessions trying to concurrently modify different rows within the same block that is in the buffer cache. This symptom is typical in applications with high DML concurrency. Unfortunately, a block can be pinned by only one process at any one time. The other concurrent processes must wait on the *buffer busy waits* wait event until the first change is complete. This is a good thing; otherwise the block will be corrupted.

Sadly, the Oracle Database 10g Release 1 drops the reason code. The P3TEXT of the *buffer busy waits* event is changed from ID to CLASS#. (Not to be confused with the WAIT_CLASS#, which represents the wait event class or category.) This CLASS# refers to the class of blocks in the V$WAITSTAT view as shown in the following listing. Class 1 corresponds to the "data block," class 2 corresponds to the "sort block," class 3 corresponds to the "save undo block," and so on. The last one, class 18, corresponds to the "undo block." Without the reason code, it is very important that you also capture the SQL statement that is associated with the *buffer busy waits* event so that you know what the context is. In other words, if the CLASS# is 1 (data block) and the SQL statement is a query, then this is similar to reason code 130. However, if the SQL statement is a DML, then this is similar to reason code 220.

> **NOTE**
> *In Oracle Database 10*g, *the* buffer busy wait *codes 110 and 120 are replaced by another wait event, namely* read by another session. *The parameters are the same: file#, block#, class#.*

```
select * from v$waitstat;

CLASS                   COUNT        TIME
------------------- ---------- ----------
data block            41476005    4743636
sort block                   0          0
save undo block              0          0
segment header           49514       3471
save undo header             0          0
free list                   97         10
extent map                   0          0
1st level bmb                0          0
2nd level bmb                0          0
3rd level bmb                0          0
```

bitmap block	0	0
bitmap index block	34033	4276
file header block	13584	2379
unused	0	0
system undo header	0	0
system undo block	0	0
undo header	309220	8021
undo block	5112402	435459

If a session spent the majority of its processing time waiting on the *buffer busy waits* event, you must find out what class of block it waited on the most, as this will help you to formulate the right solution. For example, if the *buffer busy waits* contention is mostly on a table's segment header block (class #4), then adjusting the table's PCTFREE will not resolve the problem. Prior to Oracle Database 10g, the only way to determine the class of block was by translating the P1 and P2 parameters of the *buffer busy waits* event. Only a limited number of block classes can be determined in such a manner. Perhaps this is why Oracle makes it easy for DBAs by changing the P3 definition of the *buffer busy waits* event in Oracle Database 10g. The following query identifies several classes of blocks in versions prior to Oracle Database 10g. First, it checks to see if the P1 and P2 parameters combination translates to a segment header. If not, it checks to see if they translate to a FREELIST GROUPS block. Failing this last check, the combination may be a data, index, or rollback block.

```
select 'Segment Header' class,
       a.segment_type, a.segment_name, a.partition_name
from   dba_segments a, v$session_wait b
where  a.header_file  = b.p1
and    a.header_block = b.p2
and    b.event        = 'buffer busy waits'
union
select 'Freelist Groups' class,
       a.segment_type, a.segment_name, a.partition_name
from   dba_segments a, v$session_wait b
where  b.p2 between a.header_block + 1 and (a.header_block + a.freelist_groups)
and    a.header_file      = b.p1
and    a.freelist_groups > 1
and    b.event            = 'buffer busy waits'
union
select a.segment_type || ' block' class,
       a.segment_type, a.segment_name, a.partition_name
from   dba_extents a, v$session_wait b
where  b.p2 between a.block_id and a.block_id + a.blocks - 1
and    a.file_id  = b.p1
and    b.event    = 'buffer busy waits'
and    not exists (select 1
                   from   dba_segments
                   where  header_file  = b.p1
                   and    header_block = b.p2);
```

Now we will discuss the appropriate method for treating *buffer busy waits* problems based on the reason code and the class of block.

Contention for Data Blocks (Class #1) with Reason Code 130

If the majority of the *buffer busy waits* wait events are centered on data blocks (class #1) and the reason code is 130, this shows the application runs multiple sessions that query the same data set at the same time. (You will only know this if you query the V$SESSION_WAIT view repeatedly or trace the session with the 10046 event or use the data sampling methods discussed in Chapter 4.) This is an application issue. There are three things you can do to minimize this problem:

- Reduce the level of concurrency or change the way the work is partitioned between the parallel threads.

- Optimize the SQL statement to reduce the number of physical and logical reads.

- Increase the number of FREELISTS and FREELIST GROUPS.

From our experience, it is very difficult to get the application to reduce the level of concurrency. It may not be a good idea because it limits scalability. However, there are differences between scalability and a blind attempt by the application to improve performance by spawning multiple sessions. So far, SQL tuning has worked wonderfully to reduce the occurrences of *buffer busy waits*. Check the SQL execution plan and optimize the SQL statement to use the most effective join method and access paths that reduce the number of physical and logical reads.

The following statistics from the V$SYSTEM_EVENT view are taken from a 29-hour-old Oracle 8.1.7.4 instance that is infested by the *buffer busy waits* wait event, primarily due to reason code 130. The database is a data warehouse, and the application opens multiple concurrent sessions that query the database using parallel query slaves. As you can see, processes wasted about 364 hours (131187473 centiseconds) cumulatively on the *buffer busy waits* wait event. The application may have been better off not using parallel query because slave processes that belong to different sessions compete for the same blocks. The application may also have been better off releasing the queries in stages instead of all at the same time. If you have a similar situation, you can show your statistics to the application group to communicate the problem and your solution.

```
select * from v$system_event where event = 'buffer busy waits';

EVENT                 TOTAL_WAITS  TOTAL_TIMEOUTS  TIME_WAITED  AVERAGE_WAIT
-------------------   -----------  --------------  -----------  ------------
buffer busy waits      174531409             683    131187473     .751655383
```

You may also see secondary *buffer busy waits* contention on data blocks when there are not enough FREELISTS. This is especially true when multiple sessions are concurrently inserting into the same table and the table has only one FREELISTS and FREELIST GROUPS. In this case, multiple sessions are directed to the same data block for record insertions, which creates the *buffer busy waits* contention. When a session spends a lot of time waiting on the *buffer busy waits* event, and the SQL statement that is associated with the event is an INSERT statement, you should check how many FREELISTS that table has. Of course, insufficient FREELISTS primarily cause *buffer busy waits* contention on the segment header—class #4, which we will discuss shortly.

Contention for Data Blocks (Class #1) with Reason Code 220

If the majority of the *buffer busy waits* wait events are centered on data blocks and the reason code is 220, this indicates there are multiple sessions performing DML on the same object at the same time. In addition, if the database block size is large (for example, 16K and above), it can only intensify this symptom as larger blocks generally contain more rows per block. There are three things you can do to minimize this problem:

- Reduce the level of concurrency or change the portioning method.

- Reduce the number of rows in the block.

- Rebuild the object in another tablespace with a smaller block size (Oracle9*i* Database and above).

Again, as mentioned earlier, it may not be practical to limit scalability by reducing the level of concurrency.

If the data blocks belong to tables or indexes, then consider rebuilding the objects to reduce the number of rows per block and spread the data over a larger number of blocks. For example, you can rebuild a table or an index with a higher PCTFREE. In some cases, we have rebuilt indexes with PCTFREE as high as 50 percent. The downside to this is that index range scans and index fast full scans will be slower. You can also alter the table to minimize the number of rows per block with the ALTER TABLE *table_name* MINIMIZE RECORDS_PER_BLOCK command. Starting in Oracle9*i* Database, you can move or rebuild the object in another tablespace with a smaller block size. While these actions can minimize the *buffer busy waits* problem, they will definitely increase full table scans time and disk space utilization. As the saying goes, there is no such thing as a free lunch.

Contention for Data Segment Headers (Class #4)

If the majority of the *buffer busy waits* wait events are centered on data segment headers (that is, the table or index segment header and not the undo segment header), this usually means some tables or indexes in the database have high segment header activities. Processes visit segment headers for two main reasons—to get or modify the process FREELISTS information and to extend the high watermark (HWM). There are three things you can do to minimize this problem:

- Increase the number of process FREELISTS and FREELIST GROUPS of the identified object.

- Make sure the gap between PCTFREE and PCTUSED is not too small.

- Make sure the next extent size is not too small.

The first step is to identify the segment name and type. They can be identified from the P1 and P2 parameters of the *buffer busy waits* wait event. Then you can alter the object to increase the number of process FREELISTS. If time and opportunity permit, you should also increase the number of FREELIST GROUPS by recreating the object. You should create all data segments with a minimum of two FREELIST GROUPS, by default—even in a single-instance database. Contrary to some teachings, FREELIST GROUPS are not exclusively for Oracle Real Application Clusters (RAC) databases. It costs you one Oracle block per FREELIST GROUPS, but the benefits are well worth it. Table 6-6 shows how the FREELIST GROUPS helps minimize *buffer busy waits* contention on the segment header in a single-instance database. The Oracle instance is recycled prior to each test and the same number of sessions are used to perform each load. In fact, everything is the same except for the number of FREELIST and FREELIST GROUPS.

If you do not want to mess with FREELISTS and FREELIST GROUPS, you can rely on the Automatic Segment Space Management (ASSM) feature to scatter the incoming data from the insert statements. The caveat is that this is an Oracle9*i* Database feature. As with any new feature, you should first research the known bugs on the Oracle Metalink site. ASSM is not the silver bullet. There will still be *buffer busy waits* contention. In fact, the "1st level bmb," "2nd level bmb," and "3rd level bmb" classes are related to ASSM.

Next, make sure the gap between the PCTFREE and PCTUSED of the table is not too small in order to minimize block cycling to the FREELISTS. Query the appropriate DBA views (DBA_TABLES or DBA_TAB_PARTITIONS) for the information.

Finally, you should check the next extent size of the identified segment. A high insert rate combined with a small next extent size can cause frequent insertion of new entries into the extent map located in the segment header. Consider altering or rebuilding the object with a larger next extent size. If the object resides in a locally managed tablespace, consider moving the object into a reasonable uniform-size locally managed tablespace.

V$WAITSTAT	Test #1 Freelists = 1 Freelist Groups = 1		Test #2 Freelists = 12 Freelist Groups = 1		Test #3 Freelists = 4 Freelist Groups = 3	
Class	Count	Time	Count	Time	Count	Time
data block	656432	534104	9299	6986	3045	1447
sort block	0	0	0	0	0	0
save undo block	0	0	0	0	0	0
segment header	384272	150444	72337	110850	79	6
save undo header	0	0	0	0	0	0
free list	0	0	0	0	8400	8503
extent map	0	0	0	0	0	0
1st level bmb	0	0	0	0	0	0
2nd level bmb	0	0	0	0	0	0
3rd level bmb	0	0	0	0	0	0
bitmap block	0	0	0	0	0	0
bitmap index block	0	0	0	0	0	0
file header block	1	0	0	0	0	0
Unused	0	0	0	0	0	0
system undo header	0	0	0	0	0	0
system undo block	0	0	0	0	0	0
undo header	2388	36	166	18	155	51
undo block	0	0	0	0	0	0

TABLE 6-6. *FREELIST GROUPS' Effects On Segment Header Contention*

Contention for Undo Segment Headers (Class #17)

If the majority of the *buffer busy waits* wait events are centered on undo segment headers, this indicates there are either too few rollback segments in the database or their extent sizes are too small, causing frequent updates to the segment headers.

If you use the system-managed undo introduced in Oracle9*i* Database, you shouldn't have to deal with this problem as Oracle will create additional undo segments according to demand. However, if you are still using the old rollback segments, then the following applies.

You can create additional private rollback segments and bring them online to reduce the number of transactions per rollback segment. Don't forget to modify the ROLLBACK_SEGMENTS parameter in the INIT.ORA file accordingly. If you use public rollback segments, you can lower the value of the initialization parameter TRANSACTIONS_PER_ROLLBACK_SEGMENT, which influences the number of public rollback segments that will come online at startup. Don't let this parameter confuse you; it does not limit the number of concurrent transactions that can use a rollback segment. Oracle determines the minimum number of public rollback segments acquired at startup by TRANSACTIONS / TRANSACTIONS_PER_ROLLBACK_SEGMENT. So, a smaller divisor allows Oracle to bring up more public rollback segments.

Contention for Undo Blocks (Class #18)

If the majority of the *buffer busy waits* wait events are centered on undo blocks, this usually means there are multiple concurrent sessions querying data that is being updated at the same time. Essentially the query sessions are fighting for the read consistent images of the data blocks. This is an application issue and there is nothing amiss in the database. The problem should go away when the application can run the query and DML at different times.

System-Level Diagnosis

Oracle maintains a number of instance-level statistics on *buffer busy waits*. These statistics can give you a rough idea of what you are dealing with, but the information may not be specific enough for you to formulate a corrective action. They are mentioned here for the sake of completeness.

The view X$KCBWAIT (kernel cache buffer wait) is the base view for the V$WAITSTAT view, which keeps track of *buffer busy waits* contentions by block class. The class with the highest count deserves your attention, but unless you are also monitoring the *buffer busy waits* symptom at a lower level, you don't have a clear direction to proceed. Let's say the data block class has the highest count of all. Which segment was affected most, and why were the sessions unable to pin the buffers? Did they fail to get the pins while attempting to read or change the blocks? Unfortunately, Oracle does not keep track of *buffer busy waits* by block class and reason code. We hope someday Oracle will provide a matrix of *buffer busy waits* by SQL statement, segment name, and block class. Oracle Database 10*g* keeps a history of the V$WAITSTAT view. The data can be seen through the DBA_HIST_WAITSTAT view. You can export the data into Microsoft Excel or some other charting tool for trending analysis. You should order the data based on SNAP_ID and CLASS as follows:

```
select *
from   dba_hist_waitstat
order by snap_id, class;
```

The view X$KCBFWAIT (*kernel cache buffer file* wait) keeps track of *buffer busy waits* contentions by database file. You can discover which data file has the most waits using the following query. Unless you have only one segment per data file, it is hard to pinpoint which segment in the data file suffered the most waits.

```
select b.file_id, b.file_name, a.count
from   x$kcbfwait a, dba_data_files b
where  a.indx   = b.file_id - 1
and    a.count  > 0
order by a.count;

    FILE_ID FILE_NAME                                           COUNT
---------- -------------------------------------------- ----------
        26 /dev/vgEMCp105/rPOM1P_slice2k_174               3643362
        27 /dev/vgEMCp105/rPOM1P_slice2k_175               3814756
        25 /dev/vgEMCp105/rPOM1P_slice2k_173               4296088
        24 /dev/vgEMCp105/rPOM1P_slice2k_172               5191989
. . .
```

The view X$KCBWDS keeps track of *buffer busy waits* by *cache buffers lru chain* latch that protects the LRU and LRUW working sets, as discussed in the "What Does the Latch Free Wait Event Tell You?" section earlier in this chapter.

```
select set_id, dbwr_num, blk_size, bbwait
from   x$kcbwds
where  bbwait > 0;

    SET_ID   DBWR_NUM   BLK_SIZE     BBWAIT
---------- ---------- ---------- ----------
        17          0       8192    9045337
        18          1       8192    9019887
        19          2       8192    9034296
        20          3       8192    9052245
        21          0       8192    9029914
        22          1       8192    9036767
        23          2       8192    9045665
        24          3       8192    9031014
```

The view X$KSOLSFTS is the base view for the V$SEGMENT_STATISTICS view, which keeps track of *buffer busy waits* by segments. This only tells you which segment has experienced the most *buffer busy waits*. There is an interesting column in the X$KSOLSFTS view that is not exposed in the V$SEGMENT_STATISTICS view. The column is FTS_STMP, which records the last time the value (FTS_STAVAL) was updated for the particular segment. In other words, you can know the last time a *buffer busy waits* occurred on a particular segment.

```
select *
from    v$segment_statistics
where   statistic_name = 'buffer busy waits'
order by value;
```

The V$SYSTEM_EVENT view keeps track of the instance-wide total waits and time waited on the *buffer busy waits* wait event. Always query this view in the order of TIME_WAITED to see where the *buffer busy waits* is in relation to other wait events. If it is not in the top-five list of non-idle events, you shouldn't have to worry about it.

You might think that the numbers in the preceding views would agree with each other—the TOTAL_WAITS of the *buffer busy waits* wait event in the V$SYSTEM_EVENT view should equal the SUM(COUNT) in the V$WAITSTAT view, and the SUM(COUNT) in the X$KCBFWAIT view, and the SUM(VALUE) in the V$SEGMENT_STATISTICS view. However, they do not as we prove in the following listing. Don't be surprised if you see a large discrepancy between them. This happens for three main reasons. One, the underlying memory structures are not protected by latches, and so in a busy system, simultaneous updates to the memory structures can corrupt the count. Two, the *buffer busy waits* are called from various places within the Oracle kernel, and in some places the code always adds a constant high number (for example, 100) instead of adding the actual number of waits that occurred. And three, there are no consistent reads done for these memory structures.

```
select  a.value A, b.value B, c.value C, d.value D
from    (select sum(bbwait) AS value from x$kcbwds) a,
        (select sum(count)  AS value from v$waitstat) b,
        (select sum(value) AS value
         from   v$segment_statistics
         where  statistic_name = 'buffer busy waits') c,
        (select total_waits AS value
         from   v$system_event
         where  event = 'buffer busy waits') d;
```

A	B	C	D
72749463	72668122	65914197	72751265

In a Nutshell

Congratulations! You have just read the longest chapter in this book. We discussed three wait events: *latch free, enqueue,* and *buffer busy waits.* They are the in-memory latency.

A latch is a simple locking device used to protect critical SGA memory structures. Every process that reads or modifies data in the SGA must perform the operation under the protection of latches.

An enqueue is a sophisticated locking device used to protect database resources. A resource may be shared if the lock mode is compatible. If not, the requesting process puts its lock request in a queue and it is serviced in order.

A *buffer busy waits* wait is a wait for a buffer lock or pin. A buffer must be pinned before it can be read or modified so that the integrity of its content can be preserved. A buffer can be pinned by only one process at any one time.

CHAPTER
7

Interpreting Common
Latency-Related
Wait Events

here are hundreds of wait events in an Oracle Database, but the nice thing about OWI is that you need to know only a handful of common wait events to cover most of your tuning needs. So far, you have been exposed to 10 common I/O- and lock-related wait events. This chapter covers another 6 common latency-related wait events. It equips you to diagnose and correct problems related to: *log file sync, log buffer space, free buffer waits, write complete waits, log file switch completion,* and *log file switch (checkpoint incomplete).* Oracle Real Application Clusters (RAC) related events are covered in Chapter 8.

log file sync

The *log file sync* wait event has one parameter: buffer#. In Oracle Database 10*g*, this wait event falls under the Commit wait class. Keep the following key thoughts in mind when dealing with the *log file sync* wait event.

- The *log file sync* wait event is related to transaction terminations (commits or rollbacks).

- When a process spends a lot of time on the *log file sync* event, it is usually indicative of too many commits or short transactions.

Common Causes, Diagnosis, and Actions

Oracle records both the transactions and the block changes in the log buffer in SGA, a method known as physiological logging. The LGWR process is responsible for making room in the log buffer by writing the content to log files at various schedules, including:

- At every three seconds

- When the log buffer is 1/3 full or has 1MB worth of redo entries

- When a user commits or rolls back a transaction

- When signaled by the DBWR process (write ahead logging)

Writes that are initiated by user commits and rollbacks are known as sync writes; the rest are known as background writes. A *log file sync* wait is related only to the sync write. In other words, a user process may be processing a large transaction and generating a lot of redo entries that trigger the LGWR to perform background writes, but the user session never has to wait for the background writes to complete. However, as soon as the user session commits or rolls back its transaction and the _WAIT_ FOR_SYNC parameter is TRUE, the process posts the LGWR and waits on the *log file sync* event for the LGWR to flush the current redo entries, including the commit marker, to log files. During this log synchronization, the LGWR process waits for the sync write to complete on the *log file parallel write* event while the user session waits for the synchronization process to complete on the *log file sync* event.

Once a process enters the *log file sync* wait, there are two possible exits. One is when the foreground process is posted by the LGWR when the log synchronization is complete. The other is when the wait has timed out (typically at 1 second), at which point the foreground process checks the current log SCN (System Change Number) to determine if its commit has made it to disk. If it has, the process continues processing, otherwise the process re-enters the wait.

NOTE
You must never set the parameter _WAIT_FOR_SYNC to FALSE, not even in a development or test database, because committed transactions are not guaranteed to be recoverable upon instance failure. People use this feature to cheat on benchmarks.

Typically, a *log file sync* wait is a very uneventful event. It is brief and hardly noticeable by the end user. However, a multitude of them can contribute to longer response time and chalk up noticeable wait statistics in both the V$SYSTEM_EVENT and V$SESSION_EVENT views. Use the following query to find the current sessions that spend the bulk of their processing time waiting on the *log file sync* event since logon. Evaluate the TIME_WAITED with the USER_COMMITS and HOURS_ CONNECTED. To discover who performs a lot of commits between two specific points of time, you can compute the delta using the example shown in the "How To Use V$SYSTEM_EVENT View" section in Chapter 2.

```
select  a.sid,
        a.event,
        a.time_waited,
        a.time_waited / c.sum_time_waited * 100 pct_wait_time,
        d.value user_commits,
        round((sysdate - b.logon_time) * 24) hours_connected
from    v$session_event a, v$session b, v$sesstat d,
        (select sid, sum(time_waited) sum_time_waited
         from    v$session_event
         where   event not in (
                     'Null event',
                     'client message',
                     'KXFX: Execution Message Dequeue - Slave',
                     'PX Deq: Execution Msg',
                     'KXFQ: kxfqdeq - normal deqeue',
                     'PX Deq: Table Q Normal',
                     'Wait for credit - send blocked',
                     'PX Deq Credit: send blkd',
```

```
                        'Wait for credit - need buffer to send',
                        'PX Deq Credit: need buffer',
                        'Wait for credit - free buffer',
                        'PX Deq Credit: free buffer',
                        'parallel query dequeue wait',
                        'PX Deque wait',
                        'Parallel Query Idle Wait - Slaves',
                        'PX Idle Wait',
                        'slave wait',
                        'dispatcher timer',
                        'virtual circuit status',
                        'pipe get',
                        'rdbms ipc message',
                        'rdbms ipc reply',
                        'pmon timer',
                        'smon timer',
                        'PL/SQL lock timer',
                        'SQL*Net message from client',
                        'WMON goes to sleep')
           having sum(time_waited) > 0 group by sid) c
where   a.sid        = b.sid
and     a.sid        = c.sid
and     a.sid        = d.sid
and     d.statistic# = (select statistic#
                          from   v$statname
                          where name = 'user commits')
and     a.time_waited > 10000
and     a.event        = 'log file sync'
order by pct_wait_time, hours_connected;


 SID EVENT            TIME_WAITED PCT_WAIT_TIME USER_COMMITS HOURS_CONNECTED
 ---- --------------- ----------- ------------- ------------ ---------------
  423 log file sync         13441    84.9352291        62852              15
  288 log file sync         13823    85.3535042        63007              15
  422 log file sync         13580    85.7648099        62863              15
  406 log file sync         13460    87.0239866        62865              15
  260 log file sync         13808    87.0398386        62903              15
```

NOTE
In a RAC environment, the LMS background process may register waits on the log file sync *event. This is due to the write ahead logging mechanism. When a foreground process requests a block from another instance, all the redo entries associated with the block must be flushed to disk prior to transferring the block. In this case, the LMS background process initiates the log synchronization and waits on the* log file sync *event.*

The following sections discuss the three main causes of high *log file sync* waits.

High Commit Frequency

High commit frequency is the number one cause for foreground *log file sync* waits. Find out if the session that spends a lot of time on the *log file sync* event belongs to a batch or OLTP process or if it is a middle-tier (Tuxedo, Weblogic, etc.) persistent connection.

If the session belongs to a batch process, it may be committing each database change inside a loop. Discover the module name and ask the developer to review the code to see if the number of commits can be reduced. This is an application issue, and the solution is simply to eliminate unnecessary commits and reduce the overall commit frequency.

Some application developers have learned that if they commit infrequently, jobs may fail due to rollback segments running out of space, and they get calls in the middle of the night. Those who have been bitten by deadlocks may have been told to commit more frequently. Naturally, they become commit-happy people. The right thing to do is to properly define what a transaction is and commit at the end of each transaction. A transaction is a unit of work. A unit of work should either succeed or fail in its entirety. The proper place for a commit or rollback is at the end of each unit of work. Do not introduce additional commits for the sake of rollback segments space or deadlocks. That is treating the symptom and not the problem. If none of the existing rollback segments can handle the unit of work, then you as the DBA should provide one that will. (If you are using the Automatic Undo Management (introduced in Oracle9*i* Database), then allocate enough space to the undo tablespace and set an appropriate undo retention time.)

Introducing additional commits can create other problems, among them, the infamous *ORA-01555: snapshot too old* error because the rollback (or undo) data can be overwritten. A high commit frequency also increases the overhead that is associated with starting and ending transactions. At the beginning of each transaction, Oracle assigns a rollback segment (called a rollback segment binding) and updates the transaction table in the rollback segment header. The transaction table must also be updated at the end of each transaction, followed by a commit cleanout activity. Updates to the rollback segment headers must also be recorded in the log buffer because the blocks are dirtied. Therefore, make the necessary adjustments in the application so that it only commits at the end of a unit of work. The commit statement that is inside a loop may need to be moved out of the loop so that the job commits only once instead of once in every loop iteration.

If the session that spends a lot of time on the *log file sync* event is a persistent connection from a middle-tier layer, then this is a tough case because it services many front-end users. You have to trace the session with event 10046 and observe the application behavior over time. Look for the *log file sync* event in the trace file. It may give you an idea of the commit frequency. Alternatively, you can mine the redo log files with Oracle Log Miner. This will show you the systemwide commit behavior.

In OLTP databases, you normally notice a high *log file sync* wait time at the system level (V$SYSTEM_EVENT) but not at the session level. The high system-level wait time may be driven by many short transactions from OLTP sessions that actively log in and out of the database. If this is your scenario, then about the only thing you can do in the database is to ensure a smooth I/O path for the LGWR process. This includes using asynchronous I/O and putting your log files on raw devices or an equivalent, such as the Veritas Quick I/O, that is serviced by dedicated I/O controllers—or better yet, using solid state disks for the log files. (James Morle has an excellent article and benchmark numbers on solid state disks for redo logs at http://www.oaktable.net/fullArticle.jsp?id=5) However, you only need to do this if the *log file parallel write* average wait time is bad. Otherwise, there isn't much benefit. The real solution has to come from the application.

Slow I/O Subsystem

Query the V$SYSTEM_EVENT view as follows to discover the LGWR average wait time (*log file parallel write* event). An average wait time of 10ms (1 centisecond) or less is generally acceptable.

```
select *
from   v$system_event
where  event in ('log file sync','log file parallel write');

EVENT                   TOTAL_WAITS TOTAL_TIMEOUTS TIME_WAITED AVERAGE_WAIT
----------------------- ----------- -------------- ----------- ------------
log file parallel write     6411138              0     3936931  .614076783
log file sync               6597655           9819     6534755   .99046631
```

A higher system I/O throughput can improve the average wait time of the *log file sync* and *log file parallel write* events. However, this is not an excuse for not fixing the application if it is poorly designed and is committing too frequently. You may be tempted to mess with the database layout and I/O subsystem, perhaps because it is difficult to deal with the application group or it is a third-party application. However, just because it is a third-party application does not give the vendor the right to throw junk code at your database, right? Remember, you cannot solve an application problem from the database. Any change you make in the database may give your users the impression that it is a database problem. Besides, the problem won't go away because the root cause is in the application.

That said, there are many things that you and your system administrator can do to provide some relief to the *log file sync* wait by increasing the I/O throughput to the log files. This includes using fiber channel (FC) connection to databases on SAN (storage area network); gigabit Ethernet (Gig-E) or Infiniband connection to databases on NAS (network attached storage); ultrawide SCSI or FC connection to databases on DAS (direct attached storage); private networks; high-speed switches; dedicated I/O controllers; asynchronous I/O; placing your log files on raw device and binding the LUN in RAID 0 or 0+1 instead of RAID 5, and so on. The questions you have to ask are which business unit is paying for the new hardware and how much faster the commits will be. Let's take the preceding listing, for example. The *log file parallel write* average wait baseline is 6.1ms, and the *log file sync* average wait baseline is 9.9ms. What numbers can you expect to get with the new hardware—25 percent improvement, 50 percent improvement? How does a 50 percent improvement in the average *log file sync* wait translate to the session response time? Will the users be happy? You must weigh the hardware cost with the potential benefits.

In practice, you often have to compromise because of company policies and because you don't make hardware decisions. Your log files may be on RAID 5 LUNs that are shared with other systems. This is especially true in SAN environments. The storage companies are not helping either by rolling out large capacity disk drives. Most likely, your management makes storage decisions based on cost per MB instead of performance. As a result, you end up with fewer disks. Furthermore, you may be required to manage disk utilization into the 90 percentiles. Believe us, we feel your pain!

Oversized Log Buffer

Depending on the application, an oversized log buffer (that is, greater than 1MB) can prolong the *log file sync* waits. A large log buffer reduces the number of background writes and allows the LGWR process to become lazy and causes more redo entries to pile up in the log buffer. When a process commits, the sync write time will be longer because the LGWR process needs to write out many more redo entries. Your log buffer size should not be so small that it causes sessions to start waiting on the *log buffer space* event or so large that it prolongs the *log file sync* waits. On one hand, you want a larger log buffer to cope with the log buffer space demands during redo generation bursts, especially immediately after a log switch. On the other hand, you want a smaller log buffer to increase background writes and reduce the *log file sync* wait time. How can you satisfy these competing requirements? The answer is the _LOG_IO_SIZE parameter, which defaults to 1/3 of the LOG_ BUFFER or 1MB, whichever is less. It is one of the thresholds that signal the LGWR process to start writing. A proper _LOG_IO_SIZE setting will let you have your cake and eat it too. In other words, you can have a large log buffer, but a smaller _LOG_ IO_SIZE will increase background writes, which in turn reduces the *log file sync* wait time. However, as mentioned in Chapter 5, this method is not overhead free. A more active LGWR will put a heavier load on the *redo copy* and *redo writing* latches. You may refer back to the *log file parallel write* wait event section in Chapter 5.

By default, the _LOG_IO_SIZE parameter is reduced to 1/6 of the LOG_BUFFER size in Oracle Database 10*g*. This is because the default value of the _LOG_ PARALLELISM_MAX parameter is 2 when the COMPATIBLE is set to 10.0 or higher. The default value of the _LOG_IO_SIZE in Oracle Database 10*g* is discovered by dividing the LOG_BUFFER size with the log block size (LEBSZ) and the value of *kcrfswth*, as shown next:

```
orcl> oradebug setospid 14883
Oracle pid: 5, Unix process pid: 14883, image: oracle@aoxn1000 (LGWR)
orcl> oradebug unlimit
Statement processed.
orcl> oradebug call kcrfw_dump_interesting_data
Function returned 90F42748
orcl> oradebug tracefile_name
/orahome/admin/orcl/bdump/orcl_lgwr_14883.trc
orcl> !grep kcrfswth /orahome/admin/orcl/bdump/orcl_lgwr_14883.trc
   kcrfswth = 1706

orcl> select value from v$parameter where name = 'log_buffer';
VALUE
---------------
5242880

orcl> select max(LEBSZ) from x$kccle;
MAX(LEBSZ)
----------
       512

orcl> select 5242880/512/1706 from dual;
5242880/512/1706
----------------
      6.00234467
```

NOTE
A larger PROCESSES parameter value also increases the waits for log file sync. *During every sync operation, the LGWR has to scan the processes' data structure to find out which sessions are waiting on this event and write their redo to disk. Lowering the number of PROCESSES can help to reduce the overall* log file sync *wait. Use the V$RESOURCE_ LIMIT view for guidance. According to Oracle, this problem is fixed in Oracle9i Database Release 2.*

log buffer space

The *log buffer space* wait event has no wait parameters. In Oracle Database 10g, this wait event falls under the Configuration wait class. Keep the following key thoughts in mind when dealing with the *log buffer space* wait event.

- Sessions wait on the *log buffer space* event when they are unable to copy redo entries into the log buffer due to insufficient space.

- The LGWR process is responsible for writing out the redo entries and making room for new ones.

Common Causes, Diagnosis, and Actions

In addition to the *log buffer space* wait event statistics, Oracle also maintains a session- and system-level *redo buffer allocation retries* statistic in the V$SESSTAT and V$SYSSTAT view, respectively. The *redo buffer allocation retries* statistic keeps track of the number of times a process has to wait for space in the log buffer. However, the *log buffer space* wait event is a better indicator because it contains the TIME_WAITED statistic.

If a session spends a lot of time on the *log buffer space* wait event, it is normally due to one or both of the following reasons:

- The log buffer in the SGA is too small.

- The LGWR process is too slow.

Undersized Log Buffer

A small log buffer (less than 512K) in a busy batch processing database is bound to cause sessions to contend for space in the log buffer. As mentioned in the preceding section, you can operate a database with a large log buffer if you set the _LOG_IO_SIZE accordingly. Therefore, check the current LOG_BUFFER setting and make the proper adjustment if necessary. The log buffer is not a dynamic component in the SGA, so you must bounce the instance before the new value is effective.

Slow I/O Subsystem

A slow I/O subsystem can cause the LGWR process to be unable to cope with the rate of redo generation, and this in turn causes processes to wait on the *log buffer space* event. New redo entries cannot override entries that have not been written to disks. Make sure the average wait time of the *log file parallel write* wait event is acceptable. Otherwise, you can improve the I/O throughput using the method discussed in the *log file sync* section.

So far we have focused on the database. You should also take a look at the application to see if it can be changed to reduce the logging activity. If the log buffer is the place of contention, then perhaps the best thing to do is not to go there, or go there less frequently. Where appropriate, use NOLOGGING operations, bearing in mind that objects created with NOLOGGING are unrecoverable unless a backup is immediately taken. If you intend to use NOLOGGING operations, check to see if the FORCE LOGGING option is turned on as it overrides the NOLOGGING specification. The FORCE LOGGING option can be enabled at object, tablespace, and database levels. Also, look out for bad application behavior that fetches and updates the entire row when only a few columns are actually changed. This can be hard to catch. You may discover this behavior by mining the DMLs from the V$SQL view or redo log files using Oracle Log Miner.

free buffer waits

The *free buffer waits* event has three parameters: file#, block#, and set ID. In Oracle Database 10*g*, this wait event falls under the Configuration wait class. Keep the following key thoughts in mind when dealing with the *free buffer waits* event.

- Before a block is read into the buffer cache, an Oracle process must find and get a free buffer for the block. Sessions wait on the *free buffer waits* event when they are unable to find a free buffer on the LRU list or when all buffer gets are suspended.

- The DBWR process is responsible for making clean buffers on the LRU lists.

Common Causes, Diagnosis, and Actions

A foreground process needing a free buffer scans the LRU list up to a predetermined threshold, usually a percentage of the LRU list. In Oracle9*i* Database, the threshold is 40 percent. This value is described in the X$KVIT (kernel performance information transitory instance parameters) view as "Max percentage of LRU list foreground can scan for free." If a free buffer is not found when the threshold is met, the foreground process posts the DBWR process to make available clean buffers. While the DBWR process is at work, the Oracle session waits on the *free buffer waits* event.

Oracle keeps a count of every free buffer request. The statistic name in the V$SYSSTAT view is *free buffer requested*. Oracle also keeps a count of every free buffer request that fails. This is given by the TOTAL_WAITS statistic of the *free buffer waits* event. Free buffer requests are technically buffer gets, if you will, and free buffer requests that fail can be considered as buffer misses. Yet another V$SYSSTAT statistic *free buffer inspected* tells you how many buffers Oracle processes have to look at to get the requested free buffers. If the *free buffer inspected* value is significantly higher than the *free buffer requested*, that means processes are scanning further up the LRU list to get a usable buffer. The following queries list the systemwide *free buffer requested*, *free buffer inspected*, and *free buffer waits* statistics:

```
select *
from   v$sysstat
where  name in ('free buffer requested', 'free buffer inspected');
```

```
STATISTIC# NAME                          CLASS          VALUE
---------- ------------------------- ----- --------------
        75 free buffer requested         8  3,311,443,932
        79 free buffer inspected         8    108,685,547

select *
from   v$system_event
where event = 'free buffer waits';

EVENT                  TOTAL_WAITS TOTAL_TIMEOUTS TIME_WAITED AVERAGE_WAIT
-------------------- ----------- -------------- ----------- ------------
free buffer waits          30369          15795     2187602   72.0340479
```

If a session spends a lot of time on the *free buffer waits* event, it is usually due to one or a combination of the following five reasons:

- Inefficient SQL statements

- Not enough DBWR processes

- Slow I/O subsystem

- Delayed block cleanouts.

- Small buffer cache

Inefficient SQL Statements
Poorly written SQL statements are by far the main culprits. Look for statements that perform a lot of physical reads (DISK_READS) in the V$SQL view. The statements may be performing full table scans, index fast full scans, or accessing tables via unselective indexes. Tune the statements to lower the physical read demands. Use the most effective join method and access path. Also, if appropriate for the application, make more use of direct reads and writes, such as direct loads, direct inserts, and parallel queries. Direct read and write operations bypass the SGA.

Insufficient DBWR Processes
As the LGWR process is responsible for making room in the log buffer, the DBWR process is responsible for making free buffers on LRU lists. There is a relationship between the DBWR process and the buffer cache working set. Remember, a working set is comprised of the LRU and LRUW lists. (We discussed the buffer cache working set in the "*cache buffers lru chain* Latches" section in Chapter 6.) If there is only one DBWR process, it has to service all the working sets. When there are multiple DBWR processes, Oracle divides them among the working sets. Naturally, a higher number of DBWR processes can service the working sets more efficiently and yield a higher

throughput. The following snapshot from the X$KCBWDS (kernel cache buffer working set descriptors) view shows eight working sets and two DBWR processes:

```
select set_id, dbwr_num
from   x$kcbwds
order by set_id;

    SET_ID    DBWR_NUM
---------- ----------
         1          0
         2          0
         3          0
         4          0
         5          1
         6          1
         7          1
         8          1
```

Some of you are using asynchronous I/O and may have been told to use only one DBWR process. You should know that is only the general guideline, and you can still use multiple DBWR processes with asynchronous I/O to combat the *free buffer waits* symptom. Depending on your CPU_COUNT, you can increase the number of DBWR processes with the DB_WRITER_PROCESSES parameter. However, this is not an excuse for not optimizing SQL statements with high buffer gets, if they exist.

NOTE
Quite often DBAs think they need more DBWR processes when the real problem is that they oversized the buffer cache. Just because the database is a few terabytes in size does not mean that it needs a gigabyte-size SGA. Rarely is there a need for a gigabyte-size buffer cache. Instead of increasing the number of DBWR processes, try reducing the buffer cache size.

In addition to using multiple DBWR processes, you can also reduce the number of *free buffer waits* occurrences by increasing the number of DBWR checkpoints. In Oracle9i Database, this can be achieved by shortening the mean time to recovery (MTTR) through the FAST_START_MTTR_TARGET parameter. A shorter MTTR causes the DBWR process to be more aggressive and consequently a better supply of clean buffers. However, a more aggressive DBWR process increases the chances of processes waiting on the *write complete waits* event if they need to modify the blocks that are in transit to disk. You have to find a balance based on the application behavior. We will show you how to handle the *write complete waits* event in the next section.

Slow I/O Subsystem

The DBWR performance is vastly influenced by the quality and speed of the I/O subsystem. If the average wait time of the *db file parallel write* wait event is high, it can negatively impact foreground processes causing them to wait on the *free buffer waits* event. We showed you how to handle the *db file parallel write* wait event in Chapter 5.

Delayed Block Cleanouts

After you have loaded a table, you should perform a full table scan operation on the table before turning it over to the application. This is because the first process that reads the data blocks may be penalized to perform delayed block cleanouts, which can cause *free buffer waits*. So, when you bear the penalty before turning the table over to the application, you spare the application from the misleading one-time *free buffer waits* attack. You can see this behavior in Oracle9*i* Database with the following simple test:

1. Set the buffer cache to about 20,000 blocks.

2. Set the FAST_START_MTTR_TARGET to a low number, say 5 seconds. This will cause the DBWR process to aggressively write out dirty buffers so that delayed block cleanouts must be performed when the blocks are queried at a later time.

3. Insert a large amount of rows (say, about 1.5 million) into a table with no indexes and commit the transaction.

4. Shutdown and restart the database.

5. Count the number of rows in the table. The Oracle process will perform a full table scan operation on the table. Query the V$SESSION_EVENT for this particular session. You should see many *free buffer waits* events due to delayed block cleanouts.

6. Repeat steps 4 and 5. However, this time you should not see *free buffer waits* events because the old ITLs have been cleaned out.

NOTE
Delayed block cleanout and commit cleanout—a transaction may affect and dirty many data blocks in the buffer cache. The DBWR process writes both committed and uncommitted blocks to the data files at various intervals. When a transaction commits, the Oracle process performs commit cleanouts to blocks that have not been written out by the DBWR process. Blocks that have been written out will be cleaned by the next process that reads them. This is known as delayed block cleanout. For more information see Metalink note #40689.1.

Small Buffer Cache

Lastly, processes may experience *free buffer waits* contention if the buffer cache is simply too small to handle the free buffer demands. We purposely make this our last point because nowadays it is uncommon to find an undersized buffer cache. DBAs tend to oversize the buffer cache because database servers are equipped with a "boatload" of memory. Many DBAs are still under the impression that they need to allocate 50 percent of the available memory for SGA. Before you entertain the idea of increasing the buffer cache size, you should first increase the number of DBWR processes and see if that will reduce the number of *free buffer waits* events. Then you may increase the buffer cache size.

write complete waits

The *write complete waits* event has two parameters: file# and block#. In Oracle Database 10g, this wait event falls under the Configuration wait class. Keep the following key thought in mind when dealing with the *write complete waits* event.

- The Oracle session is prevented from modifying a block that is being written by the DBWR process.

Common Causes, Diagnosis, and Actions

The *write complete waits* latency is symptomatic of foreground processes needing to modify blocks that are marked by the DBWR process as "being written." Blocks that are marked "being written" cannot be modified until they are written to disk and the flags are cleared. If a session spends a lot of time waiting on the *write complete waits* event, it is usually due to one or a combination of the following reasons:

- Slow I/O subsystem causing high DBWR write time

- MTTR is too short

- DBWR write batch size is too large

When the effectiveness of the DBWR process is impacted by the I/O subsystem, it can have a domino effect on foreground processes in terms of *write complete waits* and *free buffer waits* latencies. We have touched on the *write complete waits* event in the "*db file parallel write*" section of Chapter 5 and provided some examples. You may refer to the section again. The *write complete waits* latency is usually a secondary problem. You should focus on the average wait time of the *db file parallel write* event. Any improvement to the DBWR average write time should also minimize the *write complete waits* latency.

We have also mentioned how a short MTTR can produce a hyperactive DBWR process in the "*free buffer waits*" section earlier in this chapter. While an active DBWR process is beneficial for supplying clean buffers, it tends to write hot buffers out repeatedly. Sessions that actively perform DML operations can find themselves waiting on the *write complete waits* event. Therefore, make sure the FAST_START_MTTR_TARGET parameter is not set too low. One way to find out is to trace the DBWR process with the event 10046 at level 8 and observe the write calls (*db file parallel write*) over a period of time. If you continually see DBWR writing out before its 3-second timeout, chances are it is overly active.

Beginning in Oracle8*i* Database, the default DBWR write batch size is 204 blocks. (We provided a query output example in Chapter 5.) This is changed from 4096 blocks in prior versions. This means starting in Oracle8*i* Database, the DBWR write batch size should no longer be a factor that contributes to the *write complete waits* contention.

log file switch completion

The *log file switch completion* wait event has no wait parameters. In Oracle Database 10g, this wait event falls under the Configuration wait class. Keep the following key thought in mind when dealing with the *log file switch completion* wait event.

■ Excessive log switches caused by small log files and transactions that generate a lot of redo entries

Common Causes, Diagnosis, and Actions

If a session spends much of its processing time waiting on the *log file switch completion* event, this is because the redo log files are too small for the amount of redo entries that are being generated, causing too many log switches. The Oracle session constantly has to wait for the LGWR process to complete the write to the current log file and open a new one.

The *log file switch completion* latency can be minimized or eliminated by reducing the number of log switches. This means you need to create new log groups with larger log files and drop the old log groups. Larger log files will reduce the number of log switches and expensive conventional checkpoints.

How large should the log files be? The answer depends on the current log file size, the current rate of switching, and your goal for the number of switches per hour during peek processing time. You can find out how frequently the logs are switching using the query provided in the "*log buffer space*" section earlier in this chapter. For example, let's say the logs are switching at the rate of 60 logs per hour during peak processing time; your target is no more than 4 per hour, and the current log file size is 20M. Based on these numbers, your new log file size should be 300M (60 * 20M / 4).

NOTE
Larger log files may result in longer instance recovery time. Oracle provides the FAST_START_MTTR_ TARGET parameter to maintain the DBA-specified crash recovery time by regulating checkpoints starting in Oracle9i Database. In Oracle8i Database, you can use the FAST_START_IO_TARGET parameter. In prior versions, you can tune checkpoints with the LOG_ CHECKPOINT_INTERVAL and LOG_CHECKPOINT_ TIMEOUT parameters.

log file switch (checkpoint incomplete)

The *log file switch (checkpoint incomplete)* wait event has no wait parameters. In Oracle Database 10g, this wait event falls under the Configuration wait class. Keep the following key thought in mind when dealing with the *log file switch (checkpoint incomplete)* wait event.

■ Excessive log switches caused by small log files and a high transaction rate

Common Causes, Diagnosis, and Actions

The *log file switch (checkpoint incomplete)* and the *log file switch completion* are closely related and share the same root cause—that is, the log files are too small for the amount of redo entries that are generated. When you see one, you normally see both in the database. However, in this case, the foreground processes are waiting on the DBWR process instead of the LGWR process. This happens when the application produces enough redo entries to cycle through or round-robin the redo logs faster than the DBWR process can write out the dirty blocks to complete a checkpoint. The LGWR process cannot overwrite or wrap into the first log because the checkpoint is incomplete, so foreground processes wait on the *log file switch (checkpoint incomplete)* event. The solution is the same as for the *log file switch completion* event. You need to replace the current log files with larger ones, and you may also add more log groups.

In a Nutshell

In this chapter, we equipped you to deal with wait events that are related to user comments, log buffer, DBWR process, and log files. They are the *log file sync, log buffer space, free buffer waits, write complete waits, log file switch completion,* and *log file switch (checkpoint incomplete)* wait events.

The *log file sync* wait event is related to transaction terminations such as commits or rollbacks.

The *log buffer space* wait event is related to the log buffer. Sessions wait on the *log buffer space* event when they are unable to copy redo entries into the log buffer due to insufficient space.

The *free buffer waits* event is related to the LRU list and DBWR process. Sessions wait on the *free buffer waits* event when they are unable to find a free buffer on the LRU list or when all buffer gets are suspended.

The *write complete waits* event has to do with blocks that are presently being written out by the DBWR process.

The *log file switch completion* and *log file switch (checkpoint incomplete)* is due to high log file switch frequency.

CHAPTER
8

Wait Events in a Real Application Clusters Environment

n recent years, you may have heard Oracle say that you can use Real Application Clusters (RAC) to reap benefits of high availability, fault tolerance, and excellent return on your investment in hardware and that use of RAC is on the rise. As a DBA you may already be supporting a RAC environment. This chapter will introduce you to Oracle wait events in a RAC environment and show you how to identify and resolve bottlenecks with wait events specific to a RAC environment. We will focus on the global cache waits because those affect the entire cluster.

What's So Special About Waits in Real Application Clusters (RAC)?

Before we begin discussing wait events in a RAC environment, you need to understand how the buffer cache works in a RAC environment.

In a single database instance environment, there will be only one set of shared memory segments for the database. All I/O operations, SQL processing, and library cache operations are routed through one set of shared memory structures. In other words, the buffer cache and shared pool are local to that particular instance; at any point in time the processes attached to that particular instance will be accessing only one set of memory structures.

However, in the RAC environment, the scenario is entirely different. Multiple instances share the same database. These instances typically run on different servers or nodes. The buffer cache is split among these multiple instances; each instance has its own buffer cache and other well-known SGA structures. It is possible for a buffer (also known as a block) to be in the buffer cache of one of the instances on another node. Processes, which are local to that particular machine, will be accessing these buffer caches for reading. Other than the local foreground processes, the remote machine's background processes access the local buffer cache. The remote instance's Lock Manager Service (LMS) processes will be accessing the global buffer cache, and the DBWR process will be accessing the local buffer cache.

Because the buffer cache is global and spread across multiple instances, the management operations associated with the buffer cache and shared pool are also different from typical single-instance Oracle environments, as are the wait events.

NOTE
Real Application Clusters requires a shared disk system for storage of datafiles. This is usually achieved by using Raw devices or Cluster file system. Both allow the datafiles access by more than one node simultaneously.

NOTE
The terms block *and* buffer *are used in a similar context throughout our discussions for ease of understanding. The* block *is stored on the disk and can be loaded to a* buffer *in any of the buffer caches. A* block *can be loaded to any one of the* buffers *in the buffer cache. Oracle always accesses blocks in the buffer cache. If it is already loaded in any instance's buffer cache and can be transferred without more work from the holding node, it will be transferred to the other instance's buffer cache. Otherwise, the* block *is read into* buffer *from the disk.*

Global Buffer Cache in Real Application Clusters

In general, the data buffer cache is shared by more than one instance, and the buffer cache is called the global cache. Each instance has its own buffer cache local to that particular instance, and all of the buffer caches together create the global cache.

Because the cache is global, the consistent read (CR) processing differs from the single-instance environment. In a single-instance environment, when a process needs to modify or read a block, it reads the block from disk into memory, pins the buffer, and may modify the buffer. In the RAC environment, when a process needs a block, it also reads it from disk and modifies it in the buffer. Because the buffer cache is global, there is a good chance that the buffer may already have been read by another process and be in one of the buffer caches. In this case, reading the block from disk may lead to data corruption. The following section explains how Oracle avoids data corruption.

Parallel Cache Management

In Oracle Parallel Server, the global buffer management operation was called Parallel Cache Management (PCM) and buffer locks, known as PCM locks, were used to protect the buffers in the cache. In simple terms, a PCM lock is a data structure that usually covers the set of blocks. The number of PCM locks for a file was configured using the GC_FILES_TO_LOCKS init.ora parameter. Detailed discussion of PCM locks is beyond the scope of this chapter. Here, we will discuss the cache management in RAC environments and related wait events.

Lock Mastering and Resource Affinity

In normal cluster environments, the resources are split between various nodes, which are typically different servers participating in the cluster. Each node, called a master node, owns a subset of total resources; the control of those resources is handled from the respective nodes. This process is known as *resource mastering* or *lock mastering*. If one node wants to acquire a resource that is mastered by another node, the requesting node makes a request to the master node or the holding node to grant access to the requesting node. In this way, a resource is handled by only one node at a time, avoiding data corruption in clustered environments.

In Oracle's RAC implementation, if one node (the requesting node) wants to acquire a resource that is mastered by another node (mastering node), the requesting node makes a request to the Global Cache Service on the mastering node, and the global cache service grants access to the requesting node. The requestor does not make the request to the holding node unless it is also the master node.

In the RAC environment, the Global Resource Directory (GRD) that is maintained by the Global Enqueue Services (GES) and Global Cache Services (GCS) handles the "lock mastering" operations. They dynamically remaster the resources based on resource affinity, which enhances the performance because the ownership of those resources are localized. For example, if any instance uses a resource more frequently than other instances, that resource will dynamically be remastered to that instance. This helps the resource to be controlled from that particular instance and increases the performance of the clusters by reducing the lock management operations. This new feature is called *dynamic remastering*. The initialization parameter _LM_DYNAMIC_ REMASTERING controls the behavior of dynamic remastering; setting this parameter to FALSE disables the dynamic remastering.

A buffer can be read into the following modes in the buffer cache; the states are visible in V$BH view. The following is the list of possible state of buffers in the buffer cache:

```
FREE - not currently in use
XCUR - exclusive current
SCUR - shared current
CR - consistent read
READ - being read from disk
```

```
MREC - in media recovery mode
IREC - in instance recovery mode
WRI- Write Clone Mode
PI- Past Image
```

CR (Consistent Read) Processing

In a buffer cache a buffer can be in any of the preceding states. We will focus on the XCUR, SCUR, and CR states for this discussion. Any SELECT operation on the buffer cache will require the buffer in SCUR mode during the execution of the statement. DML commands require buffers in XCUR mode (called *current mode buffer*), and the process that makes the changes (in this case the DML operator) owns the buffers exclusively. During that time, if any other process requires access to those blocks, it will clone the buffer within the buffer cache and use that cloned copy, called a CR copy, for processing. The process of cloning increments the statistic *consistent gets* reported in V$SYSSTAT.

> **NOTE**
> *Buffer cloning is a process of making a copy of the buffer from/to the point where the buffer contents are deemed consistent using the undo vectors and called as Pre Image or Past Image abbreviated as PI.*

During the buffer cloning, there's a chance that a buffer will be cloned infinitely because of the high volatility of the buffer contents. This can cause the buffer cache to be flooded by the same buffer clones, which can restrict the buffer cache usage for the rest of the buffers. To avoid flooding the buffer cache with cloned buffers, Oracle limits the number of cloned buffers (or CR copies) to six per DBA (Data Block Address—not to be confused with database administrator). Once the limit is reached, Oracle waits for the buffer; the normal wait time is 10cs before it attempts to clone/reread the buffer. The number of cloned copies per DBA is controlled by the initialization parameter _DB_BLOCK_MAX_CR_DBA, which defaults to six otherwise. Having more CR copies will not harm the buffer cache much in management operations because the CR copies are not subject to the normal MFU (Most Frequently Used) algorithm. The CR copies are always kept at the *cold* end of the buffer cache unless the parameter _DB_AGING_FREEZE_CR is modified from default value TRUE to FALSE, or unless a *recycle* cache is configured. Note that the CR buffers in the *cold* end of the buffer cache can be flushed out anytime.

The New Buffer Cache Management

The Oracle Database buffer cache algorithm is no longer LRU/MRU (least recently used/most recently used) based. Instead, the new algorithm is based on how frequently the buffer is accessed. The most frequent buffers are always kept in the *hot* end of the buffer cache, and the newly accessed buffers (a.k.a. MRU buffers) are now placed in the middle of the buffer cache (in earlier Oracle versions they were kept in the *hot* end). This is called mid-point insertion. In this new MFU algorithm, the buffer is *heated* based on the frequency of the usage and slowly moved to the *hot* end; the buffer's *temperature* is reduced if it is not accessed (touched) for a certain period of time. Each buffer structure has a counter called a *touch count*, and a buffer is moved to the *hot* or *cold* region based on this counter. The touch count is halved if that buffer is not accessed for the default of three seconds (or the time specified in the initialization parameter _DB_AGING_TOUCH_TIME). The CR buffers are placed at the *cold* end of the buffer cache.

Having discussed the buffer cache basics and CR processing in a single database instance, we will now discuss CR handling in the RAC environments. As you saw earlier, the RAC environment will have two or more buffer caches managed by different instances. We will review how the buffer transfer occurred in the pre-RAC days and then review how it is changed in the RAC environment.

Pings and False Pings
In OPS (Oracle Parallel Server), whenever a process (belonging to one instance) wants to read a resource/buffer (we'll call it a resource for simplicity), it acquires a lock on the resource and reads it into its own buffer cache. The Distributed Lock Manager (DLM) structures keep track of the resources and owners in their own lock structures. In this scenario, if the resource is acquired and used by the other instance, Oracle sends a request to the other instance to release the lock on that resource. For example, instance A wants a block that was used in instance B's cache. To perform the transfer, instance B would write the block to disk and instance A would read it. The writing of a block to disk upon request of another instance is called a *ping*.

There is another type of disk write that happens if the block is written to disk by one instance because another instance requires the same lock that covers different blocks. This is called a *false ping*. Once the holder downgrades the lock and writes the buffer to the disk, the requester can acquire the lock and read the block into its own buffer cache. For example, instance A wants a block that shares the same PCM lock as a block in the cache of instance B. Having additional PCM locks configured will greatly reduce the *false pings*, but it would be too resource-intensive to cover every block by a lock unless it was a very small database. A single READ request can require multiple write operations as well the read, and the disk will be used as a data transfer media. True *pings* and *false pings* put a heavy load on the I/O subsystem, and affect the scalability of the system if the application is not partitioned correctly based on the workload characteristics. This is one of the strong reasons for workload partitioning in Oracle Parallel Server environments.

In addition, it puts a huge administrative overhead on allocating PCM locks for each database file based on the frequency/concurrency the administrator uses to configure the fixed, releasable, and hash locks. Improper configuration of lock objects causes the excessive *false pings*, and the systems supposedly designed for scalability never scales to the required level.

The DLM keeps track of the ownership of the blocks (attributes), such as which instance holds which blocks in shared and exclusive mode. At any point of time, only one instance can hold a block in an exclusive mode, and more than one instances can hold that block in a shared mode. During lock downgrade (or ping), the holder writes the changes to the redo log, flushes the redo to the disk, and downgrades the lock from exclusive mode to null /shared mode. The requestor can acquire the lock in required mode and read the block into its own buffer cache.

Cache Fusion

Starting from Oracle8*i* Database, the CR server processing was simplified and the new background process, Block Server Process (BSP), was introduced to handle the CR processing. In this case, when a requestor pings the holder for the CR copy, the CR copy is constructed from the holder's undo information, and is shipped to requestor's buffer cache via the interconnect (high speed and dedicated). The disk is not used as a data transfer medium. The interconnect is used to *fuse* the buffer across the caches; this data transfer method is called *Cache Fusion*. The BSP handles the cache transfer between instances.

Starting Oracle9*i* Database, the Global Cache Service (GCS) handles the Cache Fusion traffic. The current buffer (XCUR) can also be transferred through a network connection, which is usually a dedicated fast interconnect. The internals of the current mode transfer are very complex and beyond the scope of the discussion, but one interesting thing to note is that Oracle limits the number of CR copies per DBA that can be created and shipped to the other instance through the network.

There is a fairness counter kept in every CR buffer, and the holder increments the counter after it makes a CR copy and sends it to the requestor. Once the holder reaches the threshold defined by the parameter _FAIRNESS_THRESHOLD, it stops making more CR copies, flushes the redo to the disk, and downgrades the locks.

From here onward, the requestor has to read the block from the disk after acquiring the lock for the buffer from the lockmaster. The _FAIRNESS_THRESHOLD parameter value defaults to 4, which means up to 4 consistent version buffers are shipped to the other instance cache, and thereafter the CR server stops responding to the CR request for that particular DBA. The view V$CR_BLOCK_SERVER has the details about the requests and FAIRNESS_DOWN_CONVERTS details.

```
V$CR_BLOCK_SERVER
Name                      Type      Notes
----------------------    ------    -----------------------------
CR_REQUESTS               NUMBER    CR+CUR =Total Requests
CURRENT_REQUESTS          NUMBER
```

```
DATA_REQUESTS               NUMBER
UNDO_REQUESTS               NUMBER
TX_REQUESTS                 NUMBER   DATA+UNDO+TX= CR+CUR
CURRENT_RESULTS             NUMBER
PRIVATE_RESULTS             NUMBER
ZERO_RESULTS                NUMBER
DISK_READ_RESULTS           NUMBER
FAIL_RESULTS                NUMBER
FAIRNESS_DOWN_CONVERTS      NUMBER   # of downconverts from X
FAIRNESS_CLEARS             NUMBER   # of time Fairness counter cleared
FREE_GC_ELEMENTS            NUMBER
FLUSHES                     NUMBER   Log Flushes
FLUSHES_QUEUED              NUMBER
FLUSH_QUEUE_FULL            NUMBER
FLUSH_MAX_TIME              NUMBER
LIGHT_WORKS                 NUMBER   # of times light work rule evoked
ERRORS                      NUMBER
```

The column CR_REQUESTS contains the number of requests received for a particular block at a specific version or a specific SCN. Any request that involves SCN verification is called *consistent get*. The total number of requests handled by the LMS process will be equal to the sum of CR_REQUESTS and CURRENT_REQUESTS. The total number of requests will be split into DATA_REQUESTS, UNDO_REQUESTS, and TX_REQUESTS (undo header block) requests.

```
select cr_requests cr,
       current_requests cur,
       data_requests data,
       undo_requests undo,
       tx_requests tx
from   v$cr_block_server;


      CR        CUR        DATA       UNDO         TX
--------  ---------- ---------- ---------- ----------
   74300        3381      74300       3381          0
```

Light Work Rule

In some cases, constructing CR copy may be too much work for the holder. This may include reading data and undo blocks from disk or from some other instance's cache which is too CPU intensive. In this case the holder simply sends the incomplete CR copy to the requester's cache and the requester will create a CR copy either by block clean out which may include reading several undo blocks and data blocks. This operation is known as the *light work rule*, and the LIGHT_WORKS column indicates the number of times the light work rule is applied for constructing the CR blocks.

The number of times light work rule is applied will be visible in the view V$CR_BLOCK_SERVER:

```
select cr_requests,light_works
from   v$cr_block_server;

CR_REQUESTS LIGHT_WORKS
----------- -----------
  23975         133
```

_fairness_threshold

Reducing the _FAIRNESS_THRESHOLD to lower values from the default value will provide some performance improvement if the data request to down convert (downgrade) ratio is greater than 30 percent. Setting the threshold to a lower value will greatly reduce the interconnect traffic for the CR messages. Setting _FAIRNESS_THRESHOLD to 0 disables the fairness down converts and is usually advised for systems that mainly perform SELECT operations.

In Oracle8*i* Database, the holder will down convert the lock and write the buffer to the disk, and the requester will *always* have to read the block from the disk. From Oracle9*i* Database, the holder down converts the lock to shared mode from exclusive, and the shared mode buffer will be transferred to the requestor's cache through the interconnect.

```
select data_requests,fairness_down_converts
from   v$cr_block_server;

DATA_REQUESTS FAIRNESS_DOWN_CONVERTS
------------- ----------------------
        74304                   6651
```

Global Cache Waits

The most common wait events in the RAC environment related to the global cache are: *global cache cr request, global cache busy,* and *enqueue.* We will discuss these wait events in detail and explain how to investigate the problem if excessive wait times are observed with these wait events.

global cache cr request

When a process requires one or more blocks, Oracle first checks whether it has those (blocks) in its local cache. The simple hashing algorithm based on the DBA (Data Block Address) is used to traverse the *cache buffers chains,* and a suitable lock is found if it is in the hash bucket. When a session requests a block(s) that was not found in its local cache, it will request that the resource master grant shared access to those blocks. If the blocks are in the remote cache, then the blocks are transferred using the interconnect to the local cache. The time waited to get the blocks from the remote cache is accounted in the g*lobal cache cr request* wait event.

NOTE
This event is known as gc cr request *in Oracle Database 10*g. *The '*global cache*' is changed to just '*gc*'.*

The time it takes to get the buffer from remote instance to local instance depends on whether the buffer is in shared or exclusive mode. If the buffer is in shared mode, the remote instance will clone buffer in its buffer cache and ship it to the local cache. Based on the fairness value on that buffer, the lock downgrade may also happen if the number of CR blocks exceeds the _FAIRNESS_THRESHOLD counter value. If the buffer is in exclusive mode (XCUR), the PI has to be built and shipped across the buffer cache. The statistics are incremented according to whether the CUR block or the CR block is shipped.

Typically, *global cache cr request* waits are followed by the *db file sequential/scattered read* waits. During the sequential scan a few blocks may be in the remote buffer cache and the rest of the blocks may be on the disks.

Normally, the requesting process will wait up to 100cs and then retry reading the same block either from the disk, or it will wait for the buffer from the remote cache, depending on the status of the lock. Excessive waits for *global cache cr request* may be an indication of a slow interconnect. The private interconnect (the high speed interconnect) should be used for cache transfer between instances, and the public networks should be used for client server traffic. In some cases, the RAC may not pick the interconnect, and the Cache Fusion traffic may be routed through the public network. In this case you will see a huge number of waits for g*lobal cache cr request*. You can use the *oradebug ipc* command to verify if the private network is used for cache transfer between instances.

Finding the Interconnect Used for Cache Transfer
The following procedure can be used to find the interconnect used for Cache Fusion:

```
SQL> oradebug setmypid
Statement processed.
SQL> oradebug ipc
Information written to trace file.
SQL> oradebug tracefile_name
/oracle/app/oracle/product/9.2.0/admin/V920/udump/v9201_ora_16418.trc
SQL>
```

The trace file will contain the details of the IPC information along with the interconnect details:

```
SKGXPCTX: 0xad95d70 ctx
admono 0xbcfc2b9 admport:
SSKGXPT 0xad95e58 flags          info for network 0
        socket no 8    IP 192.168.0.5   UDP 38206
sflags SSKGXPT_UP
        info for network 1
        socket no 0     IP 0.0.0.0      UDP 0
        sflags SSKGXPT_DOWN
        active 0        actcnt 1
context timestamp 0
```

From the preceding trace file, you know the private network 192.168.0.5 is used for the Cache Fusion traffic and that the protocol used is UDP.

> **NOTE**
> *For some reason, if the right interconnect is not used by the Oracle kernel, the CLUSTER_INTERCONNECTS parameter can be used to specify the interconnect for cache fusion. However, this limits the failover capability during interconnect failures.*

Most of the hardware/OS vendors use proprietary high-speed protocols for the private network. The following table gives the short description of the network protocols used in different hardware/OS platforms. Other than the listed cluster servers, Veritas Cluster uses its own protocol (Low Latency Protocol) for the Cache Fusion traffic and cluster-wide traffic.

OS/Hardware	Network
Sun	RSM (Remote Shared Memory Firelink)
HP PA RISC/IA	HMP Hyper Fabric
HP-Tru64	RDG (Reliable Data Gram) Memory Channel
AIX	UDP High-performance Switch, FDDI
Linux	Gigabit Ethernet
VMS	TCP/UDP Ethernet

TABLE 8-1. *RAC Network Protocols*

Relinking Oracle Binaries to Use the Right Interconnect Protocol

By default, TCP is used for inter-instance communication. To change the communication protocol to use the high speed interconnect, you need to relink the Oracle binaries and bind them to the high speed interconnect card. For example, on a default installation, UDP is used for the cluster interconnect in HP-UX. During instance startup, the interconnect protocol information is written to the alert.log:

```
cluster interconnect IPC version:Oracle UDP/IP
IPC Vendor 1 proto 2 Version 1.0
```

To make use of high speed interconnect you need to shut down all Oracle services and relink the binaries using the following command:

```
$ make -f ins_rdbms.mk rac_on ipc_hms ioracle
```

If you want to revert to UDP you can relink the binaries with the UDP protocol:

```
$ make -f ins_rdbms.mk rac_on ipc_udp ioracle
```

The alert log can be verified to check whether the right interconnect is used. The following is reported in the alert log if the UDP is used as interconnect protocol:

```
cluster interconnect IPC version:Oracle UDP/IP
IPC Vendor 1 proto 2 Version 1.0
```

Global Cache Wait Process

When a session wants a CR buffer, it will submit the request after checking the status of the buffers and the state of the lock element for those CR buffers. It will sleep till this request is complete. This sleep is recorded as a *global cache cr request* wait event. The receipt of the buffers will wake up the session, and the wait time is recorded for this particular wait event.

In general, high waits for *global cache cr request* could be because of:

■ Slower interconnect or insufficient bandwidth between the instances. This could be addressed by relinking binaries with the right protocol or by providing the faster interconnect.

■ Heavy contention for a particular block, which could cause the delays in lock elements down converts.

■ Heavy load on the system (CPU) or scheduling delays for the LMS processes. Normally the number of LMS processes is derived from the number of CPUs in the system with a minimum of two LMS processes. Increasing the number of LMS processes or increasing the priority of them could help in getting more CPU time, thus minimizing the waits. The init.ora parameter _LM_ LMS can be used to set the number of LMS processes.

■ Slow disk subsystem or long running transactions with a large number of uncommitted (means the blocks are in XCUR mode) transactions.

Global Cache Statistics
The statistics related to global cache are available from the V$SYSSTAT view. The following SQL provides the details about the *global cache* statistics:

```
REM -- In Oracle10g global cache waits are known as gc waits
REM -- Replace 'global cache%' with 'gc%' for Oracle10g

select  name,value
from    v$sysstat
where   name like '%global cache%';


NAME                                               VALUE
-------------------------------------------------- ---------
global cache gets                                   115332
global cache get time                                 7638
global cache converts                                55504
global cache convert time                            14151
global cache cr blocks received                      62499
global cache cr block receive time                  143703
global cache current blocks received                126763
global cache current block receive time              20597
global cache cr blocks served                        79348
global cache cr block build time                       266
global cache cr block flush time                    135985
global cache cr block send time                        649
global cache current blocks served                   55756
global cache current block pin time                    811
global cache current block flush time                  159
global cache current block send time                   389
global cache freelist waits                              0
global cache defers                                     72
global cache convert timeouts                            0
global cache blocks lost                               772
global cache claim blocks lost                           0
global cache blocks corrupt                              0
global cache prepare failures                            0
global cache skip prepare failures                    4544
```

The average latency for constructing a CR copy can be obtained from the following formula:

```
Latency for CR block =
(global cache cr block receive time  *10) / global cache cr blocks received
```

Reducing the PI and CR Buffer Copies in the Buffer Cache

In the RAC buffer cache, a new buffer class called PI (past image) is created whenever a dirty buffer is sent to remote cache. This helps the local buffer cache to have a consistent version of the buffer. When the buffer is globally dirty, it is flushed from the global cache. Sometimes, because of the high volatility of the buffer cache, the CR buffers and PI buffers may flood the buffer cache, which may increase the waits for global cache. The V$BH view can be used to monitor the buffer cache. The following SQL shows the buffers distribution inside the buffer cache:

```
select  status,count(*)
from    v$bh
group   by status;

STATU   COUNT(*)
-----   ----------
cr            76
pi             3
scur        1461
xcur        2358
```

Setting FAST_START_MTTR_TARGET enables the incremental checkpointing, which reduces the PI buffers. Having more PI and CR images will shrink the usable buffers to a lower value and may increase the physical reads. Setting this parameter to a nonzero value enables incremental check pointing. The value for this parameter is specified in seconds.

global cache busy

In a cluster environment, each instance might be mastering its own set of data. There is always the chance that the other instance may require some data that is cached in the other instance, and the buffers cached in the other instance may be readily available or locally busy. Depending on the state of that buffer in the remote instance, the pin times may increase proportionally with the time it takes to service the block request.

If the buffer is busy at the cache level, you can use the following SQL to get the operations that are keeping the buffer busy. Based on the operations, you can reduce the contention for those buffers. This process can identify the *buffer busy waits* in single instance database environments also.

```
select wh.kcbwhdes "module",
       sw.why0 "calls",
       sw.why2 "waits",
       sw.other_wait "caused waits"
from   x$kcbwh wh,
       x$kcbsw sw
where wh.indx = sw.indx
  and sw.other_wait > 0
order by sw.other_wait;
MODULE                     CALLS        WAITS  CAUSED_WAITS
--------------------   ----------   ----------  ------------
kdiwh06: kdifbk           113508            0             1
ktewh25: kteinicnt        112436            0             2
kduwh01: kdusru             4502            0             3
kdiwh18: kdifind            1874            0             3
kddwh03: kddlkr           270333            0             4
kdswh01: kdstgr           139727            0            41
```

NOTE
The column OTHER_WAIT is OTHER WAIT (notice the space rather than the underscore) in Oracle8i Database.

The preceding output is from a relatively quiet system, which does not have many waits for the global buffer. Table 8-2 lists the most commonly seen *buffer busy waits* and the operations/functions causing them.

Module	Operation
Kdifbk	Fetches the single index row matching the argument key.
Kdusru	Updates the single row piece.
Kdifind	Finds the appropriate index block to store the key.
Kdstgr	Performs full table scan get row. Rows are accessed by a full table scan. Check the number of FULL table scans
Kdsgrp	Performs get row piece. Typically, row pieces are affected only in case of chained and migrated rows. Row chaining has to be analyzed and fixed.
Kdiixs	Performs index range scan.
Kdifxs	Fetches the next or previous row in the index scan.
Kdifbk	Fetches the single index row matching the agreement key.
Ktugct	Block cleanout.

TABLE 8-2. *Common Operations Causing buffer busy waits*

RAC Wait Event Enhancements in Oracle Database 10g

Starting from Oracle Database 10g, most of the RAC related wait events could be further classified into two types: place holder events and fixup events. For example, when a CR request is initiated, the outcome can be either a lock grant or a buffer. In other words, when a session is looking for a block in the global cache, it may not know whether it will get a buffer cached at remote instance or receive a lock grant to read the block from disk. The wait events tell precisely whether the session is waiting for a lock grant or buffer to arrive from other instance cache. This detailed breakup information is not available in previous versions because the complete wait time is charged to a single wait event. In the preceding example, the *global cache cr request* wait is a placeholder event. The outcome of the wait event (which could be another wait, such as a receiving message to read the block from disk) is called a fixup event. Here is a brief listing of fixup wait events and their categories:

- Block-oriented

  - gc current block 2-way

  - gc current block 3-way

  - gc cr block 2-way

  - gc cr block 3-way

- Message-oriented

  - gc current grant 2-way

  - gc cr grant 2-way

- Contention-oriented

  - gc current block busy

  - gc cr block busy

  - gc current buffer busy

- Load-oriented

  - gc current block congested

  - gc cr block congested

NOTE
The fixup events are for informative purposes; thus there isn't much to do in the way of tuning, nor has there been anything written about them in the Oracle documentation. These events merely provide additional details about the block and message transfers, and knowing them will help you understand the behavior of the resources used in the database.

Enqueue Waits

Waits for *enqueue* are not specific to RAC environments. However, they have a higher impact in performance than in the single instance environments because the enqueues are globally coordinated. Enqueue management is handled at the Global Enqueue Services (GES) layer, which is responsible for enqueue operations. The initial allocation of the GES resources is based on the following initialization parameters:

- DB_FILES

- DML_LOCKS

- ENQUEUE_RESOURCES

- PROCESSES

- TRANSACTIONS

The number of Global Enqueue Resources is approximately calculated as

(DB_FILES + DML_LOCKS + ENQUEUE_RESOURCES + PROCESSES + TRANSACTIONS + 200) * (1 + (N-1) / N), where N is the number of nodes participating in the cluster.

The actual number of GES resources allocated during the instance startup will be printed in the alert log. The same is also visible in the V$RESOURCE_LIMIT view:

```
Global Enqueue Service Resources = 4086, pool = 2
Global Enqueue Service Enqueues = 5947
```

Most Common Enqueues

Because the resources are globally coordinated in the RAC setup, tuning *enqueue* waits becomes a critical component in RAC related waits. However, you need to keep in mind that there will be a small amount of discrepancy between the values of the *enqueue* waits in the V$SYSTEM_EVENT and V$ENQUEUE_STAT. V$SYSTEM_EVENT is incremented at every *enqueue* wait, and the X$KSQST (V$ENQUEUE_STAT) is incremented only once per wait—that is, the *enqueue* wait will be incremented only once, even if it has *n* timeouts during that wait.

The enqueues that protect the dictionary, database-wide space management, or global library cache/shared pool are most commonly seen in RAC environments. These affect the scalability and performance of the application if they are not properly tuned.

CU Enqueue

This enqueue is used to serialize the cursor binding in the library cache. The parsed cursors in the library cache can be shared between processes if they are having the same bind variables. If literals are used instead of the bind variables, the init.ora parameter CURSOR_SHARING can be used to convert the literals to system-defined bind variables. Usage of bind variables is highly recommended for application scalability and performance because it greatly helps reduce the parse time for the SQL statements. The *CU* enqueue is used to protect the cursor from binding more than one process at the same time.

CF Enqueue

A control file is used as a single point of synchronization component in the database. It is updated whenever there is a structural change in the database, such as adding a tablespace or a data file, performing recovery-related operations like checkpoint and log switching, and the performing regular database maintenance operations like startup and shutdown. Few operations such as adding a data file or tablespace will require the *control file transaction CF* enqueue in exclusive mode. During that time the other processes, which requires the enqueue at the same or higher level, will wait 15 minutes and retry the operation. The timeout can be defined by the parameter _CONTROLFILE_ENQUEUE_TIMEOUT, which defaults to 900 seconds.

Contention for *CF* enqueue may affect the database operations in the RAC environment because the enqueue is deadlock sensitive. Table 8-3 shows the common operations, which require the *CF* enqueue and respective modes required.

In general, contention for *CF* enqueue may be an indication of a slower I/O subsystem/device. Excessive waits and timeouts for this enqueue sometimes terminate the instance with ORA-0600 [2103] error, especially when it has waited for the background process for checkpoint. Another reason for contention for this enqueue is the number of data files. With fewer data files, the checkpoint process has a smaller

Operation	Mode Held
Switching logfiles	Exclusive
Updating checkpoint information for datafiles	Exclusive
Opening a log file for redo reading during recovery	Shared
Getting information to perform archiving	Shared
Performing crash recovery	Exclusive
Performing instance recovery	Exclusive
Performing media recovery	Exclusive
Creating a database	Exclusive
Mounting a database	Shared
Closing a database	Shared
Adding a log file or log file member	Exclusive
Dropping a log file or log file member	Exclusive
Checking information about log file group members	Shared
Adding/dropping a new datafiles	Exclusive
Beginning/ending a hot backup	Exclusive
Checking whether datafiles are in hot backup mode after a crash (first shared, then exclusive)	Shared
Executing an ALTER DATABASE BACKUP CONTROLFILE TO TRACE	Shared
Opening the database (control file) exclusive by first instance to open, shared by subsequent instances	Exclusive
Renaming datafiles or log files	Exclusive
Marking a control file as valid and mountable	Exclusive
Handling an error encountered in the control file	Exclusive
Validating data dictionary entries against matching control file records for file entries	Exclusive
Updating control file format after a software upgrade	Exclusive
Scanning for log file info by log sequence #	Shared
Finding the highest-in-use entry of a particular control file record type	Shared

TABLE 8-3. *Operations Requiring CF Enqueue*

Operation	Mode Held
Getting information about the number of log entries and their lowest/highest sequence number and log file numbers	Shared
Looking up a control file record matching a given filename	Shared
Making a backup control file	Exclusive
Dumping the contents of the control file during debugging	Shared
Dumping the contents of the current redo log file during debugging	Shared
Dumping the contents of the redo log header	Shared
Dumping the contents of datafile headers	Shared

TABLE 8-3. *Operations Requiring CF Enqueue*

workload. Having more DB_WRITERS or enabling the asynchronous I/O will help reduce the number of waits for this enqueue.

HW Enqueue

Whenever new data is inserted into the data segment, the segment grows to accommodate the newly inserted values. High watermark defines the boundary between used and unused space in the segment. Free space above high watermark is used only for direct path inserts, bulk loads, and parallel inserts. Space below high watermark is used for the conventional method of inserts.

During heavy volume inserts, or bulk loads, the segment grows rapidly and the high watermark gets moved up. The *HW* enqueue serializes this movement. Other than the normal loads, the ALTER TABLE ALLOCATE EXTENT command also requires the *HW* enqueue to allocate a new extent. In the V$LOCK view column ID1 represents the tablespace number, and column ID2 represents the relative DBA of the segment header of the object for which the space is allocated.

Altering the storage definitions of the segment to larger extent will reduce the number of extents, which in turns reduces the number of *HW* enqueue conversions. Other than that, preallocating extents with a larger size also helps reduce the contention of this enqueue. During space allocation, the high watermark is moved by 5 blocks or multiples of 5 blocks at a time. These 5 blocks are defined by the parameter _BUMP_HIGHWATER_MARK_COUNT, which default to 5. Changing the value from 5 to a higher number will also reduce contention for this enqueue. In addition to changing the underscore parameter _BUMP_HIGHWATER_MARK_COUNT, increasing the number of freelists also helps because it moves the high watermark in the multiples of freelists.

PE Enqueue

PE enqueues are rarely seen in a well-managed RAC environment. This enqueue is used during ALTER SESSION SET *parameter=value* statements and it protects the memory structures during the parameter changes and frequent changes to SPFILE. More sessions connecting and disconnecting to the database (not using connection pooling) will also increase the contention for this enqueue. Well-defined connection management, connection pooling, MTS or Shared Servers will help reducing the contention for this enqueue.

Sequence Enqueues: SQ and SV

Sequences are Oracle's number generators that can be used in the programs or SQL statements. Contention for *SQ* (Sequence) enqueue is inevitable when too many sessions are accessing the sequence generator because the SELECT statement for the next sequence number causes an update in the data dictionary unless the sequence is defined with the CACHE option. Beware of gaps in the sequences because the cached sequences may be lost during instance shutdown or shared pool flushing. However, caching sequences greatly increases the performance because it reduces the number of recursive calls.

When the sequences are cached, each instance will cache the sequence up to cache size, but the order of the sequence number is not guaranteed. In this case, the ORDER option with the CACHE option can be used to get the cached sequences in order. When cached sequence with order is used, all instances cache the same set of sequences, and the *SV* enqueue is used to verify that the *sequence value [SV]* and the order are guaranteed.

The following options can be used for sequences, listed from good to best order:

```
NOCACHE ORDER
NOCACHE NOORDER
CACHE   ORDER
CACHE   NOORDER   --Best Performance
```

TX Enqueue

TX enqueues are used to serialize the database transactions and to get a consistent view throughout the lifecycle of the transaction. The row-level locks are implemented using the *TX* enqueue where the change vectors to reverse the transactions are written in the undo segments. The address of the undo blocks are written in the data blocks. So that the reader (or process) looking for a consistent view can follow the address and get the consistent view of that data during that time.

This enqueue is typically used during transactions and index block splits. Sometimes heavy contention for *TX* enqueue can be an indication of bad application design that unnecessarily lock the rows. The index of the monotonically increasing key increases the contention for the *TX* enqueue. Any waits that are not for ITLs (Interested

Transaction Lists) are also indicators of the *TX* waits. The waits for the transaction slots can be easily identified by querying the V$SEGMENT_STATISTICS:

```
select  owner,
        object_name
from    v$segment_statistics
where   statistic_name = 'itl waits' and value  > 0
```

If more waits are seen for the 'ITL waits' event, the objects should be rebuilt using higher INITRANS. Keep in mind each INITRANS will take 24 bytes of space in the variable header of the data block and adding more INITRANS potentially wastes space in the data blocks at the cost of concurrency. Oracle Database 10*g* has a separate wait event for ITL waits.

In a Nutshell

Real Application Clusters waits are a special case in the Oracle Database environment because of the multiple instances accessing the same set of resources. Everything you learned about wait events in the single instance environment is applicable to the RAC environment as well. In RAC environment you must know about *global cache cr request, global cache busy,* and *enqueue* wait events.

This chapter introduces you to the global cache management and the implementation of global cache in Real Application Clusters. Understanding RAC related wait events helps you diagnose the problems in these environments so you can zero in on the solution.

CHAPTER
9

Performance Management
in Oracle Database 10g

racle Database 10*g* Release 1 revolutionizes the performance diagnostic and tuning as we all know it. All the manual data collection and analysis methods we discussed in previous chapters have now been fully automated and are part of the database. The mechanism and the intelligent architecture called Manageability Infrastructure is employed by Oracle Database 10*g* to collect various statistical data. Not only does it satisfy all the requirements for a fast and accurate root cause analysis discussed in Chapter 4, but it also offers remedial solutions in terms of recommendations, advisories, and server-generated early warning alerts.

In this chapter we discuss the components of the Manageability Infrastructure that make this automatic diagnosis and tuning possible. First, we will discuss the various types of database statistics gathered by Oracle Database 10*g*.

Database Statistics

Oracle Database 10*g* gathers and analyzes performance-related statistical data to diagnose problems. The data is captured using lightweight data capture methods that do not add any measurable load to the system. It reports top problems and offers corrective actions, or advisories, for resolving them. It also reports nonproblematic areas, so you can focus only on problematic areas.

The collected statistical data can be broadly categorized into the following types:

- Time model statistics
- Wait model statistics
- Operating system statistics
- Additional SQL statistics
- Database metrics

Time Model Statistics

Time model statistics are new in Oracle Database 10*g*. As we mentioned in Chapter 2, OWI only reports the wait time for events that a session waited on. Time model statistics provide the breakdown of the time a session spent in various steps, such as hard parsing, soft parsing, SQL execution, PL/SQL execution, Java execution, and so on, while performing the actual task. These statistics are displayed by the V$SESS_TIME_MODEL view. Summarized time model statistics at the system level are displayed by V$SYS_TIME_MODEL as shown in the following example:

```
select stat_name, value
from   v$sys_time_model;
```

```
STAT_NAME                                                     VALUE
--------------------------------------------------  ----------
DB time                                               835243622
DB CPU                                                633280130
background elapsed time                              3737809876
background cpu time                                  1869951797
sequence load elapsed time                              122400
parse time elapsed                                    192685706
hard parse elapsed time                               151503406
sql execute elapsed time                              828428484
connection management call elapsed time                 856270
failed parse elapsed time                               243612
failed parse (out of shared memory) elapsed time             0
hard parse (sharing criteria) elapsed time              861810
hard parse (bind mismatch) elapsed time                 798655
PL/SQL execution elapsed time                          94173710
inbound PL/SQL rpc elapsed time                              0
PL/SQL compilation elapsed time                        94186909
Java execution elapsed time                                  0

17 rows selected.
```

The most important time model statistic is the *DB time*. It shows the total time spent by the sessions in database calls. It is equivalent to the sum of CPU time and wait times of all sessions not waiting on events classified by the *Idle* wait class. However, it is timed separately. The following breakdown of the time model statistics shows which statistics are subsets:

    1. background elapsed time
        2. background cpu time
    1. DB time
        2. DB CPU
        2. connection management call elapsed time
        2. sequence load elapsed time
        2. sql execute elapsed time
        2. parse time elapsed
            3. hard parse elapsed time
                4. hard parse (sharing criteria) elapsed time
                    5. hard parse (bind mismatch) elapsed time
            3. failed parse elapsed time
                4. failed parse (out of shared memory) elapsed time
        2. PL/SQL execution elapsed time
        2. inbound PL/SQL rpc elapsed time
        2. PL/SQL compilation elapsed time
        2. Java execution elapsed time

If the session spends less time in database calls, it is performing better. Your tuning goal should be to reduce the overall *DB time* for the session.

Wait Model Statistics

By now, wait model statistics are nothing new to you. Oracle Database 10*g* Release 1 tracks over 800 wait events to report time spent by the session waiting on those events. These are classified in 12 wait classes. This classification allows easier high-level analysis of the wait events. The classification is based on the solution that normally applies to correcting a problem with the wait event.

Operating System Statistics

Operating systems statistics provide information about system resources utilization such as CPU, memory, and file systems. In Oracle versions prior to Oracle Database 10*g*, some of these statistics were not available from within the database. You had to issue OS commands or use OS level tools to gather machine-level statistics to investigate hardware-related issues. Oracle Database 10*g* captures such statistics within the database and reports them in the view V$OSSTAT, as shown next:

```
select stat_name, value
from   v$osstat;

STAT_NAME                                            VALUE
-------------------------------------------------- ----------
NUM_CPUS                                                  1
IDLE_TICKS                                         22201887
BUSY_TICKS                                          3385285
USER_TICKS                                          2101041
SYS_TICKS                                           1284244
IOWAIT_TICKS                                          78316
AVG_IDLE_TICKS                                     22201887
AVG_BUSY_TICKS                                      3385285
AVG_USER_TICKS                                      2101041
AVG_SYS_TICKS                                       1284244
AVG_IOWAIT_TICKS                                      78316
OS_CPU_WAIT_TIME                                 9.2061E+11
RSRC_MGR_CPU_WAIT_TIME                                    0
IN_BYTES                                         123883520
OUT_BYTES                                                 0
AVG_IN_BYTES                                      123883520
AVG_OUT_BYTES                                             0

17 rows selected.
```

Additional SQL Statistics

Additional SQL statistics provide information at the statement level for wait class time, PL/SQL execution, Java execution, and sampled bind variables. Oracle Database 10*g* also introduces a new hash value, SQL_ID, as a character string for the SQL statement, which is more unique than in earlier versions of Oracle Database.

Database Metrics

As you all know, almost all of the database statistics reported by various V$ views are cumulative since the instance startup. As we discussed in Chapter 2, you have to take snapshots at various intervals to find the rate of change in the statistics values reported by these views. In performance diagnostics, this rate of change, or metric, is more important than the cumulative value of the statistics. In Oracle Database 10*g*, these metrics are readily available for a variety of units, such as time, database calls, and transactions. Most of these metrics are maintained at a one-minute interval and are exposed via various V$ views. Metrics history is exposed via various V$ metric history views. A few of the metric views are listed in Table 9-1.

New Background Processes

In Oracle Database 10*g*, two new background processes are responsible for collecting, sampling, and maintaining the statistical data. These processes are the MMON and MMNL.

V$METRICNAME	Lists the metric ID, metric name with its metric group name, and group ID. There are a total of 10 metric groups for over 180 different metrics.
V$EVENTMETRIC	Displays values of the wait event metrics.
V$WAITCLASSMETRIC	Displays values of the wait event class metrics.
V$SESSMETRIC	Displays values of the metrics for the session-level statistics.
V$SYSMETRIC	Displays values of the metrics for the system-level statistics.
V$FILEMETRIC	Displays values of the file metrics.

TABLE 9-1. *Metric Views (Not a Complete List)*

The MMON (Manageability Monitor) process is responsible for various manageability tasks such as taking snapshots of various statistical information at prescribed time intervals and issuing alerts when metric values exceed defined thresholds. The MMON process can spawn multiple slave processes to perform these tasks.

The MMNL (the Manageability Monitor—Lightweight) process is responsible for computing various metrics and taking snapshots of active sessions at every second. We'll discuss this further in the section "Active Session History."

NOTE
The database instance does not crash when MMON or MMNL process is terminated for whatever reason. The PMON process will restart the failed process. Relevant messages will be written to the alert log file.

So, how does Oracle Database 10g actually collect, report, and maintain the performance statistics data? This is collectively done by the Automatic Workload Repository.

Automatic Workload Repository

The Oracle Database kernel keeps numerous statistics that can be used to identify performance problems. Unfortunately, many database statistics are not stored on the disk. This missing history data imposes a great challenge to performance practitioners to identify and fix the problem that occurred in the past. Historical data and statistics are very important for database performance monitoring and capacity planning.

Oracle Database 10g enhances the data collection mechanism with the introduction of the Automatic Workload Repository and Active Session History, which replace the previous performance data gathering tools such as Statspack and utlbstat/utlestat. The major differences between the current repositories from previous such tools include the following:

- Earlier tools had no automated way of interpreting the collected data and results produced by supplied reports. The raw data and the formatted output from the Statspack tool required manual interpretation.

- There is no proactive monitoring in the earlier tools. The DBA could tune the database or solve the problem only after its occurrence. The Automatic Database Diagnostics Monitor (ADDM) tool in Oracle Database 10g, detects a problem before it strikes and advises possible solutions.

- ADDM works at a fine-grained level to detect problems at the database segment level. For example, if there is a hot block or hot object causing performance problems, ADDM identifies the object and provides tuning advice, while this information would not be directly captured in Statspack report.

- Problems such as excessive logins and logoffs, ITL waits, and RAC-related service issues were not captured in the Statspack report, but ADDM captures this information and offers tuning advice.

The Automatic Workload Repository (AWR) captures all the data that Statspack captured in the earlier versions of the Oracle RDBMS. In addition, it captures the new statistical data described in the preceding sections. AWR is the performance data warehouse of Oracle Database 10*g*. This data resides in the SGA and is also stored on disk.

The captured data is displayed via available views and AWR report, similar to that generated by Statspack. However, accessing this information is much simpler and easier with Oracle Enterprise Manager (EM).

Repository Snapshots

By default, out-of-box, AWR goes to work. Using MMON, the new background process, it takes snapshots of database statistics every 60 minutes. The data is stored in a set of tables under the SYS schema in the new mandatory tablespace, SYSAUX. Like Statspack, a unique identifier called SNAP_ID identifies each snapshot. By default, data older than seven days is purged. Many of these tables are partitioned by range, using the DBID, the unique database identifier, and the SNAP_ID column as their partitioning key. This partitioning strategy is very helpful in data access and maintenance operations.

NOTE
*Even if you do not have Oracle Partitioning option installed, Oracle Database 10*g *will create required partitioned tables and indexes for its internal use. You will still need to license and install Oracle Partitioning for your use.*

In Oracle Database 10*g* Release 1 there are 140 tables that store the AWR data, and they are accessible via 67 views. The table names are in the format WRI$_*, WRH$_* and WRM$_*. "WR" stands for "Workload Repository," "I" stands for "internal," "H" stands for "historical" data, and "M" stands for "metadata." There are several views that are built upon these base tables. The view names are in the format DBA_HIST_*; the asterisk (*) represents what statistics the view or table shows. For example, the view DBA_HIST_LATCH shows *latch*-related statistics for historical snapshots. This view is based on the base table WRH$_LATCH. You can use the following SQL code to list the names of these tables and views:

```
select  table_name
from    dba_tables
where   owner = 'SYS'
and     table_name like 'WR%';

select  view_name
from    dba_views
where   owner = 'SYS'
and     view_name like 'DBA\_HIST\_%' escape '\';
```

Snapshot Baselines

AWR allows creation of snapshot baselines to capture performance statistics during a particular time frame. Generally, you will create a baseline for snapshots taken when a typical workload was processed and the performance was acceptable. When the same workload is processed later and the performance is not acceptable, a new baseline for this time frame can be created to compare against the previous baseline. The difference in the performance statistics can shed light on the cause of slow performance. The baseline snapshots are also called Preserved Snapshot Sets.

Using EM to Manage AWR

Oracle EM is the primary tool to interact with AWR. However, you can also use Oracle-supplied package procedures to manage AWR functionality. The manual procedures are described in the next section.

You can access AWR from the Database Control home page of Oracle Enterprise Manager. From this page, first click the Administration link to access the Administration page and then click the Automatic Workload Repository link under the Workload heading toward the bottom of the page.

The Automatic Workload Repository page is shown in Figure 9-1. On this page you can view, edit, and manage AWR snapshots.

The General information block shows current snapshot settings and the next snapshot time. The Edit button takes you to a new page where you can change the snapshot interval and snapshot retention and also drill down to change the statistics collection level.

Under the Manage Snapshots and Preserved Snapshot Sets heading you see the total number of available snapshots and preserved snapshots that are used in baselines and the date and time of the earliest and latest available snapshot.

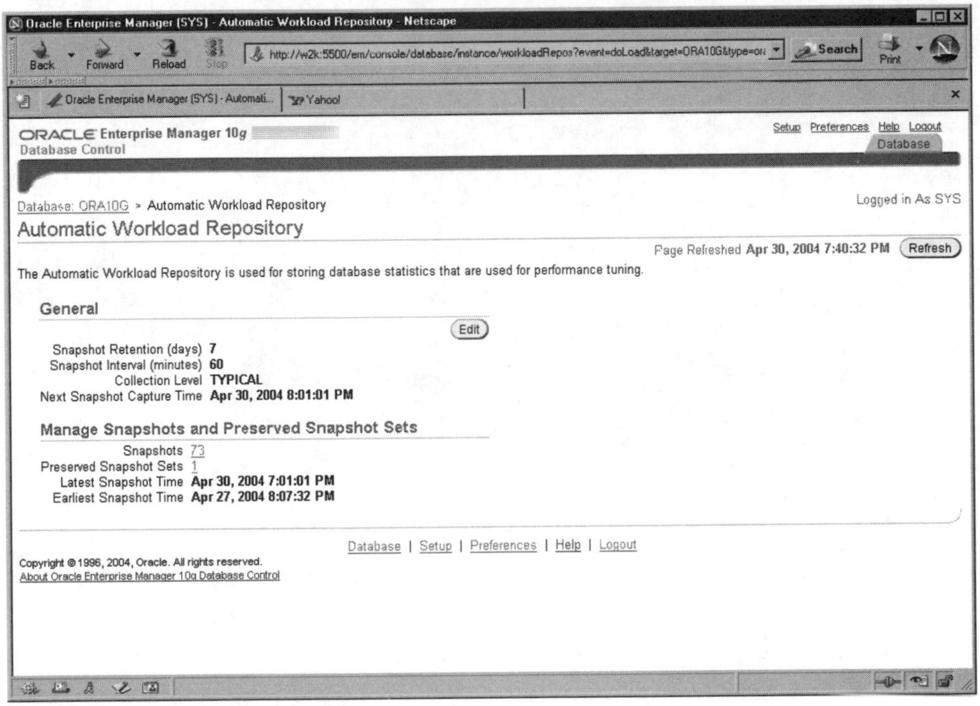

FIGURE 9-1. *Workload Repository home page*

Clicking the number shown after Snapshots takes you to the Snapshots home page, where you can view information about snapshots. Figure 9-2 shows the home page for Snapshots.

Using the pull-down Actions menu you can perform following tasks:

- Create Preserved Snapshot Set (baseline creation)

- View Report (by comparing statistics from two snapshots)

- Create ADDM task (to perform analysis against a set of snapshots)

- Delete Snapshot Range

- Compare Timelines (using two sets of snapshots from two time periods)

- Create SQL Tuning Set (to track and tune SQL statements)

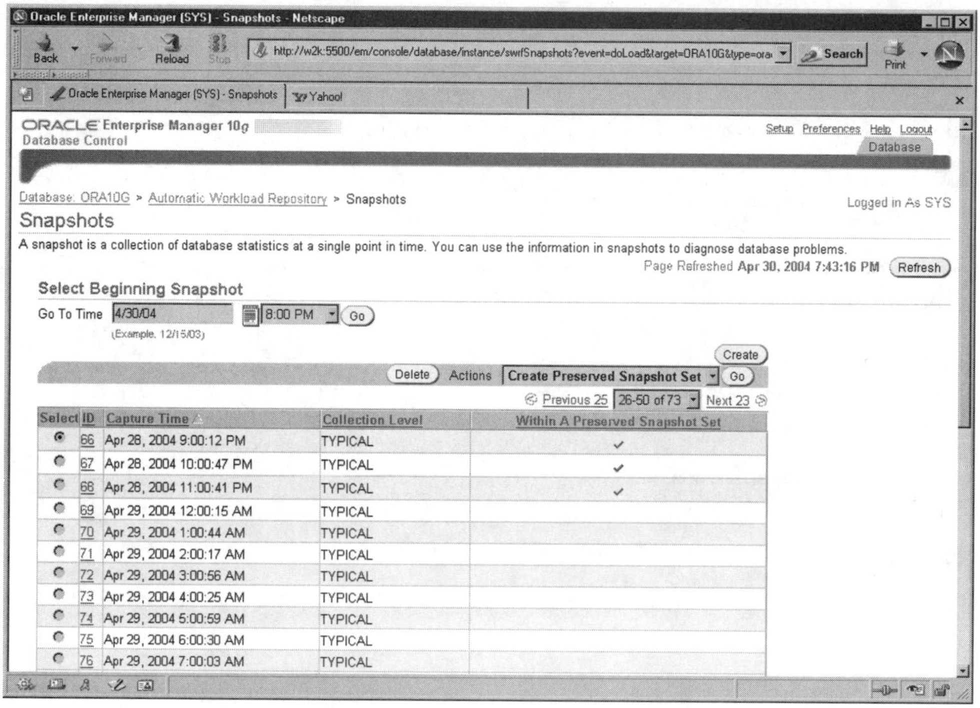

FIGURE 9-2. *Snapshots home page*

You can click the Create button to manually create a new snapshot. The Delete button deletes the specified snapshot. The Go button initiates the selected task from the pull-down Actions menu. We found the Go, Create, and Delete buttons on this page a bit confusing at first, perhaps because of their positions on the page. The column Within a Preserved Snapshot Set shows a checkmark for the snapshot IDs that are part of a baseline or the Preserved Snapshot Set.

Back on the AWR home page (Figure 9-1), clicking the number shown next to Preserved Snapshot Sets takes you to the home page for Preserved Snapshots Sets, as shown in Figure 9-3. This page lists the details of the Preserved Snapshot Sets, or the baselines, established in the AWR. The pull-down Actions menu offers you various tasks that can be performed against these baseline snapshots. Please note that the Preserved Snapshot Set ID is different from the snapshot ID. The former applies to the baselines or the preserved AWR snapshots only.

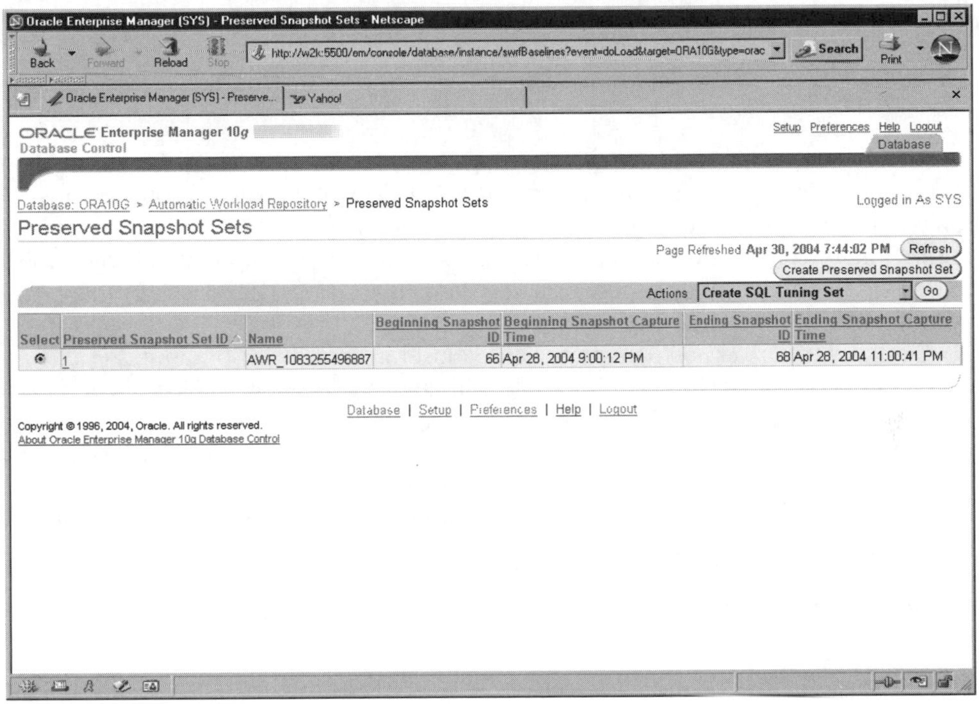

FIGURE 9-3.   *Preserved Snapshot Sets (baselines) home page*

Manually Managing AWR

The Oracle-supplied package DBMS_WORKLOAD_REPOSITORY provides several routines, procedures, and functions to manually interact with the AWR. These routines allow you to create snapshots on demand, drop a range of snapshots, create a baseline snapshot, drop a baseline snapshot, and—as we discussed in the preceding sections— change snapshot intervals and data retention period, and so on.

Modifying Snapshot Settings

The snapshot frequency, or interval, and the data retention can be changed as shown next, where the interval is changed to 30 minutes and data retention to 15 days:

```
begin
    dbms_workload_repository.modify_snapshot_settings (
                            interval => 30,
                            retention => 15 * 1440 );
end;
/
PL/SQL procedure successfully completed.
```

NOTE
Both the values interval *and* retention *must be specified in terms of minutes. That's why the retention time of 15 days is multiplied by 1440 minutes per day.*

The value specified for *interval* must range from 10 minutes to 52560000 minutes (100 years). Oracle will generate an error (ORA-13511) if the value is outside this range. However, the value zero has a special meaning: when the interval is set to zero, Oracle will disable the mechanism of taking automatic and manual snapshots. In this case, Oracle simply generates a very large number (40150 days) for this parameter.

Similarly, the *retention* parameter value must range from 1400 minutes (1 day) to 52560000 minutes (100 years). Oracle will generate an error (ORA-13510) if the value is outside this range. The value zero has a special meaning here, also. When the retention is set to zero, Oracle will retain the snapshot forever. In this case, Oracle uses a larger number (40150 days) for this parameter.

You can see the current values of these parameters as shown next. The column data is displayed in the days and hours format (+DDDDD HH:MI:SS.S):

```
col snap_interval for a20
col retention for a20
select snap_interval,
       retention
from   dba_hist_wr_control;

SNAP_INTERVAL        RETENTION
-------------------- --------------------
+00000 00:30:00.0    +00015 00:00:00.0
```

NOTE
The AWR tables reside in the SYSAUX tablespace. AWR purges snapshot data daily once the retention time has been reached. If AWR detects that the SYSAUX tablespace is running short on available space, it will perform an "emergency purge," effectively reducing the retention and will write relevant messages to both the trace file and the alert log. However, the space layer code will initiate a server-generated alert because of low space, probably long before an emergency purge is required.

Creating and Dropping Snapshots

You may need to create manual snapshots when the automatic snapshot interval is too large for diagnosing performance issues with a particularly smaller workload or job. In this case, you may want to take manual snapshots before running the job and take another one after it completes.

You can use the CREATE_SNAPSHOT routine to create snapshots on demand. This routine can be executed as a procedure or as a function. When it is executed as a function, it returns the SNAP_ID of the snapshot just created. The optional parameter *flush_level* controls the level of the statistics that is captured in, or flushed to, the repository tables for this snapshot. The default is TYPICAL. But if all of the detailed statistics are required, you must set the *flush_level* to ALL.

The following examples show the use of CREATE_SNAPSHOT as a procedure and a function:

```
REM - As a Procedure
begin
    dbms_workload_repository.create_snapshot();
end;
/
PL/SQL procedure successfully completed.

REM - As a Function
select dbms_workload_repository.create_snapshot('ALL') from dual;

DBMS_WORKLOAD_REPOSITORY.CREATE_SNAPSHOT('ALL')
-------------------------------------------------
                                            1931
```

On the other hand, the DROP_SNAPSHOT_RANGE procedure can be used to permanently drop a range of snapshots. You must know the beginning and ending SNAP_ID for this range, though. The procedure has two required parameters, *low_snap_id* and *high_snap_id*. The optional parameter, *dbid*, defaults to the local database ID. In the following example, the SNAP_ID range from 1981 to 2004 is dropped:

```
begin
    dbms_workload_repository.drop_snapshot_range (
                            low_snap_id => 1981,
                            high_snap_id => 2004 );
end;
/
PL/SQL procedure successfully completed.
```

As shown next, the DBA_HIST_SNAPSHOT view will list the information on available snapshots. In this example, we selected only the columns needed for the procedure just discussed:

```
col snap_id for 999999
col begin_interval_time for a26
col end_interval_time for a26
select snap_id, dbid, begin_interval_time, end_interval_time
from   dba_hist_snapshot
order by 1 desc;


SNAP_ID       DBID BEGIN_INTERVAL_TIME         END_INTERVAL_TIME
------- ---------- --------------------------  -------------------------
   2397 2847681843 29-MAR-04 06.00.47.194 PM   29-MAR-04 06.30.33.990 PM
   2396 2847681843 29-MAR-04 05.30.58.107 PM   29-MAR-04 06.00.47.194 PM
   2395 2847681843 29-MAR-04 05.00.07.715 PM   29-MAR-04 05.30.58.107 PM
   2394 2847681843 29-MAR-04 04.30.21.575 PM   29-MAR-04 05.00.07.715 PM
   2393 2847681843 29-MAR-04 04.00.32.191 PM   29-MAR-04 04.30.21.575 PM
   2392 2847681843 29-MAR-04 03.30.43.423 PM   29-MAR-04 04.00.32.191 PM
   2391 2847681843 29-MAR-04 03.00.57.354 PM   29-MAR-04 03.30.43.423 PM
   2390 2847681843 29-MAR-04 02.30.06.223 PM   29-MAR-04 03.00.57.354 PM
   2389 2847681843 29-MAR-04 02.00.17.503 PM   29-MAR-04 02.30.06.223 PM
```

Creating and Dropping Baseline (Preserved Snapshot Set)

The baseline, or the Preserved Snapshot Set, can be created using the CRATE_ BASELINE routine in the DBMS_WORKLOAD_REPOSITORY package. The routine can be executed as a function or a procedure. The required parameters are the *start_ snap_id*, *end_snap_id*, and *baseline_name*. The optional parameter, *dbid*, defaults to the local database ID. When executed as a function, this routine returns the baseline ID or the Preserved Snapshot Set ID. The following examples show the use of CREATE_BASELINE routine as a function and a procedure:

```
REM - As a Procedure
begin
   dbms_workload_repository.create_baseline(
                          start_snap_id => 2305,
                          end_snap_id => 2310,
                          baseline_name => 'Good Nightly Batch');
end;
/
PL/SQL procedure successfully completed.

REM - As a Function
REM - Using 2200 for start_snap_id, 2205 for the end_snap_id and
```

```
REM - 'Good Special Batch' for the baseline_name.

select dbms_workload_repository.create_baseline(
                                2200, 2205, 'Good Special Batch')
from dual;

DBMS_WORKLOAD_REPOSITORY.CREATE_BASELINE(2200,2205,'GOODSPECIALBATCH')
----------------------------------------------------------------------
                                                                     3
```

Oracle assigns a unique baseline ID to the newly created baseline. The snapshots that fall in the range of the start and end snap IDs used for the baseline will be preserved as long as the as baseline exists in the AWR. Those snapshots can only be purged when the baseline is dropped.

Oracle generates an error (ORA-13506) when the supplied snapshots IDs are not valid. Also, the supplied baseline name must be unique, or an error (ORA-13528) will be reported.

The procedure DROP_BASELINE drops the specified baseline. You must supply the *baseline_name*. The procedure has an option to either retain the associated snapshots or drop them. When *cascade* is set to *true*, all the snapshot IDs for the baseline are dropped. The default value for this parameter is *false*, meaning associated snapshot IDs will be preserved and only the baseline will be dropped. The optional parameter, *dbid*, defaults to the local database ID. In the following example, the baseline titled 'Routine Jobs' is dropped along with its associated snapshot IDs:

```
begin
    dbms_workload_repository.drop_baseline('Routine Jobs', true);
end;
/
PL/SQL procedure successfully completed.
```

AWR Reports

AWR contains a couple of SQL scripts to produce Workload Repository reports that resemble the Statspack report. However, the Workload Repository report contains much more information than the Statspack report did, since it reports all the new database statistics we discussed in the preceding sections; for example, the Time Model Statistics and Operating System Statistics. In addition, the report contains statistics at Service Name and Module Name levels.

The Oracle-supplied scripts *awrrpt.sql* and *awrrpti.sql* generate reports either in HTML or text format for the specified range of snapshot IDs. The output report from these scripts is essentially the same, but the latter script allows you to specify a particular instance in a multi-instance database environment. You need DBA privilege to run these scripts. These scripts are in the $ORACLE_HOME/rdbms/admin directory.

≥w the AWR statistics using various views. Table 9-2 lists a few of these
briefly describes their contents.

:ion to storing performance statistics data in the AWR tables in SYSAUX
tablespace, Oracle Database 10*g* also takes frequent snapshots of the active sessions
and stores that information for historical analysis. This mechanism is called Active
Session History.

Active Session History

In Oracle Database 10*g*, the current session activity can be obtained from the
V$SESSION or V$SESSION_WAIT views. The view V$SESSION_WAIT_HISTORY
provides information about the last 10 wait events that the session encountered.
However, for troubleshooting a performance issue, these views do not provide
enough historical information about what the session did. Oracle Database 10*g*
solves this problem with the introduction of Active Session History (ASH).

As the name suggests, Oracle provides historical information on active sessions.
It samples all active sessions every second to track their state and stores this information
in a buffer in the SGA.

View Name	Description
DBA_HIST_ACTIVE_SESS_HISTORY	Displays history of the contents of the V$ACTIVE_SESSION_HISOTRY view.
DBA_HIST_BASELINE	Displays information on the baselines stored in AWR.
DBA_HIST_DATABASE_INSTANCE	Displays database and instance information.
DBA_HIST_SNAPSHOT	Displays information on AWR snapshots.
DBA_HIST_SQL_PLAN	Displays information on SQL execution plans.
DBA_HIST_WR_CONTROL	Displays parameter settings that control AWR properties.

TABLE 9-2.   *AWR Views (Not a Complete List)*

The historical information is displayed by the V$ACTIVE_SESSION_HISTORY view. This view is similar to a join between V$SESSION and V$SESSION_WAIT views with historical data for active sessions.

The other important difference between the V$ACTIVE_SESSION_HISTORY and V$SESSION_WAIT_HISTORY is the archiving of the data. ASH contents are written to the database tables by AWR. This view can roughly be called the "flashback session" view as it helps perform spot analysis of the session when diagnosing problems that may have occurred in the immediate past. However, this information is not guaranteed to be available in this view at all times. In a very active database with numerous active sessions, the internal buffer can get full faster. Oracle will sample available information and write to an AWR table that can be viewed via the DBA_HIST_ACTIVE_ SESSION_HISTORY view. The view V$ACTIVE_SESSION_HISTORY acts as a single point of reference for various pieces of information such as waits events, accessed objects, time spent on CPU, details about the SQL statement such hash value, and the SQL execution plan.

What Is an Active Session?

We mentioned in the previous section that ASH samples active sessions. But what is an active session? The status ACTIVE is not to be confused with V$SESSION.STATE, which has a binary value of ACTIVE or INACTIVE. ASH considers a session ACTIVE if the user call to the RDBMS kernel falls in any of the following categories and collects the session activity data:

- PARSE or EXECUTE or FETCH operations

- Waiting for the I/O to complete

- Waiting for the message or buffer from remote instance (in RAC)

- On CPU

- Not waiting for recursive session

- If it is a parallel slave, not waiting for PX_IDLE event

- Any other wait that does not fall in the *Idle* wait class

Components of ASH

ASH does not require any initialization parameter setting or any installation script be run. It is enabled by default after creating or upgrading to an Oracle Database 10g.

The new background process, MMNL (the lightweight version of MMON), is responsible for writing the sampled data to the in-memory circular buffer in the fixed area of the SGA. The buffer contents are further sampled and written to the AWR table, WRH$_ACTIVE_SESSION_HISTORY, on every AWR flush every hour by default. The MMNL process will also flush the buffer contents to the AWR tables whenever the buffer gets full. This process does not request any latches to update the buffer contents and can keep up with database activity without any problems.

The ASH in-memory buffer, by default, has an upper limit of 30MB for its size. The minimum size is 1MB. The size of the ASH in-memory buffer depends on factors such as the number of CPUs, the size of shared pool, the value set for SGA_TARGET, and some arbitrary rounding of numbers. In Oracle Database 10*g* Release 1, the following formula derives the buffer size; however, it may change in the future releases:

```
max (min (#of CPUs * 2MB, 5% of SHARED_POOL_SIZE, 30MB), 1MB)
```

The view V$ACTIVE_SESSION_HISTORY is based on the X$KEWASH and X$ASH structures. The X$ASH structure contains the sampled details of every active session. The X$KEWASH structure contains the details about the number of samples taken in the instance.

There are a few hidden initialization parameters that change the default behavior of ASH. Do not rush to start using those. Always get approval from Oracle Support before using such parameters.

The dynamic parameter, _ASH_ENABLE, when set to FALSE will disable ASH functionality, and the view V$ACTIVE_SESSION_HISTORY will not be populated anymore. The _ASH_DISK_WRITE_ENABLE defaults to TRUE to flush the in-memory ASH data to disk. Setting it to FALSE will disable writing this data to disk. So, if for some reason you do not want to store ASH data to AWR but want to keep it in the memory, you can set this parameter to FALSE. You can also increase the buffer size by setting the _ASH_SIZE parameter to a larger value than 30MB.

V$ACTIVE_SESSION_HISTORY View

Table 9-3 describes the columns in the V$ACTIVE_SESSION_HISTORY and where appropriate relates those to columns already available in other V$ views.

The V$ACTIVE_SESSION_HISTORY view can be considered a fact table in a data warehouse with its columns as the dimensions of the fact table. The contents are in the memory; so accessing those by these columns is very fast. You can find out almost anything about any sessions' activity from this view. You can quickly answer questions such as: how many sessions waited on a particular wait event in the last five minutes and for how long? What objects sessions are waiting on the most and what for? It is important to note that this information is based on sampled data that is captured every second. As such, it will be very close to being accurate and sufficient for your analysis.

Column Name	Type	Description
SAMPLE_ID	NUMBER	ID of the sample snapshot.
SAMPLE_TIME	TIMESTAMP(3)	Time at which the sample was taken.
SESSION_ID	NUMBER	Session identifier, maps to V$SESSION.SID.
SESSION_SERIAL#	NUMBER	Session serial number, maps to V$SESSION.SERIAL#.
USER_ID	NUMBER	Oracle user identifier, maps to V$SESSION.USER#.
SQL_ID	VARCHAR2(13)	SQL identifier of the SQL statement.
SQL_CHILD_ NUMBER	NUMBER	Child number of the SQL statement.
SQL_PLAN_HASH_ VALUE	NUMBER	Hash value of the SQL plan, maps to V$SQL.PLAN_HASH_VALUE.
SQL_OPCODE	NUMBER	SQL operation code, maps to V$SESSION.COMMAND.
SERVICE_HASH	NUMBER	Service hash, maps to V$ACTIVE_ SERVICES.NAME_HASH.
SESSION_TYPE	VARCHAR2(10)	FOREGROUND or BACKGROUND.
SESSION_STATE	VARCHAR2(7)	State: WAITING or ON CPU.
QC_SESSION_ID	NUMBER	Query coordinator ID for parallel query.
QC_INSTANCE_ID	NUMBER	Query coordinator instance ID.
EVENT	VARCHAR2(64)	If SESSION_STATE = WAITING, the event for which the session was waiting for at the time of sampling. If SESSION_STATE = ON CPU, the event for which the session last waited upon before being sampled.
EVENT_ID	NUMBER	Identifier of the resource or event, maps to V$EVENT_NAME.EVENT_ID.
EVENT#	NUMBER	Number of the resource, maps to V$EVENT_NAME.EVENT#.
SEQ#	NUMBER	Sequence number, uniquely identifies the wait, maps to V$SESSION.SEQ#.

TABLE 9-3.   *V$ACTIVE_SESSION_HISTORY View*

Column Name	Type	Description
P1	NUMBER	First additional wait parameter.
P2	NUMBER	Second additional wait parameter.
P3	NUMBER	Third additional wait parameter.
WAIT_TIME	NUMBER	It is 0 if the session was waiting, maps to V$SESSION.WAIT_TIME.
TIME_WAITED	NUMBER	If SESSION_STATE = WAITING, the time that the session actually spent waiting for that EVENT will be 0 until it finishes waiting.
CURRENT_OBJ#	NUMBER	Object ID of the object if the session is waiting for some I/O-related events or for some enqueue waits, maps to V$SESSION.ROW_WAIT_OBJ#.
CURRENT_FILE#	NUMBER	File number of the file if the session was waiting for some I/O-related events or for some enqueue waits, maps to V$SESSION.ROW_WAIT_FILE#.
CURRENT_BLOCK#	NUMBER	ID of the block if the session was waiting for I/O-related events or for some enqueue waits, maps to V$SESSION.ROW_WAIT_BLOCK#.
PROGRAM	VARCHAR2(48)	Name of the operating system program, maps to V$SESSION.PROGRAM.
MODULE	VARCHAR2(48)	Name of the executing module when sampled, as set by the procedure DBMS_APPLICATION_INFO.SET_MODULE.
ACTION	VARCHAR2(32)	Name of the executing module when sampled, as set by the procedure DBMS_APPLICATION_INFO.SET_ACTION.
CLIENT_ID	VARCHAR2(64)	Client identifier of the session; maps to V$SESSION.CLIENT_ID.

TABLE 9-3.   *V$ACTIVE_SESSION_HISTORY View* (continued)

Such online analysis is possible because of the ASH in-memory buffer. The following example shows how to find what sessions waited in the last five minutes, for what wait events, for how long, and how many times they waited:

```
select session_id, event, count(*), sum(time_waited)
from   v$active_session_history
where  session_state = 'WAITING'
and    time_waited > 0
and    sample_time >= (sysdate - &HowLongAgo/(24*60))
group by session_id, event;

Enter value for howlongago: 5
old    5: and sample_time >= (sysdate - &HowLongAgo/(24*60))
new    5: and sample_time >= (sysdate - 5/(24*60))

SESSION_ID EVENT                                  COUNT(*) SUM(TIME_WAITED)
---------- ------------------------------------- ---------- ----------------
       126 db file scattered read                     276         16958032
       131 db file scattered read                     270         17728709
       131 log file switch completion                   1           418071
       133 class slave wait                             1          5125049
       133 db file sequential read                      4           151610
       138 db file scattered read                       5           354926
       138 db file sequential read                     20           974258
       138 log file switch completion                   1           418261
       138 control file sequential read                 1            27706
       153 null event                                   1            45580
       153 db file sequential read                     26          6900220
       153 control file sequential read                 4           202271
       166 control file parallel write                  8          1896634
       166 control file sequential read                 1            55883
       167 log file parallel write                      8           359185
       167 control file single write                    1            30063
       168 db file parallel write                       9           362689
17 rows selected.
```

When querying the V$ACTIVE_SESSION_HISTORY view, Oracle has to acquire all the usual latches for statement parsing, accessing the buffers, etc. If there is a parse latch related problem in a hung database, you may not be able to access the wealth of information in the V$ACTIVE_SESSION_HISTORY view that can help you diagnose the problem. However, there is another way to access this in-memory ASH information, and that is what we will discuss in the next section.

The ASHDUMP: Dumping ASH Circular Buffer
Contents to Trace File

The contents of the ASH buffer can be dumped to a trace file using the event ASHDUMP. These contents can then be loaded into a database table. The structure of this table resembles the V$ACTIVE_SESSION_HISTORY view.

You can produce the ASHDUMP trace file using the following *oradebug* command sequence after connecting as sysdba:

```
oradebug setmypid
oradebug unlimit
oradebug dump ashdump 10
oradebug tracefile_name
```

You can also use the ALTER SESSION command to produce an immediate dump of the ASH buffer as shown next:

```
alter session set events 'immediate trace name ashdump, level 10';
```

The trace file will be in your UDUMP directory. The contents of the trace file can be loaded into a table in other database. In the first few lines, the trace file lists all the column names for the data. The trace data is displayed as comma-separated values for the respective columns. This information can be used to employ SQL*Loader to load the rest of the contents of the trace file to the table for further analysis.

The following example shows the contents of the trace file from an ASHDUMP. The header information, typically found in trace files, is removed for clarity.

```
<<<ACTIVE SESSION HISTORY - PROCESS TRACE DUMP HEADER BEGIN>>>
DBID, INSTANCE_NUMBER, SAMPLE_ID, SAMPLE_TIME, SESSION_ID, SESSION_SERIAL#,
USER_ID, SQL_ID, SQL_CHILD_NUMBER, SQL_PLAN_HASH_VALUE, SERVICE_HASH,
SESSION_TYPE, SQL_OPCODE, QC_SESSION_ID, QC_INSTANCE_ID, CURRENT_OBJ#,
CURRENT_FILE#, CURRENT_BLOCK#, EVENT_ID, SEQ#, P1, P2, P3, WAIT_TIME, TIME_
WAITED, PROGRAM, MODULE, ACTION, CLIENT_ID
<<<ACTIVE SESSION HISTORY - PROCESS TRACE DUMP HEADER END>>>

<<<ACTIVE SESSION HISTORY - PROCESS TRACE DUMP BEGIN>>>
2847681843,1,6033130,"04-13-2004
07:40:58.006572000",41,597,5,"2xbhdwsp8a0zd",0,0,3427055676,1,62,0,0,16314,
1,27521,2652584166,135,1,27709,1,121,0,"sqlplus@hptest (TNS V1-
V3)","SQL*Plus","",""
2847681843,1,6033129,"04-13-2004
07:40:56.976572000",41,597,5,"2xbhdwsp8a0zd",0,0,3427055676,1,62,0,0,16314,
1,27521,2652584166,135,1,27709,1,121,0,"sqlplus@hptest (TNS V1-
V3)","SQL*Plus","",""

 . . . . . . . . . . . . . . . . . . . .
 . . . . . . . . . . . . . . . . . . . .
```

```
2847681843,1,6032838,"04-13-2004
07:35:57.196572000",49,3,0,"6q766vsk5290x",0,0,165959219,2,47,0,0,429496729
5,0,0,866018717,189,300,0,0,3007426,0,"oracle@hptest (MMON)","","",""
2847681843,1,6032837,"04-13-2004
07:35:56.166572000",49,3,0,"6q766vsk5290x",0,0,165959219,2,47,0,0,429496729
5,0,0,866018717,189,300,0,0,3007426,0,"oracle@hptest (MMON)","","",""
<<<ACTIVE SESSION HISTORY - PROCESS TRACE DUMP END>>>
```

Although this process of dumping the ASH buffer, loading the trace file data into a table, and then troubleshooting the cause of the problem may sound a bit cumbersome, it may occasionally be useful when you have a hung system. You don't need to wait for the disaster to strike. You can experiment by producing the ASHDUMP trace file using the ALTER SESSION command and keeping those scripts ready to load the data to your own ASH table!

In the preceding sections we discussed how Oracle Database 10*g* captures performance data using AWR and ASH snapshots, how to manage the data capture process, and how you can view the data. Behind the scenes, Oracle Database 10*g* is doing a lot more with this data, and that is the topic of the next section.

Automatic Database Diagnostic Monitor (ADDM)

Automatic Database Diagnostic Monitor (ADDM, pronounced "Adam") is not just another piece of software that you purchase from Oracle Corporation and install on your database server and workstation.

ADDM is a holistic self-diagnostic mechanism built into the Oracle Database 10*g*. It is an integral part of the kernel. It automatically examines and analyzes the snapshot data captured into AWR to proactively determine any major issues with the system, and in many cases it recommends corrective actions with quantified expected benefits. It is constantly monitoring and diagnosing your system.

The goal of ADDM is to identify the areas of the system that are consuming the most *DB time*—time spent in the database calls. It uses the wait model and time model statistics to find where time is being spent in the database. It drills down to the root cause of the problem using a tree-structured set of rules. These rules have a proven track record and have been used successfully over the past several years by Oracle Corporation in performance tuning engagements.

ADDM can detect and report many problems including the following types of problems:

- CPU bottlenecks due to Oracle and non-Oracle applications

- I/O subsystem capacity issues

- High-load SQL statements that may be consuming excessive system resources

- High-load PL/SQL compilation and execution consuming excessive system resources

- High-load Java applications consuming excessive system resources

- Undersized memory structures, such as SGA, buffer cache, and log buffer

- Poor connection management

- RAC-related issues with global cache management and interconnect latency

- Concurrent data access issues resulting in buffer busy waits

- Database configuration issues such as log file sizing, archiving or suboptimal parameter settings

In addition to reporting the problematic areas of the system, ADDM also reports the areas it treats as nonproblematic, so you don't spend time analyzing items that don't impact overall system performance. ADDM also recommends possible solutions to the common problems it detects. Again, ADDM recommended solutions are targeted towards achieving lower *DB time*.

NOTE
Because the recommendations from ADDM are generated by a set of predefined rules, those may or may not be applicable to all the situations. You may find some of these recommendations unsuitable to your environments. According to Oracle, ADDM does not target the tuning of individual user response times. Use tracing techniques to tune for individual user response times.

ADDM Setup

Although the Automatic Database Diagnostic Monitoring is enabled by default, there are a couple of parameters that you need to be aware of.

The initialization parameter STATISTICS_LEVEL must be set either to TYPICAL or ALL to enable ADDM functionality. It defaults to TYPICAL; setting it to BASIC will disable ADDM and many other features.

The other parameter is not an initialization parameter. It is a special ADDM-related task parameter, DBIO_EXPECTED, which ADDM uses to analyze the performance of the I/O subsystem. The value for the DBIO_EXPECTED parameter defines the average time it takes to read a single database block in microseconds. The default value for this parameter is 10 milliseconds (10,000 microseconds). If your think you I/O subsystem response time is significantly different, you may want to change this default value.

First, you must find out the average read time for random reads of a single database block for your hardware. Convert that to microseconds. For this example, let's say it comes out to be 30,000 microseconds (somewhat slow disks).

Second, use the following procedure to set the DBIO_EXPECTED value to 30,000:

```
REM - Run this as SYS user
begin
    dbms_advisor.set_default_task_parameter (
                'ADDM','DBIO_EXPECTED',30000);
end;
/
PL/SQL procedure successfully completed.
```

The value for the DBIO_EXPECTED parameter is saved in an internal table. You need to execute the preceding procedure to change it. The following SQL script shows how you can interrogate the current value of this parameter:

```
col parameter_name for a20
col parameter_value for a20
select advisor_name,
       parameter_name,
       parameter_value,
from   dba_advisor_def_parameters
where  parameter_name like 'DBIO%';


ADVISOR_NAME          PARAMETER_NAME        PARAMETER_VALUE
--------------------  --------------------  --------------------
ADDM                  DBIO_EXPECTED         30000
```

Using EM to Access ADDM

The Oracle EM Database Control is the primary interface to the ADDM. In the following series of steps you can see the results of ADDM analysis.

Figure 9-4 and Figure 9-5 show the top and bottom portion of the Database home page. Information pertaining to the database instance, host CPU usage, active session,

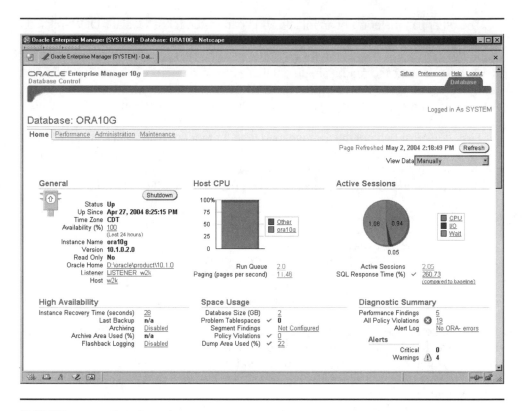

FIGURE 9-4. *Database home page top portion*

space usage, diagnostic summary, alerts, and performance analysis is shown on the Database home page. It also contains links to access other components that perform several other tasks.

In Figure 9-4, the number of ADDM performance findings for the last ADDM analysis period is shown under Diagnostic Summary toward the bottom right corner.

In Figure 9-5, those performance findings are listed under the Performance Analysis. For each finding ADDM also provided a few recommendations that are shown on the right.

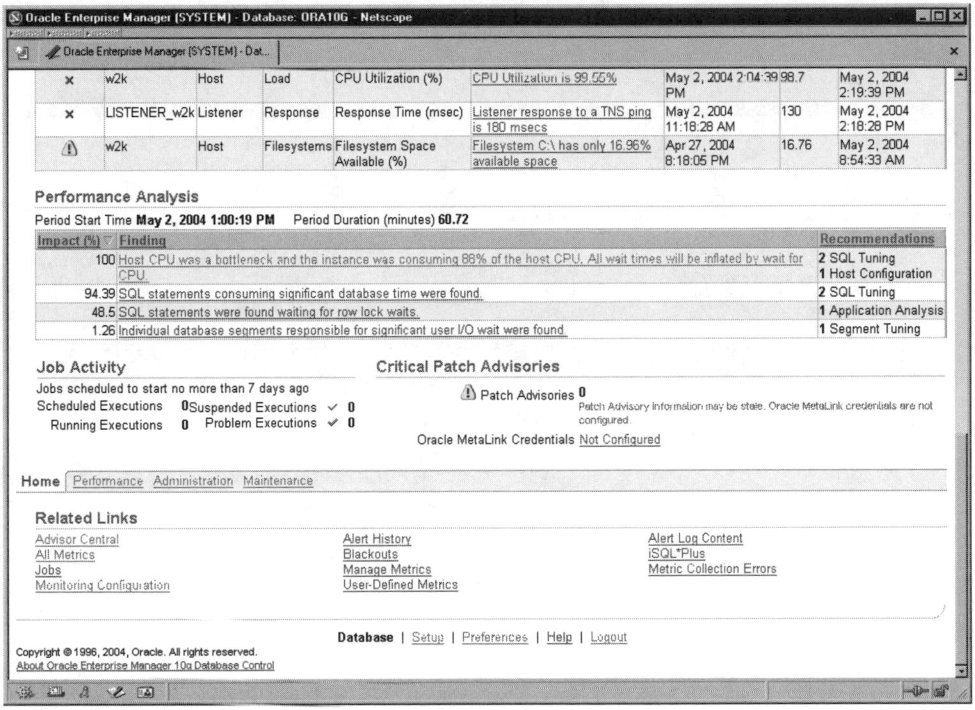

FIGURE 9-5.   *Database home page bottom portion*

The first performance finding states that there was CPU contention. By clicking the link associated with this finding, you can drill down to the details, as shown in Figure 9-6.

For the CPU contention issue, in this case, ADDM wants you to consider adding more CPUs to the server or adding more database instances, preferably on other servers, to service the load. It also identified two SQL statements that may need investigating.

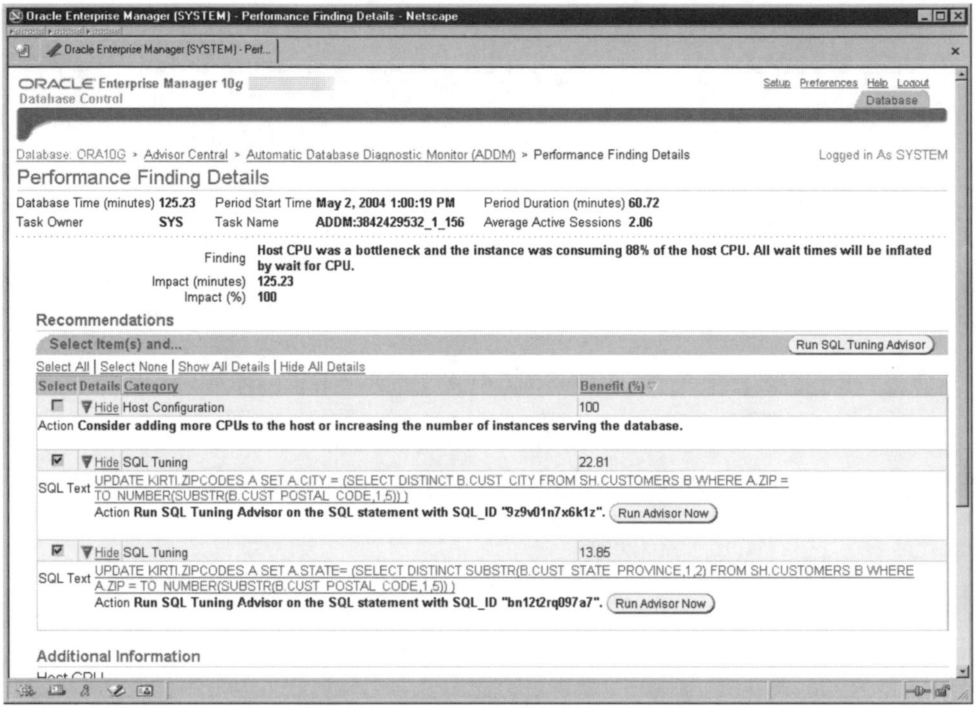

FIGURE 9-6. *Performance Finding Details and Recommendations*

Back on the Database home page, as shown in Figure 9-5, if you click the Advisor Central link under the heading Related Links at the bottom of the page, you are presented with the Advisor Central home page, as shown in Figure 9-7.

The Advisor Central home page offers a variety of advisories on almost any component of the database, from SQL tuning to undo management. It readily shows the details of the automatic advisory tasks that ADDM performed when the last AWR snapshot was taken. The latest advisor task is shown on this page. You can

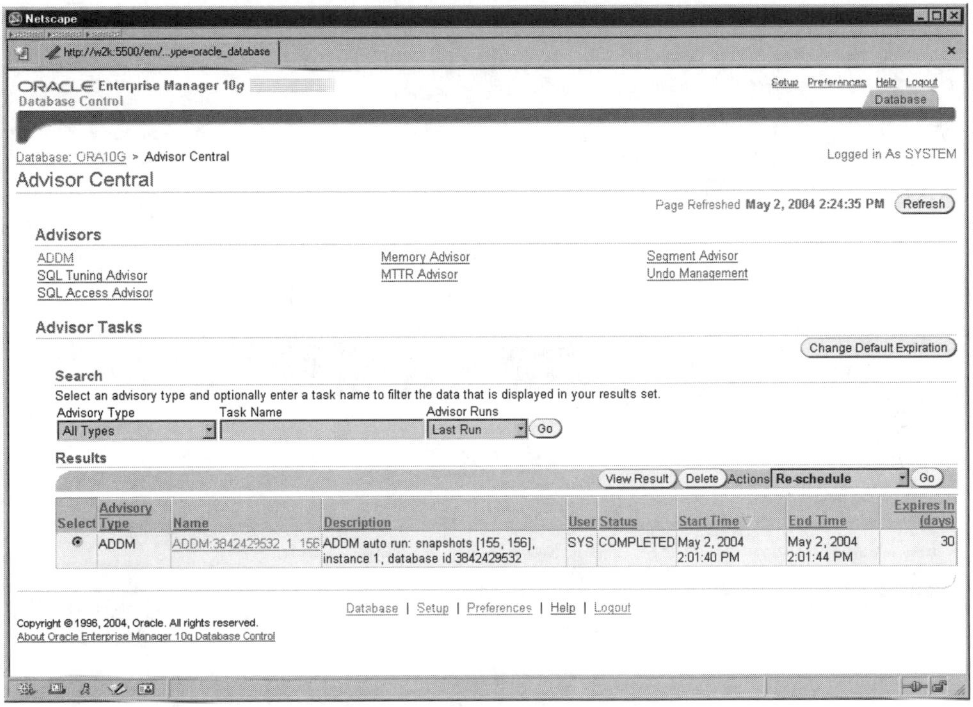

FIGURE 9-7. *Advisor Central home page*

review reports of the previous tasks using the pull-down Advisor Runs menu. You can select from the last run, the last 24 hours, or the last 7 days.

Clicking the name of the advisor task takes you to the Automatic Database Diagnostic Monitor (ADDM) page, as shown in Figure 9-8.

This page shows the database activity over the past several hours and additional information on the advisor task. To view the ADDM report for this particular advisor task, click the View Report button. The detailed ADDM report for the selected task will be displayed, as shown in Figure 9-9.

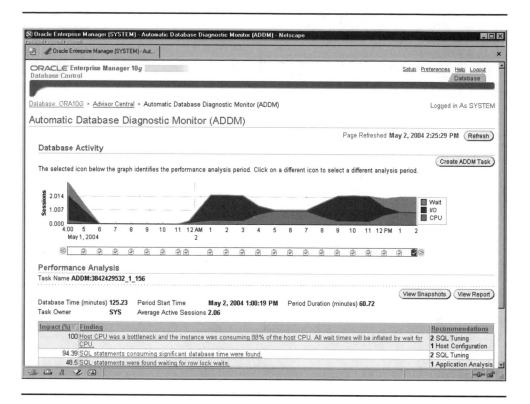

FIGURE 9-8. *Automatic Database Diagnostic Management*

All this information was readily captured and analyzed by Oracle Database 10*g*. It was easily accessible, and most importantly, ADDM analyzed the system load and offered recommendations before its findings became a real problem.

Even if you do not look at the ADDM findings immediately, you can access them later because they are stored in the database. ADDM data (and all ADDM advisor framework data) is stored for 30 days by default.

However, many a times DBAs will have to perform real-time problem diagnosis. How many times have you received calls from users stating the database is slow?

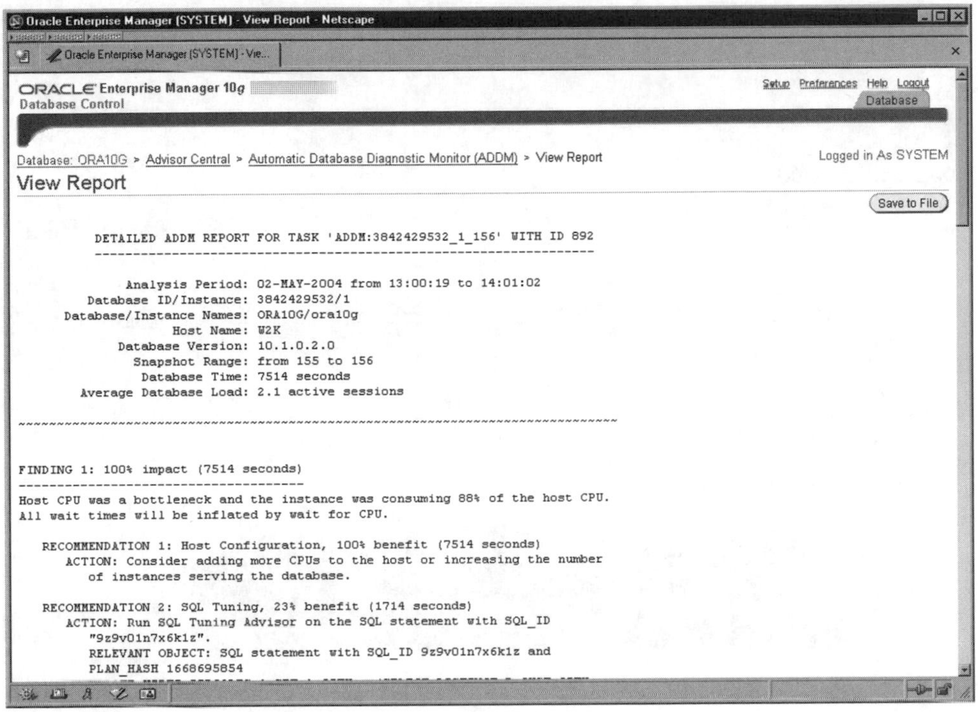

FIGURE 9-9. *Viewing the ADDM report*

With the Performance page of EM Database Control, you can now easily find out what's going on in your system. From the Database Control home page (Figure 9-4), click the Performance link to access the Performance home page, as shown in Figure 9-10.

On the Performance page, you can see how the CPU and memory resources are being used to make sure those are not the bottlenecks. You can assess the database health from the Sessions: Waiting and Working graph that shows how the CPU is being used by the sessions and if there are any sessions waiting for the resources.

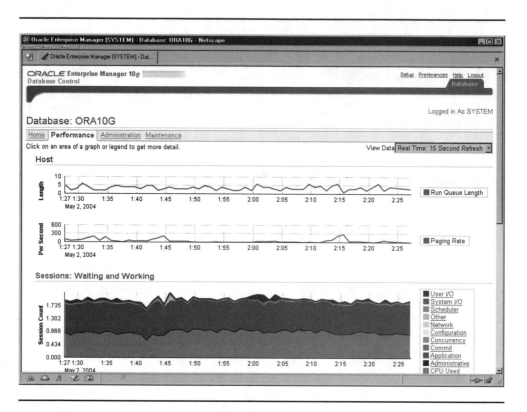

FIGURE 9-10. *Performance home page*

This graph provides quite a bit of information. It shows the average number of active sessions on the Y axis broken down by the Wait class and CPU. The X axis shows the time. The data is refreshed every 15 seconds by default. The graph uses various colors to indicate different wait classes. The larger the block of color, the worse the problem. Clicking the legend of the color scheme on the right, which is broken down by wait class, will take you to the drill-down page showing the active sessions waiting for that wait class. In the example in Figure 9-10, the Application wait class was the prominent color block. Clicking the Application legend takes you to the

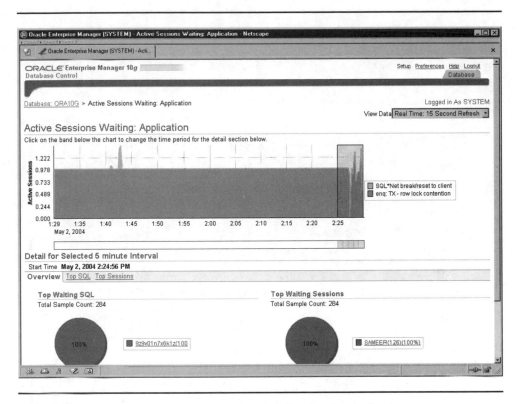

FIGURE 9-11. *Active Sessions Waiting: Application (wait class)*

Active Sessions Waiting: Application page, as shown in Figure 9-11. You see that the wait event is *enq: TX row lock contention*, so there is a locking problem in this particular application.

You can drill down by clicking the link under the Top Waiting SQL get the to SQL statement details, as shown in Figure 9-12. There you have it. This is the SQL that is waiting for the lock to be released.

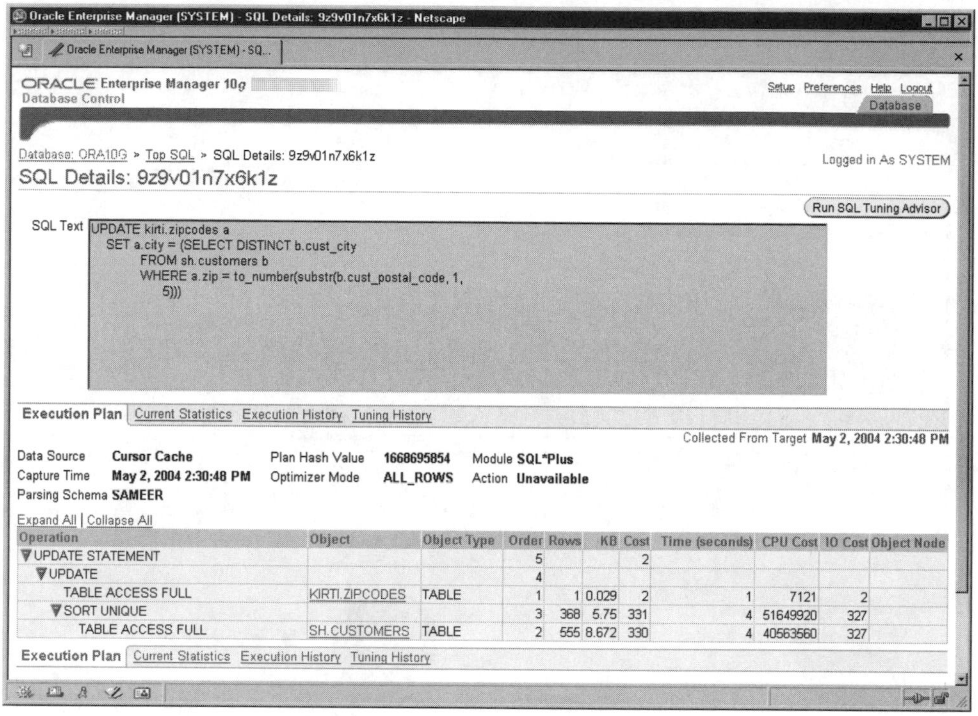

FIGURE 9-12. *SQL Details showing SQL text and explain plan*

You can also drill down by clicking the link under the Top Waiting Sessions to find the details of the waiting session, as shown in Figure 9-13. The session has been waiting on the *enq: TX row lock contention* wait event.

By clicking the Wait Events link on the Session Details page, you can see the historical wait event the session encountered. In the example shown in Figure 9-14, the session has been waiting on the *enq: TX row lock contention* for quite some time.

Manually Running ADDM Report

Running the ADDM report from within the Oracle EM is the preferred and the simplest method. However, you can use Oracle-supplied scripts and package procedures to generate the ADDM diagnosis report. You need to know any two AWR snapshots to produce such a report. The snapshots must be available in AWR and there must not be any database restarts between those snapshots.

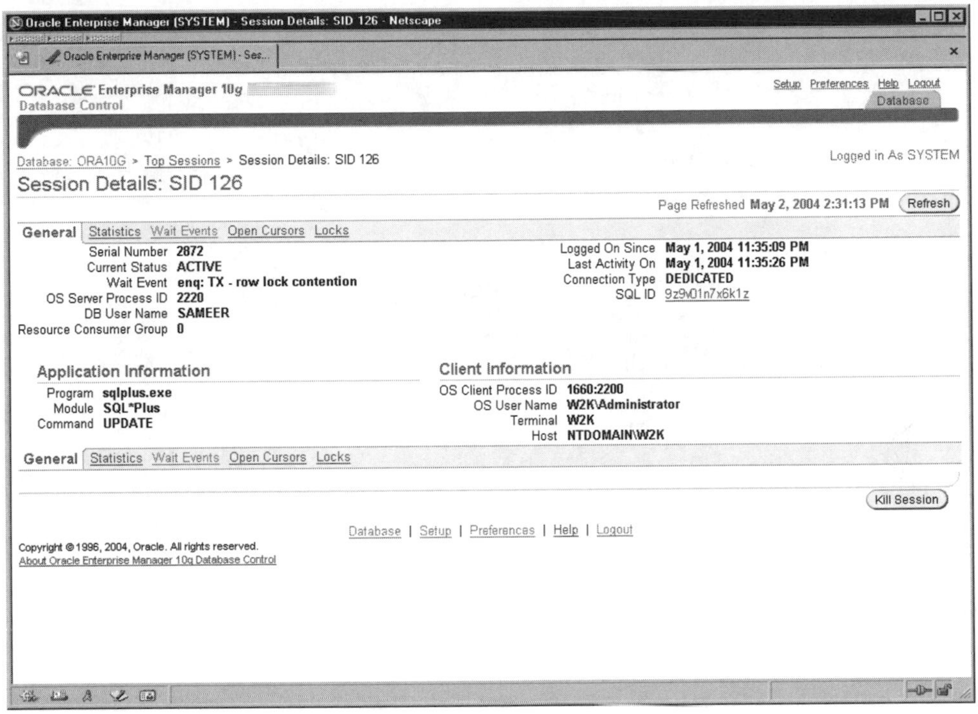

FIGURE 9-13. *Session Details showing general information*

There are two scripts in the $ORACLE_HOME/rdbms/admin directory that can generate the ADDM diagnosis report: *addmrpt.sql* and *addmrpti.sql*. The former generates the report for the local database instance, while the latter can generate the report for other instances (in the RAC environment, for example). In addition, the Oracle-supplied package DBMS_ADVISOR has procedures (API) to generate the ADDM diagnosis report.

We will briefly discuss how to use these methods to generate the ADDM diagnosis report.

To run the scripts or use the API scripts you must have the ADVISOR privilege.

When running *addmrpt.sql*, you will be prompted to provide the beginning and ending snapshot ID from a list of available snapshots and a report name of your choice. Oracle will generate the ADDM diagnosis report for the specified range of snapshot IDs. The report can also be run in a noninteractive mode. The script has instructions in it to show you how to do that.

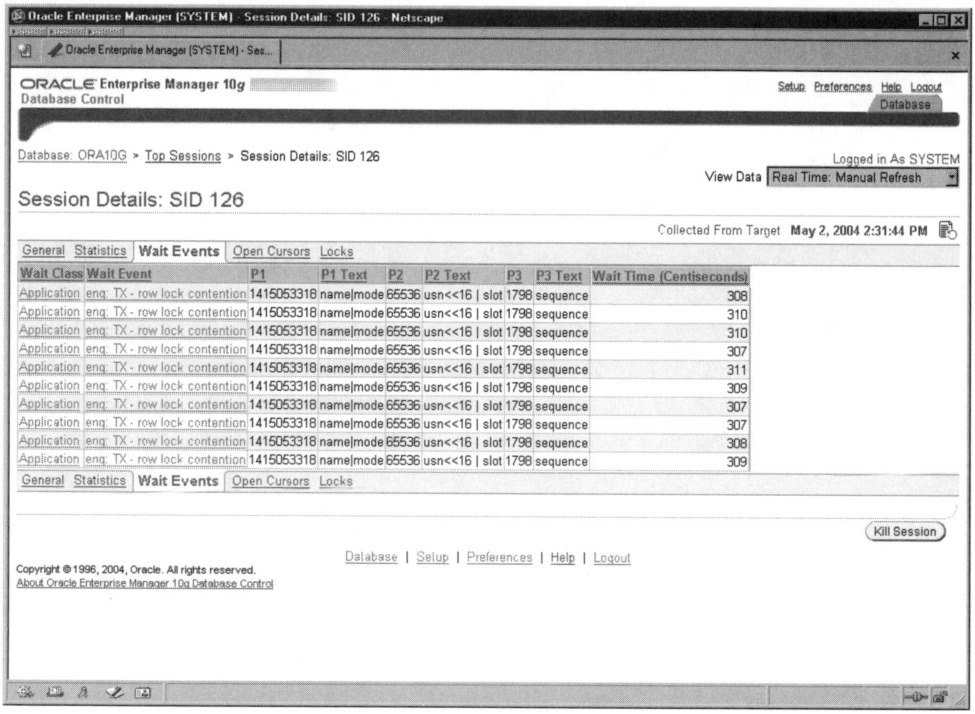

FIGURE 9-14. *Session Details showing session waits*

To generate the ADDM diagnosis report using the DBMS_ADVISOR package directly needs a bit more setup, as follows:

1. Create an advisor task of ADDM type, using the CREATE_TASK procedure.

2. Set the START_SNAPSHOT and END_SNAPSHOT parameters to run the just-created task using the SET_TASK_PARAMETER procedure. The ADDM diagnosis report will be generated for the range of these snapshots.

3. Execute the task using the EXECUTE_TASK procedure to generate the diagnosis report.

4. View the generated ADDM diagnosis report using GET_TASK_REPORT procedure.

DBA_ADVISOR_FINDINGS	Displays all the findings discovered by ADDM.
DBA_ADVISOR_LOG	Displays current state of all tasks in the database such as task progress, error messages, and execution times. There is one row for each task.
DBA_ADVISOR_RATIONALE	Displays the rationales for all recommendations.
DBA_ADVISOR_RECOMMENDATIONS	Displays the results of all completed diagnostic tasks with recommendations for the detected problems. The recommendations are ranked in the RANK column. The BENEFIT column shows the expected benefit after carrying out recommended actions.
DBA_ADVISOR_TASKS	Displays information about all existing tasks in the database.

TABLE 9-4. *ADDM Views (Not a Complete List)*

NOTE
*The Oracle Database Performance Guide 10*g *Release 1 has an excellent example in Chapter 6 in the section "Running ADDM Using DBMS_ADVISOR APIs" that demonstrates the use of the ADMS_ADVISOR package to generate and view the ADDM diagnosis report.*

ADDM Views

Oracle EM is the preferred interface to view all ADDM-related information. However, the DBMS_ADVISOR views can be used to view this information. Table 9-4 lists a few of these views and their description.

In a Nutshell

With rich features such as AWR, ASH, and ADDM, along with the Web-based Oracle Enterprise Manager, Oracle Database 10*g* revolutionizes database performance monitoring.

The mundane tasks of database monitoring and troubleshooting slow-running jobs are now completely automated in Oracle Database 10*g*. With all the historical performance data now permanently stored in the Automatic Workload Repository, and with the intelligent mechanism to analyze it, Oracle Database 10*g* knows more about your database behavior than you do!

With these powerful tools, successful performance monitoring will no longer be restricted to an elite group of consultants and experts.

APPENDIX
A

Oracle Database 10g
Diagnostic Events

vents in Oracle can be broadly classified into two groups: wait events and diagnostic events. This appendix explores Oracle diagnostic events.

Oracle Diagnostic Events

Oracle diagnostic events can be considered the most powerful tools for DBAs who are involved in debugging. Most of these events are primarily used to produce additional diagnostic information, to change Oracle's behavior, and to trace the inner workings of Oracle because these events can enable some of the undocumented features of Oracle.

NOTE
Diagnostic events should be handled with care because they can change the default behavior of the Oracle Database engine and will render the database useless and unsupported if used improperly.

Types of Diagnostic Events

Oracle diagnostic events can be classified in four major categories based on their usage as discussed in the following sections.

Immediate Dump Events

Immediate dump events will dump the diagnostic information in a trace file as soon as the command is issued. Normally *immediate* dumps are used to dump the system state, process state, and file headers (controlf, redo_hdrs, file_hdrs). *Immediate* dumps cannot be invoked by setting the EVENT parameter in the init.ora file. That is because the parameter file is read only during the instance startup. *Immediate* dumps can be better triggered by either ALTER SESSION SET EVENTS command or the *oredebug* utility.

```
alter session set events 'immediate trace name systemstate level 8';
```

The preceding command creates a trace file, which contains detailed information about every Oracle process active on the system, as well as the details about the resources held/requested by those processes. Oracle Support often requests the systemstate dump while debugging the database hang issues.

Another example of an *immediate* dump is shown here:

```
alter session set events 'immediate trace name controlf level 10';
```

More details about the different types of dumps are available in Appendix C.

On Error Dump Events

On error dump events are similar to *immediate* dump events but they are invoked only when the error occurs. They are used to dump the system state, process state, or error stack when a particular Oracle error occurs. *On error* dumps are normally set using the EVENT parameter in the init.ora file. Following example shows an entry in the init.ora file to dump the error stack to a trace file when ORA-04020 (deadlock detected when waiting for an object) is encountered. Usually the level is set between 1 and 10. It controls the amount of information written to the trace file.

```
event= "4020 trace name errorstack level 1"
```

Following are valid values for the level for an error stack dump:

- **1**   Error stack and function call stack

- **2**   Level 1 plus process state

- **3**   Level 2 plus the context area (with cursors)

On error dumps are mostly used to identify the cause of the particular error, and Oracle Support may ask you to dump the error stack for further investigation. For example, to diagnose the shared pool memory leak (ORA-04031) will need the following event set in the parameter file:

```
event="4031 trace name error stack level 10"
```

Change Behavior Events

Change behavior events are normally set using the EVENT parameter in the init.ora file. These events are very powerful events and should be used with care. These events are used to enable or disable certain functionalities of the Oracle kernel. Unlike other diagnostic events, these events do not have level numbers because these events do not create a trace file with diagnostic information written to it.

Change behavior events have an additional keyword: *forever*. Without the *forever* keyword, the event is fired only once and no subsequent actions are triggered. *Change behavior* events use a reserved set of numbers to bring about the change in Oracle's behavior.

For example, the following event disables the automatic shrinking of rollback segments by SMON process, which usually happens every 12 hours:

```
event = "10512 trace name context forever"
```

Since *change behavior* events are used to enable or disable certain features of Oracle RDBMS, they cause potential data loss or data corruption if used incorrectly. They can also be used to change Oracle kernel operations. For example, the event 10170 can be used to change the bitmap index costing algorithms.

Bitmap index access cost is calculated as the sum of the index access cost and table access cost for those blocks. Here index access cost will be a function of *blevel* and the number of leaf blocks containing the key. Once the rowids are fetched from the leaf blocks, the bitmap is constructed and table access cost is estimated. The table access cost is calculated based on the number of blocks to fetch to get all the keys. This mainly depends on the selectivity.

In the old costing model, it is assumed that all the keys could be found in same block. That is, the number of block visits is calculated by dividing the number of rows by the rows per block. So the number of blocks multiplied by the selectivity of a block is assumed to be equal to the total number of rows satisfying the condition.

For example, if you want to retrieve 100 rows from a table that has 10,000 blocks with an average of 10 rows per block, the old costing model will compute 10 blocks as the I/O cost (100 rows/10 rows per block). So the table access I/O cost is approximately 10. With the enhanced costing model, it assumes 80 percent of the rows are in the same block and the remaining 20 percent of the rows are split across all blocks (which is quite possible). In this case, the cost will be (0.8*100/10) + (0.2*10000) = 8+2000 = 2008. The difference is quite significant.

Let us take another case where an index has 100,000 rows from a table with an average of 50 rows per block (for a total of 2,000 blocks) and the result set expects 1,000 rows. In the old model, the I/O cost will be 20. In the new costing model, the cost will be (0.8*20) + (0.2*2000), which is 56 blocks.

In most cases, the enhanced (new) costing model, which is based on the Watkins formula, works reasonably well in estimating the bitmap access costs. However, the old model outperforms the new model when partitioned tables are used and when star transformation is used. In these cases, most of the rows (or all of them) will be from the same partition, and the old costing model will be more suitable than the new enhanced costing approach. Sometimes the new costing model artificially inflates the bitmap index cost where bitmap indexes could be used for transformation. The old costing mode can be enabled by setting the event 10170.

The preceding is a simple nondestructive example of the *change behavior* type events. There are many more *change behavior* events, but they are potentially dangerous to the databases. These events should be used in accordance with Oracle Support.

Process Trace Events

Process trace events are used to get additional diagnostic information when the process is running. These events are normally harmless, and they do generate a trace file. For user processes, the trace file is created in the directory defined by

USER_DUMP_DEST parameter in the init.ora file. The trace file for background processes will be written to the directory defined by the BACKGROUND_DUMP_ DEST parameter in the init.ora file. The *level* keyword is used to control the amount of diagnostic information written to the trace file.

For example, the following event is used to trace the SQL statements executed in the session:

```
SQL> alter session set events '10046 trace name context forever, level 1';
```

Event levels for event code 10046 are

- **1** Enable SQL statement tracing (the default if no level is specified)

- **4** As level 1 plus bind variable information

- **8** As level 1 plus wait event statistics

- **12** As level 1 plus bind variables plus wait statistics (highest level)

Oracle trace event 10046 is the most popular event among the performance practitioners. There is an enhancement request pending with Oracle Corporation (Req # 590463, EXTERNALISE THE EVENT 10046 BY A PARAMETER), and this event may be externalized by a parameter in future versions.

Cost Based Optimizer (CBO) operations can be traced using the Oracle trace event 10053. This event dumps the inner workings of CBO into a trace file, which is particularly helpful in understanding why CBO is not using the index or why CBO has taken a certain access path when the other path seems optimal.

Setting Diagnostic Events

Oracle diagnostic events can be set using the EVENT parameter in the init.ora file. You can also dynamically set the events using ALTER SESSION SET EVENTS command through SQL*Plus. Events can also be set using the *dbms_system.set_ev* procedure and the *oradebug* utility.

In the previous sections, you saw a few examples showing the use of EVENT parameter in the init.ora file and the ALTER SESSION command to set a particular event.

Multiple events can be set in the init.ora parameter file. When using only one EVENT parameter entry, a colon must separate multiple events, and they must all appear on a single line. However, a line continuation character (\) can be used to list them on multiple physical lines.

When using multiple EVENT parameter entries, they must be grouped together, and no other initialization parameter can be embedded within the EVENT parameter entries.

Following are all valid examples of setting two events:

```
event="\
4031 trace name context forever, level 10:\
10046 trace name context forever, level 12"

event="4031 trace name context forever, level 10: 10046 trace name
context forever, level 12"

event="4031 trace name context forever, level 10"
event="10046 trace name context forever, level 12"
```

In the following example, only the second event (10512) is set and the first one is ignored:

```
# To start SQL trace and Disable SMON posting
event="10046 trace name context forever, level 12"
user_dump_dest=/d00/app/oracle/admin/PROD/udump
event="10512 trace name context forever"
```

Setting Events Using DBMS_SYSTEM Package Procedure

You can set events using an Oracle supplied package procedure called DBMS_SYSTEM.SET_EV. The DBMS_SYSTEM package must be created by running Oracle-supplied SQL script titled *dbmsutil.sql* while logged in as SYS user. The script is available under $ORACLE_HOME/rdbms/admin directory. Privileged users should be given execute permission on the package.

The procedure *set_ev* is defined as follows:

```
procedure set_ev(si binary_integer, se binary_integer,
                 ev binary_integer, le binary_integer, nm varchar2);
```

Table A-1 describes the parameters used in the *set_ev* procedure.
You can use the following syntax to execute this procedure:

```
exec sys.dbms_system.set_ev (sid,serial#,event_code,level,'event_
action');
```

The following example shows how to enable event 10046 at level 12 in session 10 with serial 63:

```
execute dbms_system.set_ev(10,63,10046,12,'');
```

The following example shows how to disable it:

```
execute dbms_system.set_ev(10,63,10046,0,'');
```

Parameter	Description
si (SID)	Session ID of the target session
se (Serial#)	Serial # of the target session from V$SESSION
ev	event_code or event number, (for example, 10053 to trace CBO, 65535 for 'IMMEDIATE')
le	Level of information to dump. The higher the level, the more details you get. In certain cases (block dump, for example), level represents the address space.
nm	What to do when the event is triggered. For example, dump the error stack. Default is '' (NULL) which means "context forever."

TABLE A-1. set_ev *Procedure Parameters*

Setting Event Using *oradebug* Utility

The undocumented utility *oradebug* can be used to set an event for someone else's session (or for your own session).

The following example shows how to use *oradebug* to set an event in your own session:

```
SQL> oradebug setmypid
Statement processed.
SQL> oradebug event 10046 trace name context forever, level 8
Statement processed.
SQL> oradebug tracefile_name
/u01/app/oracle/product/10.1.0/admin/V10HP/udump/v10hp2_ora_9463.trc
```

An event can be set in someone else's session using *oradebug* utility when you know the session's SPID value from V$PROCESS view.

The following example shows how to trace a session with SPID value of 3574:

```
SQL> oradebug setospid 3574
Oracle pid: 15, Unix process pid: 3574, image: oracle@hptest (TNS V1-V3)
SQL> oradebug event 10046 trace name context forever, level 8
Statement processed.
SQL> oradebug tracefile_name
/u01/app/oracle/admin/V10HP/udump/v10hp_ora_3574.trc
SQL>
```

Event Specification Syntax

You must follow a particular syntax when setting events. The parameter keyword name is "event", with its value of string type. The string value is typically quoted and has the following syntax:

```
<event name> <action>{:<event name> <action>}. . .
```

The 'event name' is a symbolic name associated with the event, or, optionally an event number. There is a special name: "immediate", for an immediate and unconditional event. Oracle does not wait for somebody to post it. If a number is specified, it is taken to be an Oracle error number. If a name is specified, the parser looks it up in an event name table if it is not "immediate".

The 'action' is defined as the 'action keyword' plus the 'action qualifiers'. The 'action' keyword can be either 'trace', 'debugger' or 'crash'. The 'action qualifier' depends on the 'action' keyword.

Table A-2 summarizes the syntax for various types of diagnostics events.

TYPE	TRACE SYNTAX				
	<event name>	*<action>*			
		<action keyword>	*'name'*	*<trace name>*	*<action qualifier>*
Immediate dumps	immediate	trace	name	blockdump	level 432043242
	immediate	trace	name	redohdrs	level 10
	immediate	trace	name	controlf	level 10
	immediate	trace	name	systemstate	level 10
	immediate	trace	name	file_hdrs	level 10
On error	4031	trace	name	heapdump	level 10
	942	trace	name	errorstack	forever
	4030	trace	name	errorstack	level 10
	4020	trace	name	errorstack	level 10
	4031	trace	name	errorstack	off
Change behavior	10512	trace	name	context	forever level 12
	10235	trace	name	context	forever, level 1
Trace something	10046	trace	name	context	forever level 8
	10053	trace	name	context	forever level 1

TABLE A-2. *Diagnostics Event Syntax Summary*

A special trace name is "context", which means a context-specific trace that does not cause a debug dump operation to be invoked. Instead, it returns to the caller who posted the event and informs it whether context tracing is active for that event, and if so, what the trace level is. The trace level is used internally by the dump routines to control the level of detail in the dump. By convention, the level of detail increases with the level number, with the lowest level being 1. The caller is then responsible for invoking whatever dump operation it wants to, with whatever parameters are relevant.

Another special trace name is "all", which expands to mean all trace names that were declared at compile time through the "ksdtradv" macro, as well as the (last) "context" trace.

If more than one trace is associated with an event, at most one can be "context". Correspondingly, the last action associated with an event posting is to return the level number associated with the context-dependent trace. The event numbers need to be unique among different callers. Additionally, for trace specifications, you can specify an event named "immediate". For this case, no trace qualifiers except the trace level qualifier must be specified.

A duplicate event specification with the same action supercedes the old specification. Specifications of different actions for the same event may coexist, with the action taken according to the following precedence:

1. Context-independent traces in order of declaration

2. Context-specific trace

3. Debugger call

4. Oracle crash

If the keyword *immediate* is specified as the first keyword in the event syntax, then it is an unconditional event and the structure specified by the next qualifiers is dumped immediately after the command is issued.

The keyword *trace* indicates that the output will be dumped to the trace file. The other keywords in the second parameters are *crash* and *invoke the debugger* and are usually used internally by Oracle Development and Oracle Support.

If the keyword *immediate* is not used as a first argument in the event specification, you need to indicate how long the specified tracing should be enabled. Specifying the keyword *forever* will keep the tracing enabled for the lifetime of the session, or instance, depending on whether the event is set from the init.ora file or at a session level using the ALTER SESSION command. The last optional keyword, *level*, defines the granularity of the trace. If no level is specified, the default minimum tracing is enabled. Setting level to zero will turn the trace off. In some cases, the *level* takes some other values, for example a decimal data block address during data block dumps and index tree dumps. It specifies bit patterns representing the heap number in heap dumps.

Setting Multiple Actions for an Event

Multiple actions can also set for a single event. The following multiple actions are possible:

- **TRACE**   Dump the trace file
- **CRASH**   Crash the process
- **INVOKE THE DUBUGGER**   Invoke the debugger

Table A-3 shows the parameters supported by TRACE. Table A-4 shows the parameters supported by CRASH. Table A-5 shows the parameters supported by DEBUGGER.

CAUTION
The details about CRASH and DEBUGGER are shown purely for academic purpose. Using these parameters in a production database will cause a lot of overhead to the Oracle Database engine and may lead the database into an unsupported state.

Parameter Name	Description
Level *n*	The level keyword is used in multiple contexts. Normally, the higher the level the more details you get.
After *n* times	Starts the trace after the specified event has occurred *n* times.
Lifetime *n*	Traces only *n* number of times.
Forever	Continues the action forever.
Type increment	Sets trace level to maximum.
Type decrement	Disables the trace level (level 0).
Off	Turns off tracing.

TABLE A-3.   *TRACE Supported Parameters*

Parameter Name	Description
After *n* times	Crashes the process after *n* times.
Off	Turns off CRASH (disables).

TABLE A-4. *CRASH Supported Parameters*

In some cases, level represents a different context, such as block dumps, where it indicates the decimal block address of the DBA. In other cases it represents the object ID (for example, in DROP_SEGMENTS events it represents the tablespace number).

Internal Workings of the Events

Process events and session events group internal events. Process events are events initialized during the startup time of that process, whereas session events can be started and controlled anytime using the ALTER SESSION command. During checking for what events are set, the session events are checked first, followed by process events. The following simple pseudo code explains the search order of events:

```
if <session_event_set> is YES
execute session_event
else if
<process_event_set> is YES
session inherits the process event.
No event set.
```

An event set into one session is not visible to other sessions because the information about that event is kept in the Private Global Area (or Process Global

Parameter Name	Description
After *n* times	Starts the debugger after *n* times.
Lifetime *n*	Invokes the debugger after *n* times and turns off the debugger after that.
Forever	Invokes the debugger every time the event occurs.
Off	Turns off CRASH (disables).

TABLE A-5. *DEBUGGER Supported Parameters*

Area, or simply PGA), which is not shared among the sessions. Because of this private nature, there is no easy way to find the existence of a tracing event from another session other than going to the trace files. However, you can use an undocumented utility in the *dbms_system.read_ev* package and retrieve the information for the current session.

A simple example of *dbms_system.read_ev* call follows:

```
set serveroutput on
declare
  event_level number;
begin
  for i in 10000..10999 loop
    sys.dbms_system.read_ev(i,event_level);
    if (event_level > 0) then
      dbms_output.put_line('Event '||to_char(i)||' set at level '||
                            to_char(event_level));
    end if;
  end loop;
end;
/
```

Other than using the *dbms_system.read_ev*, the *oradebug dump events* command can be used to get the details about the events set in a particular session. The following example illustrates the use of this command.

To find out events set in your own session:

```
SQL>oradebug setmypid
Statement processed.
SQL> oradebug event 10053 trace name context forever, level 1
Statement processed.
SQL> oradebug dump events 1
Statement processed.
SQL> oradebug tracefile_name
/u01/app/oracle/admin/V10HP/udump/v10hp_ora_11262.trc
```

```
File /u01/app/oracle/admin/V10HP/udump/v10hp_ora_11262.trc contains
following:

Oracle Database 10g Enterprise Edition Release 10.1.0.2.0 - 64bit
Production
With the Partitioning, Real Application Clusters and Data Mining options
ORACLE_HOME = /u01/app/oracle/product/10.1.0
System name:    HP-UX
Node name:      hptest
Release:        B.11.11
Version:        U
Machine:        9000/889
```

```
Instance name: V10HP
Redo thread mounted by this instance: 2
Oracle process number: 25
Unix process pid: 11262, image: oracle@hptest (TNS V1-V3)
*** 2004-03-15 12:31:09.546
*** SERVICE NAME:(SYS$USERS) 2004-03-15 12:31:09.525
*** SESSION ID:(154.8244) 2004-03-15 12:31:09.525
Dump event group for level SESSION
TC Addr  Evt#(b10)    Action   TR Addr     Arm     Life
4C0200B8 10053          1       4c020148 0 0
    TR Name       TR level   TR address        TR arm      TR life      TRtype
    CONTEXT               1 0                     -1                2 135266304
```

Numbers in bold in the preceding output show that event 10053 was set at trace level 1 by this session.

NOTE
The preceding example is for illustration purposes only. To use oradebug *you must connect as sysdba.*

If you want to find out if someone else's session has set any event, you can use the session's OSPID (or ORAPID) number with *oradebug* as shown in the following example, where session 153, with an OSPID 11687, is checked if it had set any events:

```
SQL> oradebug setospid 11687
Oracle pid: 27, Unix process pid: 11687, image: oracle@hptest (TNS V1-V3)
SQL> oradebug dump events 1
Statement processed.

The trace file contained following:

*** 2004-03-15 12:52:03.518
*** SERVICE NAME:(SYS$USERS) 2004-03-15 12:52:03.515
*** SESSION ID:(153.7407) 2004-03-15 12:52:03.515
Dump event group for level SESSION
TC Addr  Evt#(b10)    Action   TR Addr     Arm     Life
4C020160 10170          1       4c0201f0 0 0
    TR Name       TR level   TR address        TR arm      TR life      TR type
    CONTEXT               1 0                     -1                2 1207959552
```

Here event 10170 is set at trace level 1 for the session.

Oracle diagnostic events should be used with care and under the supervision by Oracle Support. They can be used to get detailed trace information from the Oracle kernel during debugging. Please keep in mind that using such events is unsupported by the Oracle Corporation. These events should be never set in production databases unless advised by Oracle Support. Happy (but cautious) tracing!

APPENDIX
B

Enqueue Waits in
Oracle Database 10g

n Oracle Database 10*g* Release 1, each enqueue type is represented by its own wait event, making it much easier to understand exactly what type of enqueue the session is waiting for. You do not need to decipher the values from the P1, P2, P3, P1RAW, P2RAW, and P3RAW columns in the V$SESSION_WAIT or the V$SESSION view.

The following table lists all the enqueue waits in Oracle Database 10*g* Release 1 and describes what the enqueue is for. This information is available in the X$KSQST structure. The aggregated statistics for each of these enqueue types is displayed by the view V$ENQUEUE_STAT.

Enqueue Type	Description
enq: AD - allocate AU	Synchronizes accesses to a specific OSM (Oracle Software Manager) disk AU
enq: AD - deallocate AU	Synchronizes accesses to a specific OSM disk AU
enq: AF - task serialization	Serializes access to an advisor task
enq: AG - contention	Synchronizes generation use of a particular workspace
enq: AO - contention	Synchronizes access to objects and scalar variables
enq: AS - contention	Synchronizes new service activation
enq: AT - contention	Serializes *alter tablespace* operations
enq: AW - AW$ table lock	Allows global access synchronization to the AW$ table (analytical workplace tables used in OLAP option)
enq: AW - AW generation lock	Gives in-use generation state for a particular workspace
enq: AW - user access for AW	Synchronizes user accesses to a particular workspace
enq: AW - AW state lock	Row lock synchronization for the AW$ table
enq: BR - file shrink	Lock held to prevent file from decreasing in physical size during RMAN backup
enq: BR - proxy-copy	Lock held to allow cleanup from backup mode during an RMAN proxy-copy backup
enq: CF - contention	Synchronizes accesses to the controlfile
enq: CI - contention	Coordinates cross-instance function invocations

Enqueue Type	Description
enq: CL - drop label	Synchronizes accesses to label cache when dropping a label
enq: CL - compare labels	Synchronizes accesses to label cache for label comparison
enq: CM - gate	Serializes access to instance enqueue
enq: CM - instance	Indicates OSM disk group is mounted
enq: CT - global space management	Lock held during change tracking space management operations that affect the entire change tracking file
enq: CT - state	Lock held while enabling or disabling change tracking to ensure that it is enabled or disabled by only one user at a time
enq: CT - state change gate 2	Lock held while enabling or disabling change tracking in RAC
enq: CT - reading	Lock held to ensure that change tracking data remains in existence until a reader is done with it
enq: CT - CTWR process start/ stop	Lock held to ensure that only one CTWR (Change Tracking Writer, which tracks block changes and is initiated by the *alter database enable block change tracking* command) process is started in a single instance
enq: CT - state change gate 1	Lock held while enabling or disabling change tracking in RAC
enq: CT - change stream ownership	Lock held by one instance while change tracking is enabled to guarantee access to thread-specific resources
enq: CT - local space management	Lock held during change tracking space management operations that affect just the data for one thread
enq: CU - contention	Recovers cursors in case of death while compiling
enq: DB - contention	Synchronizes modification of database wide supplemental logging attributes
enq: DD - contention	Synchronizes local accesses to ASM (Automatic Storage Management) disk groups

Enqueue Type	Description
enq: DF - contention	Enqueue held by foreground or DBWR when a datafile is brought online in RAC
enq: DG - contention	Synchronizes accesses to ASM disk groups
enq: DL - contention	Lock to prevent index DDL during direct load
enq: DM - contention	Enqueue held by foreground or DBWR to synchronize database mount/open with other operations
enq: DN - contention	Serializes group number generations
enq: DP - contention	Synchronizes access to LDAP parameters
enq: DR - contention	Serializes the active distributed recovery operation
enq: DS - contention	Prevents a database suspend during LMON reconfiguration
enq: DT - contention	Serializes changing the default temporary table space and user creation
enq: DV - contention	Synchronizes access to lower-version Diana (PL/SQL intermediate representation)
enq: DX - contention	Serializes tightly coupled distributed transaction branches
enq: FA - access file	Synchronizes accesses to open ASM files
enq: FB - contention	Ensures that only one process can format data blocks in auto segment space managed tablespaces
enq: FC - open an ACD thread	LGWR opens an ACD thread
enq: FC - recover an ACD thread	SMON recovers an ACD thread
enq: FD - Marker generation	Synchronization
enq: FD - Flashback coordinator	Synchronization
enq: FD - Tablespace flashback on/off	Synchronization
enq: FD - Flashback on/off	Synchronization

Enqueue Type	Description
enq: FG - serialize ACD relocate	Only 1 process in the cluster may do ACD relocation in a disk group
enq: FG - LGWR redo generation enq race	Resolves race condition to acquire Disk Group Redo Generation Enqueue
enq: FG - FG redo generation enq race	Resolves race condition to acquire Disk Group Redo Generation Enqueue
enq: FL - Flashback database log	Synchronizes access to Flashback database log
enq: FL - Flashback db command	Synchronizes Flashback Database and deletion of flashback logs
enq: FM - contention	Synchronizes access to global file mapping state
enq: FR - contention	Begins recovery of disk group
enq: FS - contention	Synchronizes recovery and file operations or synchronizes dictionary check
enq: FT - allow LGWR writes	Allows LGWR to generate redo in this thread
enq: FT - disable LGWR writes	Prevents LGWR from generating redo in this thread
enq: FU - contention	Serializes the capture of the DB feature, usage, and high watermark statistics
enq: HD - contention	Serializes accesses to ASM SGA data structures
enq: HP - contention	Synchronizes accesses to queue pages
enq: HQ - contention	Synchronizes the creation of new queue IDs
enq: HV - contention	Lock used to broker the high watermark during parallel inserts
enq: HW - contention	Lock used to broker the high watermark during parallel inserts
enq: IA - contention	Information not available
enq: ID - contention	Lock held to prevent other processes from performing controlfile transaction while NID is running
enq: IL - contention	Synchronizes accesses to internal label data structures

Enqueue Type	Description
enq: IM - contention for blr	Serializes block recovery for IMU txn
enq: IR - contention	Synchronizes instance recovery
enq: IR - contention2	Synchronizes parallel instance recovery and shutdown immediate
enq: IS - contention	Synchronizes instance state changes
enq: IT - contention	Synchronizes accesses to a temp object's metadata
enq: JD - contention	Synchronizes dates between job queue coordinator and slave processes
enq: JI - contention	Lock held during materialized view operations (such as refresh, alter) to prevent concurrent operations on the same materialized view
enq: JQ - contention	Lock to prevent multiple instances from running a single job
enq: JS - contention	Synchronizes accesses to the job cache
enq: JS - coord post lock	Lock for coordinator posting
enq: JS - global wdw lock	Lock acquired when doing wdw ddl
enq: JS - job chain evaluate lock	Lock when job chain evaluated for steps to create
enq: JS - q mem clnup lck	Lock obtained when cleaning up q memory
enq: JS - slave enq get lock2	Gets run info locks before slv objget
enq: JS - slave enq get lock1	Slave locks exec pre to sess strt
enq: JS - running job cnt lock3	Lock to set running job count epost
enq: JS - running job cnt lock2	Lock to set running job count epre
enq: JS - running job cnt lock	Lock to get running job count
enq: JS - coord rcv lock	Lock when coord receives msg
enq: JS - queue lock	Lock on internal scheduler queue
enq: JS - job run lock - synchronize	Lock to prevent job from running elsewhere
enq: JS - job recov lock	Lock to recover jobs running on crashed RAC inst

Enqueue Type	Description
enq: KK - context	Lock held by open redo thread, used by other instances to force a log switch
enq: KM - contention	Synchronizes various Resource Manager operations
enq: KP - contention	Synchronizes kupp process startup
enq: KT - contention	Synchronizes accesses to the current Resource Manager plan
enq: MD - contention	Lock held during materialized view log DDL statements
enq: MH - contention	Lock used for recovery when setting Mail Host for AQ e-mail notifications
enq: ML - contention	Lock used for recovery when setting Mail Port for AQ e-mail notifications
enq: MN - contention	Synchronizes updates to the LogMiner dictionary and prevents multiple instances from preparing the same LogMiner session
enq: MR - contention	Lock used to coordinate media recovery with other uses of datafiles
enq: MS - contention	Lock held during materialized view refresh to set up MV log
enq: MW - contention	Serializes the calibration of the manageability schedules with the Maintenance Window
enq: OC - contention	Synchronizes write accesses to the outline cache
enq: OL - contention	Synchronizes accesses to a particular outline name
enq: OQ - xsoqhiAlloc	Synchronizes access to olapi history allocation
enq: OQ - xsoqhiClose	Synchronizes access to olapi history closing
enq: OQ - xsoqhistrecb	Synchronizes access to olapi history globals
enq: OQ - xsoqhiFlush	Synchronizes access to olapi history flushing
enq: OQ - xsoq*histrecb	Synchronizes access to olapi history parameter CB
enq: PD - contention	Prevents others from updating the same property
enq: PE - contention	Synchronizes system parameter updates

Enqueue Type	Description
enq: PF - contention	Synchronizes accesses to the password file
enq: PG - contention	Synchronizes global system parameter updates
enq: PH - contention	Lock used for recovery when setting proxy for AQ HTTP notifications
enq: PI - contention	Communicates remote Parallel Execution Server Process creation status
enq: PL - contention	Coordinates plug-in operation of transportable tablespaces
enq: PR - contention	Synchronizes process startup
enq: PS - contention	Parallel Execution Server Process reservation and synchronization
enq: PT - contention	Synchronizes access to ASM PST metadata
enq: PV - syncstart	Synchronizes slave start_shutdown
enq: PV - syncshut	Synchronizes instance shutdown_slvstart
enq: PW - prewarm status in dbw0	DBWR0 holds this enqueue indicating pre-warmed buffers present in cache
enq: PW - flush prewarm buffers	Direct Load needs to flush prewarmed buffers if DBWR0 holds this enqueue
enq: RB - contention	Serializes OSM rollback recovery operations
enq: RF - synch: per-SGA Broker metadata	Ensures r/w atomicity of DG configuration metadata per unique SGA
enq: RF - synchronization: critical ai	Synchronizes critical apply instance among primary instances
enq: RF - new AI	Synchronizes selection of the new apply instance
enq: RF - synchronization: chief	Anoints 1 instance's DMON (Data Guard Broker Monitor) as chief to other instance's DMONs
enq: RF - synchronization: HC master	Anoints 1 instance's DMON as health check master
enq: RF - synchronization: aifo master	Synchronizes critical apply instance failure detection and failover operation
enq: RF - atomicity	Ensures atomicity of log transport setup

Enqueue Type	Description
enq: RN - contention	Coordinates nab computations of online logs during recovery
enq: RO - contention	Coordinates flushing of multiple objects
enq: RO - fast object reuse	Coordinates fast object reuse
enq: RP - contention	Enqueue held when resilvering is needed or when data block is repaired from mirror
enq: RS - file delete	Lock held to prevent file from accessing during space reclamation
enq: RS - persist alert level	Lock held to make alert level persistent
enq: RS - write alert level	Lock held to write alert level
enq: RS - read alert level	Lock held to read alert level
enq: RS - prevent aging list update	Lock held to prevent aging list update
enq: RS - record reuse	Lock held to prevent file from accessing while reusing circular record
enq: RS - prevent file delete	Lock held to prevent deleting file to reclaim space
enq: RT - contention	Thread locks held by LGWR, DBW0, and RVWR (Recovery Writer, used in Flashback Database operations) to indicate mounted or open status
enq: SB - contention	Synchronizes logical standby metadata operations
enq: SF - contention	Lock held for recovery when setting sender for AQ e-mail notifications
enq: SH - contention	Enqueue always acquired in no-wait mode; should seldom see this contention
enq: SI - contention	Prevents multiple streams table instantiations
enq: SK - contention	Serialize shrink of a segment
enq: SQ - contention	Lock to ensure that only one process can replenish the sequence cache
enq: SR - contention	Coordinates replication / streams operations
enq: SS - contention	Ensures that sort segments created during parallel DML operations aren't prematurely cleaned up

Enqueue Type	Description
enq: ST - contention	Synchronizes space management activities in dictionary-managed tablespaces
enq: SU - contention	Serializes access to SaveUndo Segment
enq: SW - contention	Coordinates the 'alter system suspend' operation
enq: TA - contention	Serializes operations on undo segments and undo tablespaces
enq: TB - SQL Tuning Base Cache Update	Synchronizes writes to the SQL Tuning Base Existence Cache
enq: TB - SQL Tuning Base Cache Load	Synchronizes writes to the SQL Tuning Base Existence Cache
enq: TC - contention	Lock held to guarantee uniqueness of a tablespace checkpoint
enq: TC - contention2	Lock during setup of a unique tablespace checkpoint in null mode
enq: TD - KTF dump entries	KTF dumping time/scn mappings in SMON_SCN_TIME table
enq: TE - KTF broadcast	KTF broadcasting
enq: TF - contention	Serializes dropping of a temporary file
enq: TL - contention	Serializes threshold log table read and update
enq: TM - contention	Synchronizes accesses to an object
enq: TO - contention	Synchronizes DDL and DML operations on a temp object
enq: TQ - TM contention	TM access to the queue table
enq: TQ - DDL contention	DDL access to the queue table
enq: TQ - INI contention	TM access to the queue table
enq: TS - contention	Serializes accesses to temp segments
enq: TT - contention	Serializes DDL operations on tablespaces
enq: TW - contention	Lock held by one instance to wait for transactions on all instances to finish
enq: TX - contention	Lock held by a transaction to allow other transactions to wait for it

Enqueue Type	Description
enq: TX - row lock contention	Lock held on a particular row by a transaction to prevent other transactions from modifying it
enq: TX - allocate ITL entry	Allocating an ITL entry in order to begin a transaction
enq: TX - index contention	Lock held on an index during a split to prevent other operations on it
enq: UL - contention	Lock held used by user applications
enq: US - contention	Lock held to perform DDL on the undo segment
enq: WA - contention	Lock used for recovery when setting watermark for memory usage in AQ notifications
enq: WF - contention	Enqueue used to serialize the flushing of snapshots
enq: WL - contention	Coordinates access to redo log files and archive logs
enq: WP - contention	Enqueue to handle concurrency between purging and baselines
enq: XH - contention	Lock used for recovery when setting No Proxy Domains for AQ HTTP notifications
enq: XR - quiesce database	Lock held during database quiesce
enq: XR - database force logging	Lock held during database force logging mode
enq: XY - contention	Lock used by Oracle Corporation for internal testing

APPENDIX C

Oracle Dumps and Traces

ll of us have encountered ORA-0600 or ORA-7445 errors in our databases, and we all know how difficult it is to identify the root cause of such errors. Almost all the time you must contact Oracle Support to determine the root cause of these errors. Invariably, Oracle Support asks for additional trace files or various data or memory dumps, depending on the situation.

Dumping and tracing are integral parts of any advanced debugging processes. As a single piece of software, Oracle RDBMS is one of the most complex software packages, and debugging complex problems requires such traces and dumps so you can understand exactly what went wrong.

This appendix introduces you to the utilities and procedures used in producing such trace files and dumps. However, detailed analysis of the generated trace files is beyond the scope of this book.

Oradebug: The Ultimate Utility for Traces and Dumps

Oradebug is one of the most widely used utilities to set the debug events and produce dumps. Unfortunately, very little documentation is readily available on how to use it correctly. However, it does have a friendly help facility that you can use. *Oradebug* requires that you connect as a SYS user to use its commands. It has an extensive list of commands that you can use to simply trace a process, or it can be used to see the contents of the memory structures Oracle uses. Some of these commands can also change the contents. For this reason, extreme care must be taken when using *oradebug* commands.

NOTE
Incorrect use of oradebug *commands can result in data corruption, rendering your database unsupported by Oracle.*

The following is an output of the *oradebug help* command from Oracle Database 10*g* Release 1. Most of these are self-explanatory.

```
SQL> oradebug help
HELP            [command]                Describe one or all commands
SETMYPID                                 Debug current process
SETOSPID        <ospid>                  Set OS pid of process to debug
SETORAPID       <orapid> ['force']       Set Oracle pid of process to debug
DUMP            <dump_name> <lvl> [addr]  Invoke named dump|
DUMPSGA         [bytes]                   Dump fixed SGA
```

```
DUMPLIST                                    Print a list of available dumps
EVENT            <text>                     Set trace event in process
SESSION_EVENT    <text>                     Set trace event in session
DUMPVAR          <p|s|uga> <name> [level]   Print/dump a fixed PGA/SGA/UGA variable
SETVAR           <p|s|uga> <name> <value>   Modify a fixed PGA/SGA/UGA variable
PEEK             <addr> <len> [level]       Print/Dump memory
POKE             <addr> <len> <value>       Modify memory
WAKEUP           <orapid>                   Wake up Oracle process
SUSPEND                                     Suspend execution
RESUME                                      Resume execution
FLUSH                                       Flush pending writes to trace file
CLOSE_TRACE                                 Close trace file
TRACEFILE_NAME                              Get name of trace file
LKDEBUG                                     Invoke global enqueue service debugger
NSDBX                                       Invoke CGS name-service debugger
-G               <Inst-List | def | all>   Parallel oradebug command prefix
-R               <Inst-List | def | all>   Parallel oradebug prefix (return output
SETINST          <instance# .. | all>      Set instance list in double quotes
SGATOFILE        <SGA dump dir>            Dump SGA to file; dirname in double quotes
DMPCOWSGA        <SGA dump dir> Dump & map SGA as COW; dirname in double quotes
MAPCOWSGA        <SGA dump dir>           Map SGA as COW; dirname in double quotes
HANGANALYZE      [level] [syslevel]         Analyze system hang
FFBEGIN                                     Flash Freeze the Instance
FFDEREGISTER                                FF deregister instance from cluster
FFTERMINST                                  Call exit and terminate instance
FFRESUMEINST                                Resume the flash frozen instance
FFSTATUS                                    Flash freeze status of instance
SKDSTTPCS        <ifname>  <ofname>         Helps translate PCs to names
WATCH            <address> <len> <self|exist|all|target>  Watch a region of memory
DELETE           <local|global|target> watchpoint <id>     Delete a watchpoint
SHOW             <local|global|target> watchpoints       Show  watchpoints
CORE                                        Dump core without crashing process
IPC                                         Dump ipc information
UNLIMIT                                     Unlimit the size of the trace file
PROCSTAT                                    Dump process statistics
CALL             <func> [arg1] ... [argn]  Invoke function with arguments
SQL>
```

The most commonly used commands are setmypid, setospid, setorapid, dump, event, session_event, ipc, wakeup, and tracefile_name.

The dumplist command will list all available dumps, which will list contents of various internal Oracle structures. Each of these named dumps can be initiated with the use of dump command. The following example lists a few of the named dumps available in Oracle Database 10*g* Release 1. We will discuss a couple of named dumps and their application in the subsequent sections:

```
SQL> oradebug dumplist
EVENTS
TRACE_BUFFER_ON
TRACE_BUFFER_OFF
HANGANALYZE
```

```
LATCHES
PROCESSSTATE
SYSTEMSTATE
INSTANTIATIONSTATE
REFRESH_OS_STATS
CROSSIC
CONTEXTAREA
HEAPDUMP
```

In addition to the *oradebug* utility, the ALTER SYSTEM and ALTER SESSION commands can be used to produce dumps and trace files.

Data Block Dump

A data block dump shows detailed information of the contents of the block for the given datafile number and the block number. It shows you exactly how the data is stored internally. Depending on whether it is a table or index segment, the data block will list the contents of rows or index keys. The segment header block dump will list the extent map information. The undo header block dump will list the free extent pool in the undo segments. You may need to dump the contents of the data block when investigating block corruptions. In addition, complex recovery situations also warrant block dumps to check the SCN of the block.

Syntax

The following methods dump the contents of the interested data blocks to the trace file in the UDUMP directory. Data block dumps contain the actual data stored in the blocks.

NOTE
If your database instance has the hidden parameter _TRACE_FILES_PUBLIC set to TRUE, please remember that the trace file data can be viewed by anyone with access to your database server machine. It will compromise data security and confidentiality.

Using ALTER SYSTEM
The first line in the following syntax dumps the specified single block, while the second line dumps a range of adjacent blocks.

```
alter system dump datafile <file#> block <block#>;
alter system dump datafile <file#> block min <min_block#> block max
<max_block#>;
```

The following procedure can be used to dump the segment header block and the data block of a given segment. You need to identify the file# and block# for the segment. The DBA_EXTENTS view can be queried to get this information:

```
select file_id, block_id, blocks
from   dba_extents
where  segment_name = 'TEST';

   FILE_ID   BLOCK_ID      BLOCKS
---------- ---------- ----------
         1      29081           8

REM ---- To dump the segment header block
alter system dump datafile 1 block 29081;

REM ---- To dump the data block next to the segment header
alter system dump datafile 1 block 29082

REM ---- To dump both the blocks at the same time
alter system dump datafile 1 block min 29081 block max 29082;
```

Using *oradebug*
Oradebug is generally not used for block dumps.

Buffers Dump
The named dump buffers can be used to dump the buffer cache. The information produced varies. Depending on the *level* specified, the trace file will contain information pertaining to buffer headers, users and waiters of that buffer, position of that buffer, and other details, such as the object number and tablespace number. The dump file also holds the LRU information about the buffers.

The size of the trace file depends on the init.ora parameter DB_CACHE_SIZE or DB_BLOCK_BUFFERS, depending on the version of the database. You may need to dump the buffer cache if the problem is related to buffer corruption or any other buffer cache related issues. In the Real Application Clusters environment, it is required to dump the buffers in all nodes. This event can be set in the init.ora file to trigger the buffers dump when a particular error occurs.

Syntax

The following methods show how to dump the buffers.

Using ALTER SESSION

The first ALTER SESSION command below produces an immediate buffers dump at specified level, and the second ALTER SESSION produces the buffers dump when the session encounters an ORA-0600 error.

```
alter session set events 'immediate trace name buffers level <n>;
alter session set events '600 trace name buffers level 10';
```

In the init.ora File

The following event will dump the buffer contents to a trace file when an ORA-600 error occurs. You can specify any other Oracle error number to get the dump when that error occurs the next time.

```
event="600 trace name buffers level 10"
```

Using *oradebug*

The following *oradebug* command produces the buffers dump in a trace file. The level number, denoted by *n*, controls the amount of information written to the trace file.

```
oradebug setmypid
oradebug dump buffers <n>;
```

Controlling the Dump Information

The following list shows the available dump levels and the information they produce:

- **Level 1**   Dumps only the buffer header information

- **Level 2**   Dumps the cache and transaction headers from each block

- **Level 3**   Dumps a full dump of each block

- **Level 4**   Dumps the working set lists and the buffer headers and the cache header for each block

- **Level 5**   Dumps the transaction header from each block

- **Level 6**   Dumps full dump of each block

Buffer Dump

The buffer dump is same as the buffers dump discussed in the preceding session, except as regards the LRU information. The buffer dumps all the buffers in the buffer cache of the given Data Block Address (DBA) at level 10. This can be used to dump the buffers of the known DBA. Starting from Oracle8 you need to set the SET_TSN_P1 event because the address is taken as relative DBA, which is specific to a tablespace. This dump is usually taken to investigate the buffer copies of the single known buffer. Note the number of CR copies of the specific buffer in the buffer cache is limited by the undocumented parameter __DB_BLOCK_MAX_CR_DBA. You may need to use the buffer dump when the error is related to a single buffer (or a set of buffers). In this case, having the buffer dump will be a big overhead, and this will be expensive when the buffer cache is large.

Syntax

The following methods show how to dump the contents of the buffer cache.

Using ALTER SESSION

In order to enable the event, SET_TSN_P1 you need to find out the tablespace number (TS#) from V$TABLESPACE as follows:

```
select ts#, name
from   V$tablespace;

        TS# NAME
---------- -----------------------------
          0 SYSTEM
          1 UNDOTBS1
          2 SYSAUX
          3 TEMP
          4 USERS
```

The following two ALTER SESSION commands can then be used to dump the buffer.

```
alter session set events 'immediate trace name SET_TSN_P1 level <TS#+1>';
alter session set events 'immediate trace name BUFFER level <RDBA>';
```

Using *oradebug*

The following sequence of *oradebug* commands shows how to dump the buffer to a trace file. The process ID can be obtained from the V$PROCESS view.

```
oradebug setospid <process ID>
oradebug unlimit
oradebug dump buffer <RDBA>
```

Controlling the Dump Information Using Levels

Not applicable.

File Headers Dump

File header dumps will be very useful while diagnosing errors related to media recovery. These file headers will contain the various SCN numbers used for database recovery operations and hold important information such as checkpoint details, the redo information address (rba), extent information, and the high water mark for that datafile.

Syntax

The following methods show how to dump the file header information.

Using ALTER SESSION

In the following ALTER SESSION command, the file headers are dumped at level 10.

```
alter session set events 'immediate trace name file_hdrs level 10'
```

Using *oradebug*

The following *oradebug* command sequence shows how to dump file headers at level 10.

```
oradebug setmypid
oradebug unlimit
oradebug dump  file_hdrs  10
```

Controlling the Dump Information Using Levels

The file headers dump is taken between levels 1 and 10. The following output is taken from a dump of file headers at level 10.

```
DATA FILE #1:
   (name #4) D:\ORACLE\PRODUCT\10.1.0\DB_1\GOPAL\SYSTEM01.DBF
creation size=38400 block size=8192 status=0xe head=4 tail=4 dup=1
 tablespace 0, index=1 krfil=1 prev_file=0
 unrecoverable scn: 0x0000.00000000 01/01/1988 00:00:00
 Checkpoint cnt:75 scn: 0x0000.000438f4 04/01/2004 00:53:01
 Stop scn: 0xffff.ffffffff 03/31/2004 20:21:22
 Creation Checkpointed at scn:  0x0000.00000009 03/22/2004 16:46:41
 thread:1 rba:(0x1.3.10)
 enabled  threads:  01000000 00000000 00000000 00000000 00000000 00000000
  00000000 00000000
```

```
Offline scn: 0x0000.00000000 prev_range: 0
Online Checkpointed at scn:   0x0000.00000000
thread:0 rba:(0x0.0.0)
enabled  threads:  00000000 00000000 00000000 00000000 00000000 00000000
 00000000 00000000
Hot Backup end marker scn: 0x0000.00000000
aux_file is NOT DEFINED
V10 STYLE FILE HEADER:
     Compatibility Vsn = 168821248=0xa100200
     Db ID=580029651=0x22928cd3, Db Name='GOPAL'
     Activation ID=0=0x0
     Control Seq=252=0xfc, File size=38400=0x9600
     File Number=1, Blksiz=8192, File Type=3 DATA
Tablespace #0 - SYSTEM  rel_fn:1
Creation   at   scn: 0x0000.00000009 03/22/2004 16:46:41
Backup taken at scn: 0x0000.00000000 01/01/1988 00:00:00 thread:0
 reset logs count:0x1f153853 scn: 0x0000.00000001 reset logs terminal rcv
data:0x0 scn: 0x0000.00000000
 prev reset logs count:0x0 scn: 0x0000.00000000 prev reset logs terminal
rcv data:0x0 scn: 0x0000.00000000
 recovered at 04/01/2004 00:52:53
 status:0x2004 root dba:0x00400179 chkpt cnt: 75 ctl cnt:74
begin-hot-backup file size: 0
Checkpointed at scn:   0x0000.000438f4 04/01/2004 00:53:01
 thread:1 rba:(0x35.2.10)
 enabled  threads:  01000000 00000000 00000000 00000000 00000000 00000000
 00000000 00000000
Backup Checkpointed at scn:   0x0000.00000000
 thread:0 rba:(0x0.0.0)
 enabled  threads:  00000000 00000000 00000000 00000000 00000000 00000000
 00000000 00000000
External cache id: 0x0 0x0 0x0 0x0
Absolute fuzzy scn: 0x0000.00000000
Recovery fuzzy scn: 0x0000.00000000 01/01/1988 00:00:00
Terminal Recovery Stamp scn: 0x0000.00000000 01/01/1988 00:00:00
Platform Information:   Creation Platform ID: 7
Current Platform ID: 7  Last Platform ID: 7
```

Control File Dump

Control files hold the information about the redo logs and datafiles and the critical recovery information like online SCN and offline SCN of datafiles. While opening the database, the control file information is verified against the datafile header information, and the database is opened if both are in sync. Otherwise it will prompt for media recovery.

Control file dumps are usually taken to diagnose recovery-related problems. Part of the control file contents are visible in a few X$ views, such as those starting with X$KCC.

Syntax

Following methods show how to dump the control file information.

Using ALTER SESSION

In the following ALTER SESSION command, control file contents are dumped using level 10.

```
alter session set events 'immediate trace name controlf level 10';
```

Using *oradebug*

In the following *oradebug* commands the control file contents are dumped using level 10.

```
oradebug setmypid
oradebug unlimit
oradebug dump  controlf 10
```

Controlling the Dump Information Using Levels

The level controls how many records are to be dumped to the trace file. The number of records for the RMAN backups in the control files depend on the init.ora parameter CONTROL_FILE_RECORD_KEEP_TIME, which defaults to seven days. This parameter is related to RMAN when the control file is used as a recovery catalog. Setting this to higher values may increase the size of the control file, depending on the number of log switches and other recovery-related information stored in the file. The number of dumped records is $2^{(level-2)}$, as shown here:

- **Level 10**   Dumps (2^8) or 256 records
- **Level 11**   Dumps (2^9) or 512 records
- **Level 12**   Dumps (2^{10}) or 1024 records

Heap Dump

Heap dumps show details about the memory allocation and distribution in the shared pool and library cache including the details about the objects. It will also show the details about the cursors and the latch information when level 2 is used. It will have the details about the memory chunks (free, freeable, permanent, and recreatable) and their sizes. It will also have the information about the hash buckets and freelists inside the shared pool. Heap dumps are often requested by Oracle Support to diagnose shared pool related errors.

Syntax
Following methods show how to produce a heap dump.

Using ALTER SESSION
The first ALTER SESSION below will immediately produce a heap dump at supplied level number, while the second ALTER SESSION command will produce the heap dump when the session encounters ORA-4031 error.

```
alter session set events 'immediate trace name heapdump level <level>';
alter session set events '4031 trace name heapdump level 2';
```

Using *oradebug*
The following *oradebug* command sequence shows how to produce an immediate heap dump at level 10.

```
oradebug setmypid
oradebug unlimit
oradebug dump  heapdump <level>
```

Controlling the Dump Information Using Levels
The decimal value of shown in the following table can be used as *level* to control the dump information written to the trace file.

Heap	Hex	Dec
PGA	0x01	1
SGA	0x02	2
UGA	0x04	4
Current call	0x08	8
User call	0x10	6
Large pool	0x20	32

Example Output
The following snippet is from a trace file of the heap dump taken at level 2:

```
HEAP DUMP heap name="sga heap"  desc=02E1DE80
  extent sz=0x32c8 alt=104 het=32767 rec=9 flg=-126 opc=0
  parent=00000000 owner=00000000 nex=00000000 xsz=0x0
**********************************************************
HEAP DUMP heap name="sga heap(1,0)"  desc=04766E28
  extent sz=0xfc4 alt=104 het=32767 rec=9 flg=-126 opc=0
  parent=00000000 owner=00000000 nex=00000000 xsz=0x400000
```

```
EXTENT 0 addr=14000000
   Chunk 1400002c sz=         24  R-freeable  "reserved stoppe"
   Chunk 14000044 sz=     212900  R-free      "               "
   Chunk 14033fe8 sz=         24  R-freeable  "reserved stoppe"
   Chunk 14034000 sz=    3959460     perm     "perm          "  alo=3959460
   Chunk 143faaa4 sz=      12172     perm     "perm          "  alo=12172
   Chunk 143fda30 sz=       7792     perm     "perm          "  alo=7792
   Chunk 143ff8a0 sz=         24   freeable   "service names a"
   Chunk 143ff8b8 sz=         32   recreate   "fixed allocatio"  latch=130F87AC
```

Library Cache Dump

A library cache dump will have the details about the objects in the library cache, including the dependency structures and the details about the cursor, such as hash value and timestamp. This event can be used either with the immediate option, which dumps the library cache once the command is issued, or it can be triggered when an error occurs.

Syntax

Following methods show how to dump the library cache contents.

Using ALTER SESSION

The following ALTER SESSION command can be used to dump the library cache at level 10.

```
alter session set events 'immediate trace name library_cache level 10'
```

Using *oradebug*

The following *oradebug* commands can be used to produce an immediate dump of the library cache at required level.

```
oradebug setmypid
oradebug unlimit
oradebug dump  library_cache <level>
```

Controlling the Dump Information Using Levels

The following list shows the available levels and the information they produce:

- **Level 1**   Dumps library cache statistics
- **Level 2**   Dumps hash table summary
- **Level 4**   Dumps library cache objects with basic information

- **Level 8**   Dumps objects with detailed information (including child references, pin waiters, etc.)

- **Level 16**   Dumps heap sizes (can be latch intensive)

- **Level 32**   Dumps heap information

You can mix these levels to produce various pieces of information. For example, if you use level 11 (8 + 2 + 1), the dump will have the dumps of level 8, level 2, and level 1.

Processstate Dump

Processstate dumps are usually required to collect more information when diagnosing memory corruptions or dead lock errors. Processstate dumps also show the details about the shared objects used by the library cache and help in determining the process. This is very helpful in diagnosing the hanging or looping conditions. The dump can be initiated immediately or set to occur when the errors happens. Immediate invocation is not very common.

Syntax

The following methods show how to produce a processstate dump.

Using ALTER SESSION

The first ALTER SESSION command below produces an immediate processstate dump at level 10 while the second ALTER SESSION command produces the dump when the session encounters an ORA-4020 error.

```
alter session set events 'immediate trace name PROCESSSTATE level 10';
alter session set events '4020 trace name PROCESSSTATE level 10';
```

Using *oradebug*

The following *oradebug* command will produce an immediate processstate dump at level 10.

```
oradebug setmypid
oradebug unlimit
oradebug dump  processstate  10
```

Shared Server State Dump

Oracle Shared Server was called Oracle Multithreaded Server in Oracle8*i* Database and prior versions. Diagnosing the uncommon errors related to shared servers (such as process deadlocks) may warrant mtsstate or shared server state dumps, depending on the version of the database.

Syntax

Following methods show how to produce the shared server state dump.

Using ALTER SESSION

The first ALTER SESSION command below produces an immediate shared server state dump at level 10, while the second ALTER SESSION command produces the shared server state dump at level 1 when the session encounters ORA-0060 error.

```
alter session set events 'immediate trace name shared_server_state level 10'
alter session set events '60 trace name shared_server_state level 1';
```

Using *oradebug*

Following *oradebug* command will produce an immediate shared server state dump at the supplied level.

```
oradebug setmypid
oradebug unlimit
oradebug dump  shared_server_state <level>
```

Controlling the Dump Information Using Levels

The various levels available to produce the shared server state dumps are listed here:

- **Level 1**   Dumps systemwide state only

- **Level 2**   Dumps queues

- **Level 3**   Dumps circuits on the service queue

- **Level 4-6**   Dumps dispatcher info

- **Level 7-8**   Dumps shared server info

- **Level 9**   Dumps inactive dispatcher and server slots

- **Level 10-13**   Dumps info on "interesting" circuits

- **Level 14+**   Dump includes information about all circuits

Systemstate Dump

Systemstate is the one of most important dump files that Oracle Support uses to analyze the database hang conditions. This requires that the maxdump file size be set to unlimited, as this will generate large trace files depending on the size of the SGA. The systemstate dump contains a separate section with information for each process. Normally, you need to take two or three dumps in regular intervals. Expect HUGE trace files!

Syntax

Systemstate dump can be produced using following methods.

Using ALTER SESSION

The first ALTER SESSION command below removes any restrictions on the dump file size. The second ALTER SESSION command produces an immediate systemstate dump at level 10.

```
alter session set max_dump_file_size = unlimited;
alter session set events 'immediate trace name systemstate level 10';
```

Using *oradebug*

The following *oradebug* command produces an immediate systemstate dump at level 10. The *select* statement is to avoid problems on pre-Oracle 8.0.6 databases, sometimes *connect internal* may not have a complete process initialized:

```
select * from dual;
oradebug setmypid
oradebug unlimit
oradebug dump systemstate 10
```

Controlling the Dump Information Using Levels

Not applicable. Systemstate dumps are always taken at level 10. There is no code in the Oracle kernel for other levels.

Redo Log Dump

Redo logs keep the undo and redo information of every atomic database change operations. The changes are recorded as opcodes (operation codes), which are usually in the form of layer code.operation code format. For example, opcode 4.1 indicates block cleanout operation at transaction block layer.

Note, redo layers are not to be confused with Oracle's kernel layers. Redo layers are used only in conjunction with redo generation and redo logging.

Redo log dumps are normally requested by Oracle Support to analyze the data corruption (logical corruption) issues. If it is used intelligently it can be an auditing tool also. For example, if you would like to know the time and date of an extent allocated for a segment, you can dump the relevant opcodes for the extent allocation from the set of redo or archived log files and get the details that are not otherwise available in the data dictionary.

Syntax

The following methods show how to dump the redo log file contents.

Using ALTER SYSTEM

The following ALTER SYSTEM command can be used to dump redo logs. You can substitute the filters or options, depending on the requirement. If no filters are applied, the complete log file is dumped to the trace.

```
alter session set max_dump_file_size = unlimited;
alter system dump logfile 'filename'
        rba min <seqno> . <blkno>
        rba max <seqno> . <blkno>
        dba min <filno> . <blkno>
        dba max <filno> . <blkno>
        time min <ub4>
        time max <ub4>
        layer <word>
        opcode <word>
        scn min <scn>
        scn max <scn>
alter system dump logfile '/u01/oradata/oraredo/redo_01a.rdo';
```

Controlling the Dump Information Using Levels

Not applicable. Redo dumping is based on various parameters such as, rba, dba, scn, or time. Not specifying any parameters will dump the entire redo log contents to the trace file. Archived redo logs also can be dumped using the preceeding ALTER SYSTEM command.

APPENDIX
D

Direct SGA Access

ou may wonder why there is a need to access the SGA directly when friendly SQL and powerful trace facility are available. There are many benefits to accessing the SGA directly. Besides the ability to do high frequency sampling, it is possible to get processes' statistics even when the database or instance is hung and new connections cannot be established. This typically happens in very big sites with large SGAs and user populations, and the problem is normally caused by bugs in either the operating system or database. When this situation arises, the only way to get diagnostic statistics from Oracle is by accessing the SGA directly using external programs.

Overhead

Performance sampling with SQL has some overheads in the sense that the SQL statements are subject to Oracle's architecture and limits. The SQL statements must be parsed and optimized before execution. This involves dictionary lookups, latch acquisitions, etc. During the execution of the statements, the process must compete for resources as other Oracle processes. This involves latch and buffer lock acquisitions, consistent read image constructions, and various other potential waits. All these activities add to the overhead, and the overhead increases with higher sampling frequencies. But accessing the SGA directly from an external program does not introduce this kind of overhead to the Oracle instance. However, both types of access require CPU and memory to run. Performance monitoring always comes with a price, and accessing the SGA directly has a lower price tag. There is no such thing as overhead-free performance monitoring.

Security

V$ views are views that are built on top of X$ views. They do not provide all the information that is in the X$ views. To get the missing information, you have to query the X$ views directly, and this typically requires you to log in as the SYS user. In many sites, the SYS account is off limit to third-party applications for security reasons, but an external program that attaches to the SGA directly can read X$ views without logging in as the SYS user.

Speed

Oracle memory structures mutate rapidly, and SQL is not suitable for fast and repetitive access. For example, in an Oracle instance with many user connections, you may not be able to sample the V$SESSION_WAIT view 50 or more times per second. But it is not a problem for an external C program to do 50 or more read iterations per second on a memory region. (The critics of the SQL and PL/SQL sampling methods think they need such a high frequency sampling. We think it is overkill for sampling. Oracle Database 10*g* only samples once every second.) An external C program can read a memory region faster than SQL, provided there is no need to join and sort data from various memory structures.

Concurrency

SQL access to any object is subject to locking/latching issues. External programs have no need for any lock/latch, and more than one process can access the same memory region at the same time. This yields a higher level of concurrency. On the other hand, SQL access at rapid speed may increase the contention for specific latches (i.e., the row cache or library cache latches), and this overhead can be quite high in Real Application Clusters (RAC) environments.

Get Hidden Information

There is a limit to the amount of information that SQL can provide. SQL can at most provide the information that is externalized through X$ views. But there are many components of the SGA that have not been externalized or made available through X$ views. For example, you cannot write a query to display the content of a data buffer or the log buffer. Currently, you can only see the information by dumping the appropriate structure, such as the buffer cache or state objects, at the appropriate level. You must then spend a lot of time sifting through the cryptic trace files. And dumps provide only point-in-time snapshots of ever-changing Oracle memory structures. But an external program can read any Oracle memory region at any time.

Introduction to X$ Views

The SQL-less SGA access has two prerequisites: knowledge of C programming language and X$ views. Here, we will help you to better understand X$ memory structures, but C programming is beyond the scope of this book.

X$ data structures are the heart of the Oracle RDBMS kernel. They are rapidly changing memory structures in the RDBMS kernel, and they keep track of various statistics throughout the life of the instance. So if your instance has been running for several months, there is a chance that some statistic values grew too large and wrapped around. Those suspicious values can generally be ignored. The contents of X$ views always reside in memory and cannot be exported to any other database because they have no information about them in the dictionary. They do not have storage settings like those that are associated with normal tables, but they do have indexes on fixed columns.

X$ views generally start with the letter K, which stands for *kernel*. At first glance, they appear cryptic, but once you get used to them, they are easy to understand and decrypt. There is no external documentation available for the details of X$ views and their distribution across various kernel layers.

Oracle kernel comprises various layers, each of which works independently, and the control is passed from one layer to another layer. Each layer has a set of X$ memory structures that show the statuses and statistics of the functions within the layer. Most of the information is exposed in the V$ views, which are built on the X$ memory structures. Following are some of the layers in the Oracle kernel.

- Compilation layer (KK)

- Execution layer (KX)

- Distributed Transaction layer (K2)

- Security layer (KZ)

- Query layer (KQ)

- Access layer (KA)

- Data layer (KD)

- Transaction layer (KT)

- Cache layer (KC)

- Service layer (KS)

- Lock Management layer (KJ)

- Generic layer (KG)

The Compilation layer (KK) is responsible for compiling PL/SQL objects and generating explain plans based on the statistics available from the dictionary. The major component of the compilation layer is Oracle optimizer.

The Execution layer (KX) executes the compiled code from the top layer and binds the SQL and PL/SQL objects. This layer is also responsible for recursive calls to the dictionary and cursor management inside the shared pool.

The Distributed Transaction layer (K2) handles two-phase commits in the distributed transactions. A two-phase commit (prepare and commit) is the protocol used in the distributed database to ensure data integrity.

The Security layer (KZ) helps the upper two layers during compilation and execution. This layer manages roles and system privileges.

The Query layer (KQ) caches the rows from the data dictionary in the dictionary cache. The Compilation (KK) and Security (KZ) layers get the data from the query layer during compilation.

The Access layer (KA) is responsible for access to the database segments and provides information to the upper layers.

The Data layer (KD) controls the physical data storage and retrieval in the segments. It controls the formatting of data segments for storing table data and index trees.

The major component in the Transaction layer (KT) is rollback segments. This layer controls the *freelist* management, interested transaction list (ITL) allocations inside data blocks, row-level locking during the transaction, and undo generation. It also controls the rollback segment allocation and manages the consistency during a transaction.

The Cache layer (KC) manages the database buffer cache. This layer works closely with operating system facilities to manage the buffer cache and shared memory. It is also responsible for the redo generation and redo write to the redo log files.

The Service layer (KS) provides the required services to the other layers. It enforces initialization parameters in sessions and the instance. It also controls latch allocations and lock management in single-instance Oracle, and manages the wait events and statistics instance-wide.

The Lock Management layer (KJ) manages the locks and resources in a RAC environment. This layer manages the buffer locks (for global caches) which are specific to RAC and not to be confused with table or row level locks.

Before you look at the X$ views that will give you the information to access the SGA directly, let us dispel some of the myths that frequently surround them:

Myth: You should not query X$ views because they put a heavy load on the database.

Fact: It is absolutely safe to query X$ views. Almost every V$ view is based on one or more X$ views. If anything, it is cheaper to bypass the V$ views and query the X$ views directly.

Myth: You should not frequently query the X$ views because the contents will be erased once queried.

Fact: This applies only to the X$KSMLRU (kernel service layer memory-component least recently used) fixed table. The contents of this view will be erased once queried. As for the other X$ views, their contents remain.

Myth: **You should not perform DML against any X$ views, as doing so will crash the instance.**

Fact: You cannot perform DML on X$ views even if you want to. Oracle doesn't allow that. However, there are some undocumented ways to clear or reset the contents of a few X$ views. But those are not considered DML.

Myth: **In practice, you never need to access X$ views because almost all of the information from X$ views is available through V$ views.**

Fact: Only a portion of the information in X$ views is exposed in V$ views. For advanced statistics and internal information, you still need to query X$ views. The shared pool chunks sizes and block touch count information, just to name a couple, are only available in X$ views.

Myth: **The SYS user is the only one that has access to X$ views. So, to get information from the views, one must log in as SYS.**

Fact: This is partly true. You can create views based on the X$ views (as SYS) and grant SELECT on those views to any user. In this case, the users need not be a DBA to query those views.

The Necessary Ingredients

Oracle SGA is nothing more than a large and rapidly changing piece of memory structure in the eyes of an external program. From here on we will show you how to access the X$KSUSECST structure externally. The X$KSUSECST structure provides the information for the V$SESSION_WAIT view. The program needs to have the following information before it can successfully access the SGA contents:

- The shared memory identifier (*shmid*), also known as the SGA ID
- The SGA base address
- The starting address of X$KSUSECST
- The record size of the X$KSUSECST structure
- The number of records in the X$KSUSECST structure
- The X$KSUSECST view columns offsets

Find SGA ID

The SGA ID can be obtained from the trace file of an IPC dump using *oradebug* as follows.

```
SQL> oradebug setmypid
Statement processed.

SQL> oradebug ipc
Information written to trace file.

SQL> oradebug tracefile_name
/oracle/admin/REPOP/udump/repop_ora_19246.trc
```

The following is a snippet of the IPC dump trace file. The SGA ID can be found under the heading *shmid* (shared memory ID).

```
Area #0 `Fixed Size' containing Subareas 0-0
 Total size 0000000000044578 Minimum Subarea size 00000000
   Area   Subarea     Shmid       Stable Addr        Actual Addr
    0        0        1027   0000000080000000 0000000080000000
                                     Subarea size      Segment size
                               0000000000046000 000000000e406000
Area #1 `Variable Size' containing Subareas 1-1
 Total size 000000000d000000 Minimum Subarea size 01000000
   Area   Subarea     Shmid       Stable Addr        Actual Addr
    1        1        1027   0000000080046000 0000000080046000
                                     Subarea size      Segment size
                               000000000dfba000 000000000e406000
Area #2 `Redo Buffers' containing Subareas 2-2
 Total size 0000000000404000 Minimum Subarea size 00000000
   Area   Subarea     Shmid       Stable Addr        Actual Addr
    2        2        1027   000000008e000000 000000008e000000
                                     Subarea size      Segment size
                               0000000000404000 000000000e406000
Area #3 `skgm overhead' containing Subareas 3-3
 Total size 0000000000002000 Minimum Subarea size 00000000
   Area   Subarea     Shmid       Stable Addr        Actual Addr
    3        3        1027   000000008e404000 000000008e404000
                                     Subarea size      Segment size
                               0000000000002000 000000000e406000
```

Find SGA Base Address

The SGA base address can be discovered by querying the X$KSMMEM (kernel service memory management SGA memory) view. This view contains the physical memory address and value of every memory location in the SGA. This is essentially the map of the entire SGA. As such, don't be surprised if this view returns tens of millions of rows. For the purpose of direct SGA sampling, the most important piece of information from this view is the SGA base address, also known as the SGA starting address.

Following is the structure of the X$KSMMEM view and an example of how to get the SGA base address. Based on the example, the SGA base address is 0x80000000.

```
Name              Null?    Type
-------------     -------- ------------
ADDR                       RAW(4)
INDX                       NUMBER
INST_ID                    NUMBER
KSMMMVAL                   RAW(4)

select * from X$KSMMEM where indx = 0;
ADDR            INDX      INST_ID KSMMMVAL
--------    ----------  ---------- --------
80000000           0           1 00
```

Find the Starting Address of X$KSUSECST

The V$SESSION_WAIT view is built on the X$KSUSECST (kernel service user session current status) view. The full definition of the V$SESSION_WAIT view can be obtained from the V$FIXED_VIEW_DEFINITION view. The V$SESSION_WAIT (or X$KSUSECST) view provides fine-grain performance data, which is very useful for performance diagnostics and hang analyses. The information in the view changes rapidly, making it a perfect candidate for high speed sampling by an external program. The starting address of the X$KSUSECST structure in memory can be discovered as follows. According to the example, the X$KSUSECST starting address is 0x861B2438.

```
SQL> select min(addr) from x$ksusecst;
MIN(ADDR
--------
861B2438
```

Find the Record Size of the X$KSUSECST Structure

The size of a record in the X$KSUSECST structure can be determined from the starting address of any two records that are next to each other. The data type of the ADDR column is RAW and the data is in hexadecimal. You must convert the data into decimal notation and perform the calculation. An example is given here:

```
select addr
from   (select addr from x$ksusecst order by addr) a
where rownum < 3;
```

```
ADDR
--------
861B2438
861B2D50
-- 861B2438 Hex = 2249925688 decimal
-- 861B2D50 Hex = 2249928016 decimal
-- The record size is 2249928016 - 2249925688 = 2328 bytes
```

Find Number of Records in the X$KSUSECST Structure

The X$ views are C structures, and the number of records in each structure is set by a kernel variable, which gets its value from an init.ora parameter. The value of the init.ora parameter may be explicitly set by the DBA or derived from other init.ora parameters. Few structures have operating system- or version-dependent record counts. For our purpose, the number of records in the X$KSUSECST structure is set by the SESSIONS initialization parameter. The default value of SESSIONS is (1.1 * PROCESSES) + 5. If the SESSIONS parameter is explicitly set and the value is higher than the default, then Oracle will use the higher value; otherwise the default value will be used. Another way to find the number of records in the X$KSUSECST structure is simply by querying the X$KSUSECST view and counting the number of rows in it.

```
SQL> show parameter sessions
NAME_COL_PLUS_SHOW_PARAM         TYPE          VALUE_COL_PLUS_SHOW_PARAM
----------------------------     -----------   ---------------------------
. . .
sessions                         integer       300
. . .

SQL> show parameter processes
NAME_COL_PLUS_SHOW_PARAM         TYPE          VALUE_COL_PLUS_SHOW_PARAM
----------------------------     -----------   ---------------------------
. . .
processes                        integer       200

SQL> select count(*) from x$ksusecst;
  COUNT(*)
----------
       300
```

Find the X$KSUSECST View Columns Offsets

Finally, you need to find the offset of each column that is in the X$KSUSECST view beginning from the starting memory location of the view. You can get this information from the X$KQFCO (kernel query fixed tables column definitions) and X$KQFTA (kernel query fixed tables) views.

The X$KQFCO view can be considered as the data dictionary of the fixed tables. This view contains the column definitions of every X$ view, but it does not contain the fixed table names. The two important pieces of information you need from this view are the column name and the column offset, which is the starting address of the column in the memory. Without the column name and the column offset, you will not be able to access the SGA externally. The fixed table names can be obtained from the X$KQFTA view. An example of the query and its output is given next:

```
SQL> desc x$kqfco
Name              Null?    Type
--------------    -------- ------------
ADDR                       RAW(4)
INDX                       NUMBER
INST_ID                    NUMBER
KQFCOTAB                   NUMBER
KQFCONAM                   VARCHAR2(30)
KQFCODTY                   NUMBER
KQFCOTYP                   NUMBER
KQFCOMAX                   NUMBER
KQFCOLSZ                   NUMBER
KQFCOLOF                   NUMBER
KQFCOSIZ                   NUMBER
KQFCOOFF                   NUMBER
KQFCOIDX                   NUMBER
KQFCOIPO                   NUMBER

select  a.kqftanam fixed_table_name,
        b.kqfconam column_name,
        b.kqfcooff column_offset,
        b.kqfcosiz column_size
from    x$kqfta a, x$kqfco b
where   a.indx     = b.kqfcotab
and     a.kqftanam = 'X$KSUSECST'
order by b.kqfcooff;

FIXED_TABLE_NAME COLUMN_NAM COLUMN_OFFSET COLUMN_SIZE
---------------- ---------- ------------- -----------
X$KSUSECST       ADDR                   0           4
X$KSUSECST       INDX                   0           4
X$KSUSECST       KSUSEWTM               0           4
X$KSUSECST       INST_ID                0           4
X$KSUSECST       KSSPAFLG               1           1
X$KSUSECST       KSUSSSEQ            1276           2
X$KSUSECST       KSUSSOPC            1278           2
```

```
X$KSUSECST          KSUSSP1                 1280              4
X$KSUSECST          KSUSSP1R                1280              4
X$KSUSECST          KSUSSP2                 1284              4
X$KSUSECST          KSUSSP2R                1284              4
X$KSUSECST          KSUSSP3                 1288              4
X$KSUSECST          KSUSSP3R                1288              4
X$KSUSECST          KSUSSTIM                1292              4
X$KSUSECST          KSUSENUM                1300              2
X$KSUSECST          KSUSEFLG                1308              4
16 rows selected.
```

Do you wonder why some columns have an offset of 0? This shows that the column value is derived and not stored in the SGA. For example, the ADDR column of all fixed tables has an offset of 0 because it is a pointer to a memory location, and it is not stored in the SGA as a value. Similarly, the columns INST_ID, INDX, and KSUSEWTM also have an offset of 0 because their values are derived.

You may also notice that some columns share the same memory address. This means the columns share the same data, but the data may be reported in different formats or notations. For example, the KSUSSP1 and KSUSSP1R columns are associated with the P1 and P1RAW columns of the V$SESSION_WAIT view. The P1 column reports the value in the decimal notation, while the P1RAW column reports the same value in hexadecimal notation.

Attaching the SGA to a C Program

The SGA can be attached to a C program using the *shmat* system call. You can get more information about this system call by issuing *man shmat* at a Unix prompt, or from your favorite Unix programming books. The system call must be executed by a Unix user who has read permission to the Oracle SGA, and the syntax is as follows:

```
void *shmat(int shmid, const void *shmaddr, int shmflg);
The arguments are:
shmid   - shared memory identifier (SGA id)
shmaddr - starting address of the shared memory (SGA base address)
shmflg  - flag
```

CAUTION
To avoid data corruption, it is imperative that the SGA be attached as read-only. The shmflg *value must be* SHM_RDONLY. *You must never alter the memory content because it will corrupt the database.*

You must have C programming experience to develop a working application. The following programs are written by Kyle Hailey. The C program reads the X$KSUSECST structure directly. The programs can be downloaded from Hailey's website at http://oraperf.sourceforge.net/. It consists of two modules – *xksuse.sql* and xksuse.c. The first is a SQL script that prepares the *xksuse.h* header file to be included in the *xksuse.c* module, which is a C program.

```
set echo off
create or replace function to_dec (hex_input  raw)
return number
is
  input_length           pls_integer := length(hex_input);
  integer_value          number      := 0;
begin
  for i in 1..input_length loop
      select integer_value +
             (decode(substr(hex_input,(length(hex_input)+1-
i),1),'A',10,'B',11,'C',12,'D',13,'E',14,'F',15,substr(hex_input,(length(hex_input)+1-
i),1)) * power(16,i-1))
      into    integer_value
      from    dual;
  end loop;
  return integer_value;
end;
/


/*   Script:       xksuse.sql
     Author:       Kyle Hailey
     Dated:        June 2002
     Purpose:      create defines for xksuse.c
     copyright (c) 2002 Kyle Hailey
*/
set pagesize 0
set verify off
set feedback off
set echo off
spool xksuse.h
select '#define SGA_BASE  0x'||addr from x$ksmmem where rownum < 2;
select '#define START     0x'||min(addr) from x$ksusecst;
select '#define PROCESSES '||to_char(value - 1) from v$parameter where name =
'processes';
select '#define STATS     '||count(*)  from x$ksusd;
select '#define NEXT      '||((to_dec(e.addr)-to_dec(s.addr)))
from   (select addr from x$ksusecst where rownum < 2) s,
       (select max(addr) addr from x$ksusecst where rownum < 3) e;
select '#define '||
       replace(c.kqfconam,'#','_NUM') ||' '||
       to_char(c.kqfcooff  - mod(c.kqfcooff,2)) ||
       '      /* offset '|| c.kqfcooff || ' size ' || c.kqfcosiz || ' */ '
from   x$kqfco c, x$kqfta t
where  t.indx     = c.kqfcotab
and  ( t.kqftanam = 'X$KSUSECST' or
       t.kqftanam = 'X$KSUSE' or
       t.kqftanam = 'X$KSUSESTA')
and kqfcooff       > 0
order by c.kqfcooff;
```

```
select '#define '||
       upper(translate(s.name,' :-()/*''','_____'))||' '||
       to_char(c.kqfcooff  - mod(c.kqfcooff,2)+ STATISTIC# * 4 )
from   x$kqfco c, x$kqfta t, v$statname s
where  t.indx     = c.kqfcotab
and    t.kqftanam = 'X$KSUSESTA'
and    c.kqfconam = 'KSUSESTV'
and kqfcooff > 0
order by c.kqfcooff;
select 'char latch[][100]={' from dual;
select '"'||name||'",' from v$latchname;
select ' "" };' from dual;
select 'char event[][100]={' from dual;
select '"'||name||'",' from v$event_name;
select ' "" };' from dual;
select 'int users[]={' from dual;
select '0x'||addr||',' from x$ksuse;
select  '0x0};' from dual;
spool off
exit
```

The following is the *xksuse.c* C program module.

```
/*   Script:         xksuse.c
     Author:         Kyle Hailey
     Dated:          June 2002
     Purpose:        read x$ksuse direclty from the SGA
     copyright (c) 2002 Kyle Hailey

     # compile
     cc -o xksuse xksuse.c
     # run
     ./xksuse SGA_ID    (example: ./xksuse 1027)
*/
#include <stdio.h>
#include <sys/ipc.h>
#include <sys/shm.h>
#include <errno.h>
#include "xksuse.h"

#define FORMAT1 "%4s %6s %-20.20s %10s %10.10s %10s %6s %4s %10s %10s %10s %10s\n"
#define FORMAT2 "%4d %6d %-20.20s %10X %10.10X %10X %6u %4d %10d %10d %10u %10u\n"
#define FORMAT3 "%4d %6d %-20.20s %10X %10.10s %10X %6u %4d %10d %10d %10u %10u\n"

void *sga_attach (void *addr, int shmid)
{
    if ( addr != 0 ) addr=(void *)shmdt(addr);
    addr=(void *)shmat(shmid,(void *)SGA_BASE,SHM_RDONLY);
    if (addr  == (void *)-1) {
        printf("shmat: error attatching to SGA\n");
        exit();
    } else {
        printf("address %lx %lu\n",(int *)addr,(long *)addr);
    }
    return addr;
}
```

```
main(argc, argv)
 int argc;
 char **argv;
 {
  void  *addr;
  int   shmid[100];
  void  *sga_address;
  int   seqs[PROCESSES];
  long  p1r, p2r, p3r, psqla, sqla;
  unsigned int   cpu,i, tim, sid, uflg, flg, evn,  psqlh, sqlh, wtm, ctm, stm, ltm ;
  unsigned int   cur_time = 0;
  int   seq;
     for (i=0;i<PROCESSES;i++) { seqs[i]=0; }
     if (argc != 2) {
        fprintf(stderr, "Usage: %s shmid \n", *argv);
        exit(1);
     }
     shmid[0]=atoi(argv[1]);
     addr=0;
     addr=sga_attach(addr,shmid[0]);

     while (1) {
        addr=sga_attach(addr,shmid[0]);
        sga_address=(void *)START;
        sleep(1);
        printf("[H [J");
        printf(FORMAT1,"sid", "seq#", "wait", "p1", "p2", "p3", "cpu", "uflg", "stm",
"wtm", "sqlh", "psqlh");
        printf("procs %i\n",PROCESSES);
        for ( i=0; i < PROCESSES ; i++ ) {
           sga_address=(void *)((int)users[i]);
           seq=*(unsigned short *)((int)sga_address+KSUSSSEQ);
           evn=*(short *)((int)sga_address+KSUSSOPC);
           p1r=*(long *)((int)sga_address+KSUSSP1R);
           p2r=*(long *)((int)sga_address+KSUSSP2R);
           p3r=*(long *)((int)sga_address+KSUSSP3R);
           tim=*(int    *)((int)sga_address+KSUSSTIM);
           sid=*(short *)((int)sga_address+KSUSENUM);
/*
           uflg=*(short *)(((int)sga_address));
           uflg=*(int    *)((int)sga_address+KSUSEFLG);
*/
#ifdef __linux
           uflg=*(short *)((int)sga_address)>>8;
#else
           uflg=*(short *)((int)sga_address);
#endif
           flg=*(int    *)((int)sga_address+KSUSEFLG);
           stm=*(int *)((int)sga_address+KSUSSTIM) ;
           ltm=*(int *)((int)sga_address+KSUSELTM);
           ctm=*(int *)((int)sga_address+KSUSELTM-8);
           wtm=*(int *)((int)sga_address+KSUSELTM-4);
           psqla=*(long *)((int)sga_address+KSUSEPSQ);
           sqla=*(long *)((int)sga_address+KSUSESQL);
           sqlh=*(int    *)((int)sga_address+KSUSESQH) ;
           psqlh=*(int    *)((int)sga_address+KSUSEPHA) ;
           cpu=*(int    *)((int)sga_address+CPU_USED_WHEN_CALL_STARTED) ;
```

```
        if ( wtm > cur_time )  cur_time=wtm;
        if ( seqs[i] != seq  || 1 == 1) {
           if (  strcmp(event[evn],"SQL*Net message from client")  ) {
              if ( flg%2 == 1 && uflg%2 == 1 ) {
                 if (  ! strcmp(event[evn],"latch free") ) {
                    printf(FORMAT3, sid, seq, event[evn], p1r, latch[p2r],  p3r,
cpu, uflg, stm, (cur_time - wtm ), sqlh, psqlh);
                 } else {
                    printf(FORMAT2, sid, seq, event[evn], p1r, p2r, p3r, cpu, uflg,
stm, (cur_time - wtm ), sqlh, psqlh);
                 }
              }
           }
        }
        seqs[i]=seq;
     }
   }
 }
```

When the code is written and compiled, you will discover that the C program has a superb sampling performance. However, for this to be a useful application, the wait event data must be captured in a repository for future reference. You also need to capture the SQL statements that are associated with the wait events, as wait events by themselves are of little value.

APPENDIX
E

References

very effort has been made to provide you with a list of all the material we used as references for this book. Any omission from this list is purely unintentional.

Chapter 1

- Kolk, A., S. Yamaguchi, and J. Viscusi. "Yet Another Performance Profiling Method (Or YAPP-Method)." http://oraperf.veritas.com or http://www.miracleas.dk.

- Vaidyanatha, G., K. Deshpande, and J. Kostalec, Jr. *Oracle Performance Tuning 101*. Oracle Press/Osborne, 2001. http://www.osborne.com.

Chapter 2

- Millsap, C. "How to Activate Extended SQL Trace," White Paper, Hotsos Enterprises, Ltd., 2003. http://www.hotsos.com.

- Oracle Corporation, Oracle Database 10*g* Documentation, Release 1 (10.1), http://tahiti.oracle.com.

- Oracle Corporation, Oracle9*i* Documentation, Release 2 (9.2), http://tahiti.oracle.com.

- Shallahamer, C. "Direct Contention Identification Using Oracle's Session Wait Tables," White Paper, OraPub Inc., 1996. http://www.orapub.com.

- Vaidyanatha, G., K. Deshpande, and J. Kostalec, Jr. *Oracle Performance Tuning 101*. Oracle Press/Osborne, 2001. http://www.osborne.com.

Chapter 3

- Adams, S. "Oracle Performance Tuning Tips." http://www.ixora.com.au/tips.

- Holt, J. "Why Are Oracle's Read Events 'Named Backwards?'" White Paper, Hotsos, 2000. http://www.hotsos.com.

- Oracle Corporation, Oracle Database 10*g* Documentation, Release 1(10.1), http://tahiti.oracle.com.

- Oracle Corporation, Oracle9*i* Documentation, Release 2 (9.2), http://tahiti.oracle.com.

- Vaidyanatha, G., K. Deshpande, and J. Kostalec, Jr. *Oracle Performance Tuning 101*. Oracle Press/Osborne, 2001. http://www.osborne.com.

- Oracle Corporation, Oracle8*i* Database Documentation, Release 2, http://tahiti.oracle.com.

Chapter 4

- Shee, R. "10046 Alternatives," proceedings of International Oracle User Group Conference, 2003. http://www.ioug.org.

Chapter 5

- Shee, R. "If Your Memory Serves You Right," proceedings of International Oracle User Group Conference, 2004. http://www.ioug.org.

- Oracle Corporation, Metalink note #131530.1, http://metalink.oracle.com.

- Oracle Corporation, Oracle8*i* Database Documentation, Release 2, http://tahiti.oracle.com.

- Oracle Corporation, Oracle9*i* Database Documentation, Release 2, http://tahiti.oracle.com.

- Oracle Corporation, Oracle Database 10*g* Documentation, Release 1(10.1), http://tahiti.oracle.com.

Chapter 6

- Oracle Corporation, Metalink notes #30804.1, #62143.1, #131557.1, #34405.1. http://metalink.oracle.com.

- Oracle Corporation, Oracle8*i* Database Documentation, Release 2, http://tahiti.oracle.com.

- Oracle Corporation, Oracle9*i* Database Documentation, Release 2, http://tahiti.oracle.com.

- Oracle Corporation, Oracle Database 10*g* Documentation, Release 1(10.1), http://tahiti.oracle.com.

- Adams, S. *Oracle8i Internal Services for Waits, Latches, Locks, and Memory* O'Reilly & Associates, Inc., 1999. http://www.oreilly.com/.

Chapter 7

- Adams, S. "Over Committed."
  http://www.ixora.com.au/newsletter/2001_09.htm.

- Morle, J. "Solid State Disks in an Oracle Environment."
  http://www.oaktable.net/fullArticle.jsp?id=5.

- Oracle Corporation, Oracle8*i* Database Documentation, Release 2,
  http://tahiti.oracle.com.

- Oracle Corporation, Oracle9*i* Database Documentation, Release 2,
  http://tahiti.oracle.com.

- Oracle Corporation, Oracle Database 10*g* Documentation, Release 1(10.1),
  http://tahiti.oracle.com.

Chapter 8

- Pfister, G. *In Search of Clusters*, Prentice Hall, 1998.
  http://www.prenhall.com.

- Oracle Corporation, Metalink forum and support notes,
  http://metalink.oracle.com.

- Adams, S. "Cache Layer Block Types."
  http://www.ixora.com.au/notes/cache_block_types.htm.

Chapter 9

- Hailey, K. "Performance Tuning in Oracle 10*g*," proceedings of the Hotsos
  Symposium, 2004. http://www.hotsos.com.

- Oracle Corporation, Oracle Database 10*g* Documentation, Release 1
  (10.1), http://tahiti.oracle.com.

- Wood, G., K. Hailey. "The Self-Managing Database: Automatic
  Performance Diagnostics," White Paper, Oracle Corporation, 2003.
  http://otn.oracle.com/products/manageability/database/pdf/twp03/TWP_
  manage_automatic_performance_diagnosis.pdf.

Appendix A

- Gazi Unal, D. "iOraDumpReader." http://www.ubtools.com.

- Oracle Corporation, Metalink forum and support notes, http://metalink.oracle.com.

Appendix B

- Oracle Corporation, Oracle Database 10*g* Documentation, http://otn.oracle.com.

Appendix C

- Gazi Unal, D. "Microstate Response-Time Performance Profiling (MRPP)." http://www.ubtools.com.

- Oracle Corporation, Metalink forum and support notes, http://metalink.oracle.com.

Appendix D

- Hailey, K. "SGA Access." http://oraperf.sourceforge.net/.

- Gopalakrishnan, K. "Oracle9*i* Memory Structures (X$views)," *Oracle Internals Magazine*, September 2002.

Index

339

INTERNATIONAL CONTACT INFORMATION

AUSTRALIA
McGraw-Hill Book Company
Australia Pty. Ltd.
TEL +61-2-9900-1800
FAX +61-2-9878-8881
http://www.mcgraw-hill.com.au
books-it_sydney@mcgraw-hill.com

CANADA
McGraw-Hill Ryerson Ltd.
TEL +905-430-5000
FAX +905-430-5020
http://www.mcgraw-hill.ca

GREECE, MIDDLE EAST, & AFRICA
(Excluding South Africa)
McGraw-Hill Hellas
TEL +30-210-6560-990
TEL +30-210-6560-993
TEL +30-210-6560-994
FAX +30-210-6545-525

MEXICO (Also serving Latin America)
McGraw-Hill Interamericana Editores
S.A. de C.V.
TEL +525-1500-5108
FAX +525-117-1589
http://www.mcgraw-hill.com.mx
carlos_ruiz@mcgraw-hill.com

SINGAPORE (Serving Asia)
McGraw-Hill Book Company
TEL +65-6863-1580
FAX +65-6862-3354
http://www.mcgraw-hill.com.sg
mghasia@mcgraw-hill.com

SOUTH AFRICA
McGraw-Hill South Africa
TEL +27-11-622-7512
FAX +27-11-622-9045
robyn_swanepoel@mcgraw-hill.com

SPAIN
McGraw-Hill/
Interamericana de España, S.A.U.
TEL +34-91-180-3000
FAX +34-91-372-8513
http://www.mcgraw-hill.es
professional@mcgraw-hill.es

UNITED KINGDOM, NORTHERN,
EASTERN, & CENTRAL EUROPE
McGraw-Hill Education Europe
TEL +44-1-628-502500
FAX +44-1-628-770224
http://www.mcgraw-hill.co.uk
emea_queries@mcgraw-hill.com

ALL OTHER INQUIRIES Contact:
McGraw-Hill/Osborne
TEL +1-510-420-7700
FAX +1-510-420-7703
http://www.osborne.com
omg_international@mcgraw-hill.com

Sound Off!

Visit us at **www.osborne.com/bookregistration** and let us know what you thought of this book. While you're online you'll have the opportunity to register for newsletters and special offers from McGraw-Hill/Osborne.

We want to hear from you!

Sneak Peek

Visit us today at **www.betabooks.com** and see what's coming from McGraw-Hill/Osborne tomorrow!

Based on the successful software paradigm, Bet@Books™ allows computing professionals to view partial and sometimes complete text versions of selected titles online. Bet@Books™ viewing is free, invites comments and feedback, and allows you to "test drive" books in progress on the subjects that interest you the most.

GET YOUR **FREE SUBSCRIPTION**
TO ORACLE MAGAZINE

Oracle Magazine is essential gear for today's information technology professionals. Stay informed and increase your productivity with every issue of *Oracle Magazine*. Inside each free bimonthly issue you'll get:

IF THERE ARE OTHER ORACLE USERS AT YOUR LOCATION WHO WOULD LIKE TO RECEIVE THEIR OWN SUB-SCRIPTION TO ORACLE MAGAZINE, PLEASE PHOTOCOPY THIS FORM AND PASS IT ALONG.

- Up-to-date information on Oracle Database, Oracle Application Server, Web development, enterprise grid computing, database technology, and business trends
- Third-party vendor news and announcements
- Technical articles on Oracle and partner products, technologies, and operating environments
- Development and administration tips
- Real-world customer stories

Three easy ways to subscribe:

① Web
Visit our Web site at otn.oracle.com/oraclemagazine. You'll find a subscription form there, plus much more!

② Fax
Complete the questionnaire on the back of this card and fax the questionnaire side only to +1.847.763.9638.

③ Mail
Complete the questionnaire on the back of this card and mail it to P.O. Box 1263, Skokie, IL 60076-8263

ORACLE®

FREE SUBSCRIPTION